This volume is affectionately and respectfully dedicated to my late father

Thomas A. O'Rourke

And

To all C.Y.M.S. Members Past, Present and Future

Thomas Anthony O'Rourke
1911-1991

A member of the Society for sixty-six years.
Served on the Council for forty-five years.
Chairman for sixteen years.

FAMA SEMPER VIVAT

PUBLISHED BY

Breffní Publications

'Breffní Lodge', Bulgan, Glynn, Enniscorthy, Co. Wexford, Ireland.

Tel: 00 353 053 91 28872.   Email: mikeorourke888@eircom.net

ISBN 978-0-9560474-0-3

EDITIO PRINCEPS 2008

Origination and design: Michael A. O'Rourke

Text Support: Ms. Marie Mitchell

Printed by: C & R Print, Enniscorthy

Histry

of the

Wexford

Catholic Young Men's Society

1855 - 2008

Volume 1

By

Michael A. O'Rourke

SPONSORS

Breffní Publications gratefully acknowledge the generous financial support

and encouragement of the following sponsors.

~~~~~◀ ▢ ▶~~~~~

This publication has received support from the Heritage Council under the 2008
Publications Grant Scheme.

Micheál O'Rourke, Poulregan, Castlebridge, Wexford.

Ferrybank Motors Ltd., Ferrybank, Wexford

Kehoe & Associates, Commercial Quay, Wexford.

Wexford County Council Amenity & Grant Scheme 2008

The Wrens Nest, Custom House Quay, Wexford

Wexford Creamery Ltd., Rocklands, Wexford

Catholic Young Men's Society (St. Iberius Branch) Wexford

Talbot Hotel, The Quay, Wexford

Whitford House Hotel, New Line Road, Wexford

Paul Kehoe,T.D., 7 Weafer Street, Enniscorthy, Co. Wexford.

Table of Contents

Volume 1

Table of Contents
Volume 2

C.Y.M.S. Sportsmen

Billiards and Snooker History 1855-2008

Table Tennis History 1930-1980

Cycling Club History 1882-1970

History of Card Playing from 1800s to Date

Prohibited Activities in the Society

Miscellaneous

Members Photo Gallery

Members Professions and Occupations

Members' Profiles and Records

Preface

The Genesis of this Book

In August 1987 whilst enjoying my annual holidays in Wexford from Oxford, I was delighted when I was invited to accompany my late father Tom O'Rourke *'to see the new C.Y.M.S. club premises'*, as up to that time I had never been inside of the new premises in Charlotte Street, Wexford.

Having been afforded the grand tour, my eye was drawn towards a newspaper cutting in the Billiards room which related to some *'old club members'*. On noticing my interest my father proceeded to show me some other articles relating to the exploits of other *'old club members'*. These articles, although consisting of only brief newspaper accounts, nonetheless gave me some insight into the past activities of club members hitherto unknown to me in any great detail.

On our way back home that night, Dad and I had a lengthy discussion on the general activities of the *'old club'* and its various members and exploits over the years. He mentioned an exhibition match played at the club between Walter Lindrum, the Australian World Billiards Champion and Tom Newman, the British Champion. This intrigued me and I suggested to him that *'someone should write a history of the club and have it on record before all the older chaps and their memories are dead and gone and the information is lost forever to posterity'*. I had in mind that he himself should undertake this task. After all, who was more suitable to do so than he having been involved in the club's activities for over sixty odd years at that stage. He replied *'why don't you do it, you are the one interested in it'*. This retort was typical of Thomas O'Rourke portraying his humility and unassuming nature. I then suggested that he write down all his memories of past club events and we would discuss the possibility again. Each subsequent year when I came home to Wexford on holidays we would discuss it and I eventually commenced taping his reminiscences and information to have it on record.

As I became aware of the extent of the club's fame and the exploits of some of its members, I was more convinced than ever and felt very strongly that such a venture should be undertaken

So on that August evening in 1987 the idea of writing a history of the St. Iberius Branch of the Wexford C.Y.M.S. took root

His sudden death on the 21st January 1991, only four years after our initial discussion concerning the book, finally gave me the impetus I needed to proceed. Unfortunately, residing and working in Oxford meant that I could only conduct my research while in Wexford on my holidays and thus it was is excess of ten years before I could complete my research when I retired and relocated permanently to Wexford.

I was delighted with the response and co-operation when I conveyed my intention to Richard Murphy, Hon. Secretary of the club, on the 29th January, 2004. My initial task was to obtain the minute books and photo archives or any other C.Y.M.S. memorabilia available. I met Richard Murphy at the club premises and we both went through all the old books there which were located in an old filing cabinet in a damp cupboard under the stairway.

I remember thinking to myself that this was dreadful neglect of what should have been considered as very valuable assets of the club. However, I brought the books home and they improved with the warm temperature in my house. It appears that the last minute book entry recorded was dated 11th October, 2000. I was disappointed to see that the collection of photographs or any other memorabilia in the club was almost non-existent

The bulk of material for my work came from endless research through the minute books, newspaper articles, cuttings and scraps garnered here and there. I was very fortunate to have at my disposal my late Father's recordings of his sixty-six year reminiscences in the Society together with the cycling diaries and photo archives of my late brother Frank O'Rourke. I, also, conducted numerous interviews and gathered data from the memories and stories of some older members. In so doing, I have managed to rescue from oblivion valuable historical data concerning the C.Y.M.S. and local heritage so that it can be passed on to future generations of Wexfordians. Those who assisted me in compiling this data deserve great appreciation.

People like, Tom Mahon, the late Frank O'Rourke, Roy Doyle, Tommy Cullimore, and Tom O'Hara were of exceptional assistance to me in the reconstruction of the 1950s to 1970s period of the club's history while Dick Murphy, Nicky Lacey and Rodney Goggins filled in the remaining period up to the present.

I have amassed and gathered so much data that this will be a very comprehensive work which I trust will do justice to the Club and Wexford. Much of this information should be of particular interest to local historians. Having discussed the project with various printers it became obvious that the work would necessitate two volumes. One volume would not be feasible as it would be twice the size of the Wexford telephone directory ('05 Phonebook 2007') and therefore printing costs would be prohibitive.

The retail cost of the book would need to be in excess of sixty Euros merely to cover the printing costs. In the circumstances I have decided to print two volumes. Volume 1 includes the general history of the Society, intellectual pursuits, religion, finances and fundraising, social gatherings, theatrical entertainments, history of the C.Y.M.S. concert hall, and miscellaneous. Volume 2, which will be printed at a later date, will include sportsmen, billiards and snooker, table tennis, cycling, card playing, miscellaneous, professions and occupations of members, members' profiles, and photo gallery.

Michael A. O'Rourke

The Society is Born

In Ireland the history of official Catholic action, such as the Catholic Young Men's Society and other Catholic Associations dates back to a decade or so after Emancipation and was the outward expression of the resurgent spirit of Catholicism. During the Penal Days the great struggle had been to preserve the Faith, now the time had come to bring its influence to bear on the social culture and intellectual life of the people.

Pope Pius IX

The Very Rev. Dean O'Brien of St. Mary's Parish in Limerick founded the Catholic Young Men's Society of Ireland on the 19th May, 1849. It was actually named the *'Young Men's Society of the Immaculate Heart of Mary'*, and according to Fr. O'Brien, *there were not more than two dozen men present on the occasion.* Some seven years later we read in the Dean's circular letter of 1856 that *There are 400 branches of the C.Y.M.S. in Great Britain with an active membership of 30,000 and in Ireland there are 127 branches with a membership of*

10,200. This is truly an amazing success story. In January 1854 he established the first branch of the C.Y.M.S. in England was at St. Vincent's Sheffield, under the title *'The Young Men's Society of the Immaculate Heart of Mary.'* The Society in Great Britain today is not known as the C.Y.M.S. but rather the C.M.S. the Catholic Men's Society. Chris Bolger, the General Secretary of the UK Society informed me that there are fifty branches with something like 400 members in the UK today. In 1859 the Society was established in Melbourne and in May of 1861 in Grahamstown, South Africa, founded by a Wexfordman. Today (2007) there are only seventeen branches in Ireland still operational. Monsignor Dean O'Brien died 10th February 1885 aged 76 years.

The ethos of the Society was similar to that of the temperance movement of the time in that it fostered morals encouraged intellectual improvement in working-class young men. The aims of the Catholic Young Men's Society as enshrined in their Constitution are:-

The Society strives for the personal development of its members through spiritual, intellectual, social and physical activities. The basic unit is called the Branch. The Society is organised at Diocesan level and at National level by the governing body, the National Council.

Before proceeding further I must relate that whilst Fr. Richard Baptist O'Brien was at Rome in 1852 pursuing a post graduate course in Theology for the Degree of Doctor of Divinity he submitted his Constitution for the C.Y.M.S. to Pope Pius IX. The Holy Father was so impressed with the document that he commended it to his senior theologians. His Holiness sent *'his Apostolic Blessing to all the members of the C.Y.M.S.'* and further he *'granted a Plenary indulgence to all members of all branches on the festival of its Patron Saint.'* Fr. O'Brien was most gratified when His Holiness affiliated the C.Y.M.S. to the Arch Confraternity of the Immaculate Heart of Mary with full indulgences. Today members of the C.Y.M.S may gain a Plenary Indulgence every year on the Anniversary of the Foundation of the Society which is the 19th May.

Dean Richard Baptist O'Brien
1809 - 1885

Founder of the C.Y.M.S. 19th May 1849

Our story begins at a 'prayer house' in Mary's Lane, off Bride Street, where a *'few young men'* founded the Wexford Branch. These young men went to Fr. James Roche, the parish priest, with a request that he help them organise a C.Y.M.S. branch in the town. This he readily agreed to and the initial meeting was held on the Feast of the Assumption, 1855. On that evening, after Benediction, this small body of young men held their inaugural meeting with Father Roche in the chair. The opening sentence of the minutes of the meeting read as follows: *A few young men, accustomed for some time to meet together in the Oratory in Mary's Lane for the purpose of repeating the Rosary conceived the idea of forming in the town of Wexford a Branch of the [Catholic] Young Men's Society.*

Encouraged by the success of their first meeting and by the support of two such men as Father Roche and Richard Devereux it was decided to invite the founder, Dean O'Brien, to visit Wexford and formally establish the Branch. This he did on the February 10th 1856 when again under Fr. Roche's chairmanship Dean O'Brien addressed a great meeting in Dr. Sinnott's School in Georges Street which was attended by the following speakers - Dr. Anderson of the Catholic University, Dublin and Very Rev. Dr. Murray later to become Archbishop of Dublin. There were sixty members present on this evening and shortly after this it was stated that over 200 enrolled in the newly formed Society.

Founding Father
of the
Catholic Young Men's Society, Wexford Branch

Very Rev. Canon James Roche, P.P., V. F. 1801 - 1883

Patron and Spiritual Director of the C.Y.M.S. Wexford Branch 1855-1868

Parish Priest of Wexford 1850-1883

Is it not ironic that that magnificent and magnanimous duo of schoolboy pals - the joint patrons Fr. James Roche *(Spiritual Director)* and Richard Devereux, Esq. *(great benefactor)* should emerge as Princes of the Catholic Church and be foremost in the fostering of Catholicism in Wexford town having both received their primary education from a Mr. Behan, a Protestant gentleman, at his school in George's Street, Wexford. It was as if God had brought together two men with unity of mind, two devout Catholics, one spiritual and one secular to work together in unison for the Catholic faith. Was it not also fitting that when their lifetime work was over, that God should have called these boyhood school pals to their eternal reward together. Both men died in March 1883.

3

Founding Father
Of the
Catholic Young Men's Society, Wexford Branch

Richard Joseph Devereux, K.S.G., 1795-1883, (Knight of St. Gregory)

Patron and Benefactor of the C.Y.M.S. Wexford Branch 1855 – 1883

The Catholic Young Men's Society of Wexford, the St. Iberius Branch, was most fortunate in having had such Princes of the Church to lead and guide them in the early days which developed them into the foremost Catholic Action Institute of Wexford town, a Society which has survived down through the ages *(over 153 years)*.

The C.Y.M.S. of Ireland is defined as an ecclesiastically approved confraternity of religious brotherhood of Catholic young men. Founded in 1949 by Dean O'Brien of Limerick for the purpose of fostering by mutual union and co-operation and by priestly guidance the spiritual, intellectual, social and physical welfare of its members. And in obedience to and under the guidance of the hierarchy of taking part in Catholic Action. For the Glory of the Church, and the benefit of the Irish People.
– Rev. President, Fr. Sinnott speaking at the A.G.M. of the Wexford Branch on the 2nd February, 1936.

The C.Y.M.S. club was a meeting place where many of the young men of Wexford town could gather to interact with like-minded individuals. It was a place where they could enjoy themselves in a social atmosphere that was healthy for both mind and body. Here they learned to harness and channel their excess energies into healthy pastimes and sports for the greater glory of all. They learned how to meet, interact and get along with people. They acquired the attributes of good sportsmanship, how to win honourably and how to lose gracefully. They discovered what the meaning of friendship and fellowship was. In short, they learned skills and manners which shaped and developed them into some of the finest young men that Wexford town has ever produced. Many of the young men from this club went on to become some of the most respected and responsible men of the town. One has but to take a fleeting glance at the roll of honour list in this book or, at the list of Wexford business who were members of the club over the last one hundred and fifty two years to attest to this fact.

What was available and what did the members do at the club. From the very beginning all members were involved in the Guilds and all religious activities. The library/reading room was second to none and there was a vast amount of reading material available. There was a telescope in the reading room that faced out onto the Quay

where, no doubt, many of the sea captains who were members spent their latter years observing the comings and goings of the hundreds of ships in the harbour in those days. There were lectures, educational and language classes. A huge diversity of interests existed, i.e. the debating club, the annual outings and excursions, the soirées, the communion breakfasts, reunions, music, dramatic and dancing classes. There was, also, a bagatelle table and later on there was the billiards table, draughts, chess, darts, ringers, bridge club and various card games. In addition there was cycling, cricket, billiards and snooker, football, table tennis, boxing, athletics and gymnasium sections of the club. One could have one's mail or telegrams delivered to the club. Business transactions were conducted there and charitable works organised. They founded a "Burial Fund" on the 20th August 1856 to help members offset funeral expenses.

If proof is needed of just how important the C.Y.M.S. was in the 1880s I would recommend a read of 'The People' newspaper issue XXXV dated Wednesday 12th January 1887. The paper is not dissimilar to today's tabloids. The back page is comprised of four columns, three of which are reportage of the C.Y.M.S. reunion, which equals three-quarters of a page out of an 8 page newspaper. I would think that that is placing great importance on the C.Y.M.S. club

All long established clubs wax and wane in their degree of popularity and the C.Y.M.S. is no different and has had its periods of serious decline. Some say that this trend is inevitable in times of changing social habits. Most of the private social clubs that were operating in the 1950s in Wexford have vanished from the scene. The C.Y.M.S. is one of the last, if not the last one, still in existence. The new trend appears to be for clubs to specialise in one sport or interest and they are financially driven. In the vast majority of cases these clubs are business concerns conducted with the owners' interests at heart and not the members. Pubs and television have contributed their share of damage to the 'social club'. One can only hope that the club today will survive and that members with vision and leadership will surface and continue to fly the C.Y.M.S. banner high and march us into the next 150 years.

Management and Society Rules

Three fundamental rules of membership initially put in place in 1849 by the founder Dean O'Brien, also applied from the establishment of the Society in August 1855 which were:

1. **Monthly Confession and Holy Communion**
2. **No Party Politics**
3. **The Chaplain's Veto**

The great object of the Society is to create a sound Catholic spirit amongst the young men of Wexford, and in order to do this the frequentation of the Sacraments is absolutely necessary. The members of the Young Men's Society pledge themselves on entering it, to go to Confession once a month. This is the principal, The Fundamental Rule. The brother who neglects this duty is the most deadly enemy of the Society: no matter how punctually every other duty is performed, if this be not attended to, all will be wrong. --- The Very Rev. James Roche, P.P., Spiritual Director. Sunday 19th December 1858.

Throughout the life of the Wexford branch these fundamental rules were vigorously adhered to and respected by all. During the late 1950s the Wexford branch President, Fr. O'Neill, gave a series of lessons on the history of the Wexford branch. At one of those lectures he made mention of the branch changing its name and writing its own constitution. He referred to that happening as follows: *Back in the late 1890s the club changed its name and established their own constitution for some unknown reason.* Back in the 1950s I was a young man and I must

confess I did not pay too much attention to Fr. O'Neill's discourse on that matter. It was only when I began the research for this book that I came across the whole episode. As it is a part of the history and development as a branch, I feel the whole story is worth relating.

On the 11th November 1897 a special meeting of the Council was convened to discuss the rules for the management of the club, it reads: *The secretaries submitted to the meeting a copy of the rules of the 'Catholic Commercial Club', Dublin, and after some alterations a good many of them [rules] were considered and adapted.*

On the 1st December 1897, a draft of these new rules was chosen and submitted to the Council for the management of the club and with a few amendments these were unanimously adopted. We do not know what the rules were because none were recorded in the minute book and no copy of them can be located. We can with a certain degree of accuracy assume that the following rules were the ones decided upon.

ST. IBERIUS CLUB & CATHOLIC YOUNG MEN'S SOCIETY WEXFORD

GENERAL RULES OF MANAGEMENT

1. That the Club shall be called the 'St. Iberius Club and Catholic Young Men's Society,' and Catholics only (of 15 years of age and upwards) shall be eligible for Membership.

2. The objects of the Club shall be to afford to the Members the means of social intercourse, mental and moral improvement, and rational recreation.

3. The Club shall be strictly non-political, and the premises shall not be used for any purpose which, in the opinion of the Committee [council] would be opposed to the objects for which the Club has been established.

4. The Club shall be open for the reception of Members from 8 o'clock in the morning to 11.o o'clock at night. The Committee may at its discretion vary the time for closing.

5. The Club shall be under the control of a Patron, President, Vice-President, Treasurer, two Secretaries, and nine Members of Committee. The Patron shall be the Roman Catholic Bishop of Ferns, and shall possess the power of appointing the President.

6. The Vice-President, Treasurer, the two Secretaries and nine Members of the Committee, shall be elected from Members of the Club each year in the manner hereinafter specified, and they, together with the President, shall form the Committee of the Club. They shall also resign their office on the 31st day of January in each year, but will be eligible for re-election provided they comply with all the rules of election.

7. Members will be eligible for election to the Committee—(1) if they have a Subscription of Twelve Shillings and sixpence paid up to 31st day of December in the year of such election. (2) If they have been Members of the Club for at least twelve months previous to the first day of the month in which the election is held. (3) If they have been duly proposed and seconded by two Members of the Club, whose annual subscription to the Club for the year ended 31st December previous was not less than Twelve Shillings and Sixpence, and that notice of same be given to the Secretaries at least seven days before the day of election.

8. The election of the Committee shall take place at the Annual General Meeting of the Club, to be held before the end of February in each year.

9. It will be the duty of the Secretaries to have the names of the candidates for the Committee, as well as the names of their proposers and seconders, put up on the notice board at least six days before the day of election.

10. The elections for the Committee shall be by ballot, and Members only who have their subscriptions to the 1st January next following paid in full, shall be entitled to vote. Each Member entitled to vote shall be supplied by the Secretaries a few days before the day of election with a ballot paper, which should be correctly filled and put in a ballot-box, placed in the Club for the purpose, on or before the day of election.

11. At the General Meeting Scrutinizers shall be appointed, who shall make a return of the voting to the President, who shall declare the names of the gentlemen elected.

12. In the event of a tie between two candidates, both shall be declared elected.

13. The Committee shall meet at least once a month at whatever time may be found most convenient, and five Members shall form a quorum for ordinary business. All questions shall be determined by a majority of votes, and if these should be equal, the Chairman shall have a casting vote in addition to his vote as a Member of the Committee.

14. No Member of the Committee can meantime be removed from office except by a resolution of the majority of the Committee. In case of a vacancy arising during the year on the Committee, the Secretaries may summon a meeting of the Committee to fill such vacancy.

15. Any Member of the Committee who shall be absent from five consecutive meetings shall be called upon to state the cause of his absence, and if he fail to explain same to the satisfaction of the Committee, he shall cease to be a Member thereof.

16. The election of candidates for Membership of the Club shall be by ballot, and vested in the Committee of the Club. One adverse vote in five shall be sufficient to exclude.

17. Each candidate for admission As a Member must pay in advance his subscription to 31st December next following and must be proposed and seconded by Members of the Committee of the Club, who shall enter the candidate's name, address, and occupation or calling,

and add their own name and address in the book provided for the purpose.

18. The names and addresses of the candidates for Membership, with those of their proposers and seconders, shall be posted by the Secretaries in the Club three days previous to the election.

19. The election to Membership of every candidate shall be forthwith notified to him by the Secretaries. The subscriptions at present fixed by the Council are: - For Householders and Senior Clerks, Twelve Shillings and Six-pence annually: and for others, Six Shillings annually.

20. The payment of the subscription shall be understood as a distinct acknowledgment by each Member of his acquiescence in the rules and regulations of the Club and he shall not be entitled to make any use of the Club until such payment be made.

21. The Annual Subscription to the Club shall be paid in advance in January of each year. Persons elected in the last quarter of any year shall deposit such quarter's subscription and also the following year's subscription before being elected and all other Members failing to pay their Annual Subscription on or before March 31st shall be struck off the List of Members.

22. The Secretaries shall notify each Member of the Club the time his Annual Subscription is due.

23. Should the general election of any member of the Club be, in the opinion of the Committee, injurious to the character and interests of the Club, the Committee shall, after a fair hearing , be empowered to expel him from the Club, provided that notice shall be given to such Member of the intention to expel him, and that no such expulsion shall take place unless agreed to by at least three-fourths of the Committee present at a meeting specially summoned for that purpose, and at which at least eight Members of the Committee shall be present.

24. An annual General Meeting of the Members shall be held in the month of February in each year, to receive from the Committee a Report and Statement of Accounts of the Club for the previous year, and at which the Committee for the current year shall be elected.

25. The Report and Statement of Accounts shall be posted in the Club at least a week before the date of the Annual meeting at which they are to be considered.

26. A preliminary notice of each General Meeting shall be posted in the Club a week before the date of such Meeting.

27. The government of the Club shall be in the hands of the Committee, who are hereby empowered to enforce the rules, suspend from Membership or expel disorderly Members, or other objectionable persons, and from time to time to make such bye-laws and regulations as may be found necessary for the proper management and conduct of the Club.

28. The Secretaries shall attend and keep minutes of all meetings of the Committee, enrol the names of Members, and prepare the business to be laid before the Committee.

29. All cheques shall bear the signatures of the Chairman, two Members of the Committee, and one of the Secretaries, and shall be signed in committee.

30. No surplus shall be divided amongst the Members.

31. Lists of books and publications proposed to be acquired by the Club must be submitted to the Committee for approval.

32. Lectures, classes, and all entertainments must receive the sanction of the Committee, and no notice, advertisement or publication of any kind shall be placed in any part of the premises without such sanction.

33. Members are allowed to introduce strangers as visitors to the Club.

34. As soon as possible after death of a Member a day's Masses will be offered for the repose of his soul

(Signed)   William Hutchinson,   Hon. Secretary
(Signed)   Richard Goold,   Hon. Secretary

The foregoing document is the oldest set of management rules in existence for the Wexford Society and is undated. We cannot be sure of the exact date when these rules were drafted and implemented but we do know that the club's name - St. Iberius Club & Catholic Young Men's Society in this form that appears on the document was in existence from 7th February, 1909 to 14th February 1937.   We also know it was in the year 1922 when the membership subscriptions were increased from 10/- to 12/6, and rule 7 on this document mentioned the subscriptions as being 12/6.   We can, therefore, deduce that the foregoing set of management rules were created sometime within the period of 7th February 1909 and 1922.   We have also good reason to believe that these rules or similar ones were in existence since 1898, one month after the date the Council was studying the rules of the 'Catholic Commercial Club', Dublin, just prior to the club changing its name to that which appears on the document.

Throughout the years many changes were made to the constitution and management rules of the Wexford Society.   The National Council of the C.Y.M.S. of Ireland brought out their constitution in January 1934, and as Wexford was affiliated to that governing body we can assume that Wexford implemented these rules. A report in the 'Free Press' dated 3rd December 1935 mentions that the club convened an important meeting of the following - Rev. J. Sinnott, Adm. President, Richard Goold, Vice-President, Patrick Breen, John Cosgrave, John O'Keeffe, Thomas O'Rourke, Thomas Redmond and the two secretaries William Hutchinson and John J. Donohoe together with Fr. Gaul, Professor, St. Peter's College. This special Committee discussed the new National Council's directive and possible *'Improvements in the general management of the Society.'* Their report was eventually sent to the Bishop for his endorsement.

Other alterations and general changing about with the rules occurred on the 10th February 1946.   The five man committee that carried out this investigation were John Louth, Solicitor, Thomas A. Furlong, the two secretaries John J. Donohoe and John F. O'Rourke . Their advice was only implemented on the 8th February 1948. On the 1st of April 1952 the club attempted to *'Re-draft the rules of the club to bring them up to date.'* This is very interesting.   I have searched the minute books from this date to find these 're-drafted rules' and they are nowhere to be found. They simply do not exist in any written document. Therefore, one must assume that the document was either mislaid or discarded when the club relocated back in January of 1982. I find it strange and hard to accept that this could be the case as when Dick Murphy, Hon. Secretary handed over the minute books and a selection of other documents in February 2004 to me, there was among them a very worn and tattered document entitled *'St, Iberius Club & Catholic Young Men's Society, Wexford* General *Rules of Management' (See the foregoing).* I distinctly remember Dick saying to me as he gave me the document *'look after this; it's the only one we've got.'* As it happened, I did find an exact, almost new; copy in amongst the minute books. Surely if this older set of rules was able to be maintained should we not expect to have a copy of the "re-drafted" more up to date rules looked after with equal care and attention?   It is another mystery which will not be solved.

What is slightly puzzling is that whilst all this talk of drafting new rules was going on the club had already received instructions regarding the constitution of the Catholic Young Men's Society of Ireland, of which it were affiliated, and thus should have been implementing those rules. The Irish hierarchy approved the constitution of the C.Y.M.S.I. in January 1939 and subsequently the amendments in 1947, 1961, and 1984.   The National Congress amended the constitution to allow women to join in 1994 and the Society has subsequently changed its name to comply with the law.

ELECTION NIGHT AT THE C.Y.M.S.

"Look ! they've elected a new President."

Council and Management

The election of the Council members was balloted from the body of the members. For a long period of time only the higher rate subscription members were allowed a vote in this election. The apprentices, schoolboys and labourers in the lower subscription group were excluded from serving on or electing those who served on the Councils. From the 18th December, 1876 the following rule, which was already in existence, was placed in writing – *That the ordinary subscriptions of members of the Society will in future be ten shillings (10/=) per annum payable in advance, except for working men, apprentices or school boys who will be admitted at six shillings (6/=) per annum which subscription they may pay half yearly if they wish, but they cannot play on the billiard table or vote at an election of the council unless they pay their full years subscription in advance.' Only the ten shilling (10/=) members will be eligible for election as members of the Council.* This shameful class system, which was the norm

in those days, lasted until the 1920s from which time onwards every member in the club were afforded equal status with the right to vote and select the members of the Council. It would appear from the foregoing set of rules that everyone was now allowed to take part in the election of the Council whilst, in actual fact, the only change was that the 6/= members would be allowed to elect the Council members, only if they paid their subscription a year in advance. At least the Wexford Branch of the C.Y.M.S. was moving towards a democratic type of management. These Councils elected from the 10/= members were very much the cosy little coterie with very little chance that they could be unseated from their almost privileged position. But this was all to come to an end. Perhaps what you are about to read now was the beginning of the end for the class system that existed in this branch of the Society.

The most shameful night in the Wexford Society's history

Bearing in mind the aforementioned '*class system*' it is interesting to learn of the attempts of the 6/= members to revolutionise the running of the Wexford branch. The first ever dispute amongst the members took place at the A.G.M. held at 8.30.p.m. on Sunday 21st January, 1877. Because of the shameful conduct of the dissenters I shall conceal their names with the following fictitious monikers. Joe Muggins and Peter Youngfella, from 44 Yobs Place, Whipper-Snapper Hill, Wexford.

The Rev. James Browne, C.C. was in the chair with approx seventy members in attendance '*all of whom were qualified to vote for the election of Council.*'

This meeting was continuously disrupted by members objecting to everything that Robert Hanton, the Hon. Secretary endeavoured to say or do.

The real reason why this disruptive behaviour took place is not written into the minutes. It's a case of the victors not recording the issue in full. One is left to make an educated guess as to what the real problem was all about. I am of the opinion that dissatisfaction among a large number of the members related to how the club was administered by the Council. This discontent had being festering for years and when a leader appeared prepared to challenge the status quo a large number of the members were prepared to back him by voicing their opinions. I will elaborate on some points concerning the real issues:

1. A new President, Rev. James Browne, C.C., was elected only a month prior to the holding of this A.G.M.

2. The Council had just produced new rules regarding the 10/- and the 6/- members. The 10/- members consisted of mostly businessmen or persons in high paying positions and the 6/- members consisted of unskilled workingmen, apprentices and schoolboys.

3. The 6/- members were denied a vote in the election of the Council members and they themselves were excluded from sitting on the Council. If they were prepared to pay one-year subscription in advance then they could vote, but they could never sit on the council.

4. Just prior to this A.G.M. you will note that many of the 6/- members had up-graded themselves to 10/- members thereby qualifying to vote for the new Council in this election. This seems to have been a coordinated attempt to dislodge the '*Old Guard*' from the Council and replace them with new blood.

The meeting and its extraordinary proceedings

Having read the minutes of the last meeting the Secretary then proposed William Scallan and William Devereux to act as scrutinizers for the election of members for the Council. Immediately Mr. Joe Muggins objected stating that he thought that *these gentlemen were not sufficiently reliable and that they might have a bias* and Mr. Muggins went on to propose three other members namely, Messrs Breen, Cassin and O'Callaghan for scrutinizing duties.

The Rev Chairman then after much difficulty in obtaining the opportunity to speak, was successful in getting the party *who gloried in the name of 'The Opposition' to be content with having two of their appointed to go in as scrutinizers with the first two suggested by the Hon. Secretary.* It is obvious that there were two factions in the club and the '*opposition*' have succeeded in having two of their members elected as scrutinisers, contrary to the Council's wishes.

The Hon. Secretary commenced reading the new rules of the billiard room and election procedures. There ensued '*innumerable objections, the meeting becoming extremely noisy, no act of the Secretary could escape objections*'. The Rev. President attempted to bring order to the meeting so that the agenda could be proceeded with. Then one of the '*disorderly crowd*' put himself forward for a moment or two and it was thought from his attitude that he was about to recite Hamlet's famous soliloquy, '*To be or not to be*' but in this case it was not to be as he commenced to recite in a slow sensuous voice '*Seven years have now past and gone and.....*'. At this point Richard Murphy interrupted him and requested that the Rev. President should tell this gentleman that he was out of order and the young man was obliged to keep his recitation for a more congenial audience. What this silenced young man was about to say we do not know, but we can only conjecture that it related to something that happened seven years hence and thus was festering for that length of time.

The Rev. President then retired to the billiard room when the voting papers were being handed out but he was recalled as '*the opposition*' objected to the Hon. Secretary giving out the polling papers to the voters. The Rev. President asked '*What harm the secretary could do to the voting papers?*' No logical response was forthcoming and Mr. Walsh, P.C. asked what the '*factious opposition*

want'. The yelling and shouting of over thirty voices rang through the room to the disgust of the more sombre and orderly members, some of whom were connected with the Young Men's Society since its foundation in Wexford by Dean O'Brien. They had never witnessed anything to equal the present unruly scene within its walls.

The Secretary now proceeded to call out the names of those who were entitled to vote and to distribute the voting papers starting with the Rev. President, but Mr. Muggins at once objected to the Rev. President voting which caused great dismay to several members of the Council. After all, the Rev. Chairman had been elected an honorary member of the Society and President at a former meeting of the Council. The Secretary stated '*the fact he [Rev. President] had paid his subscription for 1877 alone entitled him to vote.*' The Rev. President quickly settled the matter by declining not to vote and the Secretary proceeded, in the midst of the continuous confusion and shouting, to distribute the voting papers to all on the list. At this stage several older members left the room '*protesting they would no longer continue in a Society whose members could be guilty of such disorderly conduct.*' What a sad situation it must have been to see old and respected members being forced to leave the Society. The Council was eventually elected.

Pandemonium at the A.G.M. 1877

There were two Vice-Presidents and two Hon. Secretaries elected on this council. The two Hon. Secretaries were later to be joined by yet another Secretary. To say nothing of the resignations from this Council that followed.

11

There is no doubt that two factions were at variance in the club at this period and that each appeared to have elected their preferences in the various Council positions.

At the first meeting of this new Council on the 29th January 1877 the minutes of the A.G.M. were read and presented to the then recognised Hon. Secretary, i.e. Joe Muggins to sign them off. He refused point blank to sign because he stated that *as they were not only incomplete but inaccurate also.*

Leaving aside our opinions, the facts of the case were that Mr. Muggins spoke the truth which cannot be denied. We are given no information on what dialogue then ensued.

The minutes simply continue with the next line *As the matter was not put to a vote the Rev. President signed-off the minutes.* One has to wonder why the issue was not settled with a vote on the matter. Perhaps the Rev. President was unwise in using his veto and signing the minutes when such a split in the Council existed? Then Richard Murphy stood up and resigned from the Council stating *He did not want to serve on the council this year.* Then on the 7th May, 1877 the Council received the following letter from Joe Muggins which was anything but flattering:

To the Council of the Young Men's Society

Gentlemen,

Owing to a pressure of business I beg to hand in my resignation of the post of Hon. Secretary to the Society, which was confided to me by the members.

From my little experience on the Council, I am of the opinion there is no necessity whatsoever for a Sec. [Hon. Secretary] to this Society nor a Council either. Therefore the resignation will inconvenience you but little.

I am gentlemen,

Yours,

(Signed) Joe Muggins

Mr. Muggins leaves no doubt as to what he thought of his fellow Council members. There were more casualties of the warring factions yet to come. At a meeting held on the 14th June, 1877 Peter Youngfella was ordered to send in a written apology to the President and Council for the disrespectful language he used towards them and the Society whilst giving evidence in the case of Doyle versus Busher.

On the 21st June Peter Youngfella handed in his resignation as a member of this Society. The minute book reads; *This was unanimously accepted with pleasure'* and continued with *'that his name be erased from the list of* member and went on to state that *this scurrilous document [Peter's letter of resignation] be written in full on the minutes as a standard monument of the refined mind of the* *44 Yobs Place, Whipper-Snapper Hill, Wexford , Chairman.* (Sic) Peter's highly facetious letter of resignation follows:

Wednesday 19th June 1877 Minutes

At a meeting held on Tuesday evening, 8.30 pm. in 44 Yobs Place, Whipper-Snapper Hill, Wexford. [Peter's Home] Peter Youngfella in the chair no one else present. It was unanimously ordered that the communication received by the Chairman from the Catholic Young Men's Society, Paul Quay be treated with contempt as no other action would be proper considering the facts that it came from a body not only incapable of transacting business of a trivial matter but incapable even to mind their own business and who with malice a foresight expelled unjustly the former without even a hearing well knowing that as in the case of the last election the least heard the better.

Believing the sentiment of the above resolution to be true and knowing that the idea of an apology from me emanated from the ring or clique of beings improperly and forcibly managing the Society (exclusive of a few honourable exceptions) I tender my resignation from connection with such a body as the contemptible beings I have alluded to.

I feel it an honour to remain yours in complete disjoint.

(Signed) Peter Youngfella.

What do you think of that? Peter pulled no punches and he certainly made sure that he had his say before he departed. Observe how he referred to the A.G.M election and '*the ring or clique.*' No doubt the issue of Doyle versus Busher had something to do with the dispute and Peter Youngfella was involved in giving evidence on behalf of one of the men and a heated exchange must have ensued which left Peter in the position that he found himself. No one could deny the humorous side to Peter's letter, especially if you consider some of the pretentious gentlemen that sat on those Councils back in those days. Whilst you may not agree with the content, he certainly had talent in penning a humorous letter.

1880s

In the beginning all the Council officials and members alike had to be elected. When the thirteen or so were elected they then elected or appointed their President, Vice-President, Treasurer and two Secretaries from amongst themselves. On the 22nd December 1859 the following two rules were established:

1. That member eligible to vote for the Council should be allowed to vote by proxy.

It would appear from this that some of these gentlemen were too busy to even bother to turn-up at the election of the Council. Are these guys for real or what? Some of the members who attend the meetings are denied a vote and these fellows want to do their voting by proxy.

2. That any of the Clergy (priests) can be elected President.

Sometime between February 1909 and February 1922, the Patron, the Lord Bishop of Ferns, held the authority and power to nominate the President of the society. From thereon the Presidency was always held by a clergyman, usually the Administrator of the town. Prior to this the Council appointed their own President. An example of this can be seen in the minutes of 7th November, 1864 when the Council request Richard Devereux (*one of the founders*) to become President. He declined the position of President so the Council elected him as Treasurer instead.

The next official position on the Council to become exempt from the election process was the Hon. Secretary position so from the 8th February 1948 this position became ex officio. Another interesting fact was that members were referred to as *'brother'* According to Article 61 of the C.Y.M.S. of Ireland constitution *'all members are to be addressed as brothers.'* It reads: *Members of the Branch must be addressed as brothers both at meetings and in official correspondence.*

The very first Annual Report was delivered to the members at a meeting held on the 24th December 1858 during which the Hon. Secretary, William Power reported on the statement of accounts as follows:

Receipts for the year (1858)	**£45-5-9**
Expenditure	**£44-0-11**
Balance on hand	**£ 1-1- 9**

Amongst the contributors to the Society's funds at this date were the following:

Most Rev. Dr. Furlong	**Bishop of Ferns**
Very Rev. Dean Murphy	**Parish Priest of Glynn**
Very Rev. James Roche, P.P.	**Parish Priest of Wexford**
The Very Rev. William Murphy	**Dean and Vicar General of Ferns**
Richard Devereux, Esq.	
Right Hon. Sir Thomas Esmonde, Bart.	**9th Baronet, Residence Johnstown Castle**
Anthony Cliffe, Esq.	
Stephen Ram, Esq.	
John Thomas Devereux, Esq., M.P.	**Deputy Lieutenant, Residence Rocklands.** *(Brother of Richard)*
James R. Crosbie, Esq.	

The next statement of account was delivered at the A.G.M. of the 31st March 1859. It appears that a quarterly reporting of the statement of accounts was established at this time. Up to this date the Council presented their report at each monthly meeting and later, as the business increased, this was expanded to the Quarterly General Meetings which were the forerunner to the Annual General Meetings which we are accustomed to in our times. The first Annual Report & Statement of Accounts was delivered in the late 1860s but from December 1858 the balance sheets were dealt with at each Council meeting.

The Club Name throughout the Years

One question that arises regarding the name of the Wexford branch is 'from whence dose it come?' Any first year student of Irish church history and particularly Wexford history will know that one of the first Christian teachers to evangelise Wexford town was St. Iberius. Iberius is the Latin translation for Ibar. We read in an outline history of Wexford town that our Christian heritage most certainly predates that of our National Apostle St. Patrick, as we had our own missionary Ibar, whose presence is recorded under his many variants such as Iver, Iberius, Ivory and Yvorus. Ibar was of noble birth and descended from the Northern tribe of Ui Eachach Uladh of the barony of Ivreagh, Co. Down.

In the 5th century he founded his monastery on Beg-Erin *(Little Island)* in the north of Wexford Harbour. It is now lost in the reclaimed lands of the old bay. Some of the earliest records of Viking raids on Monasteries, mention Begerin. St. Ibar carried out his missionary work from 425 to 450 in Co. Wexford. Tradition says that he died on the 23rd April, 500.

All our Branch members are granted a Plenary indulgence on this date. His Holiness, Pope Pius IX, first granted this back in 1856. In all the documents and minute books I have perused and in all the interviews I have conducted with many members and ex-members, I have never seen this written and no one has ever mentioned it to me. I am convinced; therefore, that this date and the indulgences attached to it was unknown to members and must have been overlooked.

In an Old Irish poem, Ibar is mentioned as:

'A lamp was Bishop Ibar, who attained to the head of every piety
The flame over the wave in brightness, in Erinbeg he died.'

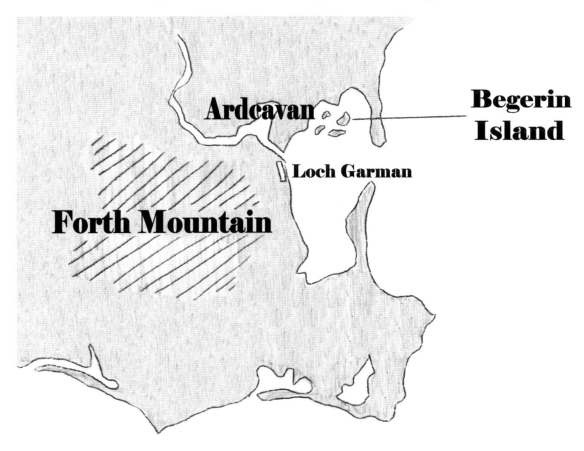

The 245-year old Church of St. Iberius, *(Church of Ireland)* on the Main Street, in the centre of Wexford town is another noted reference to this Wexford Saint's name. There was also a Parish in Wexford town named St. Iberius. In 1841 there was a population of 1,445 people living in 210 houses on its 16 acres. Another example of the use of the name in our town is the Street *'St. Ibar's Villas'*. The local cemetery at Crosstown is named *'St. Ibar's Cemetery'*. The church in Castlebridge is also named *St. Ibar's* and like the C.Y.M.S. has celebrated its sesquicentennial *(150th anniversary)* in 2005. There is also St. Ivers, a well-known rural area south of the town and finally the C.Y.M.S. premises at the corner of Common Quay Street and Commercial Quay, Wexford was known as the *'St. Iberius House'*. This premises to-day still bears that name over one of its doors. When this club changed is name in 1898 it called itself 'The St. Iberius Catholic Club' *(Wexford)*. This then explains where the branch name originated. The club derives its branch name from our local missionary St. Ibar as do other Churches and places in Wexford. We can be sure, however, that the club was not using the branch name 'St. Iberius' at the outset. The branch names were introduced later to distinguish one C.Y.M.S. club from another. There is no disputing the fact that this club was commonly called the 'Wexford Young Men's Society' or simply the 'Young Men's Society' originally. This is interesting because at the very beginning Fr. O'Brien's original title for the Society was the 'Young Men's Society of the Immaculate Heart of Mary'.

Name Change of the Club 1898

The Council changed the name of the Society from 'Catholic Young Men's Society' (C.Y.M.S.) to the 'St. Iberius Catholic Club' which is well attested at the Annual General Meeting of the 27th February, 1898. William Hutchinson, Hon. Secretary delivered the following explanation of why the *"committee"* [Council] decided to change the name and function of the club. He delivered the following speech:

On entering the new premises the name St. Iberius Catholic Club was substituted for Catholic Young Men's Society. Your committee had two reasons for changing the name.

In the first place, a Catholic Young Men's Society means not only a place for the recreation of the members, but also a place for meeting and carrying out specified religious exercises. This was the intention of the promoters of the Catholic Young Men's Society at first, and for a long time their intentions were practised until the establishment of the Confraternity of the Holy Family, which absorbed within itself all the religious exercises of the members of the Young Men's Society. Once these religious exercises had not been carried out your Institution had no claim to the name of Catholic Young Men's Society. Secondly, your committee considered the name "Young Men's Society" entirely inappropriate, because the institution is not entirely confined to young men. Her portals are also open to men of every age, even to the man whose hoary locks have stood the blast of eighty or more winters. William went on to extol the *'new premises'* the Society had just occupied, by saying: *'Though as yet unfinished, and considerably in debt your council believe that the 'St. Iberius Catholic Club' comparatively speaking, is second to none of its kind in Ireland and that it not only supplies a long felt want, but that it is in full keeping with the other splendid Catholic edifices [twin churches] in the Town. --- A.G.M. 2nd March 1898.*

William Hutchinson informed the meeting why 'they' *(the Council)* decided to change the name. He did not request permission to do this nor did he offer the membership the right to voice their opinions on this very important matter. To make matters worse he failed to inform the meeting that the discussion to change the name had already been carried out a year previously, as is reported in the minutes of May 1897.

When the Society opened a bank account on the 20th April, 1897 in order to lodge all subscriptions received for the purchase of the new club, it was opened in the name of the 'Wexford Catholic Young Men's Society', but by the time they made their first lodgement to the account on the 3rd May they had already decided to change the name of the Society and thus the bank account. At the council meeting of the above date, we read that Patrick Walsh proposed and Frank Carty seconded the following: *That the name of the 'Wexford Catholic Young Men's Society' be changed to the 'Wexford Catholic Club' and that Mr. L.S. Kennedy* (Bank manager) *get notice of same.*

Leaving this matter aside you may have noticed that within one year of the Society occupying the new premises named 'St. Iberius House' this Council had adopted "St. Iberius" as their official name which was later to develop into the Branch name when they rejoined the Federation of C.Y.M.S.I. and that title 'St. Iberius' has remained with the Wexford branch ever since in one form or another.

In the local newspapers of March 1899 the club is referred to as the *"St. Iberius Club, Wexford"* and then in the same report it is called *'St. Iberius Catholic Club'*. Some two years after they took possession of this premises they ran

The Grand Bazaar of September 1899 to raise funds to pay for the new club. From this date onwards there can be no doubt that the club was using the St. Iberius name. This information is attested in the verse written by an honourable fellow member, Simon McGuire who wrote under the pen name of 'Milligan'. His humorous verse concerning St. Iberius *(the club's new premises and new name)* reads as follows:

Souvenir of Iberion

Simon McGuire

"Milligan" Having discovered that Iberius is a noun of the second or O declension declines it in this fashion:

Nominative:

If you're wanting a saint who lived easy and grand,
With a fine slated house and a good bit of land,
With a cow in the byre, and a pig in the sty,
A joke on his tongue and a wink in his eye;
I'll tell you of one, and for long it was said,
That Protestant notions he'd got in his head,
But the Young Men's Society saw the mistake,
And when wanting a patron himself did they take.
Saying "There isn't in Heaven a saint to suit us
Or safeguard our club with you I—BER – I –US."

Genative:

And the saint mighty pleased with the honour conferred—
He was fond of his fun with the boys, as you've heard—
Said he felt precious lonely up in the Main-Street,
And owned 'twas a pleasure gay fellows to meet;
But one thing he couldn't come under at all,
Says he, " Boys I've heard you've not paid for the Hall,
" And mighty unpleasant about the small debt;
"Go get up a bazaar, and leave yourselves free" ---
Faith that was the notion of I – BER – I – I.

Dative:

The council then met and they pondered awhile,
As they feared that bazaars mightn't just be the style,
For gaming and singing and flirting and such
Go on at those times, But the saint said " Not much!
"And we're heavy in debt, and I'll tell you, Begor,
"you'll have to look after the 'to' and the 'for'
"you've got to get money, so lay down your pomp,
" Let the young people all have an innocent romp;
" Just get up the bazaar and side shows put on,
" And you'll rake in the sheckles", said I – BER – ION.

17

Accusative:

The council went at it as hard as they could,

And the people assisted as Wexfordmen should;
The prizes were glorious and tickets were sold,
Till the saint sat with pride on a big pile of gold ---
" But wait till next Sunday and Monday," said he,
" And then maybe something like pluck you will see;
"And I'd like very much to be able to boast
"That the prizes will go to the men who spend most.
" But I'm certain the ladies will make the place hum;
"If not I'll be flummoxed", said I – BER – I – UM.

Vocative:

Said the Saint "You'll be needing some music, no doubt,
"A good band no leading bazaar is without;
"But in your case I think you could manage with two,
"And the Gorey and 3rd Royal Irish will do;
"While for song and amusements what could you ask more,
"Than those boys of your own, numbering nearly three score;
"They can sing, dance and whistle, strum string or sound reed,
"And an excellent concert they'll give you, indeed.
"Now, boys are you willing to sing, dance and play ?"
And they answered, "Of course we are", I – BER – I – E.

Ablative:

So the fun was arranged and the stalls are all bright
With a glitter and show that would dazzle the sight,
For the prizes stand out on the tables of plush,
And the people will come on both days with a rush;
The rattle of dice and the spin of the wheel,
And the eyes brightly flashing will make one's head reel,
But as to who the fairest or loveliest there,
You'd better not say, if you're wanting your hair.
For the ladies can do as they please, now you know,
They've got special permission from I – BER – I – O.

Sad Case:

There's a case of my own you've not heard of before,
But you'll know it quite well when the gay fate is o'er;
You'll enter the Market with pockets quite full;
And now and again an odd shilling you'll pull;
You'll be highest for this and lowest for that,
Till you notice the purse that once bulged is quite flat;
Then, perhaps, you will find you've won many a prize,
Or else that you're trapped by those bright flashing eyes—
And if you are one of the lot that is BUST
You can lay all the blame on Saint I – BER – I – UST !

----- **By "Milligan" (Simon McGuire), a club member. Printed by 'The People Wexford' 1899.**

In the first verse Milligan alludes to St. Ibar's meagre monk's life-style and pokes harmless fun at the rich Protestants for using his name on their magnificent church building that had stood on the Main Street for over 139 years at that time. He then states that the C.Y.M.S. is reclaiming the name back for themselves *(the Catholics of the town)*. In verse three he pokes fun at the C.Y.M.S. itself for its strict rules and stance against gambling and flirting etc. Ladies were not allowed in the club at this time and gambling was not considered a suitable way of raising funds for the Society. Milligan urges them to reconsider this policy and thereby look after the finances of the everyday running expenses of the club.

Two Examples from the Society's Documents

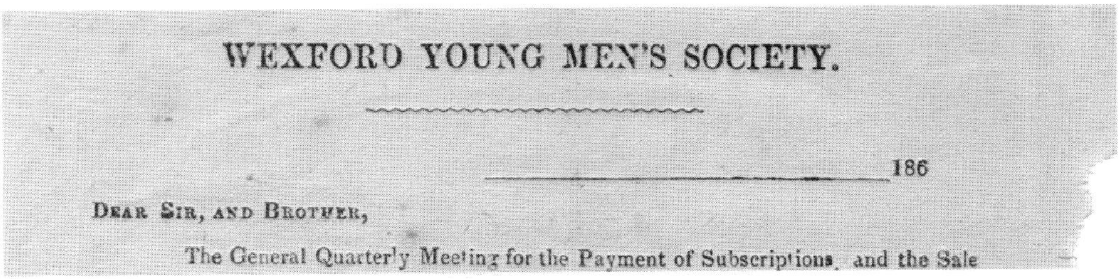

WEXFORD YOUNG MEN'S SOCIETY.

186

Dear Sir, and Brother,

The General Quarterly Meeting for the Payment of Subscriptions, and the Sale

1860s

St. Iberius Club & Catholic Young Men's Society,

92   WEXFORD,

1920s

The very first line of the 'Minute Book dated February 1902 to January 1924' states: *'Minute Book of the 'St. Iberius Catholic Club Wexford'.'* There is no doubt as to the club's name here.

The club tinkered around making minor changes and variations to its name several times since its establishment back in August 1855 and, as already stated, in the early days (1855 – 1859) it was referred to as the 'Young Men's Society'. On the 4th February 1859 they decided to title themselves as the 'Wexford Branch Catholic Young Men's Society' or simply 'Wexford Catholic Young Men's Society'. On the 27th February 1898 they made what was a fundamental change which took them out of the C.Y.M.S. fold, by calling themselves the 'St. Iberius Catholic Club' which lasted until February 1909. After eleven years in the wilderness they decided to return to the bosom of the C.Y.M.S. flock. They then named themselves the 'St. Iberius Club & Catholic Young Men's

Society'. This lasted 28 years when on the 14th February 1937 they altered the name again to read, 'Catholic Young Men's Society (St. Iberius Branch).'

This is the name it was known by for 68 years. In 1994 the time arrived for the club to change its name again.

With the emergence of new legislation in the state, it is now illegal to discriminate or exclude women from the Society. The constitution of the 'Catholic Young Men's Society of Ireland' was amended to allow women to join the C.Y.M.S. in 1994. To have lady members would render the name Young Men's Society' a ridiculous title. The word 'Young' is also ageist considering the age profile of most of the branches. This matter was discussed at National level and some of the suggestions for the new name proposed were: 'The Catholic Men and Women's Society of Ireland' and 'The Catholic Family Society of Ireland'. The last proposal seemed to be the most likely to be accepted alas, the title 'Catholic Men and Women's Society' was chosen in 2005, and that is now the official name of the Society.

Let us now explore the Society's sources of income, subscription charges, membership numbers, procedures for membership, rules & management of the Society and the Society at National Level
.

The Society's Source of Income

The total amount of subscriptions received at the meeting dated 23rd August 1855 was 13/4 1/2p. Initially, the membership subscriptions and collections from the three Guilds, i.e. St. Patrick, St. Mary and St. Joseph were the Society's main source of income. Other revenue in the early days was derived from the numerous lectures the Society organised in the town. These lectures were given by various eminent church dignitaries and were conducted in various venues around the town such as the Assembly Rooms in the Town Hall, the Theatre in High Street and in the club's own premises. They were usually open to the general public with a fee charged at the door. Some money was, also, collected from the bagatelle table from the 1850s, the harmonium and piano in the 1870s, the first billiard table from 1871 and chess and draughts appeared on the scene in 1925.

When finances were stretched Richard Devereux Esq., who was an exceedingly kind patron to the Society, was always ready and willing to help out. Rev. James Roche, the founder, who was also joint patron with Richard Devereux, was also sought at times of financial difficulty.

In March 1883 the Society was shocked with the loss of these two men, both patrons and generous benefactors. No one seems to have been recognised as patron of the Society from then until 1909. Sometime between 1909 and 1922 the title of patron was bestowed on the Bishops of Ferns and this is written into the Society's constitution and still applies to this day.

Richard Devereux, a renowned philanthropist and Christian gentleman, continues to be a benefactor up to the present time. He bequeathed, after his death, monies from his estate to the Society and to the St. Vincent de Paul Society.

By January 1920 the Society was forced to increase the senior membership subscriptions by a whopping 2/6. The juniors were spared any increase which is hardly surprising for those days. A junior at that time would most likely have been earning only 25% of what a man would have been earning unlike the practice of to-day, where young inexperienced people are paid almost on a par with their more knowledgeable and older work colleagues.

The following two entries in the minute books will serve to illustrate just how the Council viewed and dealt with the 6/- members. The first entry is dated 23rd February, 1886 and reads: *The council unanimously decided*

Richard J. Devereux, K. G.

that all Foremen in shops should pay 10/- subscriptions to the Society per year. On the 27th July, 1905 we see; *it has been ascertained that John Browne was receiving full bakers pay. It was decided to transfer him to the 10/- [senior] list of member.*

The Council members were fully aware of the social standing of the junior members. After all, the majority of the Council were employers in the town and were very 'au fait' with the wages they were paying and had they increased the juniors' subscriptions they would, in effect, have driven all the young men from the club. The juniors simply would not have been able to afford the increased subscriptions. You will note above that as soon as a junior member completed his apprenticeship or was promoted to higher or full wages, the Council then transferred him onto the senior members list and justifiably so.

The subscription charges throughout the years were as follows:

3rd **August 1855**, **one penny per week**. *(4/4 per year), (A half penny if more than one member in one home).*

	Senior Members	*Junior Members*	
1876-	10/-	6/-	per annum
1922-	12/6	6/-	per annum
1947-	15/-	6/-	per annum
1956-	£1.0	10/-	per annum
1959-	£1-10-0	15/-	per annum
1982-	£25	£12.50	per annum
2002-	32 Euros	16 Euros	per annum
2008	40 Euros	20 Euros	per annum

(Old age pensioners pay half the going subscription fee similar to the junior members)

Other sources of revenue for the Society throughout the years changed according to their popularity at any given time. The Society's main sources of income right up until the 1870s were members subscriptions, collections from guilds, donations from benefactors and admission fees to lectures, variety concerts and 'Smoking Concerts' (*I cannot enlighten you as to what a smoking concert was).*

In September 1863 a Mr. Dunne (*Council member*) made a plucky suggestion that the society run a '*Raffle*' to generate funds. Good God such enterprise! Was the man gone stark barking-mad? From the minutes we read: *Mr. Dunne said that something should be done to raise funds to furnish the hall* (new club premises) *and he proposed a raffle.* We are not privy to the discussion that ensued after this suggestion but the records record the following *but afterwards a lecture was considered more preferable.* One must remember that in those early days

of the Society gambling was a *'no go'* area and was strictly prohibited.

In the 1890s when the Society relocated to their new premises at Common Quay Street, their big revenue generators were staging concerts, plays, bazaars, dances and renting out the shop, the stores and individual rooms. From the 1920s to the 1940s whist drives, bridge tournaments, variety concerts, dances and running sweepstakes were popular. From 1940 up to the 1960s dances were extremely popular and became the club's main money spinner. However, by far the greatest ever source of revenue was, undoubtedly, Pongo which covered the late 1950s into the 1960s. This source of income was correctly credited with saving the Society from insolvency. I am proud to say that I was one of the '*Pongo Working Committee*' members and as such I can lay claim to the fact that I was one of the few who helped to keep this club from going bankrupt in those days. *(See details of all these funding activities in their respective sections)*

Subscriptions Paid Ex-Gratia

Some professionals, the more affluent people, were also having their annual subscriptions wavered in lieu of services. According to the minutes of a meeting held on the 29th March, 1941 a motion was proposed by Eugene McGrail and seconded by William R. Turner to *'make-up the annual subscriptions'* of Joseph Busher, Accountant, and Patrick Carson, Civic Engineer, as *Paid for this year in recompense for services rendered as Auditor and Engineer respectively.* Another case of this was on the 7th March, 1944 where John Byrne had his subscription fee considered as paid in lieu of his acting as Auditor to the Society during the year. All life members or honorary members are also exempt from annual subscriptions.

Selection and Election of Members

To become a member of the Wexford branch was not as easy as some people imagined. Not everyone who applied for membership was elected. Throughout the minutes many names were rejected being deemed as *'unsuitable'*.

Some people in top professions thought that they could just walk into this club and become a member. A certain Constable thought just that but discovered that he was refused. This matter was raised at a meeting held on the 19th October, 1892 and a discussion ensued concerning the admission of members of the Constabulary. It was decided that those who decided to become members of the club, must: *'be elected by ballot in the usual way'.* There was no favouritism. I was surprised to read this last line because way back in October, 1863, the following appears: *An order having been made in the Constabulary that none of that body would be members of any Society, one, who has lately joined this Society explained this to the caretaker and his name was erased from the membership list.* Obviously the Constabulary's ruling on this had changed over the years.

The Rev. President had a lot of influence in the Society as would be expected and quite regularly they exercised their authority above the Council as they saw fit. They had the right of the veto which was one of the fundamental rules of the Society. We read on the 17th March, 1859, where the Rev. President, *(Rev. Walter Lambert)* used his influence to obtain a young man entry into the club. It reads: *Mr. Pierce was proposed as a member of the Society. The President expressed a wish in this case (He* [Mr. Pierce] *being under seventeen years) that he would be admitted as a member.* Obviously this was not the norm but an exception to the rule to please the Rev. President's wishes. Elsewhere in this work I have remarked on members being referred to as Brother. The following entry dated 13th January 1863, refers to our Society as "The Brotherhood", it reads: *James Condon be admitted to the Brotherhood, passed unanimously.*

The requirements to become a member since the 1950s were, firstly, you had to be a practicing Catholic and if you were not a member of the Holy Family Confraternity, then you would certainly be obliged to join it prior to becoming a C.Y.M.S. man. The second step would be to get a friend or relative who were existing members to invite and introduce you into the club premises. The third step was for your friend or relative to introduce you to a council member or members explaining your wishes. Your friend now is automatically responsible for recommending you and putting your name forward for membership. This alone was a big responsibility and was not to be taken lightly as the popover's reputation was now at stake. Your name, address, occupation, and age, would then be put forward for consideration at the next available Council meeting. The fourth step would be for the Council meeting to consider the proposal and often the decision would be left over until sufficient information was collected concerning the individual's character and general conduct. Only then would a decision be made.

The President (*Chaplain*) would look into the person's spiritual life or lack of it. If even two council members objected to the newcomer being enrolled in the Society, then that person would not be elected to membership. At this stage it is necessary for a Council member to propose the prospective member for membership and another to second it and if this did not happen then you were out.

There are many cases where people were rejected. I'll give you a few examples for the reader to see just what I am speaking about. When I first read the following I was gob smacked, read on: *15th December 1881, a discussion arose about how many black beans it would take to disqualify a candidate from becoming a member. It was unanimously agreed that two black beans would be sufficient to disqualify someone.* And then on the 24th October 1887, Mr. X was disqualified because he got two black beans. By December of the same year two more gentlemen were disqualified for getting two black beans. One of these gentlemen was James Neill. I name him only because of what followed. On the 2nd January 1888, *The council that black beaned* [balled] *James Neill; because he was to join the band* [this was the Society's own band]. *The Rev. President* [Rev. Nicholas T. Sheridan, C.C.J.] *took on to himself to elect him* [James Neill] *and he was duly elected a member of the Society.* Rev. N. Sheridan was certainly a hands-on President, as can be seen here; he used the Chaplain's veto. Why Mr. Neill should have been black balled because he joined the band, is beyond me.

On the 17th November 1892, seven gentlemen were up for membership six were accepted and duly elected, however, Mr. Anonymous *was not elected as two black beans were given against him.* I could hardly believe my eyes when I read the foregoing. I thought I was reading the minutes of a freemason meeting. I never knew that the Society used the secret ballot and the black balling of undesirables in the election process of proposed members.

On the 12th of June the following year there were three candidates put forward for membership but one *'was black beaned [balled]'* and some of his friends wanted the decision reversed. The records state *such and such were unanimously elected members. Mr. X was not elected as the number of black beans necessary to disqualify him were given against him.* Some members of the Council said they thought a mistake had been made and wanted to

have him balloted for a second time. The Council could not see their way to accede to this, as it would be against *the rule that has been in force a long time.* There was another sentence added to this, which was scratched out. It read as follows: *By the request of those members he was to be balloted for the next meeting.* Well all this caused one hell of a hullabaloo as the Rev. Fr. Aylward, he President, would not sign-off the minutes of the last meeting until they deleted that last offending line. Fr. Aylward insisted that this line *Be expunged from the minutes.* As Fr. Aylward did not sign-off the minutes one must assume that some sort of heated discussion took place and the good Father waked out on the meting. William J. Robinson, one of the Council members signed-off and the offending line was struck-out. Once again one must assume that he did this with the full authority of the Council.

"For God's sake Michael - a rejection from the C.Y.M.S. isn't the end of the World !"

I was very surprised to discover that a candidate for membership could be black balled by as little as two Council members. It is also obvious that this system of balloting prospective members was in force for quite some time, if not from the very outset.

This practice of balloting members is almost identical with the practice of Freemasonry. Initially the Freemason's were predominately anti-Catholic. There was a Papal Bull issued against Freemasons and secret societies over a century ago and Catholics were forbidden to join those societies. For these reasons one must assume that our founding fathers were definitely not freemasons, but can anyone doubt or deny that they were familiar with and did in fact adopt Freemason procedures for the balloting of prospective members to their ranks?

Whilst on the subject of character – at the Annual Reunion held on Sunday 9th January 1887 a guest speaker Rev. Thomas Murphy had this to say: *The fact of belonging to the C.Y.M.S. in Wexford was a passport of good conduct.* – 'The People', 12th January 1887. Enough said on this subject.

23

The Promise

Full Membership of the Society has as a basic requirement, the taking of the Promise.

(a) Before a Probationer is invited to take the promise, the Branch Committee must be satisfied that such a person (I) is a committed Catholic, (II) is fully conversant with the Society's objectives and (III) has made a commitment to the Society's work.

(b)The Promise is taken by a Probationer (*or group of Probationers*) in the presence of the Chaplain during the monthly meeting or in the course of a Church Ceremony.

The Text of the Promise

I *(Person's name)* wish to become a member of the Catholic Young Men's Society of Ireland and to enrol in the Association of the Miraculous Medal and the Arch Confraternity of the Immaculate Heart of Mary.

I promise to be faithful to the Society and its objectives and to co-operate with the members in carrying out whatever may be asked of me.

I ask you, Father Chaplain, to bless this intention. *(The Chaplain then presents the member with the Society Emblem.)*

The Society's Emblem

The Emblem has long been the Crest of the National Federation and it was initially authorised and approved at the First National Convention held in Dublin in 1932.

It was to be worn as a badge by all members and it is a composite badge of triple significance. The old Roman Lamp with Flame denotes the members' love for the light of Faith. This Faith should be a guiding light to members in their own lives. The Society's motto is inscribed in Latin; *'Fortes-in-Fide'* and translates *'Strong in Faith'*. The letters on the lamp are the first and last letter of the Greek alphabet, i.e. Alpha and Omega meaning Christ the beginning and the end. *I am alpha and omega, the beginning and the end, the first and the last* — the revelations of the Lord Jesus Christ to St. John the Apostle

(Revelations 22:13) The Greek letters 'P' and 'X', superposed on the lamp are the first two Greek letters of the name Christ. This is the Chi-Rho cross, later to be known as the Constantine Monogram. It is formed by joining the first two letters of the Greek word for "Christ" (resembling English 'P' and English 'X'). Tradition informs us that the Roman Emperor Flavius Valerius Constantinus had a vision of the Chi-Rho cross just prior to the battle of Milvian Bridge ('In Hoc Signo Vinces' in this sign thou shalt conquer) and he inscribed the Chi-Rho on his standard and ordered his soldiers to do the same on their shields. The battle was won and the rest is history.

The ring, which encloses and keeps this two-fold Love and Faith and its Divine Founder, denotes the strength of the C.Y.M.S organisation. No member is alone, with him in the mighty circle of his brothers animated with the same zeal for Faith and Fatherland. The founder, Dean O'Brien, emphasised as one of the characteristics of the Society when he spoke of *The spirit that springs from association, which makes an individual feel in himself the strength of a Community, and makes a locality feel the vigour of a Province or of a Nation.*

I would venture the chain holds us firmly in our unbreakable faith within the circle of our brotherhood.

The President of the Wexford branch, Fr. Doyle Adm., on the 28th May 1949 at the Wexford celebration for the Catholic Young Men's Society of Ireland Centenary had the following to say regarding the emblem *He appealed to all the members to wear the emblem of the Society. It was a composite badge of triple significance. The old Roman lamp with flame denoted the members love for the light of faith "fortes in Fide" Strong in Faith, was the motto of all C.Y.M.S. associations. Superimposed on the lamp were two Greek capital letters of the name Christ. This was known as the Constantine Monogram, because originally designed and used by the first Christian Emperor, Constantine. Finally the ring, which enclosed and kept this two-fold love of Faith and its Divine Founder, [Jesus Christ], denoted the strength of the C.Y.M.S. organization. The member of the C.Y.M.S., who took part in Catholic Action, was not alone. With him was the mighty circle of his brothers animated with the same seal of Faith and Father-Land.* -- Fr. Doyle, Wexford Branch President, (speaking at the May 1949 C.Y.M.S. Centenary Celebrations in Wexford).

**Emblem of the Wexford
C.Y.M.S.. Pre-1924 to 1932**

Whilst the above emblem/badge on the right has been the official emblem/badge of the Society since the first national convention held in Dublin in 1932, the Wexford C.Y.M.S. had a different badge to that one prior to that date. I am unaware if this badge was exclusive to the Wexford branch as in all the research I conducted I have only come across this badge on this one occasion and that was in an advertisement for the Wexford C.Y.M.S. 'The Grand Whist Drive' of 1924 and it was published in the Wexford People newspaper. How long this emblem was in use prior to 1924 is not known. The shield in the centre of the design bears the letters C.Y.M.S. inside the four quarters, the belt surrounding the shield bears words Catholic Young Men's Society. The inscription below is too difficult to decipher. Photocopies from newspapers are notoriously bad and it is impossible to read. If I were to hazard to guess I would say it is a Gaelic inscription mentioning Loc Garman. If it was, it would be unique to the Wexford branch, either way it is unique. I have published the emblem here for you to see and I think it is a fine design and a badge that any Wexford member would be proud to wear on their lapel.

It seems that Dean O'Brien omitted nothing when he founded the C.Y.M.S. Apart from formulating a brilliant constitution he also wrote a charter song for the Society which could well be described as the C.Y.M.S. anthem or the battle hymn of the C.Y.M.S. I am publishing it in full for the reader to peruse. One cannot help but wonder how many of our members sing it or are even aware of its existence.

Charter Song of the Young Men's Society

(The C.Y.M.S. Hymn)

by

The Very Rev. Richard Baptist O'Brien, D.D.,

1st Verse.

Chorus.
What shall the Young Men's toast be, friends,
This festive night of ours,
When Hope her flowers of promise sends,
And Faith their varying beauty blends,
To crown the joyous hours.

Solo.
The Church! Oh yes, the Church, fair Queen,
Her sceptre round *us* gathers,
What e'er of worth the world has seen,
Faith's Lights and Martyrs that have been,
The mind's illustrious fathers.

Culti Chorus.
The Church we pledge, our Mother Church,
We pledge the Church – Hurrah!
We pledge the Church – Hurrah! !

2nd Verse.

Chorus.
And Brothers, let us pledge again,
To that, the next and nearest –
The name that's dear to Christian men,
Christ's Vicar! Bless him, God! Amen!
With graces best and rarest!

Solo
The Pope! The Pope! – we bid him hail,
Whose love is always nigh us;
Though lies asperse and foes assail
His lordly reign, 'twill never fail,
We pledge the great Pope Pius.

Culti Chorus.
The Pope – we pledge the Triple Crown,
We pledge the Pope – Hurrah!
We pledge the Pope – Hurrah! !

3rd verse.

Chorus.
Then friends, this Xmas time of faith,
What spell of power can bring it?
E'en though till then we watch and wait,
And heart and soul lie desolate
We'll still expectant sing it.

Solo.
We'll pledge then, Knowledge, Self-Control,
Love, Union, Self-reliance,
The Vigour of a nation's soul,
That walks right onward to its goal
And bids all foes defiance.

Culti Chorus.
Love, Knowledge, Union, Self-Control,
We pledge, we pledge – Hurrah!
We pledge, we pledge – Hurrah! !

4th Verse.

Chorus.
Once more a pledge – to hope most dear,
It meetly crowns the others.
We pledge the earnest men who rear
Our glorious standard far and near –
We pledge our absent Brothers.

Solo.
We pledge – we pledge – the Brotherhood,
By every sea and shore;
The noblest band that ever stood
In Virtue's ranks to strike for God,
We pledge them o'er and o'er.

Culti Chorus.
The Brotherhood! - The Brotherhood!
We pledge with one cheer more!
We pledge with one cheer more!

Published in 'The Catholic Circle' (Liverpool) - 9th September 1905.

27

Methods of Enlisting New Members

No one can accuse the Council of failing to enlist new members. On the 30th September 1863 the Rev. President *urged the members to encourage new members to join to help pay the expenses of the Society. He himself said that he had being speaking to Capt. Doyle at Devereux's* [probably Richard Devereux's shipping office] *who said he would join and that he was sure of getting a few other Captains* [to join]. It was more than likely that Richard Devereux invited the President to speak with his employees. He had a large fleet operating from Wexford Quays at the time. Many of the Catholic businessmen of the town encouraged their employees to join and in some cases I wager that the employers even paid the first subscription and proposed them for membership. A novel and creative entry in the minutes states that the Council were going through their accounts and when they came to a bill from Mr. Power, New Ross for £1-19-4. The secretary was ordered *to write Mr. Power, to see would he allow £1* (his yearly subscription) *to be taken off the bill.* Now that's one way of getting members to pay up their subscriptions on time.

In 1891, the club had a circular drawn-up showing *the benefits of the Society to the young men of the town.* They had this distributed to all the Catholic shopkeepers and men of standing in the town asking them to support the Society by becoming members. In February of 1892 the exact same circular was sent out once again, only this year the club sent out a deputation consisting of James Kavanagh, Michael O'Connor, Michael Nolan, John Cosgrave and the two secretaries *visiting all the shops who got the circular and they succeeded in enlisting forty new members.* At the A.G.M. on the 10th February 1935 the membership was urged *to try and introduce new members to help the club to pay its way.* And it went on to state *With counter attractions of pictures [films], theatres, dances etc., and the club is passing through a critical period.* What on earth would they have said to day if those old chaps were here to see the 'attractions' or should I call them distractions? Nothing much had changed in the ensuing year so the Council decided to do something about it. At a meeting dated 3rd March 1936 it is stated that the *membership of the Society has fallen considerably* and as it was necessary to keep up the membership for the running of the club successfully it was decided to send out circulars again to the *principal professional and business men* of the town appealing for them to help to carry on the Society *with their subscriptions.*

Another breeding ground for potential young men suitable for the C.Y.M.S. ranks was to be found in the ranks of the Catholic Boy Scouts 2nd Wexford Troop. The Scouts ethos of caring for the community and their absolute loyalty to their organisation and Mother Church made these young men ideal candidates for the C.Y.M.S.

In 1950 the Society wrote to the Boy Scouts in an endeavour to get them to join the Society when they left the scouts on attaining the age limit. I believe that George Bridges or Tom McGuinness may well have been the men who suggested this. I have compiled a list of all Society members whom I know to have been members of the 2nd Wexford Troop Catholic Boy Scout movement. This list can be seen in the miscellaneous section at the back of the book. The Troop was founded in 1927 by Wexford chemist R. J. Sinnott, who was the first scoutmaster. Stevie Martin and Murth Joyce were also scoutmasters and all three men were members of the Wexford C.Y.M.S.

Badge of the Catholic Boy Scouts of Ireland

Non Members Using the Club

If one was to count the number of young men who were non-members who frequented or visited the club and used its facilities, one would arrive at a number far exceeding the total membership that is on the register (*approx. 4,000*). I personally knew umpteen lads who were on the C.Y.M.S. premises and were not members and never did become members. I should imagine that practically every young man in Wexford town must have been in the C.Y.M.S. premises at some time or another. Throughout the minute books there are constant references to this activity. The oldest case that I came across was dated 21st August 1883 where the Council discussed this problem and ordered a notice to be erected which read *None but members are allowed to frequent these rooms. Any member can introduce a stranger* [newcomer]. Of course a member could invite a visitor into the club for a couple of days or so before the caretaker would start asking questions. The caretaker would then ask the individual to either apply to become a member or vacate the premises and not to return.

As an example I quote the following case which was dated the 19th March 1900. *The caretaker reported that John Kirwan Jnr. from John Street, a non member, was visiting the billiards room and it was decided he should become a member or cease frequenting the club.* Young John was the grandson of Ald. John Tyghe, T.C. a long time member of the Society's ruling Council. Anyway John applied and was duly elected a member of the

Society on the 10th April 1900 in keeping with the Council's wishes.

As a matter of interest young John Kirwan was a student in Blackrock College and played rugby for the college's famous fifteen and he also represented Co. Wexford in the Leinster Rugby Games. *(See sports section in Vol. II)* At the outbreak of the First World War he patriotically enlisted in the Irish Guards as indeed did thousands more brave young Irish men. Alas, after only a few months training he was given a rifle and sent to France on the 16th August 1915. He fought in the battle of Loos, Flanders and was reported killed in action on the 30th September. He was posthumously awarded the *'British War Medal'* and the *'Victory Medal'*.
(See awards section .Vol. II) I wonder how many more of the past members had similar interesting stories to relate.

The most unlikely visitor to have come to the Wexford C.Y.M.S. as a guest was undoubtedly Ernest Stewart proprietor of *'Stewart Star Amusements'*. My father brought him to the club and gave him the grand tour and, believe it or not, I was tagging along. This story is related in full in the section concerning the carnival.

John Kirwan, jnr.

Membership Numbers

On the 8th March 1860 the Council ordered a report to be drawn-up and printed in pamphlet form and that it should contain the names and addresses of all the members for the passed year. This was the first official attempt and forerunner to the Society making a registry of its membership. Up to this time the Society had no idea just how many members was on their books. There was no members' register and the Warden's over the Guilds only maintained their own individual records. There was no real unity of effort to merge this information until this date which alas was only a once off. The first real attempt to compile a members' register was on the 30th September 1863. The findings were – the total members of the three guilds was 141 prior to 1863, and only 101 on the commencement of 1863 and to make matters worse, only 58 of those were fully paid members.

At the A.G.M. dated 14th February 1892 the club had 160 members on their books, and speaking about this the Secretary had this to say: *About one hundred and sixty members the largest number that has ever been in the list of members since the Society was established in the year 1851 [sic].* Had the secretary been able to see into the future he would have discovered that the highest number of members ever at any time was in the year 1925 when it was recorded that we had 301 members on the club books, 237 of them were senior members and the other sixty four were junior members. This was the greatest number of members that this Society ever had on its books throughout its long history. The lowest number of members occurred in the year 1987, where it was recorded that we only had 36 members in total and seven of them were life members *(non-paying)*. The average number of members in the Society at any one year would be approx 140 souls. In the 153 years of the Society's existence there were around 4,300 young men and some not so young men who were members of this great club and I have listed as many of these names as was possible throughout the history. (See profiles and the photo gallery in Vol. 2 also).

Throughout the Society's history the membership numbers have ebbed and flowed just like the tide, the numbers were up one year and down the next. The steady influx of new members which compensated for those who were leaving kept the membership numbers at an even average throughout the years as you can see from the record that follows. Whilst many have come and gone for their various reasons, there was always a vein running throughout the club's history of rock-solid committed members. Men who have joined the club as young men and who have been staunch members right up to the end of their days. There is much about such men in these pages as you progress through the book.

In the 1850s when the excursions and soirées were in full swing some members would leave the Society after having the benefit of having attended these functions. This kind of conduct was common. On another occasion, when the Council disposed of the bagatelle table, many young men left the Society. Another rule passed in September of 1863, stated *That members leaving the Society are to notify the council in writing, otherwise they are accountable to pay subscriptions when they return.* This was a common happening throughout the history of the Society when many people would just simply allow their membership to lapse and then rejoin the Society. Many others have been forced to emigrate to find work and, not surprisingly, this last group was one of the main reasons for people leaving this Society. You can find examples of this throughout the minute books. In 1901 some twenty of the club's *best supporters left ... their sphere of duty calling them away to other places ... your committee* [council] *wishes them success in their new occupation of life* and then at the A.G.M. on the 31st December 1910, we read: *there were eleven members who left under the usual circumstances such as leaving Wexford to take up employment in other parts* (meaning emigrating to England). Note the phrase used in this entry, *'Left under the usual circumstances'* surely that says it all?

In 1912 we find almost the exact same sentence regarding nineteen members leaving to *'take up employment elsewhere.'* *'Elsewhere'* being a nice euphemism for England. People have being leaving this Country for work in England since God was a boy. In the early 1950s when I was a young lad playing on the Quays in the summer evenings, I often stopped and stood to watch the trainloads of humanity being shunted-down to the ferryboats at Rosslare Harbour destined to be shipped-out to the highest-bidder in the labour markets of Great Britain. Little did I know then in my childish naivety that I too would be taking that journey in less than nine years hence.

At least fifty per cent of the young men who were members of the C.Y.M.S in my time emigrated to England for work. The number of club members leaving to emigrate to England seeking employment was a good indicator of the situation which existed in Wexford town itself and on a broader scale it portrayed the position in Ireland as a whole. The Council members were well aware and in tune with the membership regarding the unemployment situation in the town and they showed great understanding and kindness to the less fortunate members of the club in those harsh times. There are many examples where leeway was given to the unemployed members of the Society. Having said this I must relate that no such kindness or understanding was afforded the unfortunate unemployed of my day in the late 1950s and early 1960s.

On the 17th May 1922, a list of the unpaid members was sent final notices *but due to unemployment others would be dealt with in the best interest of the club.* Some promised to pay as soon as they could. However, it was discovered that many others *Had been unemployed for some time and unable to pay at present.* The Council decided to take no further action with regard to these members at the time. These were hard-times and many people *'could ill afford to pay their subscriptions.'* Many were out of work for long periods and, therefore, had no choice but to leave the club when they received the final notice to pay-up. Others lingered as long as they could until the inevitable happened and they were struck-off. This was a regular occurrence throughout the years. I doubt if there was a single year that passed when someone wasn't struck-off. The caretaker was given the unenviable task of going around knocking on the doors of members in arrears in an attempt to collect the unpaid subscriptions.

In 1912 there was a massive amount of members in arrears with their subscriptions and the caretaker was instructed to collect from all. The result of his efforts can be seen in a meeting held on the 4th of July when it was recorded that the caretaker reported back that there were *Still twenty members in arrears with their subscriptions.* The Council having heard the reasons and considered the matter then decided *Owing to the exceptional time through which the members and the people of the town in general have passed within the last year. The council decided on taking no further action with regard to the other members in arrears for some time.* So here we see that twenty members were unable to pay their subscriptions and they were given a reprieve. The "exceptional time" the people of the town had just endured was the strikes and lockouts of 1911-12.

Members, who were deemed capable of paying their subscriptions but hadn't done so, were being automatically struck-off the membership list. We read in the minutes of the 6th August 1946 that after endless warnings and final letters the Hon. Secretary was instructed that with the exception of William Ffrench, any other member of the Society who had not paid their current subscription was to have their name struck-off and the caretaker was to be instructed that: *if such members wished to renew their membership that they would have to be proposed and seconded in the usual way and pay two years subscription.* We are not informed what Mr. Ffrench's circumstances were but obviously there must have been justifiable reasons why his case was treated as exceptional.

At a Council meeting held on the 9th of December 1947 John J. O'Rourke pleaded a case of leniency on behalf of one such member who found himself struck-off. John F. O'Rourke proposed, and it was seconded by Eugene McGrail, that Mr. X, a lapsed member, is allowed to rejoin the Society without having to be re-elected on payment of two years subscription. One councillor proposed that the rule of the Society be adhered to. No one seconded him and O'Rourke's proposal was carried. To force someone to go through the indignity of applying for re-election to membership was an insult to that person and it was good to see that some Council members were trying to discard with this rule.

This harsh rule was discarded with by the 1950s and members could re-join by paying two years subscriptions without further ado. We are informed thus from the minutes of the 6th October 1952 which state *Regarding membership list, it was decided to scratch-off all members (who frequented the club) who had not paid their subs, and to inform them that they must pay two years subscription to rejoin the club.* Deleting non-subscription paying members from the list has been necessary throughout the years right up to the present time. The largest number of members ever struck-off at any one time occurred in the 1980s and the event could well be christened the 'C.Y.M.S.'s night of the long knives.' It was an absolute massacre. The minutes record *Fifty-six members were struck-off the list of members for not having their subscriptions paid for this year.* –3rd May 1883.

Membership Numbers over the Years

DATE	COMMENT	MEMBERSHIP TOTAL
3 August 1855	Feast of the Assumption	A few young men
August 1856	At the inaugural meeting in George's Street	60
24 February 1856	50 more joined	110
Late 1856	It was said that the membership was approx.	200
19 December 1858	Known from John O'Brien's farewell address to the Society that there were at that meeting	160
1858-1876	The Guild books were the only records of members being maintained and on the 30 September 1863 a census was conducted which resulted in	141
1863		141
1890	The highest number for the past ten years	135
1898	70 new members joined this year alone	240
1914	Senior 183 + Junior 21 21 members left town this year	204
1925	Senior 237 + Junior 64	301
1947	There were 2 Honorary Life members	174
1959		138
1965	Senior 42 + Junior 44 + Honorary Life 2 This was the lowest number for over sixty years	88
1982	Honorary Life members 4	108
2007	Senior 56 + Junior 3 + Honorary Life 12	71

Chronological List of the Earliest Members

All the following gentlemen were at the first meeting on the 15th August 1855.

Edward Bent, Patrick Brien, John Browne, Peter Browne, Thomas Carty, Thomas Connors, Nicholas Cousins, Richard Cousins, Thomas Cousins, William Connick, Richard J. Devereux , Pat Donovan, Robert Doyle, John Duff, Joseph Dwyer, Edward FitzPatrick, Richard Furlong, Edward Green, William Griffin, John Hayes, John Healy, James A. Johnson (proprietor and editor of the People newspaper), John Lyons, Andrew McDonald, Charles McDonald, John Murphy, Martin Murphy, Nick Murphy, William Murphy (Main Street), Pat Nowlan, John O'Brien, W. Parle, Very Rev. Canon James Roche, P.P., V.P., Ned Roche, Pat Roche, William Rossiter, William Scallan T.C. (Working at Jefferes), John Shannon (High Street), James Sinnott, Matthew Sinnott, Patrick Sinnott, snr., Patrick Sinnott, Jnr., Pat Wade, Edward Whitty, John Whitty.

The following group were paid-up members and entitled to attend the first meeting but for various reasons were absent from the first meeting.

John Byrne, Philip Dillon, Robert Devereux, John Furlong, James Gaul, John Gordon, Thomas Keating, Denis Lambert, John Magee, Patrick O'Rourke, Matt Redmond, James Roche, James Sinnott, jnr. Pat Williams.

Register No 58. James Hanlon. Cornmarket / South Main Street. February 1858.
Register No 59. Marks Rourke (Mark O'Rourke), Cornmarket. c. March 1858
Register No. 60. John Stafford, High Street. The Librarian and Caretaker. March 1858
The above three members registration numbers and dates of joining are known for certain. *(See example page from John Stafford's 'General Memoranda' in O'Rourke profiles Vol. 2.)*

The next group followed closely behind, all before 1860.

Rev. James Barry, Pat Berry (Main Street), Michael Brown (The Faythe**),** John Busher (Student.), George Codd, (South Main Street), John Codd (Main Street / John Street) John Cogley, James Condon, Joseph Connors, (Main Street), John Cousins, Nicholas Crowe, James R. Crosbie (Victoria Cottage), Denis Dowd (Common Quay), Stephen Doyle (T.C. John Street) , John Durney (Main Street), Peter Fardy (Main Street), John Fortune (South Main Street.), Martin Furlong (Main Street), John Hammond (Faythe), Martin Jackman (North Main Street), Richard Kearns (Cornmarket. Working at E. L. Doyle's.), Thomas Kelly (working at Pitt's), Thomas Laffin (Main Street).Brendan Marnell (George Street), Miles Murphy (Selskar), Richie Murphy (Faythe), William Harris (Bullring), Richard Pierce (Waterloo Place), John Pitt (Bullring),William Power, David Sinnott (Main Street), Ald. John Sinnott, (Mayor of Wexford, working at Godkin's.), Robert Sinnott (Cornmarket), Rich (Richie) Walsh (working at Cloth hall), Thomas White.

The Society's Premises

'The Oratory' and adjacent House
Situated in St. Mary's Lane (off Bride Street)

This house was the society's first premises

The house on the left with the three dormer windows was the Oratory 'Prayer House'

On the Feast of the Assumption 1855 the Wexford Branch of the C.Y.M.S. was conceived and founded in a house named 'The Oratory' situated in St. Mary's Lane off Bride Street. This house was previously used as a Chapel, school room and prayer centre for the Catholics of the town.

Tradition has it that it was used after the time of Cromwell (*approx. 1673*) by the people of St. Mary's Parish. The adjacent house beside the churchyard steps has always been associated with the Oratory and was *most likely the residence of whatever priest officiated there.* According to Fr. Berney this house became the first premises of the fledgling C.Y.M.S. Whilst the Oratory was the house where the Society was conceived it was next door that became their premises, which accommodated a Council-

room, a recreation room and a library-room. For big important occasions the Society had to acquire the use of larger premises. For instance for the inaugural meeting held in August, 1856 there were 60 members and visiting guest speakers attending so the meeting was held at Dr. Sinnott's School in George Street which was situated where Melrose Court is today.

On the 13th December 1855, John Cullen (Secretary) presented a brass lamp for suspension before the statue of the Blessed Virgin and John Sinnott erected it. Miss O'Brien and Miss Laffin presented 'very beautiful artificial flowers' for the altar. These objects were obviously presented to the Oratory and prayer house in Mary's Lane.

Selskar, Abbey Street, John Street, Church Lane, Peter Kehoe's House, Mrs. Scallan's House and Allen Street.

By the 21st February 1856 the Society's premises were located all over the town. We have a few sentences recorded which inform us that the Society's reading room, hall and various other activities were situated in the following premises:- Temperance Hall at Selskar, Mr. Kinsella's House, Abbey Street, the John Street Hall, the Church Lane House; Peter Kehoe's House, Mrs. Scallan's House and the Allen Street House and Theatre. There is good reason to believe that these premises were loaned to the Society Ex-Gratia or if not at a nominal rate.

3 Rowe Street, Cornmarket and Main Street.

The Society next moved to number 3, Rowe Street, where the club held their first meeting at *"the new house"* on Thursday 20th March 1856. They then spent a short period in a house at Cornmarket and from there they moved on to the Main Street. By December 1858 they were in possession of *'a commodious house in a central position.'* This house was situated on the Main Street and had been formerly occupied by Miss French. Thanks to the generosity of the proprietor John Coghlin, M.D. the house was given free of rent and subject only to taxes. There were several spacious apartments in this building which enabled the Council to allocate rooms to the various sections which comprised the Society. There was a reading-room, an oratory, a debating-room, a bagatelle-room, a chess-room and living accommodation.

Photo. Michael O'Rourke

3 Rowe Street

Whilst at the Main Street they employed their very first caretaker - John Stafford for the princely sum of *'£1 per year and his rooms rent free.'* His job description was to clean the house regularly, light the fires, deliver the notices and look after the library. They, also, employed a man as *"door porter"* and the Society's name 'Young Men's Society' was proudly emblazoned in bold letters above the door and also inscribed on a brass plaque.

Allen Street

By the 25th August 1859 the Society had relocated once again to a house in Allen Street *(they were still there on October 1860)*. The minutes state *The council met for the first time in their 'New House' in Allen Street at 8 o'clock, etc.* The house belonged to a Mr. Finn and the rent was set at £12-0-0 per year *free of all taxes, with liberty to give it up at three months notice.* They had a small altar and a statue of the Blessed Virgin placed under the stairway. The wall behind the statue was coloured blue with gold stars adornments and here the members could kneel in silent private prayer as they entered and left the premises.

The Society was growing in numbers and from 1860 onwards they were on the lookout for larger premises. Every house that became available for renting in the town was viewed but to no avail as they were all too small. In October 1862 the President, Rev. William Murphy, spoke to the Council members at some length concerning the building of a *'New Hall'*. Most of the prominent and wealthy members all promised to subscribe lavishly to this idea.

Richard Devereux became involved in the debate concerning a new hall and in an open letter published in the newspapers he addressed Rev. Murphy and other prominent Catholic gentlemen who had obviously been exchanging opinions about a Catholic Hall for the town. Richard more or less said, *Come on now lads, and let's stop pussyfooting around. We want a Catholic Hall or Institute for Catholic purpose; only let the Clergy and laity of Wexford meet and decides to have it, and the work will be done.* He then suggested that it be called *'The O'Connell Hall'* so the memory of O'Connell be perpetuated in the most useful way. There is no further mention of this until a meeting held on the 3rd March 1863 when the newly elected President, Rev. Jeremiah Hogan, in his maiden speech had the following to say *Referring to the possibility of erecting a hall tho [sic] he would exert himself in every manner to obtain for the Society such a beneficial desideratum, yet from the bad state of the Country owing to continued deficiency in crops he could not think the consideration of this subject advisable at present.* He went on to tell the meeting that he had been conversing with Richard Devereux and that in the course of the conversation Mr. Devereux said *he would have great pleasure in giving the recently built house on Paul Quay for the use of the Society.* This was considered very benevolent and steps were taken by the Society to avail of the generous proposition. This property was situated in the area where Stafford's yards of the 1950s and 60s were located.

The Society had not taken up residence in the Paul Quay house by the 26th May 1863 as it is recorded that the *Secretary's testimonial was deferred till the Society has possession of the new hall* and then on the 11th July the President informed the Council that *Mr. Devereux had informed him of his intention to give the recently built hall to the Society* and that the Council should take up residence and possession of the premises as soon as possible. Mr. Devereux and many other members subscribed for the purchasing of furnishings for the hall and Fr. Hogan presented the Society with a bust of His Holiness Pope Pies IX. Friday 31st August was the date decided for the move.

Paul Quay

The Council meeting dated the 1st September 1863 records that *The first council meeting was held this evening at the "New Hall" [Paul Quay] Etc. Etc.* The exact location of this hall is not known but it must have been amongst dwelling houses because the Society's band was forbidden to practice in fear of upsetting the neighbours. Whilst at these premises the St. Vincent de Paul Society began using the club's rooms for their meetings. This arrangement had been agreed between the clergy, Mr. Devereux and both the Societies. The hall was not exclusively for the C.Y.M.S. Society but was to be available for any Catholic purpose. Both the C.Y.M.S and the St. Vincent de Paul Society shared a close relationship in the town as many of the C.Y.M.S. members were involved in charitable work and held official positions in charitable organisations. For example the following is the Council of the St. Vincent de Paul Society of 1886:

Council of St. Vincent de Paul Society 1886

Rev. Luke Doyle, Adm.   Spiritual Director
(One time C.Y.M.S. President)

Ald. John Sinnott,   President
(C.Y.M.S. member)

William Connick   Vice-President
(The C.Y.M.S. Vice-President and Treasurer)

Edward Dixon   Hon. Secretary
(C.Y.M.S. member)

Michael Walsh   Hon. Treasurer
(C.Y.M.S. member)

It is worth going back in time and taking a closer look at the Paul Quay and Richard Devereux connection. The Sisters of Mercy established a house at Paul Quay in December 8th 1840. Richard owned most of the houses on Paul Quay and many on Lower King Street also. When the Sisters moved to Summerhill to take over the running of the 'Redmond Talbot Orphanage', Richard Devereux built and endowed a Convent for them and here the nuns also operated a school. There is no doubt that Richard Devereux owned the house that the nuns occupied before their departure to Summerhill and it is safe to assume that it was in that area that the C.Y.M.S. was placed thanks to the generosity of Richard Devereux.

On the 13th April 1882, some eight years later, we find the Council discussing the size of the premises as being too small once again and the Council approached Mr. Devereux and requested the use of the 'Old Hall' for special occasions. This request was granted. The Club's soirée did indeed take place in January of 1882, *In the room that was formerly occupied by this Society.* And again in January of 1883, *It was held in the original Hall which Mr. Devereux placed at the disposal of the Society.*

On the 2nd January 1883 a glowing account of Mr. Devereux's benevolence towards the Society was recorded in the minutes as follows *Mr. Richard Devereux is one of the greatest benefactors of the C.Y.M.S., it is mainly owing to him that we are enabled to have our Soirée to-night, he built a hall for the advantage of the Society, and when he found it necessary to take it away for business purposes, he did not do so without making restitution, and built us another hall, where we have at present our reading room and billiard room.* Sadly, within two months of this Richard Devereux, undoubtedly the Society's greatest benefactor and Patron since 1855, passed-away on the 6th March 1883 having served twenty-eight loyal and faithful years service to his beloved Society. The Society suffered the loss of two of its greatest friends in March 1883 with the death, also, of its Patron and Spiritual Director Rev. James Roche.

At a meeting dated the 8th May 1883 the President, Rev. Luke Doyle, informed the Council that *he expected a large hall would be built for the Society in Rowe Street.* It is recorded in the minutes dated 26th May 1885 that Fr. Doyle placed before the Council a sketch or plan of a 'New Hall' which was very much admired.

There is no further mention of this new hall in the minute books. Throughout the 1890s the Society conducted its business as usual at these premises without any further talk of moving. On the 21st July 1892 the Council discussed the possibility of building a Racket Court or Ball Alley at the back of the Hall. This meeting concluded without arriving at any decision. The 'Billiard Table Shareholders' in the Society had first discussed this idea way back in February 1875 (*See Billiard Chapters Vol. II*). The Society officially gave-up this premises on the 30th June 1897.

St. Iberius House

On the corner of Common Quay Street and Commercial Quay

The Society next relocated to the old 'Seed Warehouse' owned by Fred Woods, a farm & garden seed importer and merchant, situated on the corner of Common Quay Street and no 1 Commercial Quay. When this premises was first placed on the market the Society's Council viewed it and after some deliberations and diligent inspection they decided that in consequences of the situation of the premises and the number of spacious apartments contained therein *no place in Wexford could be better adapted for supplying the people of Wexford with a Catholic Institution* and consequently, they decided to purchase the place. It was bought on April 20th, 1897 for the sum of £500 plus £32-18-6 expenses on the carriage of sale making total purchase money of £532-18-6. A further £150 was expended on structural improvements and in May the Council invited a Mr. Dooley, the architect of the new church being built at New Ross, to visit Wexford and view the property and give them advice on the most suitable way to carry out the alterations to suit the club. They named the new premises the '*St. Iberius House*' and a part of the premises is still known by that name to day.

The club's address was always given as '*Common Quay Street*' because the single door into the club and the double doors into the concert hall were both on that Street. However, St. Iberius House itself was on the corner of Common Quay Street and Commercial Quay. The shop and storeroom were facing the Quay. These premises were, undoubtedly, the most prestigious that the Society ever occupied in all their 153 year history.

Speaking at the A.G.M. dated 27th February 1897 the Hon. Secretary in his report had the following to say concerning the purchase *The council were in no way disheartened in their project because the generosity of the people of Wexford to support them, and consequently with three other gentlemen they borrowed the money from the bank and made themselves responsible for the debt.* True to form, the people of Wexford responded kindly and 133 generous subscriptions came in at once totalling £314-16-6. The three gentlemen who signed the overdraft with the National Bank, in the presence of L. S. Kennedy, the bank manager, thus making them selves responsible for the loan were actually ten souls, not three as stated above.

A sketch of the C.Y.M.S. premises viewed from Common Quay Street in the 1950s

Their names were: William Connick, James Stafford (*the 'supply stores'*), Robert Hanton, William Scallan, Frank Carty, Richard Goold, William J. Robinson, John Tyghe, James Sinnott and John Harpur.

St. Iberius House 1898

Situated on the corner of Commercial Quay and Common Quay Street.

In September 1905 the question of *'fitting-up a ball Alley'* (*Hand-Ball Alley*) on the premises was been considered and on the 14th of November a special meeting was convened to deal with the question of its proposal. John White proposed and Michael Luccan seconded that *the sanction of the council be granted to some members of the club to have a ball ally fitted-up on the premises providing that the cash for the same be made by subscribed and not to come from the clubs funds.* It was decided by vote and the result was three votes for the ball alley and five against. There is no further record concerning a ball alley ever again.

The A.G.M. report dated 31st December 1910 states; *Some very recent repairs were carried-out in the premises during the year. Your council saw that a great deal more was required to be done. But in consequence of the unusual amount of employment which Wexford tradesmen had during the year it was considered advisable to postpone all except urgent requirement.* Did they say there was a boom in work for Wexford tradesmen in 1910? One wonder how many people knew that, certainly not the eleven members of the club who had to leave Wexford for work elsewhere as was reported in the very same address to the meeting.

The premises was in a very dilapidated state when the Society purchased it in 1897 and it literally took years for the club to attain a good standard of upkeep. This put a constant drain on the Society's funds and in the 1930s the matter of the maintenance and general upkeep of the premises was of concern and needed continued attention so much so that the Council decided to appoint a special committee to deal with the matter.

Thomas Hayes

Photograph Courtesy of Kehoe & Assoc.

When Kehoe & Associates purchased the St. Iberius House in December 1991 they immediately began refurbishing the building and tastefully preserved the facade of the old house bringing it up to it's present day splendor.

The committee appointed consisted of the following members: Thomas Hayes, Joseph Kinsella, Edward F. O'Rourke and John Brown. Their mandate was *to examine and draw-up plans and stipulations of what painting, repairs and general maintenance was needed to be carried-out on the premises.* On the 14th August 1931 a letter was received from C.J. Morris, Borough Surveyor, stating that *The water-main in Common Quay Street was being renewed in view of the Street being concreted in the near future.* He was notifying all owners of premises in the Street. *To see that their service pipes connected with the mains are in good order before the new surface is put down.*

In February of 1975 it is recorded that the club premises was broken into and considerable damage done – *It was decided to make a tour of inspection of the club premises, after which it was decided to close down the club premises for the time being, and to dispense with the services of the caretaker* – Tuesday 25th February 1975. Nothing further after this is recorded until October 1977 when the Council met to discuss the re-opening of the club. The 'St. Vincent de Paul Society' applied to rent part of the premises. That was two years and nine months from the last meeting.

The next branch Council meetings that took place sat on the 13th December 1977, 10th April and 25th July 1978 and at a meeting held on the 19th of September 1980 the Council discussed an offer of cash plus a new club to be built at the old Walkers Cash & Carry Stores in Charlotte Street. The next two meetings in October of the same year dealt with the Council's acceptance of the offer, and at the very next meeting, which was held on Tuesday 5th January 1982, the entry in the minutes opens with: *A meeting of the council was held this evening in the new club premises in Charlotte Street, Thomas O'Rourke in the chair.* This one sentence, after almost seven years of closure, is recorded as if they were only away for a week. Like a phoenix rising from the ashes they rose-up, head high and proud from the blackest period in the long history of the Wexford C.Y.M.S

C.Y.M.S

Photo Michael O'Rourke

Charlotte Street

Charlotte Street

The present building in Charlotte Street is much smaller and a more compact premises than the '*St. Iberius House*'. This move to smaller premises alone must indicate to the reader that the club had reached its zenith and was now in a decline. The new club was officially opened and blessed by the branch's President, the Very Rev. John McCabe, Adm., on the 26th April of 1982. This was followed by light refreshments organised by the ladies committee. Presently, the Society is involved in negotiations regarding the possible sale of the premises and the building of a new hall situated somewhere in the town.

The Society at National Level

1800s

Rev. Walter Lambert, President and Thomas White, the Hon. Secretary of the Wexford Branch attended the first ever National Central Conference which was held in Limerick on the 5th May 1859. The Wexford Branch also sent representatives to the following year's Conference but missed 1861 and 62 *'Due to lack of funds.'* However, the Branch did continue to remit the *'Penny Annual Subscription'* to the Central Council of Ireland Fund. This was a levy of a penny per head placed on each member of the Society to help fund the National Central Council. When the Wexford branch took possession of the new premises at *'St. Iberius House'* in April of 1897 they parted company from the National Body of the C.Y.M.S.I. by virtue of removing the name C.Y.M.S. from the Institute and renaming themselves *'St. Iberius Catholic Club'*.

Early 1900s

On the 7th February 1909 after an absence of eleven years the club again changed its name this time calling themselves *'St. Iberius Club & Catholic Young Men's Society'* and by so doing once again returned to the fold.

In 1928 Fr. Ambrose Croft O.P. of the St. Columba's Branch, Dublin established a Federation so the branches could affiliate to a *'Central Executive Committee'*. This newly formed *'Federation of Catholic Young Men's Society of Ireland'* held its first Annual Convention in 1932. In December 1930 a John Costello, Hon. Secretary of the *'Catholic Young Men's Society of Ireland Federation'*, 29 North Frederick Street, Dublin, exchanged correspondence with the Wexford branch inviting them to join the federation. On the 24th February 1931 a fee of £1-1-0 was remitted and the Wexford branch became a member of the *'National Federation of the C.Y.M.S.I.'*. The Council decided to have the Certificate of Affiliation framed and hung up in the billiards room. Sadly, like a lot of important letters, documents and photographs belonging to this Society it has disappeared. The Society sent two delegates to the historic first National Convention held at 29 North Fredrick Street, Dublin in 1932 but, unfortunately, the minutes do not record who the two men were. The Irish Hierarchy approved the constitution of the *'Catholic Young Men's Society of Ireland'* in January 1934.

At a Special National Convention held on 12th January 1936 at Columbian Hall, Dublin, for the purpose of raising funds in aid of the Enniscorthy Cathedral renovation expenses, the Wexford delegates present were Richard Goold and Patrick Breen.

1940s

The Wexford Branch attended the conventions right up to 1941 when it was held in Dublin. However, they did not attend again until 1946 *Owing to the unsettled state of the times and the difficulties of travelling.* In 1943 the Wexford Branch received a letter from the National Council requesting *All the names of new member initiated into our Branch for October 1941 to date for the purpose of having some registered into the 'Arch Confraternity of the Immaculate Heart of Mary'.* This request from the National Council proves that the Wexford Branch had neglected to send lists of new members to them since 1941. In 1944, in response to a request from the National Council for affiliation fees, the Wexford Branch Council pointed out that it opposed the motion of an affiliation fee on the basis of 1/= per member and that Wexford would not be sending any delegates due to *'transport difficulties'* and *'financial reasons.'* Whilst both of these reasons were certainly bona fide reasons during the war years, considering petrol rationing etc., nonetheless, there would appear to have been something else going on that was not entered into the minute book. It is obvious that the relationship between the National Council and Wexford was not what it should have been and matters were becoming very strained indeed. On the 6th of May 1947 the annual account of £3-3-0 affiliation fee to the National Council of the C.Y.M.S. of Ireland was *'left over' (not paid)* to the next meeting.

By June the Council had come to a momentous decision and on the 3rd June 1947 the Wexford Branch *severed their affiliation to the National Council of the C.Y.M.S of Ireland.* This time it was purely for *'financial reasons.'* To put it bluntly, the Wexford branch was broke. There was definitely no intention to either change the name or discontinue the *'Catholic Action Programme'*. Was this the end of the matter? Certainly not. The National Council reacted quickly.

By the 1st of July the Wexford Branch received a letter from none other than the Very Rev. John Sinnott, Parish Priest of Blackwater and a former President of the Wexford Branch. Fr. Sinnott enclosed a letter that he had received from the National Council detailing the Wexford Branch's intention to discontinue affiliation to it.

There was a discussion and it was decided *to leave the matter over to the next meeting.* The pressure was now on. We know that the Wexford Council's feathers were ruffled because on the 9th September they received yet another letter from the National Council which asked for their outstanding affiliation fees. This letter was *'marked as read'* and put aside *until the matter be raised again.* This was tantamount to chucking this letter into the waste-paper bin.

What the National Council did not know was that in September of 1947 the Wexford branch had only £10 in its bank account and it owed in excess of £100 in overdue bills. The branch had to go to the bank with cap-in-hand and beg and the bank agreed to an overdraft of £100. The amusements *(fund-raising)* committee had just reported the failure of its annual sweepstakes due to better sweeps being run in the town. The club was at rock-bottom and nobody was aware of it other than the Bishop and the Bank and still a brave face was put on and a donation given to the 'Fund for the Relief of the Distressed People of King Street' caused by the floods of January 1948.

On the 15th and 16th of May 1948 the National Annual Convention was held in Cork. The Wexford Branch was invited to attend and replied as follows; *Owing to the distance and difficulty of travelling to Cork, the Wexford Branch would not send any delegates this year.* The foregoing was recorded in the minutes without any further explanation as to when the affiliation fees were paid. The fact that the club felt obliged to send a reply with an excuse for its non attendance at the Convention, is evidence that the Wexford branch was now back in the fold. There is no doubt that pressure from the clergy was brought to bear on the Branch and more than likely the Bishop was involved. It is also worth noting the following,

by November 1949 the National Council brought the levy down to 6p per person for the Wexford branch.

1950s

The Wexford branch sent a delegation to the unveiling of the plaque to the late Dean O'Brien, the Society's founding father, which was held in Limerick on the 19th June 1950. The delegates were Frank Gaul (*his car was used for the journey*), Henry F. Doyle, George Bridges and John J. Donohoe. From then until the present time the branch has stayed affiliated to the National Federation and has attended all the national conventions with the acceptation of the few years when the club premises had been broken into and totally vandalised and wrecked. The names of some of the members who repeatedly represented the branch at these conventions were J. J. Donohoe, Edward F. O'Rourke, Thomas Mahon, Thomas O'Rourke, George Bridges, Wally Cleary and Harry Doyle.

C.Y.M.S. National Convention 1950s
The two delegates from Wexford are encircled
left to right; Jackie Donohoe, (Hon. Secretary.) Wally Cleary, (Council Member.)

The Annual Conference, Catholic Young Men's Society of Ireland at Windsor Hotel, Knocknagoney, Belfast, 16th May 1964. The Wexford branch had no delegates present but the encircled gentleman, Ray Flynn was the Hon. Secretary and representative from the St. Columbas branch Dublin. Ray was also a member of the St. Iberius branch Wexford at the same time.

The St. Iberius C.Y.M.S. Branch Council 1983

Seated from left: George Bridges, Thomas O'Rourke, Chairman; Jackie Donohoe, Hon. Secretary Standing from left: Matt Stafford, Myles O'Rourke and Sam O'Rourke. Missing from the main picture are Thomas Mahon and Harry Doyle.

Wexford C.Y.M.S. St. Iberius Branch Council 1995

Lt. to Rt. Myles O'Rourke (President and Hon. Treasurer), Fr. P. Cushen (Chaplin),

Nicky Lacey, Dick Murphy (Hon. Secretary), Harry Doyle.

Council of the Catholic Young Men's Society, Wexford
(St. Iberius Branch)

Back Row (Lt. to Rt.)

James Gordon

George Bridges

Eamon Cleary

Thomas Kelly

William Murphy

Sean Doyle

Front Row (Lt. to Rt.)

Edward P. O'Brien

John F. O'Rourke
Asst. Hon. Secretary

John J. Donohoe
Hon. Secretary

Revd. Patrick Doyle, Adm.,
President

Edward F. O'Rourke
Vice-President and
Honorary Life Member

Eugene H. McGrail

During the Centenary Year 1949.

45

The 24th Annual Convention

On Whitsun week-end, Saturday 28th and Sunday 29thh May 1955, the Catholic Young Men's Society's twenty-fourth Annual Convention was held in Wexford town. The occasion coincided with the celebration of the Centenary of the St. Iberius Branch, Wexford. Wexford was honoured with the convention by reason of the fact that they were celebrating their Centenary of the founding of the Society in Wexford town. It was also the ninth Congress of the Ambulance Corps of the Knights of St. John of Jerusalem and Malta. These events brought a big influx of people to the town which was welcome from the business point of view. There were upwards of 500 delegates in the town, the Hotels and Guest Houses were full and it was arranged that some be accommodated in Rosslare Strand.

The Convention was opened at 6.00.p.m. on Saturday by the Most Rev. Dr. Staunton, Lord Bishop of Ferns, who was the Patron of the Wexford (St. Iberius) branch. There were over one hundred delegates in attendance not only from the twenty-six counties but from the six Northern counties There were also representatives from the U.K. Mr. P. Browne and Rev. M.J. McCabe from Birmingham and Mr. J. Lunney from Scotland. Numerous delegates spoke and a motion was passed on behalf of the National Executive Committee *That the C.Y.M.S. take all possible steps to prevent the circulation of crime and horror literature and encourage the spread of wholesome reading.* Communism also came in for a good battering and the members were encouraged to join unions and attend all their meetings and ensure that Communism did not take control of the unions.

During the year 1959 Brother T. F. Rowley, Hon. Propagandist on the National Executive Committee gave an interesting lecture on the aims and objects of the Society to the members of the Wexford Council at their monthly meeting of the 23rd June 1959. In that same year Patrick Kelly and Thomas Mahon attended the National Convention held in Bray on Whit weekend. In the 1990s the following members represented the branch at these conventions Dick Murphy, Sean Radford and Nicky Lacey. Dick Murphy, the branch Hon. Secretary attended the N.E.C. meetings on several occasions and held an executive position on the National Council from 2000. Dick has now been elected Vice-President of the National executive of the Catholic Men and Women's Society of Ireland which is the first time that a Wexford member has served on the National council. This is the last record of the club's business with the C.Y.M.S of Ireland. Wexford is still affiliated to the national body as of this date and it is my understanding that Dick Murphy; Hon. Secretary still attends the various meetings.

Born Leaders and Organisers

In every grouping or Society down through the ages individuals emerge whose personal commitment and enthusiasm transcends the ordinary members of the group and raises them above the rest. These people are born leaders possessing organisational abilities and vision.

Let us reflect and look back on some of those fine men, the *'enthusiastic organisers'*, the stalwarts of the C.Y.M.S., the men who served the club and all it stood for with selfless dedication on a voluntary basis. Men such as James A. Johnson, John O'Brien, Laurence Rossiter, William Connick, William Hutchinson, Richard Goold, Robert Hanton, Thomas O'Rourke, Tom Mahon, George Bridges, Dick Murphy and many more. The list is far too long to mention all by name here but the ensuing chapter is devoted to these men and the various committees they served on with such devotion over the years.

When you peruse it you will realise just how privileged we all are to have known these people. Members of a club which ranked second to none, an elite club in Wexford and one that Wexford people can be justifiably proud of. The very fact that the club celebrated its sesquicentennial in 2005, which now makes it 153 years old, indicates that it has come through the test of time with flying colours. The Council members were elected annually from the main body of the membership and the complete list of the C.Y.M.S. Council from year to year commencing in 1855 up to 2007.

(See' Elected Council Members 1855 to 2008' appendix No 1, page 256)

Intellectual Pursuits

Study Groups, Lectures and Classes

Classes for Latin, French and English commenced at the very beginning in 1855. The rate of subscriptions to each class was set at 5/= a quarter. The Professor a Mr. O'Cavanagh was said to have *'held a very high position as a linguis.'* It was not recorded how many pupils attended these classes but you can be certain that both John O'Brien and James A. Johnson. Esq. attended especially the Latin class. Mr. O'Brien departed to go and study for the priesthood and Mr. Johnson left to join the Redemptorist Order. *(You can read more about both men in the Profiles Chapter Vol. II).*

On Tuesday the 21st December 1858 Dr. Nichols gave his second lecture in the Town Hall to members of the Young Men's Society and large numbers of the clergy, *'respectable inhabitants of Wexford'* and some ladies attended as on his first evening's lecture the Right Rev. Dr. Furlong, Bishop of Ferns had presided. The subject was *'The Social Life and Institutions of America.'* He covered every aspect of American life, the geography, the latitude, boundaries, population, climate, products, the life and habits of the new settlers, American liberty and intelligence, politics and military matters. He mentioned the constitution and said that *the South did not want to change or alter it, but only to withdraw from the Federation* he went on to say *there is no power in the North to conquer the South ... To conquer the South, and*

hold it in subjection, as some Countries in Europe are *held, is impossible...To bring about a peace between the North and South, a peace which will never be accomplished until the Southerners be granted what they so justly deserve, and until the inflictions of the Northern cruelty be worn out of the minds of the present generation.* The lecture concluded by *wishing that peace might be restored that he might return to his Country.*

On the motion of Alderman J. Walsh and seconded by Richard Devereux, Esq. a vote of thanks was tendered to Dr. Nichols. The young Men's Society band attended as on the former evening. Obviously Dr. Nichols was an American gentleman and from the tone of his remarks about the Northern States we can safely deduce that he was no Yankee-doodle-dandy but a staunch confederate man. War broke out the following year after Dr. Nichols had given his lecture to the C.Y.M.S and the rest is history. With hindsight Dr. Nichol's opinion on the political situation in America could not have been more wrong with his assertion and the ;peace wished for' would only be achieved after a bloody Civil War, which cost the lives of 700,000 young American men. Of course, Dr. Nichols could not have foreseen the invention of Richard Gatling's new gun in 1861 which could fire six hundred rounds a minute and greatly increase the loss of life in that Civil War.

Richard Gatling's Gun, 1861

On the 12th August 1858 it was proposed that Fr. Doyle's lectures be advertised in the People and the Independent newspapers on the two Saturdays prior to its delivery. The profit made from this lecture was £2-15-0. In April 1860 Mr. Power, a Council member, suggested that they *enquire of Mr. FitzGerald whether he would teach Latin, French and English classes in the Society* and also to state his terms. All three of these classes were still going strong in February 1863. Dr. Murray's lectures were held in the Town Hall with Bishop Furlong, the Mayor Richard O'Connor and Ald John Walsh all attending. The members of the Society were admitted free *with privilege to bring a lady each at half price.* Father Furlong's lecture was held on the 1st Dec. 1862 and was well attended by members of the Society

Father Furlongs Lecture 1 Dec 1862

Received 84 Sixpenney and 9 One shilling ticke

		Sixpenney		Oneshilling	
Mr John Dong	6	2/6	0		
Mr Francis Hore	6	Returned	0		
Mr Miles Kehoe	4	1/6 one Returned	0		
Mr Patrick Fortune	4	2/	2	1/ one Retu	
Mr Joseph Oconnor	3	three Returned	3	three Return	
Mr Richard Ryan	6	Six Returned	"		
Mr Isaac Scallon	4/6	three Returned	"		
Mr William Scallon	3/6	two Return	"		
Mr Philiph Kehoe	4	four Returned	"		
Mr Michael Brown	6/6	five Returned	"		
Mr Thomas White	3/6	two Returned	3	two Returned	
Mr Mathew Simpson	6	Six Returned	"		
Mr Joseph Lacy	6	Six Returned	"		
Mr Francis Hoare	"		2 two paid		
Mr Pott Fortune	4	1/6 one Returned	"		

The above photocopy of a list of names of the subscribers to one of Fr. Furlong's lectures held on the 1st December 1862.

In January 1873, N. Philan, Esq. delivered a lecture at the club hall with W. Redmond M.P. in the chair for the evening and he proposed a toast of thanks to Mr. Philan.

In July 1877 the Society wrote to Fr. Murphy of St, Anthony's, Liverpool to remind him of the promise that he had made in July 1878 to lecture for the Society on his next visit to Wexford. By August Fr. Murphy had replied that he had to change his visit to see Fr. Roche in Wexford due to shortages of priests in his parish, but promised to find an alternative date. On the 6th May 1878 Fr. Brown, the Rev. President, asked His Lordship the Right. Rev. Dr. Warren, Bishop of Ferns to preside at a lecture to be given by Rev. John L. Furlong of Ballygarret. He also invited Fr. James Roche, P.P. to attend together with Mr. Ryan, R.M., Richard Devereux, Esq., John J. Walsh, John J. Devereux and John Talbot. It was to be held on Monday evening the 3rd June in the Theatre in High Street at 8.00.p.m.

Fr. Furlong requested permission to lecture for his own Church under the name of the Catholic Young Men's Society. This was granted and arranged for Wednesday evening the 26th January 1879 to be held at the Theatre in High Street. The lecture to be the follow–up from his last lecture 'Revolution and Pious IX, Part 3'. Fr. James Roche was in the chair and Mayor John J. Walsh proposed a vote of thanks and Ald. Sinnott seconded.

On the 21st January 1880 His Lordship Dr. Richards delivered a lecture for the Society. His Lordship Dr. Warren took the chair and Mr. Ryan of Alma House proposed a vote of thanks. Fr. Roche seconded the vote and Ald. John J. Walsh took the second chair. Councillor Hutchinson offered the second vote of thanks and John Tennant, T.C. seconded. Fr. Roche of London gave a very interesting *Magic Lantern Exhibition* in July 1882 for the entertainment of the members and their friends.

Fr. Roche also gave an exhibition of painting or diorama (*special painting*) for the benefit of the Society which was held in the Theatre in High Street on Wednesday evening July 26th.

This is a most interesting piece of information because Fr. Roche's '*Magic Lantern Exhibition*' of July 1882 pre-dates any such exhibition of this nature (*stills or animated moving pictures*) in Wexford town. The Theatre Royal Picturedrome in High Street first operated in May 1917. The Palace Cinema in Harpur's Lane (*Cinema Lane*) only opened in 1914 and the Capital Cinema at Stone Bridge (*South Main Street*) first opened its doors in February of 1931. Having said this there was one travelling show the 'Ireland's Own Animated Picture Co.' that visited Wexford in 1902 and showed 'The renowned Edison Animated Pictures' for a trinoctial and one matinee on a Saturday at the Theatre in High Street. A Mr. Sinnott of 29, South Main Street was the agent who sold the tickets for this show. This still leaves Fr. Roche's magic lantern exhibition of 26th July 1882 twenty years ahead of anyone else in Wexford. This is another first which the C.Y.M.S. Wexford can claim they brought to the town.

The Magic Lantern Show July 1882

The 'Magic Lantern' was invented in America in the 1650s and was lit by candles at first. A new discovery, lime light, was created by pouring oxygen and hydrogen onto a piece of limestone and this then turned incandescent once the gases were lit. This Oxy-Hydrogen lime light produced a powerful light. The 'wandering lanternists' as they were called put on shows in halls, churches and private homes. They were all the rage in Great Britain between the 1830s and the 1870s. Surely, they must have been in Ireland around the same period. However, I have not come across any written document stating that there were magic lantern shows in Wexford town. If this is correct then the C.Y.M.S. provided a first for the people of Wexford with this entertainment as I have already claimed.

On the 14th February 1888 the C.Y.M.S. put on a lecture on Ireland entitled 'Her beauty and her blight' and the 'Oxy-Hydrogen lime light' illustrated it with magnificent dissolving views.

Following is the Advertisement for the C.Y.M.S. which appeared in the People newspaper of the 7th of February 1888.

CATHOLIC YOUNG MEN'S SOCIETY HALL.
PAUL-QUAY.

VARIETY ENTERTAINMENT !

The Council of the Catholic Young Men's Society
have much pleasure in announcing that an

ENTERTAINMENT

WILL BE GIVEN

IN THE NEW HALL, PAUL-QUAY,

ON MONDAY, FEB. 13, 1888,

Consisting of

LECTURE ON IRELAND,

HER BEAUTY AND HER BLIGHT;

Illustrated with Magnificent Dissolving Views
by the Oxy-Hydrogen Lime Light.

Music, Songs, &c., will be given during the Interval.

The Entertainment will conclude with the very
Laughable Farce, entitled

A RACE FOR A WIDOW;

OR, TWO GENTS BAMBOOZLED.
(For particulars see Programme.)
The Characters to be sustained by the Members of the
Dramatic Club of the Society.
The Brass Band of the Society will render a Grand
Selection of Music.
Reserved Seats, 2s.; Front Seats, 1s.
Doors open at 7.30. To commence at 8 o'clock.
The proceeds to be applied for the benefit of the Society.
Feb. 7, 1888.   (2)

In February 1888 the Rev. President said that if he could get ten members to join an evening class or a debating class he would have either of them commence at once. The evening class would consist of bookkeeping, grammar and arithmetic. He invited those who were interested to put their names forward and twelve names were enrolled for a debating class. This, obviously, was started but no more is recorded about it. In October of the same year the Society requested Sir Thomas Esmonde to give a lecture for the benefit of the Society when he visited Wexford but we do not know if this came to fruition. The Rev. Patrick F. Kavanagh, O.S.F. gave a lecture on St. Patrick's Night 1890 in the concert hall with the subject being patriotism. His Lordship Most Rev. Dr. Brown took the chair and the profits were £2-5-9.

On the 17th November 1891 in the C.Y.M.S. concert hall a Mr. Lynd gave a lecture an entertainment with his Thomas Alva Edison invention the 'Magic Lantern' and its travelling companion the eloquent and versatile 'Talking Machine' the 'Phonograph' (this invention was later called a Gramophone) both working in conjunction with each other. These were the most prolific inventions of the age and people must have been amazed at their operation. It was as near to movies as these people had ever been. First Mr Lynd explained all the workings of the machines and then began his lecture whilst pausing to illustrate and play the sounds as he continued. Incidentally. Jem Roche the boxer who fought Tommy Burns for the World title on St. Patrick's night of 1908 *(and grandfather of Wexford playwright and author Billy Roche)* used to love listening to music on his Edison Phonograph to help him relax whilst training for a fight.

Emile Berliner's Gramaphone

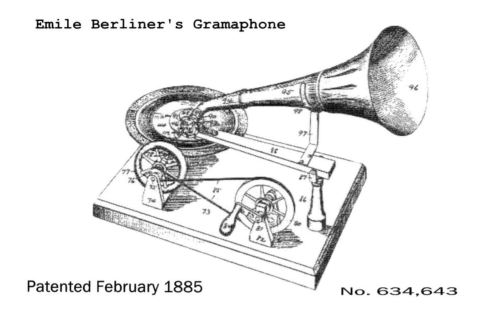

Patented February 1885   No. 634,643

Some of the sounds that Mr. Lynd played to the astonished crowd were 'A cornet sole', 'A whistle solo' by a celebrated English siffleur (whistler) and musical recordings of 'Auld Lang Syne', 'Rule Britannia' and 'The Wearin' O' the Green'. He then played the sounds of a baby crying, a puppy yelping, the Scottish Bagpipes the sound of the sea etc., etc.

At the conclusion Mr. Lynd invited various people to speak into the tube and then he would play back their voices to them. Initially people were cautious and shy to come forward but it wasn't long before many people wanted to try it out with some singing and others whistling. The night was enjoyed by everyone and it was hoped that Mr. Lynd would be back again sometime in the near future. Mr. Lynd also put on an entertainment on the 21st November at the Young Men's Christian Association in North Main Street.

A rhymester wrote the following about the new inventions:

I am the Phonograph without teeth or tongue,
I am not very old nor yet very young;
Still, I sing any song that ever was sung,
And I speak every language under the sun.

The rush of the river, the ocean's roar.
The surges thundering on the shore,
The cry of man. Or beast, or bird.
Or any sound that ever was heard;
If given to me I give again,
In all their force distinct and plain.
And yet I am dead, devoid of breath,
And my silence is like the silence of death.

On Friday 11th February 1927 the St Iberius Society organised a lecture at their hall. Madame Alicia Adelaide Needham, A.R.A.M., A.R.C.M., the well-known composer, gave the lecture. She delivered an interesting one on her travels in Italy and Germany before and after the war and afterwards she announced that the lecture was the first in a series that she intended giving in the Free State. The following contributed songs   Eva Cousins, May Sampson, Aidan Roche and John Kirwan accompanied by Miss Mary Codd, L.L.C.M.

In 1901 the following classes were held in the reading room - amusement classes, choral and dramatic classes. I do not know what constituted the amusement classes. In 1935 the Society formed a study circle under the patronage of Rev. Patrick Doyle C.C. and Rev. William Gaul, S.T.L. of St. Peter's College. This study circle met weekly in the Society and all members were welcome to attend the classes and lectures. On 21st March 1939 a *'History and Debating Class'* commenced in the Society. Meanwhile, the study circle continued to prosper under the Spiritual Directorship of the two aforementioned clergy. Alas, only nine months later the study circle had to cease through lack of support.

In this decade the World was plunged into the worst war that mankind has witnessed since its creation. Whilst Ireland remained neutral it, nevertheless, suffered from all sorts of shortages and rationing. The reader should bear this in mind as the saga of the Wexford C.Y.M.S. unfolds throughout the war years.

The Patron of the Society, the Bishop of Ferns, addressed the Annual General Meeting of 1940 *He spoke of the grave dangers of the increase of Communism throughout the World, and more patricianly since the war was brought about by Russia* [sic]. He went on to say *the only way to attack the falsehood of Communism was with the truth* and continued *This truth could only be learned by reading, debating and through the medium of the Study Circle.* He repeated the wish of the Hon. Secretary as expressed in the Annual Report *That the Study Circle should be revived as in the future it would be urgently necessary to know the truth on social and other questions. It was through discussion and at best through the Study Circle that the members should know the truth* - His Lordship, the Most Rev. James Staunton, D.D., Bishop of Ferns and Patron of the Wexford C.Y.M.S. speaking at the A.G.M. 27th February 1940.

By 1950 the Society had sponsored a member's university course fees. This matter was dealt with at a Council meeting held on the 5th October of 1950. The following is recorded *On the proposition of Tony Kelly seconded by Thomas O'Rourke; it was decided to defray the cost of the university course in the Technical School for a member of the Society and to put a notice in the case (glass case notice board) - 5th October 1950.* According to the minutes of a meeting held on the 7th November, 1950 the member who received the donation was a Patrick Kelly from Upper John Street. The last record of him that year was that he had made his application to the Technical School and forwarded the cheque to cover the fees. The next mention of Mr. Kelly is in October of 1951 where we read *A Vote of congratulations was passed with Mr. Thomas Kelly, members of the council on his having attained honours at the examinations held in the Technical School in connection with the University course* -2nd October 1951. There were two Kelly's doing these courses. Thomas Kelly, a Council member who lived at Clifford Street and worked at Stafford's Timber Company at the Crescent Quay, graduated and received his diploma in Social and Economic Studies (*Extra Mural*) at the Wexford Vocational School (*The technical School*) in early 1952. This adult education programme was the very first to be run in Wexford and was in fact a pioneer experiment. What will be of further interest to the C.Y.M.S. clan is that two of the lecturers on the two-year course were both C.Y.M.S. men themselves - Fr. Matthew Berney (*Lectured in Social Principles)* and T. D. Sinnott the County Manager

On the question of books and literature in general the following was recorded in the minute book of March 1964 *It was decided to run a best essay competition. The winner to get a gold medal.* Nothing further is recorded about this so I am unable to tell you who won the medal.

(See 'Speakers and Lecturers at the Club' Appendix No 2, Page 276)

C.Y.M.S. Debating Club

1860s

A Debating Guild was formed in the Society in 1858. It was open to all members and they met once every fortnight. Since its formation the following questions were debated:

1. Was the Invention of Printing on the whole serviceable to Society?
2. Were the Crusades of benefit to the World?
3. Which is the more useful – the Merchant or the Tiller of the Soil?
4. Which was the greater General –Napoleon or Wellington?
5. Which was the greater Orator – Curran or Shiel?
6. Has the Poor Law System served Ireland?
7. Ought there be a Guarantee for a Railway in this County?
8. Should a Harbour of Refuge be erected on the Wexford Coast?
9. Is Total Abstinence a Duty which man owes to Society?
10. Did Marshal Ney deserve Death?

The Debating Guild of the Society was re-established on the 8th May 1861 to arrange times for meetings and suggest subjects for debate. Selected subjects had to obtain the approval of the Council before the Guild could proceed with the debate. Barely fifteen days had passed when someone had complained about the newly formed club because it is recorded in the minutes *Resolved that the 'Debating Guild' be written to concerning the 'History of England' (book from the library) being torn by some of the members.* One must not think that this book was torn out of some sort of malicious intent. What most likely happened was that the book was accidentally torn when someone was studying for one of the debates. If a misdemeanour had occurred, you can be sure that the culprit or the 'Debating Guild' would have heard about it and that never happened. The fledgling club was not very lucky because they also got involved in heated discussions with other classes in the Society over which room they should occupy. This is mentioned in the minutes of the 29th April 1862 where we read that in consequence of *A little disagreement having taken place amongst both the 'Debating Guild' and Classes* it was ordered that the 'Debating Guild' occupy the Council room and the Classes are to have the room below stairs. The topic for debate on the 7th of September was *'Was James II or William III the best Monarch?'* The Council passed this as a suitable debate for the Society

1880s

The debating section of the Society was rekindled with fourteen men holding their first meeting at 9.00.p.m. on 12th March 1888. In the chair was the Rev. A. J. Sheridan C.C. and the elected Hon. Secretary was James Whelan. The other members present were: Edward Walsh, John Cullimore, Michael Nolan, Daniel J. Healy, Edward Whelan, Laurence Rossiter, William McGuire, Patrick Byrne, Patrick Cullen, Michael O'Connor, John M. Walsh and Hugh McGuire. At their initial meeting they drew-up their code of rules and dealt with arrangements for managing the section. As the years passed many other names were added to this initial group. The debates were well advertised both in and outside the Society and there was mention of non-members being present at some of them. However, the speakers were always members of the C.Y.M.S. debating club. The meetings were held mostly in the Concert Hall but on one occasion in the reading room. I must assume that the life span of this section was just three months short of seven years as the only records that are available cover that period of time.

The very first subject for debate was 'Whether Mr. Gladstone's Home Rule or the total separation of Ireland from England would be the more advantageous to both countries.' After each debate there was a show of hands to determine the outcome. In this very first debate the result was counted and found to be equal. When the result was over all strangers *(non-members)* would be asked to leave and the club would continue with its business. Most of the debates recorded in the minute books are all to do with the political situation prevailing in Ireland at that time. I have listed hereunder the titles of some of the debates and the results:

1.   'That emigration is beneficial both to the Country and the emigrant'
    Result: Negative

2.   'Will Ireland be able to compete with other Countries in manufactures, if she were ruled by a native Parliament'
    Result: affirmative

3.   'Ought members of Parliament be paid by the State'
    Result: Affirmative

4.   'Has the Gaelic Athletic Association been advantageous to the youth of Ireland'
    Result: Affirmative

5.   'Which is better, Physical Force or Constitutional Agitation'
    Result: Constitutional Agitation.

These were all the big questions of the day. Home Rule was on the minds of all patriotic Irishmen and such debates must have been very interesting indeed and, no doubt, attracted a large and varied audience. Before I proceed any further I must draw the reader's attention to what Dean O'Brien had to say in his letter to the Wexford branch on their inauguration back in 1855. The good Dean wrote *Your own good sense will tell you that inside the doors of our Societies not one word of politics should ever be allowed to enter. We need and desire a union of all, not of any class. Our training will make men honest in all politics, but partisans to none. The moment the first discussion or difference on politics takes place in a Young Men's Society Hall I feel assured of its inevitable and rapid decay, and I therefore pray most fervently that no Society will ever admit such an evil.* - Dean O'Brien's letter to the Wexford Branch 1855.

It is obvious that the membership had forgotten the advice given to them in 1855 and particularly the debating section of the Society. On 8th June 1888 the debating club formulated its own rules as follows:

C.Y.M.S. Debating Club Rules

1) Name: The C.Y.M.S. Debating Club

2) Meetings: Once a fortnight or once in three weeks according to Convenience of members

3) Place and Hour of Meetings: Sunday evenings at 8 O'clock (ProTem) in New Hall

4) Admission to Club: Club restricted to members of C.Y.M.S. Any member of the Society may become a member of this club by giving his name to the Secretary and notifying his willingness to take part in debates

5) Subject of Discussion: Any subject political or otherwise, likely to supply ample matter for discussion or prove generally interesting may be selected

6) Speakers: two or three speakers on either side to be elected by ballot the six members of previous debate being exempt.

7) Every member is expected to undertake part assigned to him unless prevented by urgent reasons, if unable to attend he should procure a substitute and to notify same to secretary as soon as possible

8) The club to suspend its meetings during the summer months

Proceedings at Meetings

a) Chairman to be appointed who will open debates and appoint succession of speakers

b) Speakers, affirmative and negative, alternate, no interruptions of speaker without special permission of Chairman

c) Chairman sums up

d) A show of hands to determine sense of audience on subject discussed, strangers withdraw, and members of club resolve into meeting

1. Reading of minutes.
2. Appoint date of next meeting and subject for next debate.
3. General discussion of matter as pertaining to club.

There was a sad note recorded on the 20th January 1889 which relates to Edward Walsh. It reads *That this club desires to express it's most profound regret at the imprisonment of Mr. E. Walsh our most respected Chairman.* Alderman Edward Walsh, proprietor and editor of 'The People' newspaper, was imprisoned for 'Anti-Establishment activities'
(See his Profile in Vol. II for a full explanation). The last recorded meeting of the debating club was in November 1894. No other written records pertaining to this section of the Society after this date could be located. I doubt if the debating club came to such an abrupt end, I feel it is more likely that the records have been mislaid.

1890s
There is no record of the Debating Club from 1888 to the 14th of February 1892, in the minutes but one cannot help but noticing that when that great Irish patriot, Edward Walsh, the backbone of the Society's debating section was imprisoned by the British authorities, everything seems to have gone very quit. It is not beyond the realms of reality to suspect that someone asked the debating class to tone down their debates, which after all were bordering on Irish Nationalist fever. Also, it has not gone unnoticed that out of original members of the debating club

of 1888, only two of these men rejoined the re-established debating class of 1892. This is no coincidence, there is a great truth hidden here which was not recorded in the minutes.

On a later date we read the debating class was reformed and is now in full working order, two debates having taken place within the last month at which a great many members were present This notwithstanding, we find that at the A.G.M. dated the 14th February 1894, that the 'Debating Class' has fallen off. But by the end of the year it had restarted once again. By November 1894 a further thirty-four members had joined the debating club as follows:

Rev. E. Aylward, Adm., Thomas Murphy, Peter Devlin, Nicholas Gahan, Francis O'Connor, J. M. Walsh, John Cleary, Peter Kearney, William McGuire, Robert Hanton, William Corcoran, Rev. Robert P. Doyle C.C., Michael O'Keeffe, Christopher Cleary, Richard Lyne, P. Doyle, W. J. Murphy, W. Sears, Myles Codd, Thomas Harpur, J. English, Thomas Lacy, Michael Kehoe, Richard Gould, Frank Carty, Richard Ryan, John Salmon, Maurice O'Shea, Mr. Duffy, Rev. Patrick Doyle C.C., A. Cullimore, J. Doyle and Charles Lennon.

At the A.G.M. dated 16th February 1896 the Council *is sorry to state that the 'Debating Club' has fallen through. Mr. O'Shea, the Hon. Secretary called three meetings during the year and only three members put in an appearance.* So the club has now ceased. At the following year's A.G.M. the Council re-iterated last year's statement concerning the 'Debating Club' being discontinued.

1930s

On 18th March 1939 the following group of members attempted a revival of the debating club in the Society - T. A. Furlong, Henry Compton, R. Turner, Albert Sherwood, Laurence O'Mahoney, Bartholomew Hickey, Richard J. Breen, James P.

Albert Sherwood

Quirke, T. D. Sinnott, John J. Donohoe, J. G. Byrne, D. J. O'Brien, P.V. Carson, Nicholas P. Corish, Thomas Keegan, Laurence Cleary and Edward P. O'Brien. The group styled themselves as 'A History and Debating Class' which was also referred to as the 'Literary and Debating Society' at the A.G.M. of 1939. They held their first session of three instructive and interesting debates: 'That the St. Iberius' Branch of the C.Y.M.S. has Failed' on the 18th March, the second 'That the G.A.A. Ban on Foreign Games should be removed' on 31st March and the third 'That Dog Racing should be Abolished' on 28th April. Their second session commenced on the 27th October but alas, only two meetings were held with a very poor response. This was in contrast to the high standard that was attained during the initial first session. Bishop Staunton in his address to the A.G.M. of 1940 bemoaned the loss of the debating Society. This is how members learned that the newly formed 'Debating Club' of last March was now defunct. Barely a year had elapsed and the debating class had run out of members' support and topics to discuss. How was it possible they had nothing to debate with the following action taking place in the world:

28th March 1939 - the Spanish Civil War ends as Madrid falls to General Franco's troops. 610,000 men died in this war.

4th April 1939 - King Ghazi of Iraq is killed in a car accident. Rioters, who suspected that the British had arranged the car accident, killed the British Consul in retaliation.

1st September 1939 - Adolf Hitler's Nazi troops, tanks and aircraft invaded Poland.

3rd September 1939 - Britain, France, Australia and New Zealand declare war on Germany.

10th September 1939 - Canada declares war on Germany.

17th September 1939 - Stalin's Soviet troops invade Poland from the East.

21st September 1939 - members of the pro-fascist Iron Guard murder Armand Calinescu, Premier of Romania.

27th September 1939 - Warsaw falls to the Germans.

28th September 1939 - Poland is partitioned between the U.S.S.R. and Germany.

13th December 1939 - the sea battle of the River Plate in the South Atlantic is fought.

9th April 1940 - Germany invades Norway and Denmark. Benito Mussolini's troops had seized Albania and the Japanese were busy beating the living daylights out of the Chinese.

And the C.YM.S. debating class had nothing to talk about !!!!!!!.

This was the last ever record of the debating section of the club and there was never any other attempt to initiate a revival to the present day. In fairness, perhaps at this time the Society was adhering strictly to Dean O'Brien's rule of not allowing any politics to be discussed in the club. It is an open secret and fact that there were people in Wexford at that time who were 'up for the Germans' to their shame. During the research for this book I have seen a photograph of a respectable Wexford businessman and long time Council member of the Society standing beside anti-British and pro-German slogans. There was no caption needed as the picture said it all. Obviously, at the outset of the war and with the bitter taste of the cruel Black and Tans still strong in many an Irishman's mouth, such sentiment was widespread at that time. So perhaps a ban on debating anything relating to the ongoing war was put in place to avoid any heated disputes which could ensue.

Society's Library and Reading Rooms

1850s

The cultural and educational needs of the Society's members were very well catered for with a well-stocked Library consisting of over four hundred volumes at its inception, which grew to approximately 2,000 volumes and were the best stocked reading rooms in Wexford Town with newspapers and periodicals.

The very first librarian was John O'Brien, who was nominated by Fr. Roche to look after the books, this was on the 16th August 1855. Mr. O'Brien's interest in books continued throughout his life. He went to the African missions as a teacher, became a priest, and founded the C.Y.M.S. in Grahamstown and built up a library for the members. I was fortunate enough to receive one of Fr. O'Brien's books from his private library which was kindly sent to me by John Reeks the archivist at Port Elizabeth.

The next librarian in the club was young master John McGee, who was appointed in early November 1855. Alas, young John resigned his position on Thursday, November 13th 1855 and it would be safe to assume that John Stafford was performing the librarian's duties from this date.

At a Council meeting on the 12th August 1858 it is recorded *It was unanimously adopted that Mr. John Stafford act as Librarian for remainder of the year.* Obviously John was already acting as librarian previous to this date. The decision to retain him was a wise one because John turned out to be an excellent librarian and luckily he produced his *General Memoranda* which thankfully furnished me with all sorts of bits and pieces of information that would have otherwise been lost for ever.

John Stafford – Society's Librarian 1850s to 1860s

Mr. Stafford maintained a small hard-covered notebook measuring 5"x 8" which he entitled '*General Memoranda*' which covered the years 1858 to 1867. John's book records the names and addresses of some of the first members registered and sometimes their professions, information which was invaluable. There are various other matters covered such as bills that have been paid and monies which had been collected. Unfortunately, like most of the other clubs books, this one is in very poor condition and falling apart, but nonetheless decipherable. John was the most meticulous of men who obviously took great pride in his work and the Society must have considered itself very fortunate to have a true bibliophile like John Stafford as the Society's librarian. It cannot have been any mean task for him to deal with all the clerical work and recording required together with his other caretaking duties.

There was a non-smoking policy for certain areas in the club from a very early time and this no smoking policy was firmly imposed on the reading-room at John's insistence as we can gather from the following letter he submitted to a Council meeting on September 8th 1859-

Gentlemen, I beg leave to suggest the propriety of doing away with the practice of smoking in the Bagatelle Room. I do believe that it tends very much to lesson the respectability of the Society and I for one do dearly wish that the very name of smoking within our walls should never go abroad.

John certainly managed to have this smoking practice stopped in the reading room as we can observe from the library rules.

Library Rules of Management

There are no set rules as such but from the following one can derive a general picture of what was allowed and what was prohibited:

1) Prior to May 1859 there had been a rule set down that *'a fine of one penny per book out over a fortnight was to be imposed.'*

2) On the 6th April 1860 a rule was imposed *'that all members were required to take-off their hats while in the reading room'.*

3) On the 14th June 1877 it was ordered that a notice be put up in the hall (*club*) requesting members *'Not to smoke in the reading room or spit on the floor.'*

4) On the 11th May 1882 we see *'That no member will keep the 'Evening Telegraph' more that five minutes in the morning if any other member is waiting to see it.'*

5) In March 1888 we read that *'No member can keep a paper longer than 15 minutes if another member is waiting to see it'* and also *'Members are not allowed to take any papers out of the reading room without permission.'*

6) On the 11th January 1927 it is recorded that *'Members are to observe strict silence in the reading room. Should an unavoidable conversation take place it must be brief and carried on in an undertone.'*

Unfortunately, rules are made to be broken as the old adage goes, and sure enough, rules will be broken no matter what age or era we live in. In September 1904 we read that there had been a report *That some members have been smoking in the reading room.* A notice was put up *'Forbidding the practice in the reading room.'* The smoking ban is not new to this Century. In all the time that I was in the club I never knew there to be a smoking ban anywhere other than over the billiards tables. In June 1905 there were complaints made concerning people smoking in the reading room again and a notice was subsequently erected prohibiting the practice. There were also complaints about people talking in the reading room and thereby distracting other members who wished to read in silence so it was decided to put up a code of rules on the 11th January 1927 to prevent such conduct in the future. The Council penned the following *Members are to observe strict silence in the reading room. Should an unavoidable conversation take place it must be brief and carried on in an undertone.*

Books Donated to the Library

It was Richard Devereux Esq., a patron of the Society, who first established and stocked the Society's library. His benevolence towards the Society is well documented throughout the minute books whilst his generosity to the Catholic establishment in general is also well documented. He presented 123 Volumes to every parish in the Diocese of Ferns which was approx. 4,920 volumes and he assisted over 80 public Catholic libraries in the Diocese. He established libraries in many Catholic schools, clubs and societies throughout Wexford town. Throughout the years many club members and clergy also donated books to the Society:

The Very Rev. Dean Murphy donated forty four numbers of 'Dublin Review' and nine numbers of 'Brownson's Review' in 1858

John Bransfield, Esq. Donated four volumes of 'Chambers' Journal' and one volume of 'Selections from French' in 1858

J. Crean, Ksg., M.D. Donated 'Lewis Topographical Dictionary' with Atlas in 1858

In 1861 **Brother Murphy** presented 'Pleasures and Puzzles' for the library room

In November 1863 a Wexford doctor (*name unknown*) donated eighteen books

Mr. Devereux of George Street donated twenty five books

M. J. McCann donated seventeen books

James Roche donated seventeen books

Richard O'Connor donated one book.

James M'Ardle (McArdle) donated four volumes - 'The Adventures of Owen Evens', 'The triumph of Perseverance', 'The War trail' and 'Life of? (*Title undecipherable*) by Francis Hore, five vols. of Cassell's 'Science Popularly Explained'

William Scallan donated four vols. - Longfellow's 'Hyperion', 'Essays' by Davis, 'Irish Volunteers' and 'The (Breanison?) of Shakespeare'

Richard Murphy donated four vols. - 'The Merchant Prince', 'Life of Thomas Moore', 'Disappointed Ambition' and 'Fathers of the Desert'

Bartholomew Murphy donated five vols. - 'Shakespeare's Complete Works', 'The Rise and fall of the Irish Nation', 'Moore's Poetical Works', Moore's Life' by Lord Byron and 'Jasper in (search) of a Father'

Unnamed donated five vols. - 'The Tales from Blackwood' in three Vols. and 'The Church of the Bible', and 'The Two Roads of life'

In 1882 both **Fr. Kelly** and **Fr. Crean** donated £7-10-0 worth of books

In 1890 **Myles Gaffney** and **Frank Harpur**, South Main Street presented the Society with 164 book of fiction. The secretary commenting on this said that *"we will have the best library in town we have a 1000 books at present"*.

Pat Doyle donated an undisclosed amount of books

In February 1894 **John Harpur**, South Main Street presented the library with *"Thirteen very fine works of fiction"*

It is recorded that on the 11th July 1911 **Mr. Hutchinson** donated a number of books, some of which he thought may have been suitable. Mr. Frizille and Mr. White, two members of the library committee, inspected these books and placed a value on them, as indeed they did with all the library books and they then decided to remunerate him for them.

The Library Story

In the early days the library was open from 12.00 noon to 1.00.p.m. from 4.00.p.m. to 5.00.p.m. and from 7.00.p.m. to 10.00.p.m. Occasionally some books were mislaid or removed without authority so the Council decided that all the books had to be numbered and labelled with the C.Y.M.S. printed on them *'In case they are lost'* and when found they could then be returned.

Only the finest books of the period were presented to the library thanks to the fine Council and library committees which the Society was blessed with throughout its existence. All books presented were meticulously vetted for suitability whilst ensuring that a Catholic ethos was being upheld

In.1859 there was a total of 845 books recorded in the library and by 1886 this figure had reached 1,053. By 1895 the library had 1,100 and of these 1,060 were borrowed by members during the year. The library was described by the secretary as *'the best library in the town.'* It is my understanding that there was only one other library of its calibre in the town at the time and that was the Mechanics Institute on Main Street at the top of Anne Street. That Institute was credited with having a marvellous library.

The Council set high standards for the library from its very establishment and saw that it expanded and was kept up-to-date through a series of grants of various amounts of cash given to it over the years. The Committee were nominated by the ruling Council and given a mandate to manage the affairs and everyday running of the library.

As early as October 1858 the Council gave a grant of £4 for the purchase of new books and James Cullen was paid £5 to arrange and catalogue all the books A similar grant was given the following year with a stipulation that it was to be utilised chiefly for the purchase of books of a historical or scientific nature. These grants from the Council to the library committee continued on an annual basis until the period of World War II when the grants appear to have ceased. The library would appear to have stagnated from then on for many years prior to the enviable run-down of its stocks began and the Council had to contemplate selling-off the most valuable books in their possession.

In September of 1867 a Captain Doyle introduced six Captains and four others to the club membership. All were seafaring men and most likely all employees of Richard Devereux, Esq. This influx of seamen to the Society led to the question arising of *How long could the seamen keep the books out for without having to pay the fine?* The Council decided *That Captains and sailors would be allowed to hold books as long as they need, due to the long voyages.* This meant that the C.Y.M.S. library books were amongst the most widely travelled books in the world. The C.Y.M.S. had their fair share of seafaring men in the Society which is hardly surprising when one considers that Wexford was one of the busiest seaports in Ireland in the 19th century with many of the town's inhabitants involved in maritime pursuits. *(See 'Ship Owners and Sailors' lists in Vol. II)*

From time to time it was inevitable that books would be lost or misplaced. In January 1893 the Council berated the poor caretaker harshly concerning lost books. They intimated that any books lost were his responsibility and that he should pay for them. This seems a bit severe but books were costly and they had to be looked after. In August of the following year two books were lost from the library. The two members who had the books out on loan were a Mr. Green and Patrick O'Brien and both gentlemen were requested to purchase new books to replace those lost by them

In October 1897 when the Society relocated to new premises the caretaker was given the loan of the mail van from Mr. Hanton so that he could transfer the books. The move was a vast undertaking and took almost a week to complete. When the Society moved to the new premises on Common Quay Street they had a reasonably sized reading room at their disposal from which to organise a book storage area. This reading room was up two flights of stairs over in the St. Iberius House side of the club. It was an elongated room with two large windows facing out on to the quays. There was a long mahogany table with several large leather bound chairs so people could spread out the newspapers on the tabletop to read. This was prior to the tabloid days.

There were two elongated glass fronted book cabinets one on each side of the doorway as you entered the room. The top section was shelved and had lockable glass doors where many old books were stored. The bottom cupboards were also locked and I believe that the larger outsize volumes were stored in these in a flat manner as some of them were far too high to be erect. Various newspapers and magazines would be placed around the table.

Courtesy of an anonymous donor who provided these photocopies.
The book was the eight edition published in 1840 and bears the official rubber stamp of the C.Y.M.S. pre 1898. The acronym A.M.D.G. printed in old English lettering which appears in the centre of the design and stand for Ad Majorem Dei Gloriam, meaning 'For the greater glory of God' The book was number 961 on the club library list.

WEXFORD CATHOLIC
A.M.D.G.
YOUNG MEN'S SOCIETY

THE

NATURAL HISTORY

OF

SELBORNE;

WITH

OBSERVATIONS ON VARIOUS PARTS OF NATURE,
AND THE NATURALIST'S CALENDAR.

BY THE LATE

REV. GILBERT WHITE, A.M.

FELLOW OF ORIEL COLLEGE, OXFORD.

WITH EXTENSIVE ADDITIONS BY

CAPTAIN THOMAS BROWN, F.L.S. &c.

ILLUSTRATED WITH EIGHT ENGRAVINGS.

EIGHTH EDITION.

LONDON:

JOHN CHIDLEY, 123, ALDERSGATE STREET.

MDCCCXL.

From 1907 to 1913 the Library Committees were in charge of the 'library book' this was the index list of books and records of the goings and comings of books. Their mandate was to look after the library and carry out any improvements which they considered necessary. They received a yearly grant to purchase books.

They purchased 'The History of Ireland' in six Vols. by the Rev. D. Dalton at a price of £32-2-0. On the 18th May 1911 the committee purchased 9 books at a cost of 7/4p. The committee's intentions were to purchase several small lots of books in this way throughout the year.

1913 commenced with the appointment of a new library committee which took place on the 25th February. The chairman was the Rev. James Codd, C.C. and his second in command was Michael Bolger. The other committee members were - Joseph Fennell, John Dunne and James J. Kehoe. Their mandate was *With power to add to their number, to inspect the books in the library and purchase any new books that they considered necessary.*

By October Fr. Codd was *empowered to use his own judgement in the purchase of books* for the library. This committee worked hard at sorting out the problems with the library and in their annual report presented to the A.G.M. held on the 2nd February 1914 one can see just how busy these men were. Their report stated *We beg to report that as directed we made a through inspection of all books in the Fiction Department of the library and selected over seventy volumes which we considered could with attention be put right by having them re-bound. We've obtained a tender for the work, but found that the cost would be at least £6 and as this amount seemed excessive. We decided that it would be better to purchase new works and discard the dilapidated books. We've therefore purchased a new edition of Dickens works in twenty volumes and also procured other up-to-date fiction from the Simes Book Club and from Messrs. Gill & Son at a cost of £7-6-0.*

A commencement has thus been made in re-furnishing the library but a still large outlay is required and we consider that in the current year a further sun of at least £10 should be devoted to this purpose and that a sum of at least £5 should be spent every future year in purchasing the latest works. We also recommend that all the worn and tattered books which we have discarded should be burned so that space might be found for new ones which may be purchased from time to time.

--Rev. James Codd, C.C.
--Michael Bolger

Having perused the foregoing, I now realise where all the first editions disappeared to. Up in a cloud of smoke over Wexford harbour in early 1914. The caretaker must have been busy for weeks with seventy books to burn and fuel the fires of the club - it would have put Dante's Inferno in the shadows. Quite frankly, I was a little shocked when I realised that many first editions may well have been destroyed in that burning exercise. Surely first editions should have been refurbished?

There were 1,156 books borrowed from the library this year which was a massive increase in the use of the library and no doubt was due to the hard work the committee had undertaken together with the additional new books available for the members. Both Rev. Codd and Mr. Bolger deserved the gratitude of all the members for their endeavours in bringing the library back to the standard of its former days.

At the Annual General Meeting of February 1943 Joseph A. Fennell suggested that something should be done with the library in the reading room with a view to having *the books which are of no value* either given to the Red Cross or sold for the benefit of the Society. He went on to say *the books should be valued as it was possible that there might be some valuable editions amongst them.* A case of closing the gate after the horse has bolted ?

It was decided that a small sub-committee under the

chairmanship of Edward O'Brien, should look into the matter and report to the Council. Joseph Fennell and Thomas Hayes both catalogued all the books in the club's library and by May the Council had contacted Miss Connolly the librarian at the County Library concerning the purchase of the books. There is no doubt that this Council had decided to rid itself of the books and contacted various parties that may be interested.

In March of 1944 they contacted Fred Hanna Ltd. to see if they would be interested in purchasing any of the books from the extensive list that they had sent to them and they replied stating *the only books that they would be interested in were the 'Series of Mermaid Plays' and they offered 2/= each.* In view of the inadequacy of this offer the Council decided to retain the books. In June it was decided to sell 'Hore's History of Wexford' and the matter was put into the hands of Patrick G. Lambert, Auctioneer, Anne Street who was a member of the Society. Patrick came back with an offer by July and the sale of 'Hore's History of Wexford' was approved for £19. They also sent lists to several book firms in Dublin enquiring if they were interested in purchasing any of the books.

In March of 1948 Patrick Hynes, 59 Bullring, a member of the Society, inquired if it was possible for him *to purchase an old account book in which his grandfather and father's names appeared.* He wanted it as a souvenir and the Council unanimously agreed *to make Mr. Hynes a present of the book free of charge.* In late 1948 the club ordered one dozen copies of the 'Life of Dean O'Brien' the founder of the Catholic Young Men's Society.

On the 11th June 1974 the club accepted an offer of £50 for the remaining books in the reading room from a Kilkenny buyer and the bookcases were also sold off by the end of the year.

Records of Books Loaned by the Library

Records from 1897 to 1916 are all intact. Unfortunately, no records were kept after 1916. In the year 1901 there was 1,095 books borrowed which made this year the second best year on record for borrowing. Between the years 1903 to 1913 the average amount of books borrowed each year was 500 and the best year recorded was the year of the start of the Great War in 1914 with a massive 1,156 books borrowed. Perhaps this tells us something. Were people burying their heads in books while the world was blowing itself to smithereens? The worst year on record was 1912 with only 327 books borrowed.

Reading Material Supplied to the Society

Newspapers pre 1800s had a stamp duty levied on them and as a consequence newspapers became very expensive to purchase. Unlike today where you can just pop into a newsagents and purchase newspapers willy-nilly, in those days most newspapers sold would be to regular order customers and that was sufficient and a good way to sell newspapers as far as the newsagent was concerned. The expense of reading material was still a strong concern when the Society began in 1855.

The Council devised a unique way of obtaining reading material cheaper for the reading room. As you continue reading this chapter you will see that the Society's custom was to auction off all the old newspapers and magazine to the highest bidder in order to save funds. On other occasions some of the more affluent members who subscribed to various magazines or newspapers would volunteer to hand those over to the reading room when they were finished with them. But by far the most unique idea that the club contrived was undoubtedly that whereby a member, who wished to have his particular choice of magazine or paper added to the list, could offer to purchase that publication in advance of the auction for half price. This meant that the club could add this publication to the list at only half the cost to themselves. This system of taking on new publications became popular and the Council requested members to use this system to obtain their choice of reading material. In January 1897 a Capt. Smith offered to supply the *'Shipping Gazette'* to the Society at a cost of 10/- per year which would save the club £4-1-0 per year. The Society already had this publication on their supply list and were paying full price for it so needless to remark they jumped at Capt. Smith's kind offer.

Newspapers that were purchased regularly by the Society in the 1850s were as follows:

'Annals of the Faith', 'Catholic Telegraph', 'Catholic World', 'Daily Graphic', 'Daily Mail', 'Evening News', 'Freeman's Journal', 'Harpur's Magazine', 'Herald Wexford', 'Independent', 'Institute Magazine', 'Irish Times', 'London Daily Mail', 'London Magazine', 'London Opinion', 'Morning News', 'Telegraph An Post'. 'The Boys Monthly', 'The Celt',' The Field', 'The Illustrated London News', 'The Irishman', 'The Lamp',' The London Times', 'The Month', 'The Nation',' The People Wexford', 'The Shamrock', 'The Tablet',' The Telegraph', 'The Times', 'The Weekly Register', 'Times Pictorial' and 'Weekly Independent'.

That was quite a collection of reading material available to the members and newspapers that was added to the regular purchase list pre 1870 were as follows: 'Dublin Evening Telegraph', ' Evening Telegraph', 'Irish Sportsman', 'London Daily Telegraph', 'Northern Press' and 'The Weekly Times'.

In June 1877 a Mr. Hutchinson offered to *read the trial of six papers for the benefit of the Society*. Obviously, papers and magazines ordered for a Catholic Society had to be studied carefully to see if they were suitable for the club. This could be classed as censorship and there can be no doubt but that the clergy would also have done this type of reading.

From the 12th May 1881 Martin White supplied the *'Shipping Gazette'* to the club free gratis. By the 1890s the club was supplying seven dailies, two bi-weekly, sixteen weekly and five monthly papers and magazines. This was a massive amount of reading material. At the A.G.M. dated 10th February 1895 the following was stated: *The reading room is as well supplied with papers and magazines as any room in town, if not better and the council are well pleased...*

Newspapers added to the regular purchase list pre 1900 were as follows:

'Black and White', 'Cornhill Magazine', 'Daily Chronicle', 'Daily News', 'Dublin Illustrated Journal', 'English Illustrated', 'Free Press', 'Harpur's Monthly', 'Insuppressibly', 'Irish Catholic', ''Irish Cyclist', 'Irish Fireside', 'Labour World', 'Lloyds Weekly', 'London Daily News', 'London People', 'London Universe', 'Longman's Magazine', 'Pall Mall Magazine', 'Pictorial World', 'Punch', 'Review of Reviews', 'Speaker', 'Star', 'St. Peter's Magazine', 'Sunday Sun', 'Tablet', 'The Nation', 'The National Papers ???', 'The Field', 'The United Ireland', 'The Word', 'Truth', 'Weekly Freeman', 'Westminster Gazette' and 'Young Ireland'.

From the 4th of January 1904 to 13th December 1918 the following were placed on the list - 'Morning Leader', 'The Tattler', 'Answers', 'Tit Bits', 'Pearsons Weekly', 'Pearsons Monthly', 'Windsor Magazine', 'Harmsworth', 'Irish Daily Independent', 'Irelands Monthly', 'Freeman's Journal Weekly', 'The Leprechaun', 'The Grand' and 'The All Story'.

The People.

Registered at the General Post Office as a Newspaper.

ONE HALF-PENNY STAMP WILL TAKE *THE PEOPLE* TO ANY PART OF THE UNITED STATES, CANADA, OR THE CONTINENT OF EUROPE. A PENNY STAMP IS REQUIRED FOR TRANSMISSION TO AUSTRALIA, BUENOS AYRES, AND THE CAPE OF GOOD HOPE.

VOL. XXXV.   WEXFORD, WEDNESDAY, JANUARY 12, 1887.   **PRICE 2½D.**

THE Anniversary Office and High Mass for the repose of the soul of the late NICHOLAS ANDREW KEATING, Ellerslie, will be held in the Church of the Immaculate Conception, Wexford, on Monday, Jan. 17, at 11 o'clock.

THE Month's Mind Office and High Mass for the repose of the late MICHAEL WALSH, Cornmarket, will be held in the Church of the Immaculate Conception, Wexford, on Tuesday, January 18th, at Eleven o'clock.

WEXFORD NATIONAL LEAGUE.

THE Monthly General Meeting of this Branch, which was to be held on WEDNESDAY, JAN. 5th, has been postponed to WEDNESDAY, JAN. 12th, when all members are requested to attend. Hour of meeting, 8 p.m.

THE Raffle to aid an Evicted Tenant, named for January 6th, is unavoidably Postponed to JANUARY 18th. Holders of Tickets will kindly take notice thereof.
JOHANNA RYAN, Mulmitira, Taghmon.

THE KILLINICK HARRIERS.

THE Killinick Harriers will meet on the following days during the Month of January, 1887:—4th, Sledagh; 7th, Ballymore Church; 10th, Lightwater; 13th, Lady's Island; 17th, Bridgetown; 20th, Tagoat; 24th, Taghmon; 27th, Tacumshane; 31st, Killinick.

WANTED, two men with grown-up sons—one as general farming man, the other must have a knowledge of gardening. Apply to PETER PRICE, Belmont, Wexford.   (2at)

THE Friends of a young country lad wish to apprentice him to the Grocery or Hardware business. Can be well recommended. Apply to the Rev. Superior, Christian Schools, Enniscorthy.
Dec. 14, 1886.   (i-1m)

FIRST-CLASS NURSE WANTED—(one from the country preferred)—to take charge of two young

---

SALE BY WALSH & SON.

WRECK SALE.

TO BE SOLD BY AUCTION, For account of whom it may concern, On WEDNESDAY, 12th JANUARY, 1887,
IN THE PACKET-YARD,
7 Casks of Beef and Pork, 9 Casks of Flour, 1 Cask of Tallow, Hams, about 200 Tins and Cases of Preserved Meats, Fish, Peas, Vegetables, 5 Cases of Soap, Preserved Apples, a superior Ship's Boat, Brushes, &c.; a quantity of Ropes and Cordage.
ALSO,
AT THE CUSTOM-HOUSE,
1 Case of Brandy, 2 Cases of Whiskey, 6 Cases of Lime Juice, 4 Boxes of Tea, 2 Bags of Coffee, 179lbs. of Tobacco, 6lbs. of Cigars, 56lbs. of Raisins, Currants, &c., being Stores of the Barque "Samasco."
Terms—Cash. Sale at the Packet Yard at 1 o'clock, at the Custom House at 2 o'clock.
For further particulars apply to
WALSH & SON, Auctioneers; or to
E. RUNDEL, Esq., Underwriters Rooms, Liverpool.
Wexford, January 7, 1887.

SALE BY R. H. SHAW.

INTEREST IN HOUSE.

TO BE SOLD BY AUCTION, On THURSDAY NEXT, 13th Inst., at 12 o'clock Noon,
AT THE OFFICE OF THE AUCTIONEER,
The Interest for a Term of Years in the House with Yard and Stabling at the rere, situate in SOUTH MAIN-STREET, WEXFORD, opposite the Post-office, and at present held by Mrs. NUGENT, who, owing to failing health, is anxious to dispose of her Interest in same. The premises are subject to the Yearly Rent of £9 16s.

XMAS PRESENTS AND NEW YEAR'S GIFTS.

THE Latest Novelties in Watches, Clocks, Jewellery, &c.—which will be found suitable for presentation—are now on view at this Establishment.
Intending purchasers are recommended to inspect them before buying elsewhere.
WATCHES.—Upwards of 500 in stock, from 18s. 6d.
CLOCKS.—From 3s. 9d. Over 10-0 to select from.
REAL GOLD JEWELLERY. STERLING SILVER JEWELLERY.
BIRMINGHAM JEWELLERY, unrivalled for cheapness, durability, beauty of finish, and elegance of design.
BRITISH GARNET JEWELLERY in all the fashionable colours, including Black, Cardinal, and Moonlight.
Lucky Wedding Rings and Massive Gold Keepers !!!
Gold, Silver, and Diamonds bought or taken in exchange.
NO SECOND PRICE.

AMBROSE R. FORTUNE,
WATCHMAKER & JEWELLER,
55A & 56, NORTH MAIN-STREET, WEXFORD.

THE CHEAPEST HOUSE IN THE TRADE
FOR
ROOM PAPERS,
PAINTS,
OILS,
COLOURS,
STAINS & VARNISHES,
WINDOW GLASS AND SASHES,
AT
PETER HANTON'S,
3, MAIN-STREET, WEXFORD.
P.S.—Special quotations for quantities.

EXCELSIOR.

ENCOURAGED by last year's success, I am now in a position to offer the Public the largest and greatest variety of Goods I have ever had since I commenced Business, which include Ladies' and Gents'

COUNTY OF WEXFORD CONVENTION.

A CONVENTION OF DELEGATES, representing the National League Branches of the County of Wexford, will be held in the ASSEMBLY ROOMS, WEXFORD, on WEDNESDAY, JANUARY 12th.
The rule by which the number of delegates to be sent to the Convention is to be determined is as follows:—
"That each Branch consisting of any number under 100 members send two delegates, and that an additional delegate be appointed for each fifty members over the first hundred."
Cards of Admission may be had at THE PEOPLE Office, on the morning of the Convention, by any member who shall produce his President's or Secretary's order for the required number.
The Clergy of the Diocese are respectfully invited to attend ex-officio.
Hour of Meeting—One p.m.
The Convention is called for general purposes, including the raising and distribution of the Pay the Members Fund.   P. KENNY, P.P.
P. DOYLE.
(gjl)   E. WALSH.

A MONSTER INDIGNATION MEETING AT ENNISCORTHY.

A GREAT MONSTER INDIGNATION COUNTY MEETING
WILL BE HELD
AT ENNISCORTHY
On SUNDAY, JAN. 16, 1887,
For the purpose of protesting against the unconstitutional action of the present Tory Government towards Messrs. John Dillon, M.P.; Wm. O'Brien, and other members of the Irish Party; and also for the purpose of taking into consideration the present depressed state of the country; to protest against rack-rents, evictions, and extermination, and to promote the National cause in general.
John E. Redmond, Esq., M.P.; Sir Thomas H. G.

There was very little mention of the library and reading rooms during this period which covered the Great War and the 1916 rising. The reader should keep this in mind when perusing the next entry concerning the reading rooms. Remember thousands of young Irishmen had perished in the trenches in Europe fighting for the British Empire whilst the dreaded black and tans were running amok on Irish streets. The Society was very careful not to mention the war or politics in its minuets as these were dangerous times and discretion and prudence was the order of the day.

At the A.G.M. held on the 16th February 1919 it is recorded that on the suggestion of Edward F. O'Rourke the meeting decided that the supply of the following newspapers and magazines to the club should be discontinued 'The London Times', 'Weekly Freeman', Weekly Independent', 'Illustrated London News', 'Answers', 'Tit Bits', 'London Opinion', and the 'London Magazines'. He suggests that the 'Enniscorthy Echo' and 'Catholic Bulletin' should be supplied to the club instead. All this was agreed to and placed in motion. Are we witnessing a little smidgen of anti-British retaliation here from old Ned aimed at British publications?. Furthermore,

anyone who is familiar with the times will know that the 'Enniscorthy Echo' was the hotbed of Irish nationalism at that time.

On the 24th February 1931 we read; *In consequence of the blasphemous article which recently appeared in the 'London Daily Mail' it was decided to discontinue getting this paper for the reading room.* Obviously the Catholic Faith had been under attack by this publication and the Society responded immediately by discontinuing purchasing this paper.

The regular newspaper list was reduced drastically in 1947 and there was some discontent from members regarding this. They wanted more newspapers and periodicals placed on the table. It was only the previous year that the Council had reduced their intake of newspapers. The outcome was that the following magazines appeared on the table by April 1948 - 'Illustrated Practical Mechanics', 'Table Tennis Review' and a new publication titled 'Fiat'. From 1951 to 1956 the club decided to add the following magazines to the list: 'Readers Digest', 'Black and White', 'Old Moore's Almanac', 'Catholic Digest', 'Catholic Herald' and to cancel the 'Times Pictorial'.

THE ILLUSTRATED LONDON NEWS

ANDREW BEST DELLO&LEIGHTON

No. 114, Vol. V.] FOR THE WEEK ENDING SATURDAY, JULY 6, 1844. [SIXPENCE.

WITH SUPPLEMENT, GRATIS.

SESSIONAL SYMPTOMS.

VERY sign of the beginning of the end of the session is distinctly visible; the indications of the period so desired by all parties —by the Ministers who represent her Majesty, and by the members who represent the people—are abundant, decisive, and not to be mistaken. We have before spoken of, a fatality that overtakes measures that are still left pending, about the first week of July. It is a legislative epidemic, periodical in its visits, unvarying in its effects, and this week has set in, as Canning once said of the English summer, "with its usual severity."

There are two ways of getting "rid" of business; one is by talking as little and doing as much as possible: this is the mode pur-

darkness of a Select Committee by the twin measure of Lord Brougham, who would rather see a bad law disgrace the Statute Book for ever, than permit any one but himself to have the credit of reforming it. Where is the County Courts Bill? Stopped in its progress by the loss of Lord Cottenham's bill; for it was at first delayed, in consequence of the more comprehensive measure of the Ex-Chancellor rendering the more local enactment in many points unnecessary: thus one evil creates another.

There is no doubt that much of this, delay and disappointment as to the carrying through of proposed measures, is unavoidable as a Legislative Assembly; it is one of the evils that must be submitted to for the sake of the compensating good arising from free discussion—an advantage that would be but ill exchanged for all the celerity that the machinery of an absolute power, fixing every thing by an ukase, or a decree, could afford. That the evil is in some respects unavoidable, seems proved from its existing alike under two Governments, so differently circumstanced, as those of Sir R. Peel and Lord Melbourne. The Whig Ministry had a bare majority in the Commons, and a united and powerful opposition; while in the Lords it could scarcely carry a single

measure: it, therefore, did nothing. The present Government has an overwhelming majority in the Commons, where the opposition to it is broken and divided; while in the Lords, it has the powerful support of the Duke of Wellington, and Lord Lyndhurst, and the good will, in the main, of the majority of the Peers. Yet, strange to say, the strong, Government does almost as little as the weak one. There are so many events, beyond the control of a Ministry, giving rise to discussions it cannot prevent, that some expenditure of time is inevitable. But the mischief is in a great degree to be attributed to the Ministry not pressing its own measures forward at the early part of the Session, when the greater number of nights are occupied, we will not say wasted, in discussions on every imaginable subject. We think it possible to combine the advantages of free and full discussion with a greater dispatch of business, provided the Government would attempt, less, know with more certainty its own intentions, and exhibit a little more determination and earnestness as to all the measures they take in hand. It is possible to talk and work at the same time, but no example of the double process is furnished by the Session of 1844.

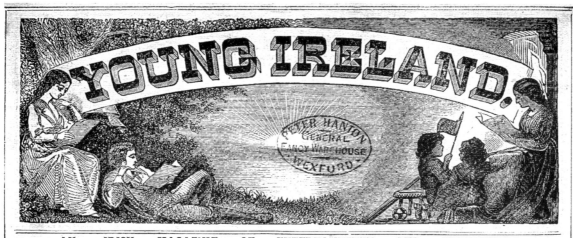

YOUNG IRELAND.

AN IRISH MAGAZINE OF ENTERTAINMENT AND INSTRUCTION.

Vol. III.—No. 27.   Dublin, Saturday, 7th July, 1877.   Price, One Penny.

"Connor looked straight down into her face, but not a muscle of it changed."—(See page 344.)

CASTLE DALY:
THE STORY OF AN IRISH HOME THIRTY YEARS AGO.

By Miss Annie Keary,
Author of "Oldbury," &c., &c.

CHAPTER IV. (CONTINUED.)

There were many murmured "True for ye, Kitty," as the lookers-on flocked after the sick boy and his bearers into the kitchen, leaving Pelham alone in the court-yard to secure Lictor's broken chain, and coax him to subside quietly into his kennel.

He was bitterly vexed and annoyed at what had happened, and in the midst of his real concern for the principal sufferer his heart swelled high with indignation at the ill-will that had been shown to himself. Those people had looked at him as if he were a sort of Cain, and he could not see that he was in any way responsible for the accident, or had done or said anything blameworthy. He felt it very hard to be so capriciously and unjustly judged; yet, before he had made the link of the broken chain secure, he had taken what appeared to him a magnanimous resolve. The prejudices of these people should not prevent him from doing what he considered his duty in this matter; neither more nor less. All proper precautions against future accidents he would enforce himself, but he would not give up

The 'Young Ireland' magazine 7th July 1877. Note Peter Hanton's stamp underneath the title.

The Vanishing Newspapers

Allow me to refer now to a matter which was a recurring problem for the Council for a long time and which finally forced them to take drastic action to combat it. There was an investigation into the matter in an attempt to catch the culprit's, the first ever instance of which occurred back in 1906.

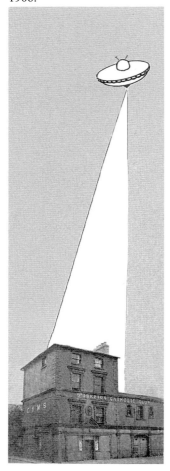

In December 1906 there was a report that *some magazines were being removed from the reading room and not been returned* A notice was erected stating that no magazines or newspapers were to be taken out of the reading room. However, the same thing happened again in November 1941 and the Council responded with *any person found removing papers from the Society would be severely dealt with.* This occurred again on the 6th March 1945 even though the caretaker was rubber-stamping all the reading material. The Council put up another notice, which stated *If this practice continues the council will place the matter in the hands of the Guards.*

Eight years later in September of 1953 unacceptable behaviour was again taking place in the reading room. The newspapers were disappearing once more. This was in the days of the UFO phenomenon.

The question arose - was there an intergalactic flying saucer hovering over Common Quay Street aiming a blinding beam of probing pulsating light down on the reading room and abducting the precious reading matter? Or was some dirty rat stealing the newspapers? The fact is the Council in its infinite wisdom decided that it was the latter. The result of all this was that a notice was erected on the back of the reading room door to the effect that *The council was considering closing the reading room due to papers being taken* – 1st September 1953.

This order was reinforced in October so it was decided that if the papers continued to be taken then they would be placed in the billiards room. This then was the beginning of the end of the reading room as it has been known in the Society for over 98 years. The '*unofficial removal*' of reading material from the reading room had being going on for some time now. It happened in 1906, 1941, 1945 and 1953 so it was an ongoing problem. The occurrence of theft in the Society was practically nonexistent. Obviously there were only a couple of individuals removing these papers as the majority of the members of the Society were of the highest calibre, good honest and decent people and this fact was well attested and well known throughout the town of Wexford.

Oliver Hickey proposed and William Murphy seconded that the reading room be transferred to the billiard room from Monday November 12th 1956. The proposal was carried unanimously. At the next meeting all the above was finalised and the reading material was transferred to the billiard room. The papers and reading material were now placed on the round table which I will deal with anon. This table now constituted the C.Y.M.S library as the reading room proper was closed and put under lock and key. This was the end of an era. Exactly one hundred and one years had passed since the Society had established a library and reading room and a few blackguards had sealed its fate for the sake of a few pence.

The Round Table

The large *"round table"* in the corner of the card area of the billiard room was used as the *"reading table"*. This table replaced the reading room function in 1956 right up to the time the club at Common Quay Street was closed. I can remember seeing old Eugene McGrail sitting there with pipe in mouth reading the newspapers. He would always sit with his back to the wall in the corner. Rumour had it that he did this because he wore a toupee. This, of course, was rubbish and nothing more than scurrilous slander put about by jealous bald-headed, C.Y.M.S. members. Others said that he was in the habit of dying his hair black. Now as he was a man of advanced years and had pitch-black hair, perhaps there was some validity in this accusation.

Enough digression now back to the 'round table'. I cannot recall exactly the names of which newspapers were on the table, nor can I recall what magazines were regularly purchased but I do remember that they were few and far between. It was a damn shame that this round table in the corner of the card room was all that remained of the magnificent library and it certainly does not say much for the intellectual leanings of the members as the club moved into the so-called modern age. We can get an idea of the papers that were being purchased in 1965 from the following meeting during which it had been decided to reduce the newspapers. It read *Decided by the council to reduce the newspapers being delivered by obtaining the local paper alternatively weekly to cut out the 'Daily Mail' and 'The Readers Digest'.* As far as I can recall the cycling magazine and the 'Reader's Digest' were the last two magazines that the club was ordering.

Sale of Newspapers and Periodicals

The other item of interest in John Stafford's book was the quarterly sale of the old newspapers. From Mr. Stafford's notes it becomes clear that the club purchased a vast amount of reading material both newspapers and magazines on a regular basis. These papers were then offered to the highest bidder and sold of to the members in that manner. It is quite clear that this was common practice as there were several pages recording this type of sale and this is also well documented throughout the minute books. These sales occurred every quarter i.e. 1st January, 1st April, 1st July and 1st of October each year. It is obvious that this was a well-established practice from the outset. A practice I might add that was still in vogue right up to our times. At some stage between 1850 and 1938 the sale of the papers changed from quarterly to half yearly sales and from the 13th December 1938 the sale of newspapers and magazines was to be held on an annual basis instead of half yearly. This was around the time when the cost of newspapers had reduced considerably and most people could afford to purchase them. Thus there was no need for newspapers in the auction.

In the early days of the Society the Council members were the ones who conducted the sales of the newspapers and periodicals. For example, Mr. Tucker conducted the auction on the 6th April 1862. Why and when the sale of the papers was handed over to the professionals is not clear but the following entry in the minute book is interesting. On the 20th May 1884 in connection with the selling of our old newspapers and magazines etc. it is recorded that *The secretary was threatened with a prosecution for selling the papers in the 1st April, auction.* The Inland Revenue decided that it would not proceed with the prosecution on account of the particular circumstances of the case. Alderman Walsh, on learning what happened, offered to sell the papers and magazines at any time that the Council wished. John J. Walsh was a Professional auctioneer and a member of the Society and it is reasonable to assume that he offered his services free of charge. From June 1884 Alderman John J. Walsh, Auctioneer conducted the sales and John J. Kehoe another professional Auctioneer and member took charge of the sales from 1910.

By the 1890s the club appears to have organised the auction of the papers in a more professional manner. I discovered one of the *'Auctions of Papers and Magazines'* handbills which were obviously distributed to the membership. The full list of all the reading material that was in the auction is listed in the handbill and it is from this handbill that we glean this otherwise lost information. The keen-eyed reader will also note that the Society's premises at this time (1890s) was at Paul Quay. This practice of auctioning off the reading material continued right down through the years to our day.

When we peruse the minutes of the 8th December 1885 we discover that the reversion of the papers for the next three months was to be held before Christmas and *an advertisement was to be put in the local newspapers and it was to be open to the public.* Mr. Walsh the auctioneer conducted the sale. This is the first mention of these sales being open to the public. Perhaps that is the way it was conducted in the early days. On 20th February 1902 the auction of the newspapers and magazines took place in December; the Auctioneer being J. J. Walsh Esq. The auction for the newspapers and magazines was held on the 19th of December 1911 with John J. Kehoe as the auctioneer.

Daily Papers.

National Press,   Evening Telegraph,
Freeman's Journal,   Pall Mall Gazette,
Irish Times,   Star,
   Daily Graphic.

Bi-Weekly.

The People,   The Independent.

Weekly.

The Free Press,   The Shamrock,
The Nation,   Irish Catholic,
The Weekly National   Truth.
Press,   The Illustrated London
Sport,   News,
Fun,   Sporting and Dramatic
Punch,   News,
Catholic Times,   The Field,
Young Ireland,   The General Advertiser,
   The Canadian Gazette.

Monthly.

Catholic World,   Irish Monthly,
Catholic Fireside,   Review of Reviews,
   Cassell's Family.

Catholic Young Men's Society,

PAUL QUAY.

Wexford, ——————— 189

....

DEAR SIR,

THE AUCTION OF PAPERS AND MAGAZINES,

FOR SIX MONTHS,

commencing the   *and ending*

the   *, 189 , will take*

place this Evening, at 9 o'clock. I hope it may

suit your convenience to attend. Annexed you have

a List of the Papers and Magazines.

     Yours faithfully,

         Hon. Sec.

A sample page from John Stafford's 'General Memoranda'.
Recording the auction of reading material 1st April 1863.

At the Annual General Meeting this year *the reversions these two same magazines were sold for 5/= for the 'Readers Digest' and 4/= for the 'Black & White'* - A.G.M. 11th February 1951. On Friday the 8th of January 1952 the reversion of newspapers was held at 10.00.a.m. There is absolutely nothing else recorded this year regarding the reading room. The reversion of newspapers and magazines was still being conducted right up to the 1980s but the reading material available at this time was minimal indeed and quite frankly I cannot for the life of me see what they had to sell. Unlike the old days when people would be glad to be able to purchase old newspapers, in the 1950s everyone could afford a newspaper so who would want old newspapers?

See appendix No 3 for the full list of businesses that supplied newspapers and periodicals to the Society. See also the Librarian and library committees from 1855 to 1944.

(See 'List of Suppliers of Newspapers and Periodicals' to the club. Appendix No 3, Page 277)

Miscellany

The Library Telescope

There was a telescope on a tripod situated at one of the windows in the library room situated on the second floor of 'St. Iberius House' facing the quayside. This was for the use and pleasure of the members and many of the older members *(some of whom were old sea-dogs)* would sit and espy the schooners coming and going in the busy Wexford harbour of the 1800s. There was many a retired sea Captain in the Society *(see full list in the chapter on 'Ship owners and sailors' Vol. II)* and no doubt these men would have great interest in watching the activities in the harbour and the business being conducted on the Quays.

On the 4th September 1906 *A Master Holbrook,* [young man] *a non-member of the club had accidentally knocked the spy glass* [telescope] *out through the window.* The telescope was badly damaged together with a pane of window glass which was broken. The boy's mother Mrs. Holbrook was informed of the instance and she expressed her *willingness to pay a reasonable compensation for the damages.* The telescopic glass was sent to an optician to see if it could be repaired and at what cost. The optician obviously advised the club to send it to a specialist because on the 4th of June 1907 we read that an *Estimate from Mr. McGregor, Dublin to repair the telescope and make it as good as new for the sum of £5.* The club decided to have the work carried out and although it is not recorded it would be reasonable to assume that Mrs. Holbrook did actually pay the bill as she had promised she would. This was not the first time that the telescope was damaged as on the 19th February 1884 we are informed that the telescope was repaired for £2-10-0.

On the 21st of May 1913 there was another episode with the telescope. The caretaker reported *The telescope was broken on the 13th May by Frank Horan.* At a Council meeting the Secretary stated *Frank Horan told him that he was taking one of the parts out to clean the glass when it fell out of his hands and broke part of the lenses in the fall.* It was decided *the damage had been done through an accident, and Mr. Horan was exonerate.* The telescope was once again sent off to Mr. McGregor in Dublin and it cost 25/6 to have it repaired. This was the third time that this telescope was broken which proves that it was in constant use by the members. As a child in the late 1940s and early 50s I was in the library room with my father and there was definitely no telescope there at that time. I can assure you that if there was a little fellow like me would have noticed it and would most defiantly have wanted to get my hands on it. There was no telescope at that time so it must have been broken beyond repair or was sold but there is no further record of a telescope in the minute books since the May 1913 incident.

Lighting in the Reading Room

At the end of 1907, a couple of weeks away from Christmas, it is recorded that the Council decided *to procure a 'Fixed Gas Pendant' for the reading room as the present one is unsuitable for the Incandescent Burners.* This was the age of gaslight and it would be some years yet before the club's members would be perusing their reading material with the luxury of electricity. *(See also 'Public Utilities' on page 225).*

R E L I G I O N

Pope Pius IX gave his blessing to the establishment of the Catholic Young Men's Society

Of the eleven Popes who reigned since the C.Y.M.S. was established, His Holiness Pope Pius IX did more for the C.Y.M.S. and its members than any other Pope.

Pope Pius IX

Pius IX
16th June 1846 – 7th February 1878.

The fourth son of Count Giovanni Maria Mastai-Ferretti was born at Senigallia on the 13th May 1792 and studied at Viterbo and Rome. He was ordained priest in 1819, served 1823-5 with a Papal mission to Chile, took charge 1825-7 of the Hospice of S. Michele, Rome, and was Archbishop of Spoleto 1827-32, Bishop of Imola 1832-40. Named Cardinal in 1840 and elected Pope 16th June 1846. After the defeat of his newly formed army at Castelfidardo 1860 *(Irish papal brigade included)* Pope Pius saw all his dominions, with the exception of Rome and its immediate environs, annexed to the new kingdom of Italy. Pope Pius never set foot outside the Vatican again regarding himself as a prisoner. His Pontificate was the longest in history.

In 1852 when Fr. O'Brien, the founder of the C.Y.M.S. was in Rome he presented his constitution for the C.Y.M.S to Pope Piue IX. The Holy Father had the document studied by his senior theologians and advisors and he was so impressed with the document that he gave it his blessing there and then. The Apostolic Blessing was bestowed upon all who became C.Y.M.S. members and a Plenary Indulgence was granted to all the members on the festival of their branch's Patron Saint (*St. Ibar, Wexford*). The Holy Father also affiliated the C.Y.M.S. to the Arch Confraternity of the Immaculate Heart of Mary with full indulgences. That was the first gesture by this Pope.

The second gesture was *Mr. N.J. Tucker, a long serving member of the society was presented with a gold medal brought by the Rev. President, Walter Lambert, C.C., from the 'Holy Roman Empire'(sic) and created a knight of the Catholic Young Men's Society.* The foregoing statement is an extract from the minute books of the Wexford branch C.Y.M.S. dated 20th March 1871. There are a few questions which must be asked concerning this. Who wrote *'Holy Roman Empire'* in the minutes? Was it Robert Hanton, the Hon. Secretary or was it dictated by Rev. Walter Lambert the President, as it would appear. Whoever, it was not correct as there was no *'Holy Roman Empire'* at that date. It should have read *'Rome'* or even *'The Vatican'* which would have been more correct. The other puzzling question relates to the title of *'Knight of the C.Y.M.S.'* Mr. Eamon Hennessy, the President of the

C.Y.M.S. of Ireland informed me that the title is unknown at the C.Y.M.S.I. Headquarters. I have never heard of such a title and I have never come across it again in all the documentation that I have researched which was very extensive. It should also be noted that the minutes from all meetings would have been signed-off by the President, Rev. Walter Lambert, C.C., Mr. Tucker himself was on the ruling Council the year he received the honour.

The third gesture was that Richard Devereux, K.S.G. was created a Knight of the order of St. Gregory by Pope Pius IX who also gave him a gift of St. Adjutor which Richard brought back to his home in Wexford. When Richard died in 1883 St. Adjutor was removed to the Franciscan Church where it remains to this day. These three gestures to the C.Y.M.S. all took place during Pope Pius IX's Pontificate.

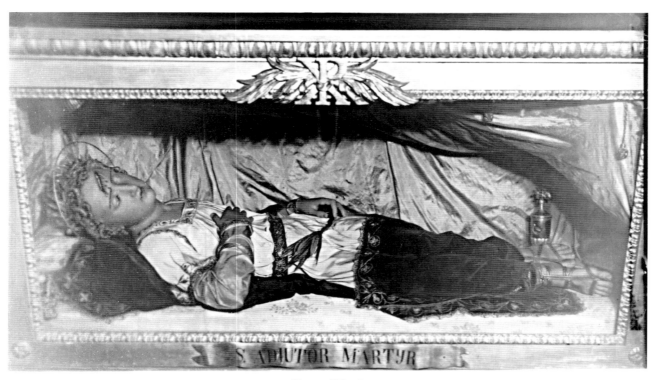

St. Adjutor

Bequeathed to the Franciscan Church 1883

The photograph depicts the reliquary of St. Adjutor. This glass fronted casket or container was taken back to Wexford and installed in Richard's home. It was bequeathed to the Franciscan Church in March 1883 on Richard's death.

People of my vintage or older will remember viewing it in the Friary. It was situated under the right hand side altar. When I was a kid I often went in to look at it and there were certain times when it was lit-up for viewing. At other times you were allowed to on to the altar area for closer viewing.

Chronological List of Bishops of Ferns and Patrons of the C.Y.M.S. St. Iberius Branch 1855 - 2008

Bishop Myles Murphy

Most Rev. Dr. Myles Murphy. D.D., Lord Bishop of Ferns
(1787–1856)

A native of Ballinoulart and a nephew of Father Michael Murphy one of the 1798 rebellion leaders. He was the first President of St, Peter's College and the first President of the Catholic Seminary that was opened at Michael Street Wexford in 1811.

Fr. Murphy was appointed Bishop on 11th November 1849 and was consecrated on the 10th of March 1850. He died on `13th August 1856 aged 69 years. Although he was Bishop of Ferns, it would appear that Bishop Murphy was not Patron of the Society as the tradition had not yet been established.

Very Rev. James Canon Roche P.P.V.F.
(1801-1883)

Very Rev. James Roche, P.P.,V.F.

Fr. James Roche was the first Patron and Spiritual Director of the Society but it is unclear when exactly he relinquished the title of Patron in favour of Bishop Furlong. Fr. Roche was the son of Thomas Roche one of the old Wexford merchants who had come as a boy from Levitstown to Wexford to serve his apprenticeship. His wife was Elizabeth Murphy of Gibberpatrick, sister of Fr. Michael Murphy, PP, Tomacork and of Very Rev. William Murphy, Dean of Ferns and pastor of Taghmon. James Roche was brother of Very Rev. Thomas Roche, PP, Our Lady's Island and Rev. John Roche, OSE. He was uncle of Dr. Abraham Brownrigg, Bishop of Ossory and cousin of Very Rev. Nicholas Roche, Dean of St. John's, Newfoundland. He was granduncle of Rev. James Rossiter, PP. Ferns and Rev. Michael Rossiter, PP Cushinstown.

Fr. Roche was born on the corner of Oyster Lane and South Main Street, Wexford on 21st August 1801 and received his primary education under Rev. Behan a Protestant gentleman who kept his school in George's Street, Wexford. In 1811 he entered the old Seminary and then went on to Maynooth College in 1819. He was ordained on 25th May 1826 and was appointed a curate in Enniscorthy on 8th September 1827.

He was promoted to Parish Priest of Ferns in 1840. During the period of his pastoral charge of Ferns, in the famine period of 1847-48, he received a donation from Pius IX for distribution among his flock. He was transferred to Wexford on 27th May 1850 where the famous 'Twin Churches' are monuments to his work. The foundation stones for the churches were laid on the 27th June 1851.

In 1854 Fr. Roche paid a visit to Rome and was received in private audience by Pope Pius IX. He received an Apostolic Blessing for all parishioners who made donations towards the new churches in Wexford. On the 18th April 1858 he celebrated the first Mass in the Church of the Assumption *(Bride Street)*. Bishop Furlong solemnly dedicated the Church of the Immaculate Conception, Rowe Street on the 3rd October 1858 and consecrated the Church of the Assumption, Bride Street, on 5th September 1860. Fr. Roche celebrated his Golden Jubilee in June 1876 when the parishioners presented him with a congratulatory address. He died on Wednesday March 14th 1883 *(aged 82)* at his residence St. Aidan's, Waterloo Road and his remains were removed to Rowe Street church on Thursday morning. He then had a public funeral with all the schools and trades of the town turning out. The 1,000 men of the Confraternity bearing their banners marched in the procession. The

'Catholic Young Men's Society' was well represented. On Friday morning the remains were removed to the Church of the Assumption when after High Mass and Office he was interred opposite the altar of the Blessed Virgin within one hundred yards of the spot where he was born.

It was decided to erect a statue to his memory in the grounds of the Church of the Immaculate Conception. The work was entrusted to Mr. Farrell of Dublin and having been erected it was solemnly unveiled on the 17th March 1887 by his Lordship Most Rev. Dr. Browne. This statue still stands in the Church grounds, now sadly a car park, and can easily be viewed by anyone wishing to do so.

Mr. Richard J. Devereux, K.S.G.
(1855 - 1883)

Richard J. Devereux was a Patron and a kind benefactor to the Catholic Young Men's Society from its beginning right up to his death in March 1883. The Society is still benefiting from his estate. Further details of Mr. Devereux can be seen in the profiles section of Vol. II.

Most Rev. Dr. Thomas Furlong. D.D.,
Lord Bishop of Ferns
(1857 - 1875)

Born in Mayglass circa 1800. Educated Mayglass and the Latin School at Ballyfane Cross. He spent five years at the Roman Catholic Seminary in Wexford and then went to Maynooth College in 1819 and was ordained there on the 22nd May 1826. He was appointed junior Dean in Maynooth College and over the next thirty years was successively Professor of Sacred Scripture, Hebrew, Dogmatic and Moral Theology. He was appointed Bishop of Ferns on the 9th January 1857 and consecrated on 22nd March. During his episcopate he established many religious houses in Wexford, the St. John of God Convent, and the Convent of the Sisters of Reparation, later known as the Sisters of Perpetual Adoration, and saw the building of the "twin churches" in Wexford town.

In 1870 he attended all the sessions of the First Vatican Council. The dogma of the Papal Infallibility was debated during this Council. Bishop Furlong was not in full agreement with this definition but accepted the majority decision. He was also present at the National Synod of Maynooth in 1875. He died at St. Peter's College, Wexford on the 12th November of the same year.

Most Rev. Dr. Michael Warren D.D., Lord Bishop of Ferns
(1875 – 1884)

Born in Clonmore near Glenbrien in 1826. Educated at St. Peter's College and entered Maynooth College in August 1849. He was ordained in 1853. He was appointed curate in Templeudigan on the 1st of February 1854 where he remained until November 1856 when he went to Ballygarrett for a few months. He was then transferred to Coolfancy in April 1857 and sent to Enniscorthy in September of that year, where he remained for the next nine years.

In 1866 Bishop Thomas Furlong established the Missionaries of the Blessed Sacrament in Enniscorthy, and Fr. Warren was one of four founding members, the others being Fr. James A. Cullen *(who later, as a Jesuit, was to found the Pioneer Total Abstinence Association)*, Fr. Thomas Cloney, both curates in Wexford town, and Fr. Abraham Brownrigg, a member of the staff of St. Peter's college. Fr. Warren was the first superior of the community and was to occupy the position for ten years. Fr. Warren was consecrated Bishop of Ferns on 7th April 1876.

Bishop Warren instituted a Temperance crusade to advance the work commenced by Bishop Furlong and appointed Fr. James A. Cullen as organising secretary. On the 1st November 1876 the 'Catholic Total Abstinence Association' was established in Enniscorthy and soon spread to every parish in the Diocese. Bishop Warren died on the 22nd April 1884 after a short illness.

Most Rev. Dr. James Browne. D.D., Lord Bishop of Ferns
(1884 –1917)

Was born at Bigbarn, Mayglass on the 28th August 1842. He received his education locally and then entered St. Peter's College, Wexford, and then on to Maynooth College where he matriculated on 27th September 1861. When he reached canonical age he was ordained on Christmas Eve 1865 by Bishop Furlong. From 1866 to 1867 he was on the staff of St. Peter's college, and was appointed curate in Barntown on the 5th November 1867. In 1869 he was transferred to Wexford town and in September of 1880 he was made parish priest of Piercestown.

Bishop James Browne

In June 1884 he was appointed to succeed Bishop Warren and was consecrated on 14th September and took up residence in Wexford, which had been made a mensal parish the previous year. In keeping with his predecessor, he too recommended the change from Rockfield to the vicinity of the Church of the Assumption at Bride Street for the Convent of Perpetual Adoration. It was constructed at a cost of £8,000, and occupied by the nuns on the 1st May 1887. Bishop Browne died on 17th June 1917 aged 75 years.

Bishop William Codd

Most Rev. Dr. William Codd, Lord Bishop of Ferns
(1917 – 1938)

Born at South Main Street, Wexford on the 6th July 1865, Son of a shipwright, John Codd, and his wife Annie *(nee Rossiter)*. He received his early education in the Christian Brothers and in St. Peter's College. He then went to the Irish College, Rome where he was ordained in 1889. On his return to Wexford he was appointed professor of Dogmatic Theology in the newly established Faculty of Theology at St. Peters and became President of the college in 1903 and was appointed parish priest of Blackwater on the 15th March 1912.

He was consecrated Bishop of Ferns on the 25th February 1918. He was an excellent golfer and yachtsman and it was said that he was 'above average' on the billiard table. It is not stated if he ever visited the C.Y.M.S. premises for a game in the club that he was Patron of. He underwent surgery in February 1938 and died on the 12th of March the same year.

Most Rev. J. Staunton, D.D., Lord Bishop of Ferns
(1938 – 1983)

Born on 20th February 1889 in Ballyoskill, Ballyragget, Co. Kilkenny. Educated at St. Kieran's College, Kilkenny and went to Maynooth in 1906 and was ordained there on the 22nd June 1913. He was then appointed professor of Dogmatic Theology in St. Kieran's College. He went to Freiburg in Germany to study for the degree of Doctor of Divinity in 1918 to 1921, when he returned to St. Kieran's to teach. In 1923 he was appointed Junior Dean in Maynooth College until in 1928 he returned to St. Kieran's as President.

He was appointed successor to Bishop Codd on the 10th December 1938 and was consecrated on the 5th February 1939. He died on 27th June 1963 the day that President John F. Kennedy visited Wexford town. It was planned to issue a souvenir album to mark the Silver Jubilee of the Episcopal ordination of Dr. Staunton on the 4th February 1964 but owing to his death it was issued as a memorial.

Most Rev. Donal J. Herlihy, D.D., L.S.S., Ph.D.
Lord Bishop of Ferns (1964 - 1983)

Born in November 1908 at Knockmagree, Co. Cork where both his parents were teachers. As a youth he had received a bullet wound in the back from a Black-and-Tan gun. Educated at the local National School and then went to St. Brendan's Seminary, Killarney and then to the Irish College, Rome. In 1925 he was ordained in the Basilica of St. John Lateran on the 4th April 1931. He continued his studies at the Pontifical Biblical Institute. On his return to Ireland he taught at the Jeffers Institute in Tralee until 1939. Appointed Professor of Sacred Scriptures in All Hallows College, Dublin up to 1947 when he became Vice-Rector of the Irish College in Rome and four years later he was appointed Rector. In 1964 he was appointed successor to Bishop Staunton and was consecrated in the Lateran Basilica on the 15th November and was enthroned in St. Aidan's Cathedral on 31st December 1964.

To mark the fiftieth anniversary of his ordination to the priesthood a special *"Golden Jubilee"* Commemorative Book was issued on the 4th April 1981 and in the following June special celebrations were held in St. Aidan's Cathedral. On the 10th June 1981 Wexford Corporation honoured him by making him a Freeman of the Borough of Wexford. He died on Holy Saturday on the 2nd April 1983.

Most Rev. Brendan Comiskey D.D.
Lord Bishop of Ferns
(1983-2002)

Born on 13th August 1935 in Tasson, Clontibert, Co. Monaghan. He was ordained in the Congregation of the Sacred Hearts at Tanagh, Co. Monaghan on the 25th June 1961. On the 20th January 1980 he was ordained Bishop at St. Andrews, Westland Row in Dublin. He succeeded Bishop Herlihy as Bishop of Ferns on the 20th May 1984. Both Patron of the C.Y.M.S. Wexford Branch and the Wexford Festival Opera, he was made a Freeman of Wexford town in June 1990. He resigned his position as Bishop of Ferns in 2002.

Most Rev. Eamon Walsh, Bishop of Dublin. Apostolic Administrator of the Diocese of Ferns (2002 –2006)

He was appointed the Apostolic Administrator of the Diocese of Ferns in 2002 as there was no Bishop of Ferns at this time due to the resignation of Bishop Comiskey.

Most Rev. Dr. Denis Brennan
Lord Bishop of Ferns
1st March 2006

Fr. Brennan was born in the Parish of Rathnure, Enniscorthy on the 20th June 1945. He attended the National school at Kiltealy and then St. Peter's College, Wexford. He entered St. Peter's Seminary Wexford in September 1964 and was ordained for the Diocese of Ferns on the 11th May, 1970. After his ordination he was appointed to the House of Missions, Enniscorthy and for 16 years he conducted Parish Missions and Retreats in Ireland, England and Canada. He was appointed Administrator of St. Senan's Parish, Enniscorthy in 1986, a position he held for 11 years. He was appointed Parish Priest of Taghmon in 1997. He was announced as Bishop-Elect for the Diocese of Ferns on the 1st March, 2006. Monsignor Brennan is the former Diocesan Delegate for Child Protection and was previously Vicar Forane for the Wexford Deanery. Monsignor Brennan was ordained Bishop of Ferns in St. Aidan's Cathedral, Enniscorthy on Sunday 23rd April, 2006. As Patron of the Society he launched the 'History of the Wexford Catholic Young Men's Society 1855 -2008' on the evening of the 7th November 2008.

Clergy Who Were C.Y.M.S. Members

Very Rev. Laurence Allen, P.P. (1895-1962) Joined the Society in 1926 and left in 1934 after he was transferred to Boolavogue in September 1933

Very Rev. Jeremiah Anglim P.P. Joined the Society in 1950. Left when he went to Tacumshane 19th September 1955. He died 30th September 1978

Very Rev. Edward Canon Aylward P.P. (1848-1912) Joined 1889 and left to become parish priest of Blackwater in 1897

Rev. James Barry Joined about 1857

Very Rev. Matthew J. Berney, Adm. Joined 1970 to 1972 (*See members profiles Vol.2.*)

Very Rev. Victor Bridges, P.P. (*See members profiles Vol.2.*)

Rev. Bulger Joined 28th October 1897 (*honorary member*)

Very Rev. Dean Thomas Busher (1825-1907) Joined the Society prior to 3rd June 1862 and probably left around the 1880s

Rev. James Butler, C.C. Joined about 1923 and left 1929

Rev. Jeremiah Anglim, C.C.

Very Rev. Nicholas Cardiff, P.P.

Very Rev. J. Canon Codd, P.P., V.F.

Rev. John Butler C.C. (1874-1936) Joined prior to 1926 and left 1936. He transferred to Glynn on the 10th June 1913

Very Rev. John M. Butler Adm. Joined 1923 and left 1954 (*See members profiles Vol.2.*)

Rev. J. Brown, C.C. Joined about February 1876

Rev. Michael Cardiff. Joined about 1926 and left 1932

Very Rev. Nicholas Cardiff , P.P. (1892 – 1973) Joined the Society prior to 1920 and left later than 1946

Very Rev. Martin F. Clancy, P.P. Joined 1955 and left 1969 *(See President's List)*

Very Rev. Thomas Canon Cloney, Adm. (1838 -1895) Joined 5th February 1910 (*See members profiles Vol.2.*)

Very Rev. Dean Thomas Cloney, P.P. (1863 -1955) Joined 14th February 1898 and left 1911. He was a nephew of Rev. Thomas Canon Cloney, Adm.

Very Rev. James Codd, Adm. Joined 1913. He resigned the Presidency in September 1925 *(See President's List)*

Very Rev. John Codd, P.P. and Dean of Ferns (1886-1977) was made an honorary life member (*See members profiles Vol.2.*)

Rev. Robert Cooke, C.C. Joined November 1862

Rev. P. Corish, Joined 19th January 1886

Rev. Cullen, Joined 11th May circa 1866

Very Rev. James Cummins P.P. Joined the Society in 1946. He left in 1972 when he moved to Duncannon

Very Rev. James B. Curtis, P.P. He was President of the Wexford C.Y.M.S. in 1973-75 and was gone from the scene in 1976

Very Rev. Patrick Cushen, P.P. He was the Branch Chaplain for 1995 and 1996 and he left in August 1997 to take up the position of Parish Priest of Marshalstown

Rev. Fr. Doran, He was made an honorary member 1st July 1861

Rev. Patrick Cushen.   Rev. Thomas Eustace, C.C.   Rev. Matthew J. Doyle

Rev. F. J. Doyle, C.C., Joined about 1876 and left 1926?

Very Rev. Luke Canon Doyle, P. P. (1849 – 1915) (*See members profiles Vol.2.*)

Very Rev. Matthew Canon Doyle P.P. Joined 1942 and he resigned the Presidency in 1970 (*See members profiles Vol.2.*)

Very Rev. Patrick Canon Doyle, P.P. (*see members profiles Vol.2.*)

Very Rev. Patrick Doyle P.P. Joined 1926 and left 1951 (*See President's list*)

Rev. Patrick Doyle, C.C. Joined 15th October 1888 and left late 1940s

Rev. Robert P. Doyle, C.C. Joined about 1890

Very Rev. Thomas Eustace, P.P. Joined the Society in 1962 and left in 1963

Very Rev. James Fegan Adm. Joined in April 1998 and was the Wexford C.Y.M.S. President and Chaplain in April 1998

Very Rev. Matthew Fanning, P.P. Joined the Society on the 20th December 1883. Died 1st July 1908

Very Rev. John Furlong, O.S.F. (1860-1900) Joined the Society prior to 1860. Was made a life member on the 15th October 1888

Rev. James Gaul, C.C. (1877-1926) (*See members profiles Vol.2.*)

Very Rev. Cannon John Furlong, P.P.   Rev. D. A. Kavanagh, C.C.   Rev. John McCabe, C.C.

Rev. William J. Gaul Joined about 1935 and left 1948

Rev. Fr. Hanning Joined 20th December 1883

Rev. William Hanton (*See African Missions and members profiles Vol.2.*)

Rev. Jeremiah Hogan, C.C. Joined 1st March 1863 and left 1864 (*See President's List*)

Very Rev. Thomas Hore, P.P. Joined the Society in 1920. He left in 1922 to take up the position of parish priest of Monageer
Very Rev. David A. Kavanagh, P.P. Joined 1898 and left 1905
Very Rev. Matthew Keating P.P. (1877-1950) Joined the Society in the early 1900s and remained a member up to the time of his death on the 2nd of April 1950
Rev. Fr. Kelly Joined on the 13th February 1881
Rev. John J. Kennedy C.C. (1874 – 1907) Joined the Society prior to.1890
Very Rev. James Canon Lacy, P.P. (1800 – 1884) Joined the Society on the 20th May 1862

Rev. Chaplin, Thomas Murphy

Rev. Edward J. Murphy, C.C.

Rev. J. W. O'Bryne, C.C.

Rev. Nicholas Lambert C.C. (1853 – 1895) Joined the Society prior to January 1875
Rev. Walter Lambert, C.C. (1818 – 1903) *(See members profiles Vol.2.)*
Very Rev. John McCabe, P.P. Joined 1982 and left 1989
Rev. Thomas (Tom) Moran Joined about 1900
Very Rev. Edward Murphy Adm. Joined the Society on the 26th August 1941 and had left by 1970
Very Rev. George J. Murphy, P.P. (1886-1973) *(See members profiles Vol.2.)*
Rev. John Murphy, Joined 1st July 1861
Very Rev. Joseph Canon Murphy, P.P. Joined the Society on the 4th January 1886
Rev. Thomas Murphy, C.C., (1839 – 1922) Joined the Society on 19th January 1889
Very Rev. Thomas Murphy, Adm. (1913 – 1972). Joined 1942 and left 1969 *(See President's list)*
Very Rev. William Canon Murphy, C.C. *(See members profiles Vol.2.)*
Very Rev. Hugh O'Brien, Adm. *(See members profiles Vol.2.)*
Rev. Greg O'Byrne, Joined about 1965 and left 1970s
Very Rev. Hugh O'Byrne, P.P. Joined 1990 and left 1994 *(See president's list)*

Rev. Henry Sinnott, C.C.

Rev. M. Wickham, C.C.

Very Rev. James W. O'Byrne P.P. (*See members profiles Vol.2.*)

Very Rev. Mark Canon O'Byrne, P.P. Joined the Society prior to 1920 and left when he was transferred to Askamore on 24th April 1922. He died on 29th May 1950

Rev. Bartholomew O'Connor C.C. Joined the Society in 1951 and remained a member up to his death in a Dublin Nursing Home on Friday 22nd November 1954

Rev. Martin O'Connor C.C. (1892 – 1941) Joined about 1920 left 1941.

Very Rev. Patrick O'Connor Adm. (1861-1908) (*See members profiles Vol.2.*)

Rev. Thomas O'Connor, C.C. (1860-1955) (*See members profiles Vol.2.*)

Rev. John O'Dowd (1838 – 1914) Joined the Society prior to May 1912. He died at a private nursing home in Wexford on Sunday, 2nd November 1914

Very Rev. Mark Canon O'Gorman, P.P. (1838-1919) Joined the Society on the 13th January 1885. He died on 9th June 1919 aged 81 years

Rev. Patrick M. O'Leary, C.C. (*See members profiles Vol.2.*)

Very Rev. Michael J. Canon O'Neill, P.P. (*See members profiles Vol.2.*)

Rev. Brother O'Reardon he was made an honorary member on the 12th January 1887

Rev. Brendan O'Rourke, C. Ss. R. (*See members profiles Vol.2.*)

Very Rev. Francis E. O'Rourke, P.P. (*See African Missions* and *members profiles Vol.2.*)

Very Rev. James Canon Roche P.P.V.F. (1801-1883) (*See members profiles Vol.2.*)

Rev. Thomas (Tommy) Roche, Ph.D. (*See members profiles Vol.2.*)

Rev. A, J, Sheridan, C.C. Joined 12th March 1888

Very Rev. Nicholas T. Canon Sheridan, P.P. (1854 – 1924) (*See members profiles Vol.2.*)

Very Rev. John Sinnott, Adm. Joined about 1900 and left 1942

Very Rev. John Canon Sinnott, P.P. (1883 -1964) (*See members profiles Vol.2.*)

Very Rev. Henry Sinnott PP. Joined the Society 1959 and left in 1971 when he was transferred to Caim

Rev. Fr. Walsh Joined in 17th November 1885

Very Rev. James Walsh, P.P. He was made an honorary member 10th June 1862

Very Rev. Matthew Wickham, P.P. (*See members profiles Vol.2.*)

Chronological List of Presidents of the C.Y.M.S. Wexford

Aug. 1855	Very Rev. James Roche, P.P. V.F.The Society's first Spiritual Director and its first Patron (He nominated the first officials)
Aug. 1855	Mr. Thomas Alphonsus Hoope, Director of the Christian Brothers. Acting Chairman
16th Aug. 1855	James A. Johnson, Esq. Elected President
1st Mar. 1856	Rev. William Doyle Nominated President
18th Feb. 1856	Richard Keating Nominated President
1857 - Nov. 1858	Rev. James Barry

Rev. Thomas Cloney, Adm.

Rev. Patrick O'Connor, Adm.

Rev. James Codd, C.C.

3ʳᵈ Nov. 1858 - 1861	Rev. Walter Lambert
1862 - Feb. 1863	Rev. William Murphy

Rev. William Murphy, S.T.L.

Rev. Walter Lambert

Very Rev. Cannon Luke Doyle, P.P.

1865 - 1875	Rev. Walter Lambert
1876 to Dec. 1876	Rev. J. F. Doyle
Dec. 1876 to 1880	Rev. J. Browne, C.C.
1881 to May 1885	Rev. Luke Doyle, C.C.
1885 to Oct. 1888	Rev. Nicholas T. Sheridan,C.C. Left in October to take up a position at St. Peter's College

Rev. Patrick Doyle, P.P.

Very Rev. Edward Canon Aylward, P.P.,

Very Rev. N. T. Sheridan, B. C. L,

Oct. 1888 to 1890	Rev. Patrick Doyle, C.C. Was gone by August 1890
Aug. 1890 to 1897	Very Rev. Fr. E. Aylward, Adm.
1898 to 1907	Very Rev. Patrick Doyle, Adm.
Apr. 1907 to Jan. 1908	Very Rev. P. O'Connor, Adm.
1909 to 1911	Very Rev. T. Cloney, Adm.
1912 to 1922	Very Rev. Thomas Hore, Adm.
1923 to 1925	Very Rev. James Codd, Adm.
1926 to 1941	Very Rev. John Sinnott, Adm. Resigned in 1941 to become Parish Priest of Our Lady's Island
1941 to 1947	Very Rev. George J. Murphy, Adm. Left town in April 1947. He was Parish Priest of Rathangan
in 55	

1948 to 1951	Very Rev. Patrick Doyle, Adm.Parish Priest of Kilmore 1955
1952 to 1954	**Very** Rev. J. M. Butler, Adm. Parish Priest of Cushinstown 1955
1955 to 1961	Very Rev. Michael J. O'Neill, Adm.

Rev. John Sinnott, Adm.

Rev. Patrick Doyle, Adm.,

Very Rev. John M. Butler, P.P.

Rev. Michael J. O'Neill, Adm.

Rev. Matthew Berney, C.C.

Rev. Thomas Murpth ADM.,

Rev. Martin F. Clancy, C.C.

Thomas O'Rourke

Rev. H. O'Byrne, P.P.

1962 - 1969	Very Rev. Thomas Murphy, Adm.
1970 to 1972	Very Rev. Matthew J. Berney, Adm.
March 1972	Rev. Fr. Clancy Acted as stand-in for a short period
1973 to 1975	Very Rev. James B. Curtis, Adm. Thomas O'Rourke was Chairman
1976 to 1981	Thomas O'Rourke
1982 to 1989	Very Rev. John McCabe, Adm. Thomas O'Rourke was Chairman
1990 to 1991	Very Rev. Hugh O'Brien, Adm. Thomas O'Rourke, Chairman died in office on 21st January
1991 to 1993	Henry F. Doyle
1994 to 1996	Myles O'Rourke Rev. P. Cushin acted as Chaplain to the Society
1997	Sean Radford
1997	Nicky Lacey
1998 to 2008	Liam Gordon Chairman. Very Rev. James Fegan, Ad m. Chaplain

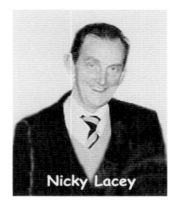 

Book of Guilds 1850s to 1860s

The first reference to Guilds and their record books is dated July 1858. It appears that there had been a discussion on the whole question of how the Guilds should be operated and a set of rules can be gleaned from these discussions which were:

1. *A senior Warden to be appointed over each Guild with a junior Warden as assistant*

2. *A fine to be imposed on members who miss the monthly Guild meetings and Confession and Holy Communion to be obligated.*

3. *The Warden of each Guild was to hold the key to the locked Guild box for the collections and contributions.*

4. *The Wardens to give notice to as many members as possible of Guild meetings.*

5. *Any member missing from a Guild meeting must submit a written explanation.*

6. *No person can become a member of the society without first having been proposed by a Warden or Council member.*

7. *Wardens to record member's names and addresses in their record books and take account of attendance and amounts paid in collections.*

On the 26th August 1858 it was recorded at a Council meeting *'that books for Guilds are got'* and continues *Wardens were required to make out a report each month of their Guilds and have it passed by the Council.* The Guilds were ordered to hold their meetings on the first Sunday of each month. St. Patrick's Guild in the Reading Room, St. Mary's Guild in the Bagatelle Room and St. Josephs in the Council Room. Wardens had to be elected to the position each year and the Guilds received Holy Communion on the third Sunday of each month. If a member of the Guild died the Warden was to notify all the members of the Guild who were expected to attend the funeral.

In July 1859 the Society purchased three banners for the three Guilds. These would have borne the name of the Guild and displayed a painting of the Patron Saint of each Guild. They, also, purchased a large Crucifix at an auction for 15/9 on the 23rd February 1860. The ensuing two entries give us an idea as to how the Guilds operated. On the 4th February a resolution was passed *That all the members meet together in the 'Lady's Chapel' on a particular day* to be decided by the Council for the purpose of approaching together to 'Holy Communion'. I wondered where the 'Lady's Chapel' was but I didn't

have to wonder for long. On the 8th March 1860 the Council resolved:
That all the members of the society going to 'Holy Communion' on the 3rd Sunday of each month meet at the 'Lady's Chapel' in Rowe Street Church at 8 o'clock Mass for the month of March. In the Friary at the same place, same hour for April, and in Bride Street Church at same place and hour for May and do so in each of three Churches alternately.
So now we know where the 'Lady's Chapel' was situated, it must have been one of the three altars and we also derive an insight into how the Guilds catered for the spiritual needs of the members.

A very interesting survey was ordered on the 30th September 1863 regarding the members of the Society. This is the first time the Society took note of the membership numbers on their books. In 1858 the Guild books were introduced and the Wardens of each Guild kept his own record of member's names. Then the Council decided they wanted to know the extent of the membership. Having gathered and analysed all the information they reached the conclusion that at the commencement of 1863 there were 141 members many of whom were in arrears with their subscriptions. The Council concluded that, in actual fact, there were only 58 paid up and active bona fide members

Guild, and resolved that it be inserted on the Minutes.

First Monthly Report of St Patricks Guild for 1864–

Members who have paid up in full for Jany 1864 } 38

Members who have not paid Jany quarter 14

Members who have not paid for Octr 1863 and Jany 1864 } 7

Members who have not paid for July, Octr 1863 and Jany 1864 } 14

Total Members in the Guild 73

There was a meeting of the Guild on Sunday 7th Feby. when Mr Robt Hanton was elected Junior Warden, 17 Members attended—

Report of the Guild of St Mary for Jany 1864

No of Members in the Guild 41

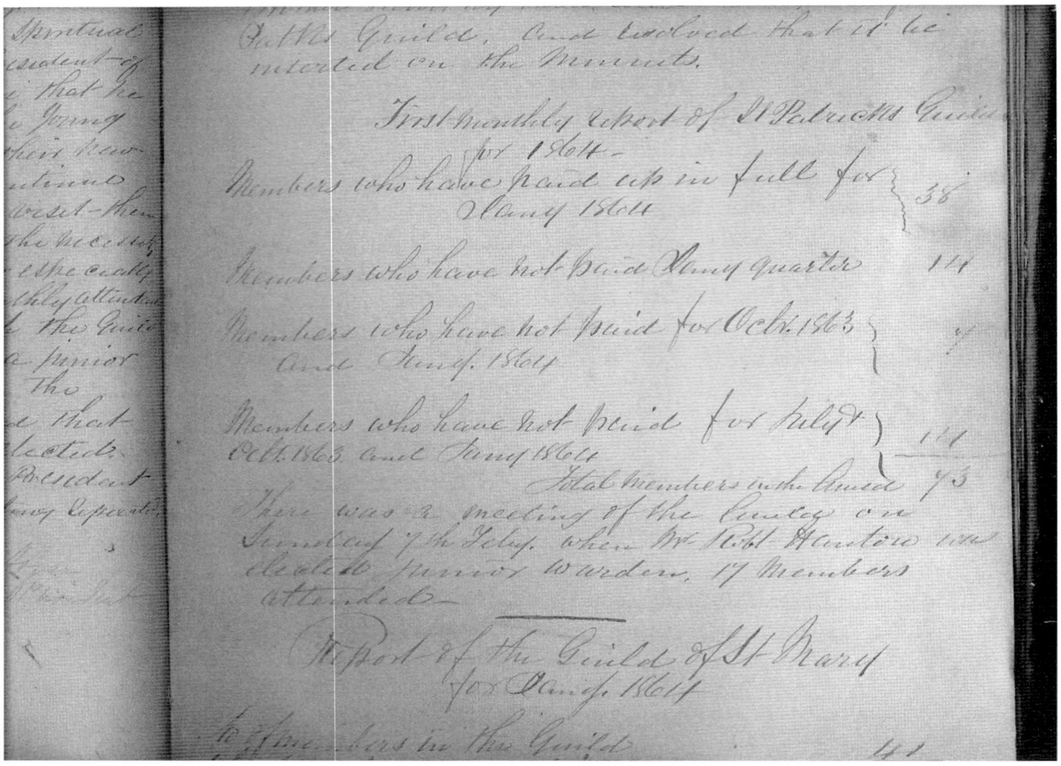

Example Page from the Guild Book

The guild books recorded the following:

Prior to 1863	**Guild of St. Patrick Members 64**
Commencing 1863	**Guild of St. Patrick Members 50**
Actual Paid-up Members	**Guild of St. Patrick Members 27**
Prior to 1863	**Guild of St. Mary's Members 44**
Commencing 1863	**Guild of St. Mary's Members 34**
Actual Paid-up Members	**Guild of St. Mary's Members 23**
Prior to 1863	**Guild of St. Joseph Members 33**
Commencing 1863	**Guild of St. Joseph Members 17**
Actual Paid-up Members	**Guild of St. Joseph Members 8**

Aggregate	**Prior to 1863**	**141**
	Commencing 1863	**101**
	Actual Paid-up Members	**58**

The only Guild book which has survived the passage of time is the one which originated with and was prepared by William Scallan in September 1863. It covers three Guilds: St Patrick's, St. Mary's and St. Josephs. There are one hundred and seventy six (176) names recorded in the book under their respective Guilds.

The Warden's duty of each Guild was to urge his members to observe the 'Rule' of the monthly Confession and Holy Communion. This rule was known as '*The Fundamental Rule of the Society*' and everyone complied with it. There was one entry with 'band' written after the name that being Thomas Murphy, of St. Joseph's Guild. Obviously Thomas was a member of the club's band. The Guild system must have preceded the Confraternity in looking after the religious and spiritual welfare of the members. The Guild book in question ended abruptly in 1864. Initially I thought that this was when the Confraternity took over. However, having completed my research, I discovered that the Mens' Confraternity was established in the Church of the Immaculate Conception during a Mission in Lent of 1868 some four years later. One can only wonder, therefore, why the guild book ended when it did. It would be interesting to know where the other Guild books disappeared to also.

On the 5th February 1866 the Council decided *that The Guild of St. Mary's was to be abolished and that the members be divided between St. Patrick's and St. Joseph's Guilds.* This was the start of the end for the Guilds and within two years the Guild system would be replaced by the Holy Family Confraternity.

Wardens Elected to the Guilds

NAME	GUILD	DATE
William Murphy, snr.	St. Louis Conzaga	16th August 1855
John Shannon, jnr.	St. Louis Conzaga	16th August, 1855
William Scallan, snr.	St. Louis Conzaga	13th September, 1855
John Shannon, jnr.	St. Louis Gonzaga	13th September, 1855
Robert Doyle, snr.	St. Josephs	13th September, 1855
Nicholas Cousins, jnr.	St. Josephs	13th September, 1855
John O'Brien, snr.	Holy Angels	13th September, 1855
Mathew Simpson, jnr.	Holy Angels	13th September, 1855
Nicholas Cousins, snr.	St. Alphonsus Lignori	23rd September, 1855
James Scallan, jnr.	St. Alphonsus Lignori	23rd September, 1855
Matthew Simpson, snr.	St. Patrick's	13th June 1857
Thomas White, jnr.	St. Patrick's	13th June 1857
James Sinnott, snr.	St. Mary's	13th June 1857
William Harris, jnr.	St. Mary's	13th June 1857
Richard Ryan, snr.	St. Patrick's	24th March 1861
Frances Hore, jnr.	St. Patrick's	24th March 1861
W. Brown, snr.	St. Mary's	24th March 1861
James McArdle, jnr.	St. Mary's	24th March 1861
Mr. Dempsey, snr.	St. Josephs	6th October 1861
Mr. Browne, snr.	St. Mary's	5th January 1862
Mr. Hore, snr.	St. Josephs	5th January 1862

The Confraternity of the Holy Family

The Men's Confraternity of the Holy Family was initiated in the Church of the Immaculate Conception *(Rowe Street)* during a Mission that was given in Wexford during Lent 1868. The Rev. James Roche was the Spiritual Director of both the Confraternity and the C.Y.M.S. The whole Corpus Christi procession held in June 1868 was almost entirely composed of members of the Confraternity and all members of the C.Y.M.S. were members of the Confraternity.

The first consecration of members of the Confraternity took place on Tuesday 8th September 1868. Approx. 1,500 men and boys of the town solemnly promised to be faithful members of the Holy family Confraternity and every one of the one-hundred plus membership of the Catholic Young Men's Society at that time were present. The C.Y.M.S. with their various Guilds were in fact the forerunner of the Confraternity and many of the club's members were prefects and sub-prefects of the various sections in the newly formed Confraternity. In affect senior and junior wardens were replaced by prefects and sub-prefects and the Guilds became sections representing the various trades etc. with Saint's names as their titles, as indeed the old C.Y.M.S. Guilds had previously been.

On the following two pages you will find lists of C.Y.M.S. men, who were prefects and sub-prefects in the Men's Confraternity during the period 1868 up to 1918.

C.Y.M.S. Prefects & Sub-Prefects – Mens' Confraternity
1868 - 1918

NAME	SECTION	STATUS
Charles Adams	St. Columbanus	Prefect
Thomas Bent	St. Anne	Prefect
Capt. James Blake	St. Stanislaus	Prefect
James Breen	St. Catherine	Prefect
Edward Byrne	St. John the Baptist	Prefect
James Byrne	St. Celestine	Sub-Prefect
John Clancy	St. Peter	Sub-Prefect
Thomas Clarke	St. Catherine	Sub-Prefect
John Codd	St. Joachim	Prefect
Nicholas Codd	Our Lady of Perpetual Succour	Prefect
Nicholas Cosgrove	St. Joseph	Sub-Prefect
John Devereux	St. Columbanus	Sub-Prefect
Michael Devereux	St. Stephen	Prefect
Edward Dixon	St. Ignatius	Prefect
James Donnelly	St. John the Baptist	Sub-Prefect
John Doran	St. Kevin	Prefect
John Dunne	St. Dominic	Prefect
Andrew Furlong	St. Dymphna	Sub-Prefect
James Furlong	St. Anne	Prefect
John Furlong	St. Cecilia	Prefect
Nicholas Furlong	St. Ignatius	Prefect
Patrick Furlong	St. Ignatius	Sub-Prefect
Peter Furlong	St. Agnes	Prefect
Nicholas Gahan	St. Iberius	Sub-Prefect
Nicholas Gaul	St. Ligouri	Sub-Prefect
Richard Goold	St. Virgilius	Sub-Prefect
Matthew Harpur	The Sacred Heart	Prefect
George Holbrook	St. Dominic	Sub-Prefect
James Hore	St. Francis Xavier	Prefect
William Hutchinson	St. Virgilius	Prefect
Luke Hynes	St. Ligouri	Prefect
Patrick Hynes	St. Agnes	Prefect
William E. Jeffares	Immaculate Conception	Prefect
James Kehoe	St. Vincent de Paul	Sub-Prefect
John J. Kehoe	St. Agnes	Sub-Prefect
Martin Kehoe	St. Vincent de Paul	Prefect
Joseph Kelly	St. Michael	Prefect
Michael Kelly	Our Lady of Victories	Prefect
Michael Kelly	St. Thomas	Sub-Prefect
John Kinsella	St. Malachy	Prefect
James Kirwan	St. Stephen	Sub-Prefect
John Lacey	St. Celestine	Prefect
Denis Lawlor	St. Agatha	Sub-Prefect
Patrick Lawlor	St. Agatha	Sub-Prefect

John Leary	Imaculate Conception	Prefect
Timothy McCarthy	St. Patrick	Prefect
John Murphy	Our Lady of Lourdes	Sub-Prefect
Michael Murphy, snr.	St. Coleman	Prefect
Michae Murphy, jnr.	St. Coleman	Sub-Prefect
James Neill	St. John the Baptist	Prefect
Edward O'Connor	St. Paul	Prefect
John O'Connor	The Sacred Heart	Sub-Prefect
Laurence O'Grady	Our Lady of Victories	Prefect
Thomas O'Grady	St. John the Baptist	Sub-Prefect
James O'Neill	St. John the Evangelist	Sub-Prefect
Joseph Redmond	Our Lady of Victories	Sub-Prefect
William Redmond	St. Vincent de Paul	Sub-Prefect
John Roche	St. Brigid	Prefect
Patrick Roche	St. Vincent de Paul	Prefect
Richard Ryan	St. Malachy	Sub-Prefect
James Scallan	St. Rose of Lima	Sub-Prefect
Patrick Stafford	St. Joachim	Sub-Prefect
John J. Sutton	St. Dymphna	Prefect
Thomas Sutton	St. Thomas	Sub-Prefect
Thomas Underwood	St. Aidan	Prefect
John Wadding	St. Francis Xavier	Sub-Prefect
Patrick Walsh	St. Agnes	Prefect
Patrick Walsh	St. Ligouri	Prefect
Patrick Whelan	St. Bernard	Prefect
John White	St. Anne	Sub-Prefect
Thomas White	St. Anne	Sub-Prefect

The C.Y.M.S. membership attended all retreats held in the town and at the Annual Retreat closing ceremony renewal of Baptismal Vows was affirmed. Everyone would have their candle at the evening devotion and at a given sign each man in the church would light-up and hold it aloft in his right hand and renew their fealty to their Lord and Master and promise once again to be loyal faithful children of Christ.

William Hutchinson

At this point, the priest would shout out

Do you renounce the devil and all his works? Immediately the whole congregation would reply with passion and conviction 'We do!' The priest would then ask Do you promise to give-up drunkenness, company keeping, impurity, etc, etc, and everyone would shout in unison 'We Do.' The priest would then bless their good resolutions, impart the Papal Benediction and after Solemn Benediction of the most Holy Sacrament the devotions came to an end.

Both the Confraternity and the Catholic Young Men's Society suffered a great loss on the death of their very efficient Secretary Laurence Rossiter. His death occurred on the 12th July 1897at the comparatively early age of 43. Only the previous year the members of the Society made him the recipient of an address and in that address it was stated We beg leave to express the hope that the link which has bound us together may long remain unbroken, and to say that whenever the day of separation comes, it can only come to us with regret. The Societies lost in him an efficient zealous worker.

Both Richard Goold and William Hutchinson joint secretaries in the C.Y.M.S. and the Confraternity succeeded him. Here then is yet more proof of how the C.Y.M.S. was at the vanguard of the Confraternity even in 1897, some twenty-nine years after it was first established with a large, loyal active C.Y.M.S membership.

The Redemptorists conducted one of the most successful retreats in the history of the Men's confraternity in May 1917 when upwards of 2,000 men attended the closing ceremonies with most of the C.Y.M.S. membership in attendance as a body.

In April 1918 Fr. Wickham requested that the members of the branch take part in the celebrations of the Golden Jubilee of the Men's Confraternity on Sunday 21st April. The President, Fr. Hore, made the suggestion that all members of the club meet on the premises and march en masse to the grounds of the Church of the Assumption from where the Confraternity procession would commence and this was indeed executed as suggested.

In the 1950s and 60's I personally can recall attending the Confraternity evenings which were comprised of the rosary, prayers, sermon, benediction of the Blessed Sacrament and the collection. I attended with my Father and brother at the Church of the Immaculate Conception or 'Rowe Street Church' as it was commonly known. Everyone had our own section where you had to sit. These sections were marked by staffs with a shield shaped top with the section's number and the saint's name emblazoned thereon. The C.Y.M.S. had several of these sections allotted to them and the Garda Síochána had a section which was always located at the door on the Rowe Street side should they need to leave in a hurry. I should imagine other emergency workers such as the fire brigade would have had the same facility.

One very pleasant aspect of the service which I recollect was the aroma of the incense during the benediction, it was a feast for the nostrils. Everyone loved the aroma of the incense in their nostrils. I often wondered were the vestry boys high on it. The other aspect which comes to mind occurred at the conclusion of the service when the congregation would all sing a rousing rendition of our battle hymn 'Faith of our Fathers'. This hymn was a declaration of our faith and patriotic pride and it was sung with gusto and conviction. The words of this hymn stirred the blood of all true Irishmen and only an Irishman could have understood why. The congregation was so inspired and aroused after singing this hymn that I doubt Satan would have been brave enough to show himself.

The prefect's duty was to record all who attended and were absent at each service and collect the money. This was all recorded in the little black book and if you were absent on say two or three occasions then you would qualify for a visit from Rev. M. J. Berney, C.C., Spiritual Director over the men's section of the Holy Family Confraternity who was designated with that duty. There were separate Spiritual Directors over men, women, boys and girl's sections.

Rev. M. Wickham, C.C.

My prefect, as far as I can recollect, was none other than Lar Roche, a good C.Y.M.S member and a sound man, as the saying goes.

The branch Council were forever passing new directives regarding attendance at the Confraternity in an effort to keep young bucks in line.

On 8th April 1950 the club Council decided to hand-over to Fr. Berney, the Spiritual Director, a list of club members who were not attending the Confraternity. In the early 1950s and late 60s, we young lads looked at this practice as tantamount to having to appear before your sergeant – major on a charge.

In April 1954 a rule was passed which stated that *to become a member of the society you must first be, an active member of the Confraternity and you must produce prove oft this.* From time to time down through the years some members would flaunt the rules.

The offenders would be duly cautioned regarding the matter and reminded of their duty as good C.Y.M.S. members. I am only aware of one chap who challenged the Council's ruling on the matter and when he refused to comply with the ruling he was given every opportunity to recant, which he doggedly refused to do. He was promptly expelled from the Society.

In 1968 the Wexford Branch of the Confraternity Centenary (1868 - 1968) was celebrated in Wexford Town. This was a very big occasion and many Wexford people took part in the procession which included six bands, the Holy Family Confraternity Band being the main one. All the sodalities paraded in the procession leaving both the twin churches simultaneously converging on Wexford G.A.A. Park.

The Spiritual Directors at that time were Rev. M. Doyle, R.C.A. (*women's' branch*), Rev. M. J. Berney, C.C. (*men's branch*), Rev. J. Cummins, C.C. (*boy's branch*) and Rev. E. Murphy, C.C. (*girl's branch*). The procession converged at the Wexford Park where an open-air Mass was the highlight of the ceremonies. The Local Defence Force was in attendance in the grounds helping organise the groupings on the pitch. His Lordship the Most Rev. Dr. Herlihy, Bishop of Ferns and Patron of the Society was the principal concelebrant. Other church dignitaries present were Rev. M. Doyle, R.C.A., Wexford; Very Rev. M. J. O'Neill, P.P., Kilanerin, Rev. E. Murphy, C.C., Wexford: Rev. M.F. Clancy, C.C., Master of Ceremonies; Rev. W. Anglim, C.C., Raheen; Very Rev. J. M. Butler, P.P., Cushingstown and Rev. T. Murphy, Adm., Wexford. Most of these priests were members of the Society and two of them were former Presidents. The Rev. Richard Breen, C.C., Castledockrill, a native of Wexford Town preached the sermon. This man was a brother of Jackie Breen the well-known and loved fellow member. Needless to remark the C.Y.M.S were well represented in this Centenary procession and would have provided a large turnout. The Comfraternity had its own hymn which is published in full below.

The Hymn of
The Confraternity of the Holy Family

Confraternity Men to the fight:
And raise up your banner on high:
Jesus, Mary, and Joseph in sight,
In our battles their names be our cry.

Hark, the sound of the fight hath gone forth,
And we must not tarry at home,
For our Lord from the South to the North
Has commanded his soldiers to come.

Confraternity Men, Etc.

We must on with our banner unfurled;
We must on: 'tis Jesus who leads;
We must hasten to conquer the world,
With the sign of the Lamb who bleeds.

We must march to the battle with speed,
Upon earth our duty is strife;
O! blest are the soldiers who bleed
For the Saviour who died to give life.

Origins of the Confraternity Band and the Boy's Brigade

To discover the origins of the 'Confraternity Band' one must go back some 148 years to the time when the C.Y.M.S. first conceived the notion of establishing a band. In Fr. Berney's *'Centenary Record of Wexford Twin-Churches, 1858-1958'* he claims that the C.Y.M.S. had a fife and drum band from the very outset and that statement is near enough true. He is also credited with stating that the confraternity band was founded in 1926 by Rev. Martin O'Connor, C.C. and I would dispute this last statement. Whilst I know it has become a tradition to claim 1926 as the band's origin, I hope here to correct this fallacy and disclose the authentic founders of the band.

Band – First Attempt

On the 16th June 1859, some four years after the Society (C.Y.M.S.) was first established, the Council attempted to establish a band. In his regard, they approached a Mr. Smith *'about the formation of a band'* and by the 3rd of November the question of establishing a band was raised again and was discussed at great length. A collection for a fund to purchase the band instruments was initiated and the first *'Band Committee'* was appointed to deal with the project. Fr. Jeremiah Hogan was elected as the Chairman, with John Brown J.P.C. elected as secretary. It was proposed *that two members of each of the three Guilds* (the C.Y.M.S. forerunner to the Confraternity) *should be on this committee and also that two members of the Council be ex officio*. However, by the 12th January 1860 some Council members were all for abandoning the idea of a band due to the lack of interest from the members and by the next meeting, held on the 15th January, the Council decided to disband the *'Band Committee'* and return all subscriptions collected to their respective benefactors. This then was the first attempt to establish a band in the Society.

Band – Second Attempt

On the 23rd March 1861 the second attempt to re-start a band was made. This time Fr. James Roche took control and he subscribed £5 to the band fund himself. All members who were interested in joining a band were invited to place their names on a list and by May it was intended to make a selection of those suitable. On the 7th May Mr. Dunne and Mr. Ryan were deputised to meet Mr. Jones on the following Thursday to select and arrange members for the band. On the 16th May the minute's state *It was considered inexpedient to proceed with the joining of a brass band at this time*. On the 23rd May the idea of the band was again being discussed and the Council subscribed £2 towards the band instruments. The band's formation could not have been progressing very well because on the 4th July someone reported that there was *'a German band in town.'* This band was duly employed at a fee not to exceed 10/-. The Society hired this visiting band for some occasion which is not recorded in the minutes.

On the 15th August 1861 the Society offered Mr. Jones 5/- a week to teach band members the flute and 2/6 was offered to Mr. Bolger to teach the drums. By September it is recorded that Mr. John Sinnott, the Mayor and a member of the Society, kindly allowed the band to practice at the Theatre in High Street (*later to be named the Theatre Royal*). In October the club was seeking the use of the Temperance Hall for their band practice as the theatre was engaged and on the 16th of December 1861 the C.Y.M.S. band had its debut in the Town Hall. The band members conducted a raffle to assist in the accumulation of some funds that month also. They played in the St. Patrick's Day parade of March 1862 and again that evening. They performed at Ballytrent on Sunday the 3rd May and by the 6th May J. H. Talbot, Esq., gave four drumheads and a dozen braces to the band, valued at more that half a guinea. By the 27th May the band was using the Christian Brothers School yard at George Street for marching and band practice. They performed at Enniscorthy on Sunday the 10th June and in the same month Michael Walsh kindly donated a new drum to the band.

On the 1st September 1863 the Rev. President, Fr. Jeremiah Hogan and the Council ruled that as *it would be against the wishes of the people of the neighbourhood the practicing* (of the band) *would be withheld till some more adapted place be found*. The next reference to the band is January 1871, 8 years later, when they played at the 'Dramatic Corps' entertainment held at the old concert hall (*located at Paul Quay*). They took part in the St. Patrick's day parade in March with the title of Confraternity band. It is not known how long the band continued but it is obvious it disbanded sometime between 1871 and 1886. The reason for its discontinuation would appear to be partly due to a lack of a venue for practice.

Band – Third Attempt

The next reference to the band was at a meeting dated the 13th August 1886 when the Council discussed and decided to re-start a band in the Society. They acquired the band instruments belonging to Fr. Keating's band and it was decided that the members should contribute weekly to pay the teacher. They acquired eleven brass instruments in September and in January 1887 purchased six more instruments at a cost of £6. In March they purchased a leading cornet at £3-10-0 and two other instruments at £5-12-0. so once more they were up and running.

At the Annual General Meeting of the Society held on the 26th February 1889 it is recorded that the band had great success on several occasions during the year performing at processions in Bride Street and Rowe Street Church grounds. The Council then decided to make the band independent and responsible for their own finances and they decided the following *That the band have a separate fund to open to subscribers from members of the Society and outsiders' and that the expenses that might be incurred by the Society are recouped from the band fund.*

The Council further passed the resolution *That the band sub-committee see Mr. R. Curran to ascertain his views regarding the conducting of the band* and that *the sub-committee be empowered to incur expenses not to exceed £10 per annum reorganizing the band.* Something must have occurred to upset the apple-cart so to speak because in April the Council tried hard to encourage the band members to stay put by *electing R. Curran, Kelly and Lucking Honorary Members so long as they remain members of the band.* The Council also paid 30/- for repairs to instruments that were broken.

On the 29th October the secretary reported that members of the band had not met for practice since the sports at Crosstown and he thought it futile to try and get them organised especially after the way they had got on at the sports. One wonders what happened ? The Rev. President said that he would speak to the band members and try to get it organised. At the A.G.M. dated 25th February 1890 it is simply stated *"the band is finished"*.

Fr. Patrick O'Leary's Confraternity Band

The next reference to the band is on 14th December 1893 when Fr. Patrick O'Leary made an application through the Rev. President for the loan of the brass instruments, as he was about to form a band in connection with the Confraternity. He also requested the use of the concert hall for the band to practice in. As the Society's own band was now defunct the Council decided to giver the instruments on the following conditions.

1. That the instruments would be returned to the Society should they require them at any time.

2. If the band (confraternity band) ceases at any time that the instruments be returned to the Society.

3. That the instruments be surrendered in the same good condition as they were loaned to Fr. O'Leary when forming the band.

Rev. Patrick M. O'Leary, C.C.

Myles Connick, Robert Hanton, John Tyghe and the secretaries were appointed on a committee to meet Fr. O'Leary and obtain a guarantee from him that these conditions would be fulfilled. Fr. O'Leary's band was to accompany the members on their forthcoming annual trip set for the 1st July but whatever happened the trip was cancelled. On the 12th September 1894 the Society's 'Dramatic Club' held a dramatic entertainment at the

'Theatre Royal' for the benefit of Fr. O'Leary's confraternity Band and a profit of £18-2-6 was made. By September 1896 Fr. O'Leary had departed Wexford due to ill health and the Confraternity band had been disbanded. The Society received the following letter from Charles E. Vize and John Sinnott, Confraternity representatives and both valued C.Y.M.S. members which read:

Band Room,
Francis Street.
7th September 1896

To Laurence Rossiter, Esq., Hon. Secretary, Catholic Young Men's Society.

Dear Sir,

As you are no doubt aware the Confraternity has ceased to maintain the band. We are directed by the members to communicate with you as to the instruments, which we have, belonging to your Society, according to the terms of agreement or any reasonable undertaking your Society may require. Before concluding we may add that it is our intention to assist at the processions as heretofore.

Trusting your Society will favour our request and so help to keep up our band, which in the past has been a source of much pleasure and benefit to our town folk.

We remain dear sir,

Very Faithfully Yours

Charles E. Vize
John Sinnott

Charles E. Vize

The Council decided unanimously that the instruments be returned to the Society as the band had ceased to be a Confraternity band.

Boy's Confraternity Band (The Boy's Brigade)

On the 25th June 1903 Fr. O'Byrne requested the club to give him the band instruments for the purpose of forming a band for the Boy's Confraternity. This request was acceded to and the newly formed band was known by June 1905 as the 'Boy's Brigade'. In November of the same year Fr. O'Byrne was appointed director of the 'Boy's Brigade' and was receiving cooperation and support from the C.Y.M.S. On the 6th January 1904 he was given the Concert Hall and the Billiards-Rooms free gratis for a performance by the boys. This must have been a success as he again requested the use of the Concert Hall for the purpose of staging an entertainment in aid of the 'Boy's Confraternity, for three nights on the 26th, 27th and 28th of April 1904. The Society granted his request but Fr. O'Byrne later cancelled this as he was given the better venue of the Town Hall for the three evenings. On September the 14th of the same year Luke Hynes (*Society member*) requested the use of the hall to put on an entertainment in aid of the Boy's Confraternity and this was also granted free gratis. That is the last entry concerning the Confraternity Band in the minute books for the following 26 years. Then on the 31st March 1930 a

Miss D. Sullivan had the use of the Concert Hall free gratis for the purpose of a Jumble Sale in aid of the Confraternity Band fund. It can be safely deduced from the foregoing that the Confraternity Band was well established, organised and conducting their own affairs independently of the C.Y.M.S. at this time.

Rev. James W. O'Byrne, C.C.

A report in the People newspaper dated 16th February 1957 had the headline *'Wexford Confraternity Band Thirty-First Annual Reunion'* which gave the impression that the band only commenced in 1926. I would imagine that if you asked one of the old members of the band when did it start they would answer around 1920s. They will, however, be enlightened after perusing this article and know that the band took part in the St. Patrick's day parade in 1871 with the title of Confraternity band. Having said that, I would suggest that the 1890s was the more authentic period for its origin and that the C.Y.M.S. actively promoted it. The C.Y.M.S. band fulfilled all the same functions as the Confraternity band, i.e. marching in church processions and being in attendance at other occasions as required. The C.Y.M.S. band evolved into the Confraternity band. Whilst not undervaluing in any way the marvellous work carried out by Fr. Martin O'Connor in establishing the band, I trust I have set the record straight and given long overdue recognition and honour to those long forgotten priests, Fr. Patrick O'Leary and Fr. O'Byrne who were the original forerunners in the founding of the Confraternity band in Wexford.

The Confraternity Band Leading the Corpus Christi Procession
Passing the Garda Barracks on Roche's Road in the 1950s

It might also be worth mentioning that throughout the years some C.Y.M.S. members have been members of the confraternity band from time to time. T. Higgins, Aidan Kelly, J. Quirke, P. Tierney and T. Wafer. *(See following photograph).* I have not researched this matter in any detail whatsoever but from memory I can recall some of my contemporaries who were both C.Y.M.S. and Confraternity band members around the early 1960s. Three which come to mind are Ollie Hall who lived in Carrigeen and both Derek and Fergus Gaddren from Davitt Road. There can be no doubt that there were many more. *(See Appendix no 4 for 'Band Members and Committees' from 1859 to 1926, on page 280).*

97

Confraternity Band 1926

Back Row, Lt. to Rt: J.O'Byrne (later Fr. Wilfred.OFM); J. Quirke, A.O'Leary (Hon.Sec.); M.Murray, M.Noctor, G. Molloy, P. Quirke, Br. Markey,CBS.

Third Row: Aidan Kelly, W. Rattigan, K. Byrne, A. Clarke, J. Clancy, P. Tierney, T. Forde, R. Murphy, T. Wafer.

Seated: J.O'Neill, J. Malone, T.Higgins, T. Lucking, Mr. Arnold (Band Master); Fr. Martin O'Connor, M.Kelly, D.Horan, Tom O'Neill.

Front Row: Tom Parle, Kevin Kehoe, John Gallagher, William Cloake.

The Holy Family Confraternity Band – 2008

Photo courtesy of the Confraternity Band.

Back Row. Lt. to Rt. Deirdre Creevy, Shane Ffrench, Seamus Mahoney, Alan Mahon, Sean Welsh, William Macken. Shauna Moran, Maureen O'Neill, Robyn Whitmore.

Middle Row: Margaret Murry, Philip Gaddern, Aisling Welsh, Gemma Coughlan, John Moran, Paul Glynn, Rory Mahon, Sean Coughlan, Davy Heinz, Seamus McManus, Michael Coughlan, Tom Cadogan.

Kneeling: John Walsh, James Warren, Martin McDonald

The 'Twin Churches' of Wexford

Very Rev. James Canon Roche P.P.V.F.

© 2008 O'Rourke.

This year is the sesquicentennial of the twin-churches in Wexford and as such I feel it my duty to make mention of the part that the C.Y.M.S. played in their beginning.

On Friday the 21st June 1851 the foundation stones of both churches were laid. The ceremonies opened at Bride Street on the site which was known as the South Church. The Bishop, clergy and people then proceeded to the Rowe Street site where a similar ceremony took place. The work of constructing the two churches took almost seven years. Alas, Bishop Murphy did not live to see the work completed as he died on the 13th August 1856.

In October 1856 the first general collection for the building work of the proposed 'twin churches' began. There was a small chapel rent collection. The Guilds in the club collected regularly for the work. Throughout the 1850s contributions for the twin church project were being collected and there is good reason to assume that the Society would have played a leading role in collecting subscriptions throughout the town. Fr. James Roche was the Society's first Patron and Spiritual Director and as such it would be very strange indeed if this powerfully persuasive leader of men would not have mustered his own brigade of Catholic soldiers, the 'Catholic Young Men's Society' to form the vanguard and assist him in every way possible.

The generosity of the Wexford people and indeed people from all over Ireland and from the many Wexford exiles throughout the World was unparalleled. Records of the time inform us that contributions came from as far a field as London, Liverpool, Wigton in Scotland, Neufchatel, Switzerland, Athens, Greece, Ahmednuggar and Calcutta, India, Tenerife, Porto Rico in the West Indies, Ionian Islands, Ibrail, Constantinople all in the Black Sea, St. John, Newfoundland, Barnabuco, Brazil, Monto Video, Buenos Ayres, Argentina; Pennsylvania, Baltimore, Philadelphia, Brooklyn, San Jose, St. John in New Brunswick, in the United States; Prince Edward Island, Canada.

Monies were sent back via the Wexford seafarers and by post from all these places. There were regular collections made on the Quays from the visiting seamen.

Some eminent Protestants are known to have subscribed to the project also. Various items for the Churches were donated by generous people including the following five C.Y.M.S. members - Rev. James Roche, P.P., Richard Devereux, Esq., Rev. Walther Lambert, Dr. Creane and Ald. John Tyghe who donated windows, church furniture and various gold and silver items for the altars of the Church of the Immaculate Conception.

The official opening of Bride Street church took place on the 18th April 1858. One week later on the 25th April 1858, Rowe Street church was opened. Prior to 1858 there was only one Catholic Church in Wexford, the fine old structure belonging to the Franciscan fathers. The first person to receive Holy Communion at Bride Street Church was a C.Y.M.S. member named John O'Brien; He was one of the Hon. Secretaries on the Council of 1857 and he attended the opening of the 'New Church' at Bride Street in that capacity. He was honoured with being the first person to receive 'Holy Communion' in that church.

Surely the fact that this C.Y.M.S. official was honoured in this way is proof that the Society had done marvellous work for the 'twin churches'.

My research shows that John O'Brien worked as a shop assistant at Jeffares in the Bullring Wexford in the 1870s although Canon Gahan in his 'The Secular Priests of the Diocese of Ferns' states that John served an apprenticeship at Patrick Hynes's drapery shop in the Bull Ring. In 1858 John travelled to the Cape with the missionaries as a lay teacher, he later took Holy Orders and served the remainder of his life there as Rev. Fr. John O'Brien.

On 3rd October 1858 the church of the Immaculate Conception (Rowe Street) was solemnly dedicated by Dr. Furlong, the lord Bishop of Ferns. The dedication of the Church of the Assumption (Bride Street) took place on the 5th September 1860.

On the 19th February 1885 the 'Catholic Young Men's Society' donated £3 towards the Father Roche Memorial Fund (statue) which was erected in the grounds of the Church of the Immaculate Conception.

John O'Brien

Special Religious Occasions

The Visit of His Excellency Monsignor Persico to Wexford

On the 3rd of October 1887 it was unanimously resolved that an address be presented to Pope Leo XIII's Papal Envoy, His Excellency Monsignor Persico and it was also decided that the address be signed by the Rev. Patrick Doyle, C.C. President of the Society, Mr. William Connick, Vice- President and Mr. Laurence Rossiter, Hon. Secretary. . I do not have an actual copy of the address but the text of the address presented to His Excellency was as follows:

His Excellency Monsignor Persico

May it please your excellency we the members of the 'Catholic Young Men's Society' gladly come to wish your excellency a most hearty welcome to Wexford and to our ancient Diocese of Ferns and to express the feelings of happiness with which our souls are replete at seeing in our midst a reprehensive of our beloved Holy Father Leo XIII, we believe that the visit of your excellency is the outcome of the loving sympathy and sincere regard which possesses the heart of His Holiness for his Irish children.

Your mission amongst us we accept as a message of love from the Eternal City and we see in your Excellency as it were the right hand of Christ's Vicar raised to bless, support, and assist us. We rejoice therefore in having this opportunity of expressing with the most profound veneration and respect, the sentiments of our devoted and undying attachment and respect to the See of Saint Peter, and to the learned and accomplished Pontiff – the infallible master who sways the destinies of our Church.

To the arduous task you have undertaken, and the wearisome labours undergone in visiting so many Counties of our old land, and in studying the many intricate and complex problems, which disturb the serenity of our social life.

Now that your historic mission is drawing rapidly to a close we beg to wish your Excellency a safe and pleasant journey to sunny Italy.

Signed on behalf of the 'Catholic Young Men's Society' Wexford

Rev. Nicholas J. Sheridan, C.C., **President.**

William Connick, **Vice-President.**

Laurence Rossiter, **Hon. Secretary.**

In August 1909 the Council were discussing the forthcoming celebrations of the Silver Jubilee of the Bishop of the Diocese, the Most Rev. Dr. Brown. The address to the Bishop was adopted and it was decided to have *it Prepared and nicely embossed on parchment in scroll form for presentation to the Bishop.* By October this had changed when Alderman John Tyghe proposed and Capt. Busher seconded *that the address be done in album form and illuminated professionally.* A Miss Fitzpatrick, artist from Dublin was hired and entrusted with the contract to complete the work at a cost of five guineas.

The on the 15th January 1918 when Rev. Dr. Codd became Bishop of Ferns, the club arranged to have an address printed and illuminated to present to the Bishop. They invited tenders for the execution of an illuminated address from local artists - the Misses Carty, Codd, Harpur and Haughton. The Miss Codd mentioned was none other than the celebrated Mary Codd, L.L.C.M. the very creative artist who was one of the most talented musicians in Ireland. She served Wexford well in her capacity as organist and choir mistress in the Church of the Immaculate Conception *(Rowe Street)* for many years. She was sister of Dean Codd.

Archbishop Mannix

On the 12th February 1918 the President, Rev Fr. Hore,

applied for six admission tickets for the members of the Council to attend the Cathedral in Enniscorthy on the occasion of the consecration of the Most Rev. Dr. Codd as Bishop of Ferns.

In 1925 the club received a letter from Alderman Richard Corish, Mayor of Wexford and T.D. Sinnott secretaries of the *'Archbishop Mannix Reception Committee'* inviting the members to participate in the procession which was being organised for the reception of Archbishop Mannix on his arrival in Wexford on Wednesday evening the 2nd September 1925 at 7.30 pm. for the purpose of receiving the Freedom of the Borough. A large number of the members took part in the procession as requested by the Council.

On the 12th May 1936 the Society received a letter from the Hon. Secretary of the Eucharistic Congress to be held at the end of June inquiring if the Society were sending any delegates to the congress. The matter was left in the hands of the Bishop and the clergy.

On the 14th March 1938 a special meeting was called *'as a mark of respect'* to the memory of the Society's Patron, the Most Rev. Dr. Codd, Bishop of Ferns who died on the 12th March. Notes of condolences were passed to the clergy of the Diocese and to his relatives on their great loss and a one-minute silence was observed. It was agreed that any member of the Society who could possibly attend the High Mass and office for the repose of His Lordship at the Cathedral in Enniscorthy should do so

The printed address on the next page was presented by the C.Y.M.S. to His Most Rev. Donal J. Herlihy, D.D., L.S.S., Ph.D. Lord Bishop of Ferns on his consecration in 1964. His Lordship is also welcomed as the Patron of the Society. You will note the days are long gone of those beautifully hand crafted illuminated addresses

October 1949 saw the Wexford people and the various religious societies all out in vast numbers for the Commemoration Ceremonies for the 300th Anniversary of the Cromwellian capture and the civilian massacre of October 1649. A week of various ceremonies ended with a large procession thought the streets of the town converging on the Bullring.

Fr. Michael O'Neill, later to be parish priest of Kilanerin, preached the main sermon to the vast crowds which included all the usual clubs and Societies and many bands took part. The boy scouts formed the guard of honour with Christian Brother schoolboys, white veiled schoolgirls, the Local Defence Force and the National Foresters. The ladies and gents confraternities were present in large numbers as was usual on these occasions, the men's ranks being filled with many C.Y.M.S. members.

The Catholic Young Men's Society
of Ireland
(ST. IBERIUS BRANCH)
Wexford

PRESENTED TO

The Most Revd. Donal J. Herlihy, DD., L.S.S., Ph.D
on the occasion of his
Consecration as Lord Bishop of Ferns.

MAY IT PLEASE YOUR LORDSHIP

ON BEHALF OF THE MEMBERS OF THE CATHOLIC YOUNG MEN'S SOCIETY
OF IRELAND (ST. IBERIUS BRANCH), WEXFORD, WE BEG TO TENDER TO YOU
OUR MOST HEARTFELT CONGRATULATIONS ON YOUR ELEVATION TO THE
EXALTED OFFICE OF BISHOP OF OUR ANCIENT DIOCESE OF FERNS.

SINCE THE FORMATION OF THE WEXFORD BRANCH OF THE SOCIETY ON
THE FEAST OF THE ASSUMPTION OF OUR LADY, ONE HUNDRED AND NINE
YEARS AGO, THE BISHOP FOR THE TIME BEING OF THE DIOCESE OF FERNS
HAS ALWAYS BEEN OUR PATRON, AND TO THAT OFFICE WE NOW GIVE YOU
A MOST HEARTY WELCOME, PROMISING YOU THE SAME LOYALTY, CO-
OPERATION AND OBEDIENCE GIVEN TO YOUR PREDECESSORS.

IT IS OUR EARNEST HOPE AND PRAYER THAT GOD IN HIS GREAT WISDOM
MAY LONG SPARE YOU TO RULE WISELY AND WELL, IN THE EPISCOPAL
CHAIR, THE HISTORIC SEE, TO WHICH YOU HAVE BEEN ELEVATED.

(SIGNED)

Thomas Murphy PRESIDENT

John J. Donohoe HON. SEC.

Prayers on the Club's Premises

From the very outset each Council meeting commenced and concluded with a prayer. Religion played a prominent part of life on the club's premises. In March 1954 it was decided that the Rosary be recited every night in the billiards room at 9.30 p.m. Fr. Butler agreed to say it after the Council meetings.

Members recited the Angelus every Sunday at noon and from February 1961 onwards it was also recited at 6.00. p.m. on Sundays. I recall it being said on Sunday at noon when I was a little lad in the club with my father because it was the signal to go home for Sunday dinner once the Angelus was over. In those days Rowe Street church bells toiled at Angelus time and it was the practice for people to stop what they were doing and pray.

Fr. McCabe, the Society's President, celebrated Holy Mass at the club's premises in Charlotte Street prior to the Annual General Meeting at 7.30 p.m. on the 10th February 1986.

Pioneer Total Abstinence Association

In the mid 1800s Father Matthew was on his crusade throughout Ireland preaching the virtues of temperance and warning against the *'demon drink'*. He visited Wexford in April of 1840 and addressed a large rally in the Franciscan churchyard. Soon after this a Temperance Society was established in the town. Temperance Clubs were formed and non-drinkers now had a place to gather and meet like minded friends to socialise with without having to resort to the public houses.
I wonder if these clubs were the forerunner to the founding of the C.Y.M.S.? After all, this was precisely why the C.Y.M.S. was established - to foster clean and healthy social intercourse and to look after the spiritual welfare of its members.

The *'Nationwide Catholic Abstinence Society'* later to become the *'Pioneer Total Abstinence Association'* (P.T.A.A.), was founded in St. Francis Xavier Church, Gardiner Street, Dublin on the 28th December 1898 by Fr. James A. Cullen and co-founded by four women: Mrs A. Egan, Mrs M.L. Bury, Mrs A.M. Sullivan and Miss L. Power. This was because the PTAA membership in the early days was confined to women. However, in 1899 men were admitted to the Association. By the year 1916 there was a membership of 285,000. In the 1920s there was an increase in the temperance movement in Wexford and many members of the C.Y.M.S. became committed members of the PTAA. Lectures were given in the club and in 1929 Father Finn, S.J. gave a temperance lecture in the concert hall in Common Quay Street which was open to members of the Society and the general public.

My father Thomas O'Rourke was enrolled in the 'Pioneer Total Abstinence Association' when he was a young man and held true to it all his life. He was introduced and proposed for ennoblement by his cousin Thomas Hayes, another staunch Catholic and C.Y.M.S. and PTAA member. A great many C.Y.M.S. members joined the PTAA and because of this and the fact that such people as these devout men are very scarce to day, I am publishing Thomas's old Certificate of Membership into that Association for all to see. I wager that few people will have ever seen such a document.

Fr. James A. Cullen

105

The Family Rosary League

The *'Family Rosary League'* was very popular in the 1950s thanks to Fr. Peyton *'The Rosary Priest'*. My father

Rev. Patrick Payton

Thomas enrolled the whole family in the league in 1954 which meant that he promised to recite the rosary each and every night with the entire family present. As a matter of interest I have published his certificate of registration. Allow me to relate an amusing anecdote concerning this. Anyone who knew my father Tom would know that he was a devout Catholic and very religious man who took his religion very seriously. Each evening after the tea we would all have to say the rosary prior to being allowed to leave the house

and go out. There were three sets of mysteries - the Joyful, the Sorrowful and the Glorious. To be quite frank, they were all a mystery to me at the time. I was 14 years of age and that would have been equivalent to a ten year old of today as we were all pretty naive and innocent back in those happy days with no television, etc. to corrupt our impressionable young innocent minds.

Anyway, to continue with the story there were five in total in our family and each one of us would have to take our turn at reciting the rosary. It was said in the living room and we would all kneel down on our chairs around the room all facing into the wall with our backs to each other. My sister Marie and I used to fool around behind my father's back without his knowing it, needless to say. We would get up to things like nudging one another or looking over and making faces or something silly like that. We got caught sniggering and laughing one evening and we were severely chastised so we were being very careful and conducting ourselves all prim and proper on this evening.

106

It happened to be my turn to recite the rosary and it was *'The Sorrowful Mysteries'*. Dad wouldn't allow us to read them off the leaflet and we had to learn them off by heart prior to reciting them. So I started with the first mystery – *The first sorrowful mystery the agony in the garden* says I as proud as a peacock as I made sure not to look in my sister's direction in case she tried to make me laugh and cause me to make a mistake. Then I arrived at the second mystery and as confidently as you like I began loudly *the second sorrowful mystery the whipping at the pillar.* At this, my sister burst out sniggering and laughing and my mother's body was shaking violently with suppressed laughter. I didn't for the life of me know what was wrong and foolishly I started to smile and snigger too. Big mistake! The room fell sharply into silence and the smirk on my face was quickly wiped off it when my dad's open hand smacked me in the ear-hole as he blamed me for causing this outburst of irreverence. I was ordered to start again from the beginning and to pay more attention to the holiness and reverence of prayer. I did as I was told and I don't remember making any more mistakes but if I had I would have only half heard it anyhow, as my ear was still aching and throbbing and I could hear bells ringing in it And I can assure the reader that they were not joy-bells. Okay! I made a mistake, I said whipping instead of *'the scourging at the pillar.'* Whipping, scourging or lashing are all the same to the man who was unfortunately having them perpetrated on his back I would imagine. I didn't see, quite frankly, what was so wrong with a bit of paraphrasing but after that night I knew exactly what *'The Sorrowful Mysteries'* really meant. They were certainly sorrowful for me anyway.

The Family Rosary League Certificate of Registration

Pilgrimage to Our Lady's Shrine at Knock

The C.Y.M.S. annual pilgrimage to the Marian Shrine at Knock, Co. Mayo was another event but I am unsure just when the Society initiated their pilgrimages there but I would venture it was possibly in 1899.

Photograph of the old Parish Church at Knock

Pope John Paul II at Knock in 1979

Monsignor Horan welcomes the Pope to Knock. Also in the picture is Archbishop Cunnane, the Archbishop of Tuam from 1969-1987, a native of Knock.

On the 21st August 1879 fifteen people witnessed an apparition of Our Lady, St. Joseph and St. John the Evangelist at the South gable of the Knock Parish Church and since that time millions have visited the shrine. The first organised pilgrimage to Knock was in March 1880. Devotion to the shrine was endorsed with the indelible seal of Vatican approval with the personal pilgrimage of Pope John Paul II in 1979. Mother Teresa of Calcutta visited the shrine in June of 1993.

The branch council gave donations on a regular basis to help with the expenses of those who were going on the pilgrimage. The C.Y.M.S. was responsible for sending many invalids to knock over the years.

Daily Mass Crusade

Members of the Branch attended a one-day retreat organised by the Legion of Mary in St. Peter's College on the 12th July 1957. There was a daily mass crusade for a week commencing on the 27th July 1959 and the Branch members were requested to attend the Holy Masses throughout that week. Whilst no actual figures are available it is believed that the members co-operated with the wishes of the Council. Another daily mass crusade was conducted the following year for a period of one week also.

On the12th July 1959 the members attended the one-day retreat organised by the Legion of Mary in St. Peter's College. C.Y.M.S. members attended a daily mass crusade which was held for the branch during the week commencing on the 2nd July 1961. Breakfast after Mass and Communion was another practice at the club but only on special occasions - these events are covered in the social gatherings section.

The Papal Order of St. Gregory the Great

Throughout our 153 years history, two of our members have been conferred with the honour of the Papal Order of Knight of St. Gregory. Following is brief explanation of this Order and its various grades.

Pope Gregory XVI founded the Papal Order of St. Gregory on the 1st September 1831. To reward the civil and military virtues of subjects of the Papal States.

Pope Gregory XVI

It therefore, has a civil and military class. The order is now conferred on persons outside the Papal domain on persons who are distinguished for personal character and reputation, and for notable accomplishments.

Originally there were four classes: - Knights Grand Cross (1st Class) and (2nd class), Knights Commander and lastly Knights. The regulations concerning the grades and uniform were explained in a Bull dated 30th May 1834. Pope Pius X further reformed the Papal Orders on the 7th February 1905. The grades of the Order were modified by the addition of a Star for the higher category of Knights Commander and the suppression of the 2nd class of Knight Grand Cross. Pius X also assigned to the Papal Knights a particular place in Papal Processions and in ceremonies of the Church.

The Highest rank, that of Grand Cross is an exceptional award and few citizens have received this honour. Usually it is awarded to those who already hold a knighthood of the lower rank. Knights Grand Cross wear a more elaborate uniform with more extensive silver braid, a white plumed hat instead of the black plumes common to the lower ranks, with the badge worn from a broad ribbon of the Order on the left hip and the breast Star.

Knights Commander wear a less elaborate uniform, with the badge worn suspended from the ribbon of the Order around the neck, while the higher rank (Knight Commander with Star) also wears the breast star. Knights wear a simpler uniform without the braid on the collar and sleeves, with the badge worn from a ribbon suspended on the left breast.

The Catholic Young Men's Society of Wexford (St. Iberius branch) has the singular distinguished honour of been able to boast having two members of its branch that were conferred with the Most Holy Order of St. Gregory the Great. Namely, Richard J. Devereux (1795 –1883), and James J. Stafford, (1885 – 1971) Once again, I ask, is there any other branch of the C.Y.M.S. anywhere in the whole World that could claim such a great honour? Most certainly not! We were the crème de la crème.

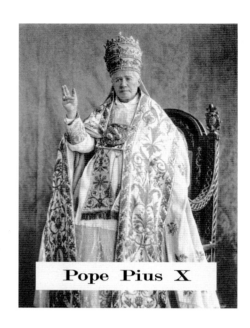

Pope Pius X

The Cross

The decoration of the order is an eight-pointed red enamelled gold cross. In the centre of which is a blue medallion on which is impressed in gold the image of St. Gregory the Great. At the side of his head near the right ear is a dove signifying divine wisdom. In a circle around the image appears in golden letters. ' S. GREGORIUS MAGNUS.' On the reverse side is the device: 'Pro Deo et Principe.' And in the centre around it: 'GREGORIUS XVI. P. M. Anno I.'

The Badge

The badge is the cross of the order surrounded with silver rays. It is worn with the ribbon of the order (red with orange borders) on the left breast. The cross-worn by a knight of the civil class is surmounted by a crown of gold oak leaves enamelled in green.

The Uniform

The costume of ceremony is a dress coat of dark green open in front and covered on breast and back with embroideries in the form of oak leaves. Trousers of the same colour, with silver side-stripes and oak-leaf decoration. A bicornered hat ornamented with small white tassels at the tips, black plume and Papal cockade, together with the knightly sword complete the costume. All the buttons are of silver and carry the cross of the order.

The Sword

The sword is attached to a silver belt, and has the cross of the order engraved on its hilt. The hilt itself is of mother-of-pearl and gold, and ornamenting it there is a cord with golden tassels. The scabbard, of black leather, likewise has its casing and tip made of gold.

Following you will find my depiction of the uniform, hat, cross, badge, and sword as I envisaged them from the above text. It is my understanding that both Mr. Devereux and Mr. Stafford would have worn this costume of ceremony when they were conferred with the knighthood of the Most Holy Order of St. Gregory the Great.

110

The Uniform of the Papal Order of St. Gregory the Great

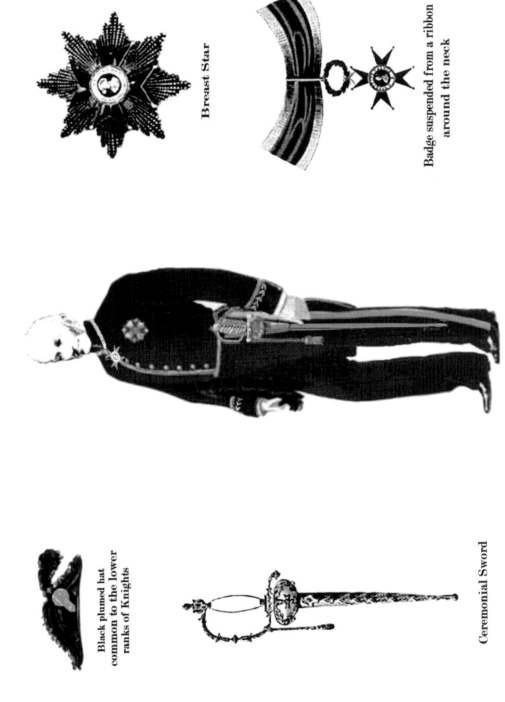

Breast Star

Badge suspended from a ribbon around the neck

Black plumed hat common to the lower ranks of Knights

Ceremonial Sword

© 2006 O'Rourke.

A depiction of Richard J. Devereux, K.G., in the early 1880s

111

C.Y.M.S. Flags Medals and Pins

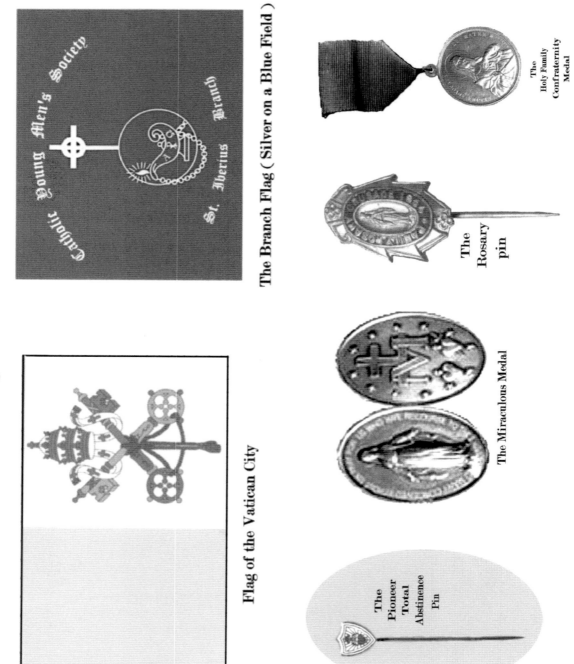

The Branch Flag (Silver on a Blue Field)

Catholic Young Men's Society
St. Iberius Branch

Flag of the Vatican City

The
Holy Family
Confraternity
Medal

The
Rosary
pin

The Miraculous Medal

The
Pioneer
Total
Abstinence
Pin

112

The Irish Papal Brigade

In March 1860 Pope Pius IX called upon the young men of Ireland to help preserve the sovereignty of the Papal States which were threatened with annexation by the armies of Piedmont – Sardinia. The first contingent of the Irish Papal Brigade, consisting of approx. 1,000 volunteers recruited for the Papal army and lead by Major Myles O'Reilly arrived in the Papal State to amalgamate with various other groups all flocking to defend the Pope and his dominions against the invasion of King Victor Emmanuel of the Italian State of Piedmont, who had embarked on a plan of uniting all Italy under his rule. Whilst many Italians were sympathetic to the Piedmont-backed revolutionary forces of Garibaldi, they viewed the continued existence of the Papal holdings as an impediment to a united Italy.

Victor Emmanuel II

After preliminary training at Spoleto the Irish brigade was assigned to General Schmidt for the defence of Perugia. As a military operation it was a totally hopeless undertaking, the defenders were outnumbered by ten to one and the equipment was obsolete. In September of the same year hostilities broke out in Ancona and Spoleto. The Irish volunteers, however, were singled-out for praise by both sides and covered themselves with glory. They spent approx. eight weeks in captivity and when London was informed by the newly formed Italian State that they held some 1,200 British *(practically all Irish)* prisoners of war, the British *(true to character)* replied that any of their subjects who had fought for the Pope had thereby forfeited their British citizenship and they cared little what happened to them. There was an immediate reaction from the Irish people *(true to their character)* and they somehow collected sufficient funds to enable them to charter the steamer 'Dee' owned by the Royal Mail Navigation Company, which set sail from Southampton destined for Havre to pick up the entire Irish Brigade, a detachment of the defeated Pontifical Army, and transport them to Cork.

The prisoners were shipped from Italy to Marseilles by boat and from there to Paris by the Lyons Railway. They were met in Paris by zealous Catholics who fed and clothed them having been forewarned of the tattered and deplorable state these poor men were in. This was due to the disgraceful treatment they had suffered and endured in captivity at the hands of the Piedmontese. After the capitulation of Ancona, they were imprisoned in an uncovered open space at the mercy of the elements both rain and sun. The soldiers who were guarding them *(for want of a better word)* meanly stole any money they had to purchase some little comfort (food), with full knowledge of their officers. They were fed a small ration of stale biscuit and water for their nourishment just sufficient to sustain life and prevent them from dying of hunger. They were further humiliated and insulted by the population on their journey to the boat by been obliged to purchase glasses of water.

When news first reached Wexford of the British Government's attitude towards the prisoners, the people in the town were outraged and they sprung into action immediately and to whom did they turn to for support and leadership in their endeavour – none other than the C.Y.M.S. On the 25th October 1860 the following letter was sent to the 'Friends of the Irish Brigade' which read
We the undersigned request a meeting of the 'Friends of the Irish Brigade' at the 'Young Men's Society' rooms in Allen Street on Thursday evening the 1st November at 8 o'clock for the purpose of organizing a collection on their behalf. The Society arranged a general meeting of its members for the 4th November for the purpose of collecting for the 'Irish Brigade'. The C.Y.M.S. did not stop there as on the 8th of November the following resolution was unanimously adopted *That a public banquet be given to the soldiers of the 'Irish Papal Brigade' belonging to the County Wexford on Thursday evening next [15th November] in the Town Hall.* This date was later changed to January 1861.

The Brigade received a hero's welcome at Cork and the Wexford people gave them such a welcome that the 'Wexford Independent' described it as follows: *We may safely aver that since the Liberator's visit in 1845, such a vast assemblage never met within the walls of Old Wexford.* Major O'Reilly, his officers and the Co. Wexford contingents came from Enniscorthy in the morning and were met at Ferrycarrig with a band and a multitude which burst into applause on their appearance. The Wexford delegation there to meet them consisted of the Mayor, John Sinnott, Esq. attended by his Mace bearer, the Very Rev. James Roche, P.P., Ald. Richard Walsh, the Rev. Walter Lambert, the Rev. Thomas Busher and many more dignitaries.

Triumphal arches were erected in the principal streets and flags and bannerettes expressive of welcome floated from several windows. Mottos, significant of love and attachment for His Holiness the Pope, were interspersed in different quarters and large banners bearing the words 'Welcome home Irish Brigade' and 'Irishmen know how to die but not surrender' appeared in different quarters. The ships in the harbour were decked out with flags of every conceivable colour. The procession moved on from Ferrycarrig towards the town entering at Westgate, Ram Street, along the Quay, Williams Street, Maudlintown, the Faythe, Main Street, Hill Street, John Street and stopped at the residence of John Thomas Devereux, M.P. in Upper George Street where the Major and his officers entered.

The Banquet

In the evening the entertainment and banquet were held in the Town Hall and the catering was supplied by Robinson's and every delicacy of the season and wines of the purest vintage were served. The soldiers present were: Major O'Reilly, D.L., Captain Coppinger and Lieuts. Crean, Lynch, Luther, McSwiney, and Mulhall, the Revd. Mr. McDivett, (Chaplain), and the County Wexford Contingent – Privates Bogan, Dempsey, Devereux, Howlin, Redmond, Rickaby, Stafford, and the two Singleton brothers. Amongst the general company present were - the Right Worshipful John Sinnott, Esq., Mayor (C.Y.M.S. member), Rev. James Roche, P.P. (C.Y.M.S. Spiritual Director), Richard J. Devereux (C.Y.M.S. Patron), Alderman Richard Walsh (C.Y.M.S. Honorary Life member), Rev. Walter Lambert (C.Y.M.S. President), Rev. Thomas Busher (C.Y.M.S. member), James Devereux (C.Y.M.S. member), Matthew Myler, Rev. Jeremiah Hogan (C.Y.M.S. member), Rev. William Murphy (C.Y.M.S. member), Rev. Thomas Furlong, S.P.C. (C.Y.M.S. member), Rev. James Barry (C.Y.M.S. member), James Peirce, Stephen Doyle (C.Y.M.S. member), Peter Murphy, T.C., Patrick O'Connor (C.Y.M.S. member), Thomas White (C.Y.M.S. member), Thomas Roche (C.Y.M.S. member) and Stephen Doyle (C.Y.M.S. member). Robinson's Catering Co. as mentioned above was owned by David Robinson a C.Y.M.S. member who owned a confectionary and grocery shop at 34, North Main Street. The Society's influence and involvement in this occasion is undeniable. Incidentally, General De La Moriciere and William Power, Esq., both wrote letters of congratulations and offered their apologies for not been able to attend the occasion.

Before concluding this paragraph allow me to remind readers that Pope Pius IX could be described as the Pope of the C.Y.M.S. As I have already outlined it was he who gave his blessing to the Catholic Young Men's Society in May of 1849 and it was he who knighted Richard Devereux, K.S.G. the favourite son of the Wexford Branch.

Wexford C.Y.M.S. Protest Letter to the Communist Government of Hungary - 1949

Cardinal Joseph Mindszenty

In 1949 Cardinal Jozsef Mindszenty was <u>charged</u> with treason and sentenced to life imprisonment on his own confession. It was widely believed at the time that he had been drugged and induced to confess falsely whilst in a confused state.

Cardinal Jozsef Mindszenty (6th March 1892 – 6th May 1975) *(pronounced phonetically as Yo-zhef Meend-sen-ti)* was a 20th century Hungarian Cardinal and steadfast clerical opponent of Communism in general, and of the regime in Hungary in particular. He was born Jozsef Pehm on the 6th March 1892 in Csehimindszent, Austria-Hungary. He adopted his new name which formed part of his home village's name in 1911.

Tortured by Sleep Deprivation

After his arrest he was questioned for hours on end with his tormentors working on a rota system. One session lasted for eighty-two hours without rest. On the fifth day of non-stop quizzing the poor man's mind and body had endured all that it could bear and he collapsed and became unconscious. The police doctors revived him by delivering 'stimulant pills' *(probably Aktedron)* dissolved in water and forcefully administered to him. His resistance was broken and he gave the answers which his tormentors wanted. He was forced to write his confession. The pills had completely broken his will. The after affects for him were violent headaches, total dullness, a confused mind and a weak and frail body. Whether by drugs or otherwise Mindszenty whilst in prison was reduced to a state of insanity and while in this condition he wrote his 'confession' now in the Hungarian Government's yellow book.
It was this outrageous mock trial of a Prince of the Catholic

Arpad Szakasits
Hungarian President 1948 - 1949

Church which spurred the Wexford C.Y.M.S. into writing their letter of protest to the Communist Government of Hungary in 1949. The entry in the minute book states -

On the proposition of Henry J. Doyle, seconded by Edward O'Rourke (Vice-President). It was decided to send a letter of protest to the President of Hungary [Arpad Szakasits] on the imprisonment of Cardinal Mindszenty, and to forward a copy of the letter to his Lordship the Bishop – Minute book, 18th January 1949.

I have tried my utmost to obtain a copy of the letter but I have been unsuccessful. Fr. Seamus De Val, Archivist. Diocese of Ferns could not locate it nor could Dr. Eva Kisasszondy, Archivist of the National Archives of Hungary. She searched the archives of the Prime Minister's Office, the State Church Office and the Ministry of Foreign Affairs Office but was unsuccessful. I have never seen the actual text of the letter but I would hazard a guess that the C.Y.M.S. Council barely contained themselves stopping short of calling the Hungarian President a dirty Red Commie **"NULLIUS FILIUS"** even though they probably thought that he deserved to be called one.

The Religious Welfare of an Emigrating Family

Just how hard the clergy and others connected to the Catholic faith worked to protect the flock is well attested in the next little story that was gleaned from the minutes. I have not ascertained the identity (*surname*) of this family but who the family were is not what is of importance but what is of interest is what the C.Y.M.S. was prepared to do to assure the spiritual welfare of the family of one of it's members.

The story began in the minute book dated 3rd October 1944 where we are informed that the Hon. Secretary was instructed to write to the Hon. Secretary of the National Federation of the C.Y.M.S. of Ireland and, also, to write to Fr. O'Neill to see *if anything could be done to safeguard the Catholic Religion of the [Family Name] children who were going to England.*

These were hard times for working class people. There was very little work in Ireland and thousands had to leave their home and families and it must have been particularly heart breaking having to leave just prior to Christmas time. By the 7th November Fr. O'Neill's letter was read out to the Council and it read as follows: *The question of the [Surname] Family had been referred by him to the Archbishop of Cardiff.* Even better news was received on the 5th December from the National Council of the Federation of the C.Y.M.S. in Dublin stating: *That the welfare of the [surname] children was being looked after by the C.Y.M.S. in England.* It is nice to see this story finish on a happy note. It is also nice to know that this Society took action in a matter such as this.

While on the subject of emigration I should mention that Eugene McGrail one of our most eminent council members was appointed a delegate to act on the 'Catholic Social Welfare Bureau' in the town in conjunction with the Legion of Mary and the St. Vincent de Paul Society *For the purpose of supplying the Bureau in Dublin with the information which they required regarding any emigrants going to Great Britain* - Dated 2nd September 1942.

Wexford C.Y.M.S. Men
and their
African Missions Connections

The Diocese of Ferns played a very important part in the development of the African Missions and St. Peter's College has been described as the *'First nursery of Irish missions'*. Wexford provided many African missionaries and I am proud to relate that some C.Y.M.S. members and associates were connected and involved with this exemplary work from the outset.

From as early as 1820 the Catholic Church in South Africa was gaining strength and organising itself in Cape Town with an Irish priest named Fr. Patrick Scully. An Irish Dominican named Patrick Raymond Griffith was Bishop in the Cape Colony in 1838 and he got assistance with the arrival of Aidan Devereux and Thomas Murphy who were sent out from St. Peter's College, Wexford where they had been recruited for the missions.

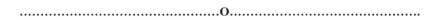

....o...

Thomas Murphy (1812-1872) from Shielbeggan, Arthurstown, Co. Wexford was ordained by Bishop Griffith on his arrival and Aidan Devereux (1805-1854) born at Poulmarle near Taghmon was ordained in 1826. Fr. Devereux was consecrated Bishop in Cape Town on the 20th December 1847 and another Wexford man, a young student named Mr. Brownrigg, arrived in 1840 but died in April of that year.

James David Ricards (1825-1893) who was born in the Bull Ring, Wexford responded to the call of Bishop Devereux while he was a Sub-Deacon and he too arrived in the Cape. He was ordained Deacon and Priest a month after his arrival in 1850. He received his Doctor of Divinity degree in 1857 and he was appointed Vicar Apostolic and Bishop of the Eastern Province of the Cape of Good Hope in 1871.

In 1858 John O'Brien, a very devout Catholic and pious man, who was the Hon. Secretary of the Wexford C.Y.M.S. decided to respond to the call for missionaries in Africa and in January 1858 he landed at Algoa Bay, South Africa in the company of Ricards and an Irish Nun, Sister Mary Frances. *(See Biography section for John O'Brien's story Vol. 2)*

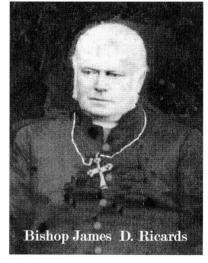

Bishop James D. Ricards

Ricards established a boy's college "Little" St. Aidan's at Grahamstown which was achieved with the assistance of his connections back in the Diocese of Ferns. Through the influence of a relative he managed to secure the help of the English Province of Jesuits to staff the new college and with the benevolence of the wealthy pious Wexford businessman Richard Devereux, who generously donated £1,000 to the college, the establishment was placed on a firm financial footing. John O'Brien was the first student together with Thomas Lynch to "enter" St. Aidan's in 1859. John was both student and teacher at the school.

The foundation stone for St. Aidan's College "Proper" was laid in 1873 and Fr. John O'Brien, Parish Priest of Uitenhage at this time attended the ceremony. Bishop Ricards had installed three Jesuit Fathers and two brothers at St. Aidan's College by 1875 to carry on the work which he himself had initiated at "little" St. Aidan's in 1850. His hope was that St. Aidan's would prosper and develop on the same lines as St. Peter's College, Wexford and would be a seminary as well as a High School. He assumed, however, that it would also be open to non-Catholics. From its origin the College provided for Catholics only and it never did become a seminary. It was once the only Jesuit College in South Africa.

Some of the eminent Aidanites who were educated at the college were Sir Charles Coghlan, first Premier of Rhodesia, Chief Justice Stafford, Count Wilmot of the Cape Parliament and three Bishops and numerous other prominent people. Prof. Frank Coleman of Rhodes University wrote a comprehensive history on St. Aidan's College from which the forgoing information is derived.

116

St. Aidan's Boys School 1859

St. Aidan's College, Grahamstown, South Africa

The Jesuits withdrew from the college in 1967 due to the South African Government's apartheid policy and in 1973 the College was forced to close due to financial difficulties. It lay derelict for almost twenty years with some out buildings being rented out from time to time and in 1980 Geoff Vetch, a Grahamstown entrepreneur, acquired the building but alas due to other commitments and finances it lay derelict for a further 14 years. At this time Mr. Vetch began the restoration to transform the building into a hotel and it opened in February 1994.

In 1875 the Rev John Allen (*later Dr. Allen*), curate of Newtownbarry (*Bunclody*) and Rev. Nicholas Fanning, both from Wexford town, sailed for the Cape accompanied by Ricards. As a matter of interest, Fr. Fanning was presented with a silver chalice from the Holy Family Confraternity on his departure. It would appear in the early days that Bishop Ricards was busy accompanying recruits for the missions travelling back and forth between Wexford and South Africa, so it is understandable why he had hoped that St. Aidan's would develop into a seminary as well as a High School.

Rev. William Hanton

Rev. Frank O'Rourke

In 1880 Rev. William Hanton and Rev. Francis O'Rourke, both Wexford town men, joined Ricards in South Africa accompanied by three Postulants, i.e. Annie Nolan, Castlebridge, Mary Anne Cosgrave, Ballenvarry and a Miss T. Doyle, Enniscorthy.

In 1893 the Rev. James Cullen SJ, from New Ross, the founder of the Pioneer Total Abstinence Association and one of the founding priests of the House of Missions at Enniscorthy, visited South Africa on a Missionary tour for over a year.

While these Wexford priests were in the Cape Colony the 'Kaffir' Wars had being raging on sporadically since the 1830s. At that time settlers began to encroach and farm Kaffir (Xhosa) land. The burning of white farms near Grahamstown and Port Elizabeth and the stealing of cattle by the marauding 'Kaffir' (Xhosa's) was a constant threat and worry to the settlers. In Grahamstown, St. Patrick's Church (*erected in 1844*) had to be fortified during these Xhosa or 'Kaffir' wars.

The British army invaded Zululand (1879) and within a month the terrible news of the massacre at Isandhlwana reached the Colony followed by reports of the other battles that were fought over the remainder of the year. Then the first Boar War broke-out which lasted barely a year ending in 1881. These wars seemed like a skirmish to what was to come. The Great Boar War broke-out in October of 1899 and ended on May 31st 1902 with the signing of the Treaty of Vereeniging. While these wars were fought far away to the North-East of the Cape Colony, nonetheless. It must have been very unsettling and of great concern to everyone at that time.

I have discovered five men with Wexford C.Y.M.S. credentials who were involved with the missionary work. Richard Devereux, a C.Y.M.S. founding father and benefactor who funded the new college at Grahamstown. He also financed the construction of 'The House of Missions' in Enniscorthy in 1866 for the missionary fathers. John O'Brien, a former Hon. Secretary of the Wexford C.Y.M.S. branch and the two newly ordained

priests William Hanton and Francis O'Rourke, both from Wexford town families with strong C.Y.M.S. connections. The fifth is a priest in the Cape called Maurice O'Byrne, who was Parish Priest of Port Elizabeth. He was brother of Rev. James W. O'Byrne, a member of the Wexford C.Y.M.S. who served on its Council. He also wrote the 'The History of the Holy Family Confraternity' Wexford. Both brothers were born in Cushinstown.

An interesting observation is that the very first C.Y.M.S. branch to be founded in South Africa was at Grahamstown in the year 1861. That was only two and a half years after Mr. John O'Brien had arrived in South Africa in January 1859. As already pointed out John was a dedicated C.Y.M.S. man since the branch's establishment in Wexford in 1855. John was a student, preacher and teacher at "Little" St. Aidan's, Grahamstown from 1859 up to the time of his ordination in 1868 when he was transferred to Port Elizabeth which placed him firmly in the unique position to be the founder of the C.Y.M.S. branch at Grahamstown.

Questions I was forced to ask myself were - did John O'Brien take his C.Y.M.S. organising skills with him to Africa? Were the Wexford C.Y.M.S. men responsible for introducing the C.Y.M.S. Society into South Africa along with the missionary brethren? If my suspicions were correct then this would explain why a photograph of Fr. John O'Brien was sent back to the C.Y.M.S. at Wexford from Uitenhage after his death in July 1896.

My thinking on the matter was that if a Wexford C.Y.M.S. man was responsible for establishing the South African C.Y.M.S. I intended to see to it that he and the branch receives full recognition for it. I could not possibly let this rest, I needed to get to the bottom of it and thus I started corresponding with South Africa and conducted an

Fr. John O'Brien
Ordination Day 1st January 1868
St. Patrick's. Grahamstown, South Africa.

in-depth research into the matter. My correspondence involved contacting Anneliese Beckers *(Diocesan Secretary)* and John Reeks *(Archivist)* both at the Catholic Diocese of Port Elizabeth.

I relayed my inquiries and suspicions to them concerning John O'Brien being the possible founding father of the South African C.Y.M.S. Mr. Reeks, who knew very little about the C.Y.M.S., on hearing of my task in writing the history very kindly agreed to assist me. I am deeply indebted to him for all his help and the time which he so generously afforded me free gratis.

The replies which I received from Mr. Reeks confirmed my suspicions. There is no doubt now that Mr. (Fr.) John O'Brien was the founder of the C.Y.M.S. at Grahamstown in May 1861. This was the first C.Y.M.S. to be established in the South Africa colony barely 12 years after the founding of the Society in Ireland and it would appear that all the other branches in South Africa have emanated from Grahamstown.

In Mr. A. Wilmot's book 'The Life and Times of the Right Rev. Dr. Ricards' (published 1908 in S.A.) the following quotes appear:

'One notable feature of this period was the very successful management of the Catholic Young Men's Society, established under the presidency of Mr. (afterwards Father) John O'Brien'

And further on…………

' ..A really splendid Library was secured by means of the funds obtained from houses crowded by people of all religious and degrees who listened delightedly to the lectures and readings of Dr. Ricards…'

From the 'Chronicon' of the Diocese, which keeps a day-to-day record of the happenings within the Diocese, we glean the following gems:

'May 1861, in this month the Catholic Young Mens' Society was established under the direction and presidency of Mr. John O'Brien.'

Another entry in the 'Chronicon' dated 1863 reads as follows:

*May. in this year - the school room at
St. Patrick's Grahamstown, was enlarged
in order to afford more accommodation to
the members of C Y Mens' Society. That
is the enlargement was begun, this
was finished in May the following year
The first meeting of this Society was
attended by only 26 persons -
September 20 Bishop Moran conferred Minor Orders on O'Reilly*

'**May 1863, in this year the schoolroom at St. Patrick's Grahamstown [Church] was enlarged in order to afford more accommodation to members of the C Y Mens' Society. That is the enlargement was begun, this was finished in May of the following year. The first meeting was attended by only 26 persons.**'

Three Wexford priests in the Cape Colony 1880s

I believe the foregoing evidence is sufficient to declare my suspicions proven beyond any doubt. What a marvellous discovery this is. Another feather in the Wexford branch's hat. I am unaware of how many branches of the C.Y.M.S were eventually established in South Africa but I do know that Port Elizabeth established their 'Young Men's Society (Y.M.S.) St. Augustine's branch in February 1904. They were still active in 1935 and ceased sometime in the 1960s. East London and Port Alfred had Catholic Men's Societies (C.M S.) in 1937. Durban, Pietermaritzburg and Cape Town all had branches at some time. Mr. Reeks placed an open letter in the 'Southern Cross' (*the South African Catholic newspaper*) on my behalf requesting old C.Y.M.S. sodality members to contact me. The fact that the features editor had to telephone and ask *'what was the C.Y.M.S.?'* says it all. It is obvious that the Society in now unknown in South Africa even to Catholics working in the media.

The photograph depicting three Wexford priests was taken at Uitenhage, South Africa in the 1880s.

Photo taken at Uitenhage in the 1880s. Lt. to Rt. Fr. Nicholas Fanning, of the Holy Family Confraternity fame. Fr. Francis E. O'Rourke, later P.P. of Glynn, Wexford. Fr. John O'Brien, former Hon. Secretary of the Wexford C.Y.M.S. and founder of the C.Y.M.S. at Grahamstown, South Africa in May 1861.

Extraordinary General Meeting

1940s

It would be impossible for a Society like the C.Y.M.S with a history stretching back 153 years without having some form of criticism levelled against its Council at some stage. There have been a few occasions when this has happened in relation to the Society's catholic action record.

A few people saw fit to accuse the Council of not doing sufficient in this respect. The following account is the full report of one such case and I will leave it to the reader to judge for him or herself. Quite frankly I never found the Society wanting in this respect.

Minutes of Extraordinary General Meeting held on the 9th March 1941

The notice of motion which was proposed by Nicholas P. Corish and seconded by J. J. Cosgrove and handed in at the A.G. M. of the 9th February 1941 was read:

That it is the opinion of this General meeting of members that an Extraordinary Meeting of all the members be called within one month from this date, 9th February. That members be asked to express fully their opinions as to the apathy which is so apparent and that a Select Committee be appointed to consider the best means to bring our Society to the position of the foremost society in town. Also to determine not in word, or to break-off connection with the C.Y.M.S. Federation and become a Social Club with no desire to publicly participate in Catholic Action principles as laid down by our Bishops as part of the functions of C.Y.M.S. branches.

I will pass on many of the points which Mr. Corish covered and only deal with his remarks relating to the spiritual wellbeing of the Society. He suggested :

a)   **That all members of Catholic Action should be members also of The Holy Family Confraternity**

b)   **That a quarterly communion be held for members.**

c)   **That an annual mass be celebrated for the Society and a weekend retreat held once a year**

d)   **That the study circle be revived**

The Chairman replied to the various points raised by Mr. Corish saying *With reference to religious practices there was the Annual Retreat for the Parish...The Study Circle had failed* Both points mentioned in the Chairman's statement are completely true. Mr. Edward O'Brien said:

The motion implied censure on the Spiritual Director (President) and on the Branch Committee...it was nonsense to say that there was apathy amongst the members regarding Catholic Action and it was scarcely   Mr. Corish's duty to point-out to the Spiritual Director of the branch what Catholic Action they should adopt.   Patrick Breen said *Many members of the 'St, Vincent de Paul Society, the 'Legion of Mary', the 'Pioneer Total Abstinence Association', the 'Boys' Club Committee', the 'Confraternity of the Holy Family', and many of the Marshals who assisted at the Annual Procession of the Blessed Sacrament were members of the C.Y.M.S. And he looked on the C.Y.M.S. in Wexford as the very centre of Catholic Action.*   The Hon. Secretary said: *Regarding Masses, the C.Y.M.S. had six days' Masses offered for deceased members in 1940 and seven days' Masses offered for deceased*

members in 1938. The Chairman then spoke again saying *He was in Wexford for over fifty years and he never saw any Catholic Action that a large number of C.Y.M.S. members did not take part in.*

Then Nick Barnwell stood-up and said *When a circular was received from the C.Y.M.S. Federation in 1939 regarding Catholic Action. Rev. J. Sinnott, Adm., the respected President of the Society in Wexford, very ably described how Catholic Action was taken care of in Wexford.* T. D. Sinnott then suggested *That a proposition be put to the meeting, to the effect that it did not consider the appointment of a Select Committee necessary.* Mr. Furlong made the suggestion that the only way to bring the meeting to a close was to table a motion *That no apathy existed in the Society and that there was no justification for appointing a Select Committee.* Thomas Hayes seconded the motion and it was passed by twenty eight votes on a show of hands. There can be little doubt from the foregoing that the Society was heavily involved in Catholic Action in Wexford town.

Thomas David Sinnott

Nicholas Corish was a devout Catholic and a valued and committed member of the Society and no one could deny this. On this occasion he took a beating and there is no doubt in my mind that Mr. Corish was influenced by circulars and directives coming from the 'National Federation' in Dublin which were frequently being distributed to the branches. I have observed on several occasions that such material was sent to Wexford and it is my understanding that this advice on how Catholic Action should be implemented was not always welcome. Sometimes questionnaires were attached that queried what the Wexford branch was doing concerning Catholic Action etc. Is it any wonder that some of the Council members considered this as an insult. After all who wants to be told that they are not good enough Catholics? The Council usually handed this material over to the President *(the Spiritual Director)* for him to deal with the matter and that action in itself speaks volumes. The reader will note that Nick Barnwell made mention of the very same thing.

This matter raised its head again at the A.G.M. held on the 10th February 1946 and at the A.G.M. of 1956 when a certain individual inferred that the club was not living up to its responsibilities in the promotion of Catholic Action. His actual words were that it was not *'Striving to live-up to our obligations.'* All the members of the Society in those times were good Catholics. Everyone went to Sunday Mass, received Holy Communion weekly and attended the Holy Family Confraternity. Everyone attended the retreats when they came to town and marched in every religious procession. Many walked after the funerals of deceased members and often in heavy rain from the Church all the way out to Crosstown cemetery. I disagree strongly with anyone who believed that club members were not doing enough in Catholic Action. What on earth did these people expect from members? The men in the C.Y.M.S. when I was there in the 1950s and early 60s were the finest that you could possible find anywhere. They were decent, upright, honest and Christian men who <u>should have been praised and not censured for their exemplary lifestyles.</u> Perhaps if the National Federation Council had been aware of the Wexford branch's charitable work they might have been more restrained in asking *'what Catholic action we were involved in.'* Of course they were totally unaware of all the good charitable works carried out by the Council in the true spirit of Christian charity because the club never publicised what it was doing. It was conducted discreetly and not discussed outside the Council chambers.

Allow me to inform the reader exactly what the Society did for Wexford town. I have gleaned from the minute books a collection of some examples of charity carried-out by the society and please bear in mind that on many occasions when the society was helping others it was in financial difficulties and yet still gave and helped others. If that's not Catholic Action, I don't know what is.

The term *'Catholic Action'* arose in the early 20th century to designate the organised work of the laity that is performed under the direction of mandate of the Bishops in the fields of Dogma, Morals, Liturgy, Education and Charity. In 1927 Pope Pius XI gave the term its classical definition as *'The Participation of the Laity in the Apostolate of the hierarchy.'*

C.Y.M.S. Charitable Work

('If a man has enough to live on, and yet when he sees his brother in need, shuts up his heart against him, how can it be said that the divine love dwells in him ?' – 1 John 3:17 N.E.B.)

During the research for this book I came across many incidents of acts of charity carried out by the Society. So much so that I thought it best to make a note of it and write a paragraph on it. However, as I continued with my research I was struck with the extent of the club's involvement in helping-out not only charities in the town but also everyone and anyone who asked and who were shown to be a deserving case. The Society's readiness to help other clubs in the town speaks well of it and the Christian men who were entrusted with its management and every-day running throughout the years. Their benevolence towards the Wexford people is unequalled by any other social club in the town and all members both past and present should be proud to have been associated with such an institution.

I struggled with the problem of how I would write such a chapter without having to go further into researching each and every individual and organisation mentioned. Such research would be beyond the sphere of this book so I settled on the idea of recording a log of the happenings in chronological order giving the details of the dates, names of both individuals and the organisations involved. Every request or application asking for help from the club recorded in the following list was granted free of charge. There was a nominal free charged sometimes but this was to pay the caretaker for his cleaning of the hall and for the heating and lighting used. The only cases where an applicant did not receive help free will be noted after the entry and a full explanation given.

October/November 1860
On the 25th October 1860 the following letter was sent to the 'Friends of the Irish Brigade'. It read *We the undersigned request a meeting of the 'Friends of the Irish Brigade' at the 'Young Men's Society' rooms in Allen Street on Thursday evening the 1st November at 8 o'clock for the purpose of organizing a collection on their behalf.* The Society ordered a general meeting of its members for the 4th November for the purpose of a collection for the 'Irish Brigade'. The C.Y.M.S. didn't stop there because on the 8th of November we read that the following resolution was unanimously adopted *That a public banquet be given to the soldiers of the 'Irish Papal Brigade' belonging to the County Wexford on Thursday evening next [15th November] in the Town Hall.*

13th February 1869
Resolved *It is fit and just to present an address to Mr. Thomas Petit Hogan for his services to this Society and his exertions generally in aid of the charities of the town.* The President and Council of the Society presented this to Mr. Thomas James Petit Hogan at his residence at Stonebridge.

8th November 1869
A letter was received from the Mechanics Institute Wexford, November 1869.

Dear Sirs,

At a meeting of the 'Board of Directors of the Wexford Mechanics Institute and literary Association' on this evening it was unanimously resolved *That the best thanks of the board directors be tendered to the council of the 'Catholic Young Men's Society' for their great kindness in granting the use of their splendid harmonium on the occasion of Mr. Meadow's reading in the 'Town Hall' last Friday evening.'*

Yours faithfully,

Thomas M. O'Leary
Mr. Hanton, Hon. Secretary.

St. Patrick's Night of 1871
The Catholic Young Men's Society ran an entertainment at their Concert Hall, Paul Quay. All proceeds were given to the building of the Manse fund.

19th February 1885
The Society donated £3 from its funds and requested the members to subscribe themselves toward the 'Rev. Canon James Roche, P.P. Memorial Fund'. This was Fr. Roche of the twin churches fame and the memorial was a statue that was erected in the Rowe Street Church grounds.

28th February 1889
Miss Shanahan requested the use of the concert hall *(the old one at Paul Quay)* to conduct a dramatic and concert entertainment for charity. It was granted free gratis.

February 1889
Mr. James Whelan requested the use of the concert hall for the purpose of starting a gymnasium class. Granted.

25th April 1892
A letter was received from Walter O'Brien of Clearistown inquiring if the 'Dramatic Club' would be allowed to give an entertainment for a charitable purpose. Granted free gratis.

13th March 1893
The Society's 'Dramatic Club' staged an entertainment in aid of the Christian Brothers of the town on the 13tyh April 1892.

4th December 1893
Fr. O'Leary made an application through the Rev. President for the loan of the brass instruments as he was about to form a band in connection with the Confraternity. Obviously the C.Y.M.S. band had ceased to exist by this time. The instruments were given on condition that if the confraternity band disbanded at any time, the instruments must be returned to the C.Y.M.S.

12th September 1894
The Society's 'Dramatic Club' staged a dramatic entertainment at the Theatre in High Street for the benefit of Fr. O'Leary's Confraternity Band. The massive profit was £18-2-6.

22nd April 1895
A letter was received from the 'Castlebridge Reading Room Committee' requesting permission from the Council for the C.Y.M.S. 'Dramatic Club' to put on an entertainment in Castlebridge in the course of a month for the benefit of their reading rooms. Granted.

9th September 1895
The Rev. Thomas O'Connor, C.C., Castlebridge, requested permission for the C.Y.M.S. Dramatic Club to stage an entertainment for the benefit of their reading rooms in

Castlebridge in the course of a month. This was granted free gratis and was held on the 22nd January 1896.

11th June 1896
The 'Dramatic Club' gave an entertainment for Fr. L. Doyle at Rosslare on the evenings of 28th and 29th June to help clear off the debt due on the new school at Rosslare.

On 13th August 1899
The Society's 'Dramatic Club' put on a dramatic entertainment at Kilmore in aid of the Parish Church.

3rd, 4th and 5th September 1899
The 'Grand Bazaar' held on Sunday, Monday and Tuesday 3rd, 4th and 5th September1899 was held for charity. It was mentioned in Milligan's humorous verse.

26th May 1898
The 'Camptown Serenaders', the Society's 'Dramatic Club' singing group put on an entertainment in the club for the benefit of the 'Committee of the 1897 Cycling Carnival.'

13th August 1899
The Society's 'Dramatic Club' held a dramatic entertainment at Kilmore in aid of the Parish Chapel.

26th February 1900
The 'Dramatic Class' put on a performance at the Theatre Royal in aid of the 'Wexford Clothing Society' This was a charity which distributed clothing to the *needy poor of Wexford Town.'* That charitable Society was later taken over by the 'St. Vincent de Paul Society'.

7th March 1900
A letter was received from J.G. Murphy and P. J. Murphy, the secretaries of the 'Wexford United Cycle Party' thanking the Council for the use of the Council room to hold their meetings.

16th August 1900
The '98 Memorial Committee' requested the club premises to hold their '98 bazaar'. The Council unanimously consented to this free gratis.

25th June 1903
Fr. O'Byrne requested the club's band instruments for the purpose of forming a band for the 'Boys Confraternity'. He gave an undertaking to return them when they would not be required. This was granted. Here is proof that the Society did indeed have a band but at this date it was not functioning.

22nd August 1904

Mr. Goold, Hon. Secretary C.Y.M.S. on behalf of the 'Bazaar Committee' applied for the use of the club premises for the purpose of running a bazaar for charitable purposes. Granted.

June 1905
Fr. O'Byrne wrote to the club on behalf of the 'Boys Brigade Committee' stating that they wished to present the club with a scene (*a painted scene*) for the concert hall stage as a token of their gratitude for the kindness shown to them by the club. The presentation was most gratefully accepted and the secretary was directed to convey to Fr. O'Byrne the Council's thanks. By the 14th of November of the same year Fr. O'Byrne wrote stating that he had been appointed director of the 'Boys Brigade' and he hoped the Council would continue their sympathy and support of the brigade.

Early 1908
Jem Roche (a member) the Irish boxing champion requested the use of the gymnasium for his own use to train for his "Big Fight" [Heavyweight boxing championship of the world] against Tommy Burns due on St. Patrick's Day in Dublin. This was granted.

29th of March 1910
Mr. Richard Ryan, Hon. Secretary of the 'Foresters Society' requested the loan or use of *"the mouth pieces"* of some of the band's instruments in the club. He wanted them as replacements for the Forester's band equipment. This request was granted with a proviso that they be returned at any time that the club required them.

12th November 1912
On the 12th November 1912 the records state; *The case of the Catholic workmen out of employment in Belfast owing to their religion and nationalist opinions was brought under the notice of the meeting and it was decided to send a subscription of £10 off from the club to this fund* ['Relief of the Belfast Expelled Workers'] *and that a notice to this effect be posted in the club inviting the members to subscribe towards this fund.* This matter was raised again in October 1915 when the club was asked to assist by Subscribing towards the paying off the debt incurred in the legal proceedings. Subscriptions were collected from individual members and the Society donated a further two guineas to the 'Belfast Catholic Workers Indemnity Fund'.

30th June 1913
Mr. Edward Foley, on behalf of Fr. Murphy, Crossabeg, requested the loan of the two scenes and two side wings from the concert hall for the purpose of an entertainment in connection with the Bazaar being held on Sunday the 29th June. Granted.

2nd November 1913
Walter Hanrahan wrote requesting the use of the club's gymnasium for the 'County Wexford Football Team' to practice for their forthcoming match with Kerry. Granted.

1st February 1914
An application was received from Mr. Breen, Secretary of the 'County Committee of the G. A. Association' for the use of one of the rooms to hold meetings of their committee. Granted.

April 1914
The use of the C.Y.M.S. premises was given for a meeting during which a local branch of *'The Children's League of Pity'* was established. *This was to ensure the help and sympathy of happy children on behalf of their less fortunate little brothers and sisters.* The meeting took place at the St. Iberius Hall (*concert hall*) organised by Miss Barry of Roxboro and 37 children became members.

17th of January 1915
Mr. Robert Moran, Secretary of the 'Irish National Foresters, Wexford Branch' wrote requesting the loan of trestles (*about a dozen*) for the purpose of a supper in their rooms on the 19th February.

17th January 1915
'The Castlebridge Reading Rooms Committee' wrote enquiring if the club would sell one of the old billiard cloths and it was decided to let them have one for £1.

5th September 1915
The secretary of the 'Wexford Branch Junior Mary's Needlework Guild' wrote stating the following resolution proposed by Mrs Horsburgh and seconded by Lady Maurice FitzGerald was passed by that body on the 31st August 1915. *That the best thanks of this meeting be given to the secretaries and members of the 'St. Iberius Catholic Club' for their kindness in granting the use of the concert hall for the working parties of the guild.*

16th January 1916
Mr. O'Hare D. J. wrote thanking the Council for the use of the concert hall for rehearsals and requesting the Council to let him have the use of the round table in the concert hall for the purpose of the play that the 'Operatic Society' was putting-on in the theatre.

23rd January 1916
Mr. Thomas Hayes, Secretary of the C.Y.M.S. 'Dramatic Class' applied for the use of the concert hall for the purpose of putting-on an entertainment in aid of the funds for the provision of comforts for the Irish soldiers and sailors engaged in the war. This application was unanimously granted and little did they know at the time that Ireland would have its own private war at Easter.

26th September 1916
John J. Kehoe requested permission to allow the 'Sports Company' to store some chairs in the club's premises. Granted.

14th November 1916
Mr. McGuire, Rowe Street conducted a meeting in connection with raising funds for the *"New Organ"* for Row Street church at the club premises. Granted.

15th December 1916
Mrs. John Carty, George Street applied for the use of the concert hall for the purpose of staging a concert in aid of the funds for the New Organ for Rowe Street church. Granted.

13th February 1917
Alderman Sinnott, Mayor of Wexford (*and member of the Society*) requested the use of the concert hall for Thursday evening for the purpose of giving some refreshments to the 'Irish Guards Band' on their visit to the town.

5th June 1917
Miss Barry, Roxborough wrote a letter thanking the Council for the use of the concert hall for the annual meeting of the 'Wexford Branch of the Children's League of Piety'.

4th September 1917
The secretary of the 'Irish National Foresters Local Branch' wrote requesting the loan of *"the trestles"* for the opening ceremony of their new hall.

13th May 1919
Miss Margaret Walsh, Hon. Secretary of the 'Ladies Auxiliary Amusements Committee of the A. O. H.' requested the use of the concert hall for the purpose of conducting an entertainment for a local charity on the 15th and 16th of June. This was granted on condition that Miss Walsh would satisfy the Council that the proceeds go to a deserving charity. [The ladies auxiliary which was founded in 1894 was a branch of the 'Ancient Order of Hibernians' and was a charitable organization.]

14th October 1919
'The National Foresters' requested the use of the concert hall and the piano for practice for their concert. The hall was granted but the piano was refused.

1919
Mr. Droughty on behalf of '(?) Amateur Dramatic Class' requested the use of the concert hall for a few nights from 6 to 8 pm. for practice. This was granted only when it was agreed that the proceeds go to a charity such as the 'Christian Brothers' or the 'St. Vincent de Paul Society'. Also this would be granted only for a few evenings until such time as Mr. Sinnott's store was available. There was a nominal charge made and they could not use the club piano. This piano was being looked after like it was made of gold in these days. There were few pianos around in Wexford and those who possessed one had to look after it.

11th May 1920
Miss Barry on behalf of the 'League of Pity' requested the concert hall for Thursday evening the 20th May for her meeting. Granted.

19th April 1921
Miss Barry, Roxboro of the 'League of Pity' requested the use of the concert hall for her meeting to be held on the Wednesday evening of the 20th April, Granted.

11th April 1922
Miss Barry, Roxboro of the 'League of Pity' received the use of the concert hall again this year for her meetings. Granted.

12th December 1922

Miss Irwin a teacher in the 'Workhouse' requested to rent a room for the purpose of teaching a small number of children for a few hours during the daytime. Granted.

10th October 1923
Mrs. Morgan on behalf of the 'League of Pity' requested the concert hall for their meeting to be held on the 14th October 1923. Granted.

12th February 1924
Thomas Hayes, High Street requested the use of the concert hall for his sister Mrs. Scanlon for the purpose of supplying refreshments to the delegates attending the 'Redmond Anniversary Procession' on the 9th March. Granted.

20th August 1924
Mrs Morgan of the 'League of Pity' requested the use of the concert hall for their annual meeting. Granted.

10th February 1925
Thomas Hayes, High Street (*a member of the society*) on behalf of the Christian Brothers and the Sisters of the Poor, St. John of God Convent applied for the use of the concert hall for the evenings of 12th and 13th February for the purpose of running whist drives for the benefit of charities connected with both of these institutions. Granted.

21st April 1925
The Secretary of the Local Branch of the 'Irish National Foresters' requested the club to nominate two members to represent the C.Y.M.S. on their committee for their Sports Carnival to be held in the Wexford Sports Ground on the 21st June. Thomas Kelly and Joseph Keane were appointed and Edward F. O'Rourke suggested that a subscription be given to the Foresters for the event. This was granted.

4th December 1925
Murtha Meyler, secretary of the 'Old Commercial Dance Class' ran a dance in the concert hall on the 2nd December and when the club discovered that the dance was run in aid of the poor of the town it was decided not to charge for the hall that night.

4th December 1925
John Browne was granted permission to make a small collection from the members of the club in aid of the funds of the St. Vincent de Paul Society.

12th January 1926.
P. J. Gregory requested the use of the concert hall and refreshment room for a charity dance on Tuesday evening 19th January. He also acquired it for another charity dance on the 6th April of the same year with the same conditions. Granted free gratis.

15th June 1926
P. White, secretary of the 'Irish National Foresters, Wexford Branch' requested the use of the concert hall to hold the International Convention of the Foresters during the first week of August. On the 31st of August the Society received a letter from Tom Moore, secretary of the

'Irish National Foresters' thanking them for their kindness. Obviously it had been granted.

14th September 1926
We reading in the minute book *On the motion of Mr. William Lacey seconded by Mr. John Doyle. It was decided to send a subscription of two guineas to Canon Bigley in aid of the 'Drumcollogher, Cinema Fire, and Disaster Fund'.*

A reply on the 28th December 1926 was received from the Canon thanking the club for their contribution in aid of the families connected with the cinema fire disaster.

14th September 1926
Thomas J. Roche, assistant teacher in the Christian Brothers School requested the use of the concert hall for the purpose of running a dance on Sunday night the 26th September to raise funds for the provision of books for the poor boys attending the school.

16th November 1926
Fr. Finn S. J. gave his temperance lecture at the concert hall this month open to the public free of charge.

6th December 1926
An application on behalf of Richard Corish, Mayor of Wexford and a member of the Society was made for the use of the concert hall for the purpose of holding a concert in aid of the poor of the town. Granted.

January 1927
The Society held a charity dance at the St. Iberius concert hall in aid of the deserving local charities. The Wexford Symphony Orchestra under the baton of W. Devereux supplied music.

27th March 1928
Fr. Allen applied for the concert hall for the purpose of running a Feis. Granted.

April 1930
A James Murphy on behalf of the 'Reception Committee for the Papal Nuncio's Visit to Wexford' wrote to the Council requesting a subscription towards defraying the expenses in connection with the visit. The club sent them a £3 gift.

9th April 1930
Miss D. Sullivan ran a jumble sale in the hall in aid of the 'Confraternity Band Fund'. Granted.

16th December 1930
The secretary of the 'Society for the Prevention of Cruelty to Children' requested the concert hall for a dance on the 2nd January 1931 in aid of that society. This was approved free gratis. However, it had also to receive the approved of the Gaelic League (*the sitting tenants*) for a suitable night.

16th January 1931
Nicholas Murphy, North Main Street requested the loan of some forms for a picnic to (Barruphill?) House for the bazaar fund in aid of the Convent of Perpetual Adoration Wexford. The appeal was granted and it was ordered that any other such or similar requests for this convent be given free of charge in the future.

7th September 1931
John J. Donohoe (*a Society member*) the secretary of the 'Perpetual Adoration Convent Bazaar Committee' requested the use of the club premises for the bazaar to be held on the 27th, 28th and 29th of September. Granted.

6th October 1931
The club decided to give a subscription of £5 to the 'Convent of 'Perpetual Adoration Bazaar Committee' for their funds.

22nd February 1933
Sergeant Scanlan of the Civic Guards requested the use of the concert hall free of charge for a whist drive on Friday nights during Lent in aid of the 'County Board N. A. C. A. J.' This was granted with a small charge of 10/= per night to cover the cost of lighting and cleaning of the hall.

2nd May 1933
Mrs. Elgee, secretary of the 'Children's League of Pity', requested the use of the concert hall for Tuesday evening the 9th of May from 3.30.p.m. to 5.00.p.m. to hold the Annual General Meeting of the League as was formerly granted for the same purpose in the past. Granted.

THE CONVENT OF PERPETUAL ADORATION, WEXFORD

6th June 1933
A letter was received from the secretary of the 'Wexford Athletic Club Sports Committee' soliciting a prize from the club for the sports to be held on Sunday 18th June. It

was decided that as the 'Wexford Athletic Club' had not paid the charge of 5/= per night for the use of the concert hall for the nights they held their whist drives that the Council would make them a present of the amount due for the use of the concert hall to purchase a prize for their sports.

6th June 1933
Mr. Corish on behalf of Michael O'Rourke jnr. applied for a loan of the whist tables for the purpose of holding a whist drive at Castlebridge in aid of their local club. Granted.

8th August 1933
James Roche, Skeffington Street requested the loan of six or eight forms for use in the Theatre Royal on Monday the 14th August. Granted.

19th September 1933
At the request of the Rev. President the use of the concert hall was granted free of charge to Mary Codd, Organist for the purpose of holding practice sessions for school-children for a concert entertainment to be held in December in aid of a charitable purpose.

December 1933
The 'Knights of St. Columbus' were given a loan of the Society's card tables and in December of 1934 the club wrote to them asking for the return of same. Over a year had passed and still the tables were not returned. The Society was not only kind but patient also.

21st March 1935
The 'Children's League of Pity' was given the use of the concert hall for their A.G.M.

October 1935
The club obviously got the tables back from the 'Knights of St. Columbus' because in October of this year the Civic Guards applied for the loan of our Whist Drive Tables for a whist drive that they were to hold shortly. Granted.

December 1935
Mr. O'Flaherty, a Solicitor from Enniscorthy inquired if the C.Y.M.S. would loan him the Card Tables for a whist drive that was been held for the purpose of helping to raise funds to carry out necessary repairs to *'the Cathedral'* in Enniscorthy. This application was also granted. At the same time it was recorded *owing to the falling-off of the receipts of the club during the year. It was decided that Fr. Sinnott and other members of the council would go to the Professional and other important people of the town and solicit subscriptions from them for the upkeep of the Society.* On the one hand the Society was giving and helping various groups and on the other soliciting for funds for the club.

January 1936
Mr. Byrne, Secretary of the 'Legion of Mary' inquired if the club would sell them some of the whist drive tables. They were offered to them at 5/= per table.

18th December 1937
The C.Y.M.S. ran a carnival to raise funds to help them pay for the extensive renovations that needed to be carried out on the premises. They offered to donate all the funds from the last night to the Mayoralty Fund for providing food, etc., for the poor of the town.

1939
The Society sent invalids to Lourdes in September of each year on a regular basis. 'The National Federation of the C.Y.M.S. of Ireland' organised this Pilgrimage and most of the branches would send around two invalids who were attended by a Doctor or medical staff. Forty- Eight pounds was raised from a whist drive and a 'sweep on the Derby' to pay for the 1939 pilgrimage. By the 23rd May the Society had forwarded both names of the invalids, the medical carers and the required medical details to the National Council. The two invalids selected to go were Matthew Murphy, Distillery Road, Wexford, and Thomas Heron, William Street. The pilgrimage was set to leave Dublin on the 6th September but the outbreak of war forced the C.Y.M.S. Federation to cancel it. To help the National Council to off-set some of their expenses due to the arrangements connected to the pilgrimage it was decided to pay them 12/6 for each invalid's booking.

1939
The Society responded to a request from the 'Loc Garman Brass Band' who requested a subscription towards their upkeep. The Society gave them 10/=.

June 1940
The Society gave a subscription of £5 to Miss J. Doyle, Hon. Secretary of the 'Catholic Girls Club' towards the expenses of five invalids sent on a pilgrimage to knock on Sunday 23rd June 1940.

Enniscorthy Cathedral

October 1940
The military authorities made an application on the 8th October requesting that the Society allow soldiers stationed in Wexford to have free use of the C.Y.M.S. club during their stay in Wexford. On the 15th October this request was granted subject to the rules of the Society.

1941
A contribution of £6 was made to the *'Fund for the Purchase of seed Potatoes for the poor of the town'* organised by the St. Vincent de Paul Society.

January 1943
Bridie Byrne, Hon. Secretary of the 'Glynn Branch of the Irish Red Cross' was granted the loan of the whist drive tables on the 12th January 1943.

January 1943
An application was made by the J.O.C's for the use of the Concert Hall for the holding of their annual entertainments. Two of their representatives George Bridges and John Keegan were invited to a Council meeting where they were given the terms and the hall was given free of charge.

1944
The Society's solicitors Messers Kirwan & Kirwan contracted them regarding the leases and the increase in the rents. The Society agreed with the advice given and whilst agreeing with a £4 increase on the property on Paul Quay they stipulated
It was not to take effect so long as the premises were being used by the Nuns of the St. John of God, for the purpose of providing 'Penny Dinners' for the poor of the town.

4th July 1944
The Hon. Secretary wrote a letter to the Local Defence Force inviting the military and members of the L.D.F. attending 'Summer Camp' in Wexford, *to the use of the club premises during their stay in Wexford.* On the 5th September Capt. M. Bates, Area Commander L.D.F. Wexford Area wrote thanking the Society for placing the club at the disposal of the L.D.F personnel attending the 'summer camp', Wexford Barracks.

June 1944
A circular was read from the Mayor of Wexford relating to the fund for the 'Brother Edmund Ignatius Rice Centenary'. The Society forwarded a subscription of one Guinea to the Hon. Secretary.

Brother Edward Ignatius Rice

10th February 1946
At the A.G.M. held on the10th February 1946 the Hon. Secretary read a circular received from Dr. George Hadden in connection with the formation of a 'Swimming Baths for Wexford'.

The Society appointed the Hon. Secretary as the Society's delegate to attend the meeting with the message *that the Society will give the project its full support.*

In September 1946
The Society wrote to the Franciscans inviting the friars to use the club premises freely as they wished. The Rev. Fr. Charles, O.F.M., Guardian wrote a letter of thanks to the Society regarding same.

7th January 1948
To end this decade it is recorded that on the 7th January 1948 the Society gave a subscription of £1-1-0 to the Manager of the National Bank for the 'Fund for the Relief of the Distressed People of King Street' caused by the recent flooding.

12th June 1951
The old table tennis table was given to the 'Catholic Boy scouts'. Also, 'the club presented the new boxing club with a boxing platform. Also this year the Society gave £12 to Sister Philip to be distributed by her among the deserving poor sick of the town. Sister Philip was a qualified nurse who attended the poor and needy and saw to it that they got food and medical attention when they needed it. This was prior to the establishment of the welfare state days, when everyone had to pay for their medical treatment.

12th February 1952
At the A.G.M. of the 12th February 1952 the following is recorded *The society expressed their sympathy with the members of the 'Crescent Boat Club'. On the loss they sustained in the disastrous fire to their club premises some few days before. And an invitation was extended to the members of the club to join the society in a temporary capacity until such time as they had rebuilt their premises or obtained alternative premises.*

26th March 1952
Hadden's of North Main Street requested the loan of chairs for the 26th of March. The club supplied these as requested. I wonder what was on at Hadden's that day. Here is evidence that the club even helped out some businesses in the town also.

October 1953
The 'Girl Guides' and the 'Apostolic Work Society' had a loan of the concert hall granted.

6th July 1954
The 'Catholic Boy Scouts' requested the use of the concert hall, table tennis room and the Council room for their reunion. It was agreed to let them have the use of these rooms for a nominal charge of £2 to cover the lighting and cleaning.

November 1954
'The National Council of the Blind *(Wexford Branch)'* was allowed to hold a jumble sale there at a nominal charge of £1 for lighting and cleaning.

December 1954
'The Apostolic Work Society' was back again and held a jumble sale in the concert hall. Granted.

Thursday 12th January 1956
The concert hall was given to the 'Catholic Boy Scouts' and the 'Girl Guides' again.

17th January 1956
The following letter was read out at the Council meeting. *Letters of thanks from Sister Philip and Sister Mary of the Sacred Heart and also from Sister Baptist for donations received.*

On the 3rd July 1956
The Society decided to donate £5 to the Barry Memorial Committee.

4th September 1956
The minutes record *It was decided to grant a request from the 'Loreto Convent Building and Repair Fund Committee' for a weeks Pongo. The dates to be September 21st to September 26th inclusive.*

2nd October 1956
The Loreto Convent Building Fund Committee were given the concert hall for Thursday night at a nominal charge of 10/= for lighting and cleaning. The 'National Council for the Blind of Ireland' had to be refused as they wanted bookings for the 16th and 17th October. The hall was fully booked-up and the Pongo was also running at this time.

1st October 1957
A letter from the 'Wexford Festival Council' was read *asking for the use of the shop premises for the three weeks prior to the Festival for the storage of costumes. On the proposition of Thomas O'Rourke and seconded by H.F. Doyle, it was decided to grant them the use of the premises free of charge on condition that it was used at their own responsibility.*

7th January 1958
A letter was read from Rev. Fr. McCartan O.F.M. Guardian, Franciscan Friary, Wexford *acknowledging the sum of seventy four pounds £74 from the Pongo Committee during the months of November-December.* On the same date another letter was read from Sister M. of the 'Sacred Heart, House of Mercy Laundry', Summerhill, Wexford. *Thanking the society for £10 worth of Christmas gifts which was donated to the girls of the House of Mercy.*

November 1959
In November 1959 members co-operated fully with the Irish Red Cross Society in the World Refugee collection. The C.Y.M.S. members acted as collectors at the various Masses.

1962
Throughout 1962 'The Prevention of Cruelty to Animals', 'the little Willie Committee' and 'The Girl Guides' all ran jumble sales in the concert hall free gratis.

The C.Y.M.S. of Wexford has good reason to be proud of its members considering all the charities that the branch has donated to over its history. Even in bad times when matters were not going too well for the club the Society still responded kindly to any good cause that approached it for donations. It was fortunate to have amongst its ranks giants of good men like Richard Devereux and James J. Stafford, two very charitable benefactors who were knighted by Popes for their good works.

To conclude this religious chapter, I would hope that the Wexford branch of the C.Y.M.S. of Ireland would live up to the faith of its founders and that its members continue to live worthy as guardians of Wexford Catholic tradition. It is a matter of great satisfaction for all to see that this branch has weathered the stress and strain of 153 years and is still flourishing. The C.Y.M.S. of Wexford gave unbroken service to the Catholic church in Wexford and to the Wexford people for over 153 years and let us pray that this marvellous tradition can be upheld and that a suitable legacy be left to the coming generations, as our forbearers did for us.

Finances and Fundraising

Donations to the C.Y.M.S.
(Incomplete)

August 1855
Fr. Roche gave books to the Society that was donated to the Bishop by Mr. Devereux for the parish and William Devereux contributed a glass case for the books valued at £5.

13th December 1855
John Cullen presented a brass lamp for suspension before the statue of the Blessed Virgin and Mr. Sinnott erected it. Miss O'Brien and Miss Laffin presented very beautiful artificial flowers for the altar.

20th March 1856
An anonymous gentleman promised to pay half of the £23 rent for the new house at Rowe Street for the Society.

21st October 1862
Brothers Rich Ryan, John Dunne and William J. Tucker subscribed liberally to the fund for the new hall.

November of 1862
Fr. Robert Cooke contributed £5 towards the new hall and Richard Devereux donated £100

31st August 1863
Fr. Hogan presented the club with a bust of His Holiness Pope Pius IX.

1892
Myles Gaffney and Frank Harpur of South Main Street donated 164 books to the Society's library.

29th July 1893
Fr. Hanton (*of the South African missions*) gave a picture of Fr. O'Brien the very first Hon. Secretary of the Society.

A.G.M. 1899
There were 133 subscriptions totalling £314-16-6 donated by the people of Wexford for the C.Y.M.S. fund to help them pay off the debt for their new premises at St. Iberius House, Commercial Quay.

20th February 1902
The Society received a donation of a 5/= postal order in an anonymous letter.

1942
A gift of £20 was given to the C.Y.M.S. for their funds from Mr. G. McDonald, Amusements Proprietor, and Rosslare Strand.

1949
A cheque for £50 for the branch and a cheque for £2 for the table tennis club was received from the estate of the late Capt. John Murphy a former member of the Society. Capt. Murphy had died in 1948.

February 1955
P. O'Brien, a member who died in September 1954, left the club a legacy of £25. It was stated by Jackie Donohoe that *Mr. P. O'Brien was the third member of the branch who had left money to the club.*

. . . .

Money from the Devereux Estate

4th February 1880
The following one liner *Temple Bar was ordered to give up.* Is in the minute book on this date with no discussion or explanation as to what was happening. It is Obvious that they either owned or held the lease on the property in order to have the authority to give such an instruction.

27th November 1928
Michael Kehoe, the Society's Vice-President & Treasurer and Richard Goold, the Society's Hon. Secretary, were appointed to represent the St. Iberius Catholic Club (*C.Y.M.S.*) at a meeting of representatives of the 'St. Vincent de Paul Society' and the 'Wexford Clothing Society' to be held in the Temperance Hall, Francis Street on Sunday at 11.30.a.m. for the purpose of discussing the position of the societies concerning the Devereux bequests and to ascertain what steps should be taken to clarify the matter in the interest of all concerned.

29th January 1985
The branch received a letter from Messrs Kirwan & Kirwan, Solicitors in connection with the Society's one-third share of the proceeds of the sale of the free sample interest in the Devereux estate in respect of Mr & Mrs Jeremiah and Jean Callaghan's premises at 27 South Main Street, Wexford. The cheque was for £1,703.66.

5th March 1985

The branch received a letter from Messer's Kirwan & Kirwan Solicitors seeking the Council's permission to pay the sum of £2,400 to Dr. Annie Stafford This was the valuation figure of Raymond Corish & Co. Ltd. for the purchase of the fee simple on a premises situated at Paul Quay held by Dr. Stafford under a 60 year lease from 25th March 1944 at an annual rent of £20. The Council agreed to this.

9th January 1993

Messrs Kirwan & Kirwan, Solicitors contacted the Hon. Sec. regarding the sale of 'The Raven Bar', one-third of which was bequeathed to the club by the Devereux estate. One third was bequeathed to the Wexford Clothing Society and the remaining one-third to the St. Vincent de Paul. The Vincent de Paul had at this time taken over the Wexford Clothing Society. The amount offered was £10,000 of which the club would receive one third and the Solicitors informed the club that the St. Vincent de Paul has already accepted the amount. At a further meeting of the branch Council on 8th February 1994 concerning the Devereux estate, it was decided to accept the offer of one third (£3,333.33) of the £10,000 offered by the sub-tenants Messrs. Clooney and Smith.

War Loan Investments 1915

On the 13th July 1915 a special meeting was called to consider the possibility of investing in the *'new war loans'*. The entry states *This meeting was called for the purpose of considering the advisability of investing a portion of the surplus funds of the club in the 'New War Loan' or other security.* Having carefully considering the matter it was unanimously decided to invest the sum of £100 in the new war loan and Rev. J. Hore, Administrator, Robert Hanton J.P., Laurence Harpur and William Hutchinson were appointed as trustees for the purpose of this investment.

The Entertainment/Amusement Committees for Raising Funds 1900s

In 1901 the committee staged a Smoking concert and on the 2nd February 1902 another Smoking concert was held in the concert hall for which the takings were £10-3-7 with expenses of £9-8-7 leaving a profit of 15/= for the Society. In the same year the Camptown Serenader's contributed a sum of £11-0-1 towards the club's funds. On the 1st April 1902 the secretary of the Amusement Committee requested the secretary of the Campdown Serenader's to ascertain *if it was possible to put on an entertainment for the benefit of the Society.* but they were unable to help at the time. Later in the year we read *There was no incidental aid such as plays, concerts etc., this year.* In 1907 the annual Smoking concert was held *of which there was an average attendance of eight members.* I cannot enlighten you as to what exactly a smoking concert is and furthermore if a total of eight people was the average attendance it doesn't sound like much of a concert does it? In the same year John White the organiser of the amusements held in the concert hall reported takings of £14-10-7 with expenses of £10-10-7 leaving a profit of £4 for the Society's funds.

1910s

On the 7th of April 1918 it is recorded that *Capt. Busher and P. J. O'Connor (snr.), were elected as a Visiting committee for the month of April.* There is no explanation as to what the Visiting committee was for or

what function they performed. On the 14th of April the *Preparation of the various rooms and concert hall were to be organized by the Visiting committee.* One must assume that they were in charge of dealing with the visitors and ladies coming into the club for the whist drive and the dance that was now to be held on the new date of 25th April instead of the 5th May. We are informed that the Amusements Committee was also working with them on this project.

1920s

On the 13th of February 1923 mention is made of the fact that for three years the club was suffering financially and in an effort to generate some funds the following members were appointed to a new Amusements Committee with *a mandate to devise some means of entertainment that would provide some extra income for the club.*

Edward F. O'Rourke

The committee was made up of the following - Rev. P. Doyle C.C., Edward F. O'Rourke, and Joseph Fennell.

On the 22nd of March 1927 yet another Amusements Committee was appointed with the power to control the renting out of the concert hall. The committee consisted of the following members - Thomas Hayes, Edward F. O'Rourke, William Hynes, James Kelly, Michael Kennedy, John Cullimore, John Doyle and Martin O'Connor.

1930s

The Society organised a sweep held on the Grand National this year. The club's funds were increased by £28. First

Martin O'Connor
1862 - 1938

prize was £7 won by James T. Kehoe, second prize was £3-10 won by Rev. G. Murphy and the third prize of £2 went to A. Wickham. William Hynes won £1 as seller of the winning ticket. In February 1930 the Thrift Fund was initiated whereby members could save money. The fund was organised and managed under the patronage of the Rev. President and the Vice-president Mr. Kehoe. The idea was to encourage thrift among the young members and to give them the opportunity to save. The saver could lodge whatever amount he wished and could withdraw whatever they wished whenever they wished. In less than twelve months there was over £300 lodged in the savings account.

In 1935 the committee organised and ran a Football Pool which made a profit of £1-5-0 for the Society. They ran it again the following year and made a profit of 10/= which was less than half the previous year's profit. *The Entertainments Committee were praised by the Council for their past year in running Dances, Billiards Handicap, Snooker Handicap and Cards Handicap. (Sic)* - A.G.M. 2nd February 1936. Does anyone know what a *Cards Handicap* is? The committee ran a Whist Drive and a Sweep on the Derby to raise funds to send invalids to Lourdes in 1938.

1940s

In the 1930s the most popular method of raising cash for the club was holding Card Drives and in the 1940s the Amusements Committee changed to Horse Racing and began running sweeps on the various races. In 1941 they ran a Sweep on the Manchester November Handicap. On the 15th December 1942 the Amusement Committee ran a Sweep on the Nass Chase and the profit on this was £30-10-0. The committee handed in over £50-18-8 to the Council from its profit making activities during this year.

The Amusements Committee organised a Sweep on the Leopardstown £1,000 Chase on the 24th October 1943. The Entertainments/Amusements Committee was revised in September 1946 after a lapse of two years (*see members listings*).

On 21st January 1947 the Amusements Committee decided to run a Sweep on the Grand National. Tickets were to be 1/= and prizes of £10 for first Prize, £5 for second, £2 for third and 5/= for each starter with £1 for the seller of the winning ticket and £1 for the seller of the greatest number of tickets. Unfortunately, by the 4th March, John F. O'Rourke, the Hon. Secretary of the Amusements Committee, informed the Council that the aforementioned sweep mentioned at the last meeting could not proceed as *there were other sweeps in the town for the same race offering more attractive prizes and for a smaller priced ticket.* This was a big disappointment to the Council as they badly needed funds and we read that on the 9th September the Hon. Secretary of the Council made a report to that meeting which stated that *The Society was in a bad way financially and* that there were *accounts owing totalling over £100 and that we were only £10 in credit at the bank.* In November it was decided to approach the National Bank and enquire if it was possible for the club to be facilitated with an overdraft due to the financial position. By the 9th November the Bank Manager had replied and given permission for an overdraft facility of £100

1950s

The Concert Hall Committee or the Whist Drive Committee ran a whist drive in 1952. The Pongo Working Committee, of which I was a member for some years, took over all the fund raising activities from 1955 to 1964. The Pongo story is covered in a separate section. The committees were the money generators of the Society and without these men the Society would have been in financial ruin. Therefore, we should be grateful to all the members of these various working committees throughout the years. They gave freely of their leisure time to serve the club so admirably. It would be hard to meet a more dedicated and altruistic group of men who so conscientiously performed their allotted duties. Without the selfless dedication of these men the club would not have survived throughout the years.

(See Appendix No 5, on page 281 for the list of 'Entertainment / Amusements Committees' for raising funds (1907 to 1964).

The Iberian Grand Bazaar 1899

On the 15th February 1899 the following thirteen members comprising some of the most impressive and influential gentlemen of Wexford were appointed to form the 'Bazaar Organising Committee':

Bazaar Organising Committee

Michael J. O'Connor, Esq., Solicitor
Michael A. Ennis, Esq., J.P.
Patrick Ryan, Esq., Mayor of Wexford
James E. Berry, Esq., J.P.
John J. Walsh (snr.), Auctioneer
John J. Walsh (jnr.), Auctioneer
Frank Walsh, Businessman
Martin Pierce, Proprietor Iron Works
M. McKenny
Hugh McCarthy, Proprietor Whites Hotel
John FitzSimmons, Businessman
John M. Walsh, the People Newspaper
James McGuire, the Free Press

Having taken possession of the new premises 'St. Iberius House' in Common Quay Street, the Society had to raise the finance to pay for it so on the 31st August 1899 a meeting was called to make arrangements for the proposed bazaar. The Bazaar Committee invited the Mayor and members of the Corporation to the opening ceremony and it was arranged that all the club's Council members would attend at 2.00.p.m. on the Sunday to receive the Corporation. The Iberian Grand Bazaar as it was called took place on Sunday, Monday and Tuesday of the 3rd, 4th and 5th of September 1899.

Pupils from the Presentation, Mercy and St. John of God schools took part in the amusements of the bazaar. There were two bands present – The Gorey Band and the Military Band. There was, also, a piano and other music, a lottery table, a roulette table and refreshment stalls. Many ladies organised and managed the various stalls as per the list below. The bazaar made a profit of £711-13-5 which was an astronomical amount of money for that time and was a godsend to the Society which paid for the new premises. Out of all the tickets sold in the bazaar there were thirty-eight prizes awarded and I was amazed when I perused the list of winners, 23 to Wexford, 3 to Dublin, 2 to Killurin, 1 to Cork, 1 to Enniscorthy, 1 to Newtownbarry, 1 to Ballygalvert, 1 to Ballykillane, 1 to Grange, 1 to Shillelagh, 1 to Liverpool, 1 to Birmingham, and 1 to Newport in Wales. The number of tickets sold must have run into thousands in order to accumulate that amount of profit.

A Summary of the Proceeds of the Various Stalls

TABLE NO.	MANNED BY	TICKET SALES	TABLE SALES
No. 1	Misses Mernagh	£3-2-0	£22-6-0
No. 2	Misses Somers	£21-10-0	£50-10-0
No. 3.	Misses Hutchinson	£16-0-0	£29-10-0
No. 4	Miss Gregory	£24-16-1	£32-11-1
No. 5	Mrs. Dr. Pierse	£20-0-9	£30-0-9
No. 6	Miss Harpur	£21-10-0	£22-0-0
No. 7	Mrs. O'Connor and Mrs Hanton	£36-1-8	£69-4-8
No. 8	Mrs. D. Keating	£9-3-0	£33-18-9
No. 9	Mrs. Corcoran	£24-15-9	£37-19-0
No. 10	Mrs. J. J. Kehoe	£31-0-0	£34-10-0

The Flower Stall was run by Mrs Frank Carty and sold £7 worth of tickets whilst the 'Art Union' sold £4 worth. Some of the people who subscribed cash amounts were:

The Right Hon. Lord Maurice FitzGerald, Johnstown Castle
Surgeon Major Stafford
John M. Walshe, the People Newspaper
Patrick Byrne, Bullring
Rev. P. Doyle, Administrator
James Sinnott, South Main Street
Michael J. O'Connor
John J. Walsh, Wellingtonbridge
Michael A. Ennis, Ardruagh
Frank O'Connor, North Main Street
William Hutchinson
John Harpur
James O'Rourke
Edward O'Rourke
Patrick Ryan, Mayor
Martin Pierce, Iron Works, Mill Road
Matthew Doyle, Charlotte Street
John Tyghe, John Street.
Michael O'Rourke, School Street
Most of the members of the Society also gave donations

Room Rental

The Reading Room

The Bridge Club must have occupied this room for some time as the Hon. Secretary was requested *to write to the secretary of the bridge club. Informing them that their rent for the reading room on Tuesdays and Fridays would be increased to 7/= per night as from the 1st October 195.* The bridge club did not accept this and requested that their rent be set at 12/= for the two nights and the Council agreed. The Reading Room was rented to Celtic Soccer Club for their committee meetings. The Branch Council held their meetings there on a regular basis and also the Gaelic League rented it for a while. The Wexford Credit Union used it to collect their deposits from members and the Ladies Bridge Club had it one night per week in 1962. A Mr. D.F. Kennedy, Area Inspector and representative for The Provident Clothing & Supply Co. Ltd., 28 Dunham Road, Liverpool was most interested in having this room as an office in the area. The Wexford Passion Play Group also rented it in 1964. There was a Painting Exhibition held there over the Wexford Festival week one year. The Mentally Handicap Children's Committee was there in June 1965 and Cathal O'Gara, Chairman of the Dramatic Group had the room above the Reading room at one stage.

The Gymnasium Room (later to become the Table Tennis Room)

The famous Jem Roche, a member of the club, had hired this room for his training for the big fight in 1908 and he also rented it on and off for years for training young boxers. On the 2nd November 1913 the County Wexford Football Team had it for training and practice for their forthcoming match with Kerry. Incidentally, Jem Roche helped the team with their training. The Wexford Cycling & Athletic Club rented it for 3/= per week in 1934, 1936 and 1937 and the Young Christian Students Club had it for 3/6 per week in February 1940. On 23rd of September 1941 Dermot Cadogan, South Main Street requested the Gymnasium to use for rehearsals for a Pantomime. This was refused because the Council understood that *"Ladies were to take part in it"*.

A Mr. Clarke made an application for the room on behalf of the Catholic Youth Association in December of 1941. They wanted to use it as a boxing room and they got it for 2/6 per week. The J.O.C. had it by March 1943 at a weekly rent of 5/= *(3/6 and 1/6 for light)*. There was a proviso that the electric bulbs were not to exceed 60 Watts and they were also *warned that no ladies were to be allowed into the gymnasium.* The J.O.C. ran their Youth Hostel in Curracloe during the summer months so they did not require the gym then but they resumed usage in the winter months. The Knights of Malta also shared the room with the J.O.C. on alternative nights. In November 1945 a Thomas Fortune, 26 High Street looked for the gym but he was refused. V. J. McAlinden, Hon. Secretary of the R.S.P.C.A. applied for rooms in April of 1946 and this also was refused due to non-availability. Occasionally the Table Tennis Room was rented out and The Knights of Malta had it for a Children's Party on New Year's Day 1960. The Wexford Festival Event Committee occupied it in October 1964 and it was rented to William Hayes for five years next. The Catholic Boy Scouts rented it in 1974 and the Ladies Table Tennis Committee used this Gymnasium Room at one time for their meetings.

Ladies Table Tennis Room

This room was rented out from 3rd June 1958 onwards so perhaps this is the date on which the ladies Table Tennis club ceased to exist. Unfortunately, there is very little recorded concerning the ladies of the club. This room was rented to the Wexford Little Theatre Group from this date until the end of August for a charge of 10/= per week with the proviso *that they finish by 11.30.p.m. each night.* Another room located near the ladies Table Tennis room *(unidentified)* was utilised by the St. Aidan's Dramatic Class 'Muintir Na Tire' for a weekly charge of 15/= for Monday, Wednesday and Thursday nights.

The Shop

In the early 1930s both the shop and storeroom together were used as a motor vehicle garage and motor vehicles were garaged there. The insurers wrote to the club on the 28th January 1930 enquiring as to *how much petrol was to be stored there.* On the Hibernian Insurance Co. fire policy form, dated 19th February 1930, the club has filled in *Carrier and that the motor vehicles will be used for this purpose'* on the form as being the nature of the business.

A Mrs. Connors had the shop and a room rented from1934 to 1936. The minutes record that *The shop was rented to George Bridges (a Society member) for the usual rent for three weeks at Christmas.--* Minute book 4th December of 1956. George, no doubt, needed storage space for the Christmas toys, as his own shops in Selskar were quite small and would have been stocked to capacity at that time of year. His shops used to be stacked ceiling high almost George told me that his house was stacked high with toys coming up to the Christmas time. I recall being brought down there one Christmas as a child and when I saw all the toys I thought that that man was working for Santa Clause.

The following advertisement appeared in the People newspaper in September of 1957 –
Shop to Let. Recently constructed and decorated lock-up shop at the C.Y.M.S. commercial Quay Wexford. Suitable for shop or offices. Apply Hon. Sec. C.Y.M.S. Wexford. Many applications and enquiries ensued. Two of the interested parties were a Mr. Scanlan of Charlotte Street and a P. Doran of 3 Lambert Terrace. The rent for the shop was set at £100 per year. At a meeting of the Council on 8th November of the same year we read *On Mr. Donohoe's [The Hon. Sec.] Suggestion it was decided to write to the contractors for the building of the New Bridge, offering them offices and store for rent.* That is what you call using your entrepreneurial spirit. However, nothing further is recorded concerning the matter so one must assume that it did not come to fruition.

The Council Chamber Room

The Town Tenants' meetings were held there in the 1930s and Mrs English's Bridge Club tenancy began on 11th November 1947. She rented the room for two nights weekly – Tuesday and Friday from 7.00.p.m. to 11.30.p.m. at a charge of 12/= per week.

The Storeroom

On 15th July 1902 M.A. Ennis requested the Council to rent part of the storeroom to the Technical School Class until such time as the school for this purpose was built. They held an agricultural class there and paid a fee of £6 per year. In 1907 it is recorded that the parting of the manual class of the Technical Institute from the premises would incur a loss of £6 a year rent. One must assume that their new school was now built. Paddy Brady, a Society member, rented the storeroom for 7/6 per week from 1934 to November 1937 and another Society member, James A. Lambert, rented it in August 1938. He paid the going rate which was 6/= per week. Was poor Paddy Brady being overcharged then?

The Room over the Storeroom

The Gaelic Athletic club rented this room in 1928. We know this because a Mr. Corry, the treasurer of that club was £2-12-6 overdue with his rent on the 10th April of that year.

The Spare Storeroom Adjoining the Billiard Room

On the 10th December 1929 the secretary of the local branch of the Catholic Boy Scouts requested the use of *the spare store room adjoins the Billiards room* for their meetings and practices. This was placed in the hands of Fr. Sinnott, the President, to enquire as to what their requirements would be. On 17th December it had been decided to grant them the room for a rent of 5/= per week commencing on the 11th January 1930. I am not quite sure which room is referred to here but I am inclined to think that it was the room which later became the table tennis room.

Any Available Room

On the 25th September 1925 a John H. Williams, Board of Works, Waterford wrote to the club requesting the use of a room for an inspection office, the rent to include gaslights, fires and cleaning. The club's reply stated – rent of £35 per year inclusive of gas lights, fires and the service of the caretaker for lighting of fire and cleaning of the room.

The Superintendent followed up this communication offering £30 per year for the room and this was agreed and signed on the 13th October 1925. The Inspector of Telegraphs from the Office of Public Works took up residency shortly after signing the agreement

The Concert Hall

(See section on Concert Hall where Renting is dealt with)

Revenue Commissioners

On the 20th May 1884 it is recorded in connection with the club's sale of old newspapers and magazines etc.(*see Library section*) that *The secretary was threatened with a prosecution for selling the papers in the 1st April, auction.* The Inland Revenue decided to discontinue with the prosecution due to the particular circumstances of the case. Alderman Walsh, on hearing what happened, offered to sell the papers and magazines at any time that the Council wished. John J. Walsh was a professional auctioneer and a member of the Society and it is reasonable to assume that he offered his services free gratis.

On the 12th February 1924 A. O'Leary of the St Vincent de Paul Society requested the Society to confer with him regarding the income tax charged and deducted from the bequest of the Devereux estate for some years past. Two representatives from the club, Mr. Kehoe the Vice-President and Mr. Goold the Hon. Secretary, accompanied the St. Vincent de Paul people to meet with Mr. Hanton, the income tax official, regarding the matter.

Brendan Corish T.D.

On the 6th August 1946 the Hon. Secretary reported that he had received a paying order for £3-4-2 in respect of a refund of Entertainment Tax on tickets that were left over from dances. The series of dances held at the Town Hall had made a profit of £115 by September 1949. Using the charitable status the club applied for the refund of tax on this profit. Alas, they were shocked by the reply from the taxman. A letter was received from the Customs & Excise office *Refusing Repayment of Entertainment Duty* on the recent dances held at the Town hall. On the 8th November 1949 the Hon. Secretary was instructed to make further inquiries regarding the matter.

He promptly despatched a letter to Wexford's man in Government, Brendan Corish T.D. and Parliamentary Secretary at that time. Brendan replied and his letter was read out in the Council meeting held on 6th December 1949. It read: *a letter was read from Brendan Corish T.D., Parliamentary Secretary that he was making representations to the Minister for Finance with a view to having the question of refunding entertainment tax reconsidered by the Minister for Finance and the Revenue Commissioners.*

It comes in very handy knowing someone in the government and even handier having a member of the Society in the government. Brendan's intervention on behalf of the Society was successful as we see from his next letter regarding our application for refund of entertainment tax on the dances run last year. Brendan informs us *he had heard from the Revenue Commissioners that a refund of £33-3-3 was being made to us.* The Hon. Secretary was instructed to write to Mr. Corish *Thanking him for his intervention.* – 2nd May 1950.

CYMS HALL

Insurance Costs

I will not elaborate on all the costs of insurance to the Society throughout the years but I think this one piece of information might be of interest seeing as the Society is a Catholic institution.

The rising cost of insurance on the premises was a bone of contention for years so the Council decided that they would write to the **Irish Catholic Church Property Insurance Co. Ltd.**, 19 & 20 Fleet Street, Dublin, 2 to acquire a quotation for the fire insurance. If the Council thought that this 'Catholic Church Property' company would be more sympathetic to them on account of their mutual religious persuasion they were in for a rude awakening.

They replied on the 7th May 1946 and the estimate for the fire insurance premium submitted by them was much higher than the premium the club was already paying to the **Hibernian Fire & General Insurance Co. Ltd.** So naturally they decided to stay with Hibernian.

History of the C.Y.M.S. Pongo

I am sure many people think that the Lottery is a 21st century invention. Not so, as in Italy in the 1500s the Italian Government ran a state lottery entitled *'Lo Giuco De Lotto.'* So the history and origins of the game can be traced back to Italy. You can call it what you will: Lotto, Tombola, Bingo, Pongo or Housie Housie – they are all derivatives from the same source. The French had it in the 1700s and they called it *'Le Lotto'* and this game was very similar to the present day Bingo. It had spread all over Europe by the 1800s. In 1800 the German Educational Authorities used the Lotto to teach children multiplication tables. It appeared on the other side of the Atlantic as a game called 'Beano' *(Nothing to do with the comic of the same name).* It was first played in the U.S.A. at a carnival near Atlanta in the State of Georgia in 1929. The game had by now developed into something resembling the game of to-day. It was played with cardboard cards and dried beans were used to mark the numbers called out and players completing a full line would shout *'Beano.'*

A New York toy salesman observed the game and took it to New York where it was played amongst his friends. Tradition has it that one of his friends mistakenly cried out *'Bingo'* instead of *'Beano'* in their excitement. A man called Lowe promoted Bingo printing cards day and night. He teamed-up with a Catholic Priest from Pennsylvania and established the game further afield. Lowe was selling the cards and he also received one dollar per year from anyone using the game. In the depression years over 10,000 games a week were being played and the game had spread all over the U.S.A. by the 1940s. A sum of almost 90 million dollars was being spent each week on the game by the 1990s. Bingo became popular in Australia in the early 20th century where it was called *'Housie Housie.'* It was played in marquees and when you completed a full line you would call out *'House.'*

The history of the C.Y.M.S. Pongo club begins way back in the days when Bingo wasn't even heard of in Ireland. This statement must be difficult for Bingo players to envisage but nonetheless there was a time when Ireland was struggling along without Bingo. Bingo's forerunner 'Housie Housie' was run at Carnivals *(Fairs)* as a rule. I suspect the game may have being called by another name, perhaps Lotto or Tombola, I'm not too sure. This game also made its appearance in children's Christmas games *(Mr. Lowe's handiwork)* that were the popular thing of the day. The grown-ups of the household would play the housie-housie when they got fed-up playing cards. In the 1940s various clubs around the town were also starting to play this game. The C.Y.M.S. was running a 'House Game' the first mention of it was on the 14th of March 1948 where it *was permitted to let the game of 'House' be played in the Society on Sunday mornings for one hour.* The next record of it was on the 1st March 1949. At a meeting of the Council they granted the organising committee *permission for a continuation of the game of house was granted.* There is nothing further recorded as to whether this game was a success or not for another four or five years. However, it is obvious from the records that a 'Pongo Game' was being run in the town by a Mr. Redmond. This we can deduce from a meeting held on the 6th July 1954 when *it was decided to run a Pongo session one night each week* and a Mr. Redmond the proprietor of the "Pongo Booth" was approached by a representative of the Council about obtaining the same.

By October of the same year we learn that Mr. Redmond

was agreeable to allow the C.Y.M.S. have the use of the Pongo Booth. From this meeting a sub-committee was appointed to discuss the business of organising a Pongo game at the club. The names of this committee were: Thomas Hayes, G. Leahy, Thomas Kelly, Thomas O'Rourke, P. J. Roice and George and Victor Bridges. This sub-committee of seven announced that the game of Pongo would commence in the near future and that they would need the use of the Concert Hall on all available nights. Pongo had arrived, in theory at least, and it was hoped that the badly needed funds, which the club needed to survive, would soon be forthcoming.

So the Council and the 'magnificent seven' men of the sub-committee discussed the introduction of the game to the branch and how to run it as a charitable enterprise. The magnificent seven shrunk very rapidly to two men when it was realised just what commitment was required to run this Pongo game. For we read: *As none of the Council members were in a position to help out in running the Pongo, etc., etc., etc., Blah, blah, Blah.* Need I say more? As it happened Thomas Kelly and Thomas O'Rourke were the two who actually did the work at that stage and by 4th January of 1955 we read that Thomas Kelly proudly reported that the club had made a profit of £100 from the Pongo. Jackie Donohoe, the Secretary, was instructed by the Council to enquire if it was legal for a charitable organisation such as the C.Y.M.S. to continue running Pongo. All concerned were over the moon with the success of the game and what it meant for the finances of the club. God only knows what the Society would have done without this game and the profit it brought to the branch in later years. It is no exaggeration to say that the club would have had to close its doors.

An Englishman named Douglas Knox-Crichton visited Wexford in 1955 and started what could be called an '*Amusement Arcade*' at number 3, Anne Street just opposite the old Shamrock Bar. He had rented the property from Mr. Lambert. We young lads nicknamed it 'Knoxies Place.' There were slot machines, game machines, Pongo and he had the 'Fattest Lady in the World' (*or

so he claimed*) in a small room which cost three pence to see. My pal the late Michael Nolan and I paid to go in and see her. She was just sitting there smiling. With hindsight I think she was smiling at us young idiots for spending our money believing that we were going to see the 'Fattest Lady in the World' instead of just a woman in a big rubber suit. Eventually the Guards raided the place and stopped the Pongo game. In the People Newspaper dated 19th February 1955 a headline reads *Playing of 'Pongo' justice and the law. Two defendants fined a farthing each.* Mr. Douglas Knox-Crichton of 3, Anne Street and the proprietor of the rented property Mr. Lambert together with twelve named persons who were caught playing 'Pongo' on the premises by the Guards were all were brought up in court for the crime of contravening the Gaming Act of 1954, which according to Judge McDonagh was *in operation for 101 years past'* and further explained that *Pongo is the old game of "House', and is as old as the 1854 Gaming Act itself.* Judge McDonagh's remarks relating to the age of the game of Pongo are very interesting. Fintan O'Connor represented the fourteen defendants in court and managed to get Mr. Lambert and Mr. Douglas Knox-Crichton off with a farthing fine each and the good Judge applied the Probation Act to the twelve caught on the premises.

By 1955 Thomas O'Rourke was *'placed in complete charge of the game.'* Thomas had the game up-and-running military style in no time *(Tom had been a Lieutenant in the L.D.F.)* His helpers were Thomas Kelly and Lar Roche. They handed in a profit of £90 by 20th September 1955. There is no further mention of the Pongo club this year. The game was run in the old table tennis room at this time and it was later relocated down-stairs to the concert hall, which was more spacious and had an adjoining ladies toilet and cloakroom. It was also easier for people to find as the concert hall double doors opened out onto Common Quay Street almost opposite Jimmy O'Brien's public house 'The Slaney Bar'. This was handy for the lads who liked to nip over for a 'quick wan' in the intervals between games.

1956 kicked-off with a letter to the Chief Superintendent of the Garda Siochana requesting a permit to play the game of Pongo in the Concert Hall of the club. Fr. O'Neill, the branch President, was asked *if it would be alright to run the game of Pongo on the Sunday nights during Lent.* Fr. O'Neill's reply was that it was okay to run it during the week of Lent but not on the Sunday nights.

Matters were improving. This year because the Pongo made a profit of £514-0-9 for the Society. In his closing speech at the A.G.M. Fr. O'Neill congratulated and made a *special tribute to the Pongo Sub-Committee Bros. Thomas O'Rourke, William Murphy, Wally Cleary and Thomas Mahon who devoted a lot of time to making the Society financially sound.* – Rev. O'Neill, Adm. President Wexford Branch, A.G.M. 19th February 1956. You will note that our President never mentioned my name on the list. Tom Mahon told me that the reason for this was because I was under age *(I was only fifteen years of age).*

The Society received a bit of a shock on the 22nd February. The Chief Superintendent of the Garda *regretted that he was unable to grant permission for the game of Pongo.* I am unaware as to what procedures followed from this or if someone used some influence to rescind or bypass the Superintendent's decision but one thing is certain – the C.Y.M.S. Pongo game continued irrespectively.

The application for a licence for the game of Pongo was applied for in the individual name of Thomas J. Kelly, the Hon. Secretary of the Society. Another member Fintan O'Connor, Solicitor put our case forward at the District Court in Wexford on Wednesday 20th June. This application was the first such application under the Gaming and Lotteries Act, of 1955. The Corporation had adopted the Act on May 11th. In our application we had stated our intentions as follows:

Wally Cleary

1. To run the game of Pongo at a price of 2d *(pence)* per game per person and the prize would be 5/=. *(Shillings)* per time. *(Note: This was a modest request in view of the Act actually allowing 6d. per game and 10s. (Shillings) prize money).* We were going in much lower than that which was required.

2. By rigid rule no person under the age of sixteen years would be admitted (on the premises).

The committee would prepare a programme of good entertainment *(This was conditional apparently).* They intended to have Concerts that would include singing, instrumental recitals, monologues, dramatic productions and lectures.

Inspector J. H. Barr had no objections to the application and the Justice granted the application.

At the Council meeting held on the 3rd July 1956 it is recorded that *The Hon. Sec. reported that the District Justice had granted the Society a Licence under the Gambling and Lotteries Act 1956.* This was all conditional on *other forms of entertainment being provided.* The entertainment that was actually staged was simply music i.e., records and later a tape made by Tommy Carroll. Tommy was on Rattigan's Ceili Band at the time, which was known as 'Ceoltoiri Loc Garman Ceili Band'. Tommy with his piano accordion recorded a tape full of Irish music for the Pongo.

William Murphy

The Council then decided to hold the Pongo on Friday, Saturday, Sunday, Monday and Tuesday nights from 9.00.p.m. to 11.30.p.m.

The following sub-committee were appointed to take charge of it – Thomas O'Rourke Chairman, William Murphy Vice-Chairman, Thomas Mahon, Walter Cleary, and the Society's Hon. Secretary. This sub-committee was *obliged to submit a full financial report of the takings and expenses to the monthly Council meetings and also to give full details as to the concert items provided.*

The takings and general business of the Pongo Committee for the month of August this year was as follows: Profit £62-2-3 and Expenses £20. Itemised as follows – Thomas O'Rourke, William Murphy, Thomas Mahon, Wally Cleary and the ball boy *(yours truly)* all received 10/= each per week. We worked five nights from 9.00.p.m. to 11.30.p.m. which was twelve and a half hours for 10/=. If some people thought that this was good money how come they were not forming a queue to take the jobs? Oh Yes! There were the usual begrudgers and grumblers in the club who thought that we should sacrifice five nights of our lives every week for nothing. When such people were challenged to come and join us they quickly became muted.

The Pongo was a lifesaver for the club. Without the cash that was earned the club would not be in existence today. The club was encountering massive financial expense for repairs to the premises at this time and it was not making money from the membership subscriptions, the billiards room, or sufficient from the renting out of rooms.

To comply more fully with the Licensing Act the club had to put-on some other forms of entertainment besides just tape recordings and this led to the birth of the C.Y.M.S. dramatic group. The Pongo committee ran these with help from some members of the Society who had theatrical experience. So the *'Pongo crowd'* as they were known, organised variety concerts in 1956 which were staged in the concert hall. This activity had not been seen in the club for many years. After an initial success in the club, the group went *'on the road'* and the shows were staged in Broadway, Blackwater, Fethard, Oylegate, Ferns, Duncannon, Courtown Harbour and Rosslare Strand. Please consult further in the drama section.

At the Annual General Meeting held on 23rd February 1958 Fr. O'Neill in his address said *I also would like to thank the Pongo committee who came down night after night for the wonderful work they were doing, not only for the Society but for other charitable purposes as well. The Friary received the sum of £74, the Legion of Mary £33-3-10, St. Michael's Industrial School received goods valued at £10 and the Loreto Building Fund £5, and they were also sending Lar Roche on the Diocesan Pilgrimages to Lourdes this year.* – Fr. O'Neill, President of the branch address to the A.G.M. 23rd February 1958.

At a meeting in December Fr. Clancy whilst praising the Pongo committee for the large sum of money that they earned for the Society went on to warn *that the Pongo committee were in danger of making the C.Y.M.S. a gambling school.* He then suggested that they should *"limit the hours for Pongo"* and also *'limit the number of cards to be issued to each person.'*

When one reads this criticism from Fr. Clancy one wonders did he ever listen to what was being said at the club's meetings? This club was surviving on the money from Pongo and the alternative to living on this 'gambling money' was to close the club down. Fr. O'Neill our President had a similar point of view on this occasion. He

said: *A special word of gratitude was due to the Pongo committee for the funds, without which the Society would be financially embarrassed* and continued *The Society had to face a certain amount of criticism with regards to gambling or Pongo.* He went on *It is the Society's duty as a Catholic Action Organisation to see we do not encourage gambling and steps should be taken to ensure this.* That's a final statement on the matter, is it not? Up to this stage Fr. O'Neill has been very

Rev. Martin F. Clancy, C.C.

sympathetic to the club's financial dilemma, but it now seems that the Society will have to deal with the matter. It should be said that Fr. Clancy was only a temporary President for a few months at this time and quite frankly I do not feel that he was 'au fait' with the running and business of the Society nor was he sympathetic towards the Society as a whole. For instance he was one of the few priests in Wexford who never became a member of the Society so how could he be conversant with matters pertaining to the club.

The Pongo section provided a social evening and was the only outlet or entertainment for most people in Wexford apart from the three cinemas in the town and the odd concert or play now and again. The Pongo supporters evolved into a kind of unofficial social club. Many people made new friends which developed into lasting friendships at those gathering. The C.Y.M.S. Pongo nights became as important to these people as the cinema was to most other people. The Pongo Committee in its wisdom decided to make it official by turning it into a 'Pongo Club' and holding the Annual Pongo Reunion Dinner and Dance. These events were usually held around Christmas time. Mrs. Michael Mahon *(Maggie),* Mrs. Tom O'Rourke *(Fanny),* Mrs John Cullimore, Mrs. Banville , Josie Cleary and Bridie Swords all played their part on the Ladies Organising Committees for the reunions.

The Mayor Jim Morris singing at the C.Y.M.S. (Pongo Club) Reunion on Wednesday 5th April 1961, accompanying him is Mrs. H. Johnson from John Street. in the background is Tom Mahan, a club official.

Pongo Club Reunion 1959

Mrs. T. O'Rourke   Mrs. Michael Mahon

Pongo Reunion December 1959

(Lt. to Rt.) Miss Hickey - Aggie Dunne - Tom Mahon - Bill Shiggins - Jack Cullen - unidentified
Josie Cleary - Bridie Swords - Mrs. Mernagh - Mai Johnson

Tom Mahon and Bridie Swords dancing in the concert hall at the dinner and dance reunion of 1959 and to the left we have Tom's father Michael Mahon (snr.). Who gave us an exhibition of Irish dancing to the delight of the onlookers.

Pongo Club Reunion night 1959

Mr. Michael Mahon,Snr. giving a demonstration of his
Irish dancing skills in the St. Iberius (C.Y.M.S.) concert hall.

Reunion dance in the concert hall in the
late 1950's. Bridie Swords and Tom Mahon
stepping it out in fine style

...ge Working Committee, Christmas 1958

Lt. to Rt. Back Row: Bill Murphy, Tom O'Rourke, Wally Cleary, Tom Mahon.
Lt. to Rt. Front Row: Michael Mahon, Michael O'Rourke.

Christmas Pongo 1959, in Concert Hall C.Y.M.S.

Lt. to Rt. Front Row: Mrs. Bridget Roche (Abbey St.), Mr. & Mrs. Mahon (O'Connell Ave.), Mrs. T. O'Rourke (Grogan's Road), Mrs. J. Cullimore (John St.).

Middle Row: Rosaleen Furlong (Green St.), Mrs. J. Larkin (St Enda's Tee.), Mr. & Mrs. Roche (Bride St.), Nellie Rodgers (Emmett Place),

Rolaleen Quinlick (Emmitt Place), Maggie Anne Cousins (Menapia Ave.), Man at the Rear /left: Laurence Bolger.

146

Pongo Club outing - Glendalough 1959

Fr. Keating watching the "Big Poker Game"

(Lt. to Rt.) Josie Cleary - Chrissie Hayes - Maggie Mahon - Michael Mahon, Snr. - Bridie Swords - Mrs. Ahearne - Joey Anglim - Fr. Keating

The Pongo Club Annual Excursion was another very popular event which was well supported. These outings took place in the summer and visited various popular locations of the day. The two destinations that I recall visiting were Tralee and Glendalough. The Tralee visit was not repeated as it was considered too far a journey with only a short stay. However, Glendalough was visited on many occasions. The following are some photographs of those events

Pongo outing at Glendalough 1959

Tom Mahon   **Michael Mahon, Snr.**   **Maggie Mahon**   **Chrissie Hayes**

The Annual Pongo Club Excursion to Glendalough 1959

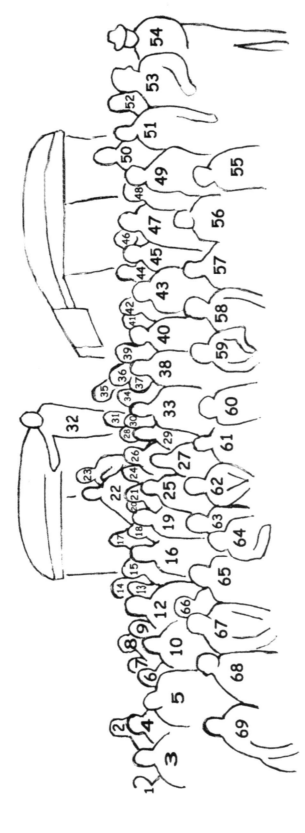

The only numbers identified are as follows:- 2 Tom O'Rourke, 3 Peter Hore, 4 Joannie Murphy (Goodison), 12 Mr. Waters, 13 Mr. Black, 17 John Cullimore, 18 Rosaleen Furlong, 22 Michael O'Rourke (myself), 23 Michael (Curley) O'Rourke, 25 Michael Murphy, 29 Kathleen Morris, 31 Bill Murphy, 32 Ray Flynn, 33 Nelly Rogers, 35 Larry Roche, 38 Maggie Dunne, 39 Miss Culleton, 42 Mrs. Kelly, 43 Chrissy Hayes, 44 Mrs. McGuire, 47 Michael Mahon, Snr., 49 Mrs. Hearne, 50 Myles O'Rourke, 51 Tom Mahon, 52 Phil Shiggins, 53 Wally Cleary, 54 Paddy Brady, 55 Mary O'Rourke (Myles daughter), 56 Mr. Hearne, 57 Michael Lynch, 58 Maggie Mahon, 59 Bridie Swords, 61 Marie O'Rourke (Tom's daughter), 62 Peg O'Rourke (Myles wife),

63 Mrs. Murphy (Talbot Street), 69 Tommy Cullimore

149

Pongo outing to Glendalough 20th July 1958

Pongo Working Committee

Tom O'Rourke   Myles O'Rourke   William Murphy   Wally Cleary   Tom Mahon

Tommy Cullimore   Michael Murphy   Michael O'Rourke

In 1959 the Pongo Club began to encounter all sorts of obstacles from outside forces. Including a series of anonymous letter to the Presbytery claiming that some people in the town were concerned *that poor people were spending money in the C.Y.M.S. Pongo that could ill afford it.* These anonymous letters continued to be discussed throughout March. The priests thought that something should be done about it *'to placate the writer'* of the letters and insure the good name of the C.Y.M.S.

Of course the correct thing to do with an anonymous letters is to throw it into the bin and give it no credence whatsoever and certainly not to placate the cowardly author. The sad conclusion to this was that both the priests and the Council capitulated to this faceless person. At a meeting of the branch Council on the 15th April 1959 the matter was comprehensively discussed and it was unanimously decided that *'a limit of 1/= per round per person should be imposed'* on the C.Y.M.S. Pongo game.

By November the takings were well down and to add further to the problems the taxman was after the Pongo money. Had some other busybody written another anonymous letter stirring things up? Fortunately by the 5th January 1960 the taxman had agreed that the Pongo takings came under charitable status. Around that time Bobby Kelly started up Pongo in Rosslare. He ran these sessions on every Sunday afternoon and evening which was further competition for the C.Y.M.S. game to compete with.

The 1960 income from the Pongo was a massive £967-4-8. and this section of the club's activities was now keeping the club afloat and the branch Council acknowledged this at the Annual General Meeting held on the 2nd December of 1960 with the following comment *If we had not an income from the Pongo it is doubtful if we would be able to carry on.* - A.G.M. Report 31st December 1960. The income for 1961 at £1,083-5-6 topped this and was the highest income since the Pongo began.

In 1963 the Parish Hall (*Dun Mhuire*) committee started their Bingo one night per week. They ran on Wednesday night in the beginning and a charge of 6/= gave you the opportunity of winning the big prize up to £100. The

club's game could not match this. On the 19th of February 1964 Joe Dillon applied at court for a Bingo licence. Now the opposition was growing and with the imposed limit on the C.Y.M.S. game our committee was playing on an uneven playing field. Due to this state of affairs, Thomas O'Rourke, the committee Chairman tendered his resignation form the Pongo Committee.

This years licence of £40 was paid and the branch Council for the first time had to expend funds to get the Pongo up and running again with William Murphy in charge. The Pongo ran at a loss once again this year and the branch Council ceased subsidising them. The Council then invited Thomas O'Rourke back as the Pongo Committee Chairman in a desperate last attempt to get things up and running and back on track. Tom went back but they struggled on for the remainder of the year with more losses. The opposition in town was hurting the C.Y.M.S. Pongo which was their only real source of income.
By 1st October Thomas reported that there was no improvement and things looked pretty grim. The Council

It would appear from 1965 onwards, as there is no record of Pongo in the club meetings, that the club had finally accepted the inevitable. It was the end of an era and the end of the Society's best earner. Apart from being a great source of income for the club, the Pongo had donated money to many charities throughout its existence.

requested they continue but in November Thomas advised the branch Council to cease the game of Pongo as the club was now incurring unacceptable losses. Most of the regular punters had deserted and gone to the bigger games like Kelly in Rosslare, Joe Dillon at the Granada Grill and the Dun Mhuire Parish Hall. Obviously the club's game wasn't big enough for the Wexford people.

BINGO
IN THE
Catholic Young Men's Society
ST. IBERIUS HALL
EVERY SUNDAY NIGHT
£70 in Prizes
BOOKS 2/6 EACH

Doors Open: 8 p.m.   Commencing: 8.45 p.m. Sharp

Advertisement in the People newspaper September 1963

C.Y.M.S. Earnings from Pongo

1955.....................£190-0-0
1956.....................£514-0-9
1957.....................£610-7-0
1958.....................£728-2-6
1959.....................£600 approx.
1960.....................£967-4-8
1961.....................£1,083-5-6
1962.....................£965-5-3
1963.....................Incurred losses
1964.....................Incurred Losses – Finished in November.

(See Appendix No 6 for full list of the 'Pongo Working Committees Throughout the Years on Page 282)

Carnival

1930s
The Amusements Committee donated £20 profit which they had earned from the McDonald's Carnival held at Rosslare in 1936 for the Society's funds. On the 5th October 1937 the Amusements Committee were contemplating running a Carnival for 10 days in December to raise funds for the Society and they requested the Hon. Secretary to write to the Corporation *asking for the use of the Market Place to erect some side-shows during the Carnival.* By the 26th October a vote of thanks was

tendered to the Mayor for the use of the Market. In November a special meeting had to be convened to consider complaints from some members concerning the proposed Carnival. Businessmen in the Society *objected to the Carnival being held two weeks before Christmas day, as it would greatly interfere with the interests of the business trades of the town.* After careful consideration of the many objections raised, it was decided on the motion of Nicholas Barnwell and seconded by James Quirke to hold the carnival from 10th to 18th December both dates inclusive. On the 30th December it is recorded that the Secretary of the Amusements Committee announced the following: *Owing to the very cold weather during the week in which the Carnival was held. We regretted to state that the receipts did not come up to the expected profits from same.* The profit handed in was £12-6-2.

1950s

Carnival at Kirwan's Field

In April 1951 the club contacted the St. Vincent de Paul Society on no less than two occasions regarding the possible renting of their field at Thomas Street for the purpose of holding a Carnival there for a period of two weeks, the dates to be arranged. The St.Vincent de Paul Society refused to rent the field with the result that the club had to look elsewhere. Kirwan's field in Carrigeen Street came to their attention.

A Mr. Stewart, of Stewart's Star Amusements and his representatives visited Wexford one Sunday morning to inspect the field to see if it was suitable for the Carnival. It needed levelling in a few places and the gateway was too small to allow access for their large vehicles and equipment. They needed a fifteen feet opening for easy access. Sam O'Rourke, the then owner of the field, was informed about the requirements and he carried out the necessary work on behalf of the club. He was paid the sum of £30 for the hire of the field but there is no mention of who paid for the work carried out.

When Mr. Stewart visited Wexford he had dinner at our house in Grogan's Road. My father Thomas was a chief official on the club Carnival Committee. Thomas had experience in organising carnivals having been one of the principal men in charge of the L.D.F. carnival at Redmond Park a few years previously. So there was no surprise that He was on the C.Y.M.S. Carnival Organising Committee. During the meal I made a general nuisance of myself asking all sorts of questions about the carnival. I was only eleven years of age and very curious about it. After dinner my Father took Mr. Stewart to inspect Kirwan's field and then down to the C.Y.M.S. club and gave him the grand tour. I was brought along at Mr. Stewart's insistence. My father had not intended that I get in the way but Mr. Stewart said it was alright. I had begged to be allowed to go along with them. In retrospect, it would be interesting to know how Mr. Stewart, a Belfast Protestant, felt being brought into the Catholic Young Men's Society, the bastion of Catholic action in Wexford, as a guest on that Sunday afternoon.

The carnival was in Wexford from the 22nd July to the 5th August 1951. There are many things I recollect about this carnival and for good reasons. The octopus was the newest and most exciting of all the rides one could avail of in the carnival of these days. It was more thrilling than the swinging boats, the chair-o-planes and the bumpers *(dodgems),* they were all old hat. I loved going in the

octopus. If my memory serves me well I think it cost six pence a ride so needless to remark I couldn't get many rides on that.

Michael Nolan and I, a school friend and a next-door neighbour when we lived on the Main Street in 1948, went to the matinee at the carnival and we had spent all our money on rides in the octopus. When our chair finally came down to earth the attendant was about to open it to let us out when Mr. Stewart appeared on the scene and on recognising me came over to have a chat. Discovering that Michael and I loved the octopus ride the attendant was ordered to leave us in it as long as we wanted. This was FREE, YAHOOO! We thought we were in heaven. After about five more rides the attendant stopped it at our chair

C.Y.M.S. CARNIVAL

Continues each night at 7.30 p.m.
AT
KIRWAN'S FIELD, WEXFORD.

Final Performance on SUNDAY, AUGUST 5th

ADMISSION 3d.

CHILDREN'S MATINEES.

saturday), and on Sunday, July 29th,

COMMENCING AT THREE P.M.

usements Half-Price for Children.

ES ALONG AND GIVE THEM THE TREAT OF THEIR YOUNG LIVES!

RCHASED ON THE GATE ON TO-NIGHT (FRIDAY) AND ON SATURDAY
UDED IN THE DRAW FOR THE SUITE OF FURNITURE.

STEWART'S STAR AMUSEMENTS.

Autodrome, Electric Speedway, Octopus, Ghost Train,
Kiddies' Joy Ride, Spinner, Shooting Range, Hoopla,
Pongo, etc., etc.

SPECIAL GATE PRIZES EACH NIGHT.

DRAW FOR SUITE OF FURNITURE ON SUNDAY NIGHT JULY 29th

Advertisement from the People newspaper 1951

and asked if we had enough. We answered 'No' and off we went again. After another two or three turns he asked us again so we were embarrassed into saying 'YES' and got out. We decided that we had pushed our look far enough. You can imagine, as two young lads, we were over the moon with our good fortune.

The financial situation relating to the Carnival was that Stewart's Amusements received 40% of the takings and the C.Y.M.S.'s share was £731-15-7 but after paying expenses, the net profit for the club was £668-13-9. Quite an amount of cash. The club must have been quite pleased with the outcome because by January of the next year we read that the club had a visit from Mr. Ernest Stewart and that he was prepared to bring his Amusements to Wexford for a Carnival in aid of the Society once again. The Council accepted his offer and they agreed the dates.

Stewart's Star Amussements

Carnival at Kirwan's field Carrigeen in the early 1950s

By 25th February the Council had received a letter from Mr. Ernest Stewart, 65 Ravenscroft Avenue, Belfast confirming the booking, Mr. Stewart also enclosed photographs of his new autodrome and list of amusements. The Council immediately booked Kirwan's field for the Carnival and also arranged public liability insurance for the duration of the event.

The Carnival organising committee for this year was: -

Thomas O'Rourke	Joint Chief Steward
George Bridges	Joint Chief Steward
John J. Donohoe	Hon. Secretary
John F. O'Rourke	Hon. Treasurer
William Murphy	Steward

Many of the membership volunteered to act as stewards as required. The table tennis section was particularly helpful with the running of the Carnival this year. The club's net profit was £667-18-4. and I assume that Mr. Stewart had the same percentage of the takings as the previous year's agreement. Apart from the two foregoing occasions, I am unaware of how many times the club held this carnival, but on the 13th January 1953 the club wrote to 'Mr. Stewart's

Star Amusements' inquiring if he would be coming to Wexford this year with his Carnival again.

I can not recall when the last C.Y.M.S. carnival was held in Kirwan's field but there were many carnivals held at that venue for many years afterwards. The following two photographs were taken at those carnivals. One picture depicts a group of C.Y.M.S. young men having a night out enjoying some harmless fun.

C.Y.M.S. Lads at the Carnival 1959
Michael O'Rourke, Peter Monaghan, Ray Flynn, Dick Fortune, Noel Roche.

The Children's Fancy Dress Competition 1951

The Childrens' fancy dress competition held under the auspices of the C.Y.M.S. Carnival was another memorable event, the results were as follows:

Winners of the Best Group, Prize £3:-
"Bound for Wales"- Boy Scouts consisting of Frank O'Rourke, Mickey Fortune, Sean Nolan, Dick Fortune and Michael O'Rourke (author). All five of us were part of the 2nd Wexford (St. Columbanus) Troop of the Catholic Boy Scouts who were bound for Wales and we would eventually all become C.Y.M.S. members when we became of age.
2nd Prize £2:
"Love on the Dole"- group consisted of Anthony Barry, Anne Hamilton, and Anne Browne.
Funniest Prize £3:-
"Mai West" - May Lalor
2nd Prize £2:-
"Annie Get Your Gun" – Evelyn Keegan and Frances Keegan
Prettiest Costune Prize £3:-
(Title ?) Gene Carley
2nd Prize £2:-
"Hawaiian Lady"- Marie O'Rourke
3rd Prize £1:-
"Lee Cream" – Eileen Marrow
4th Prize £1
"Trottie True"- Rose Mary Cullen

Special Prize £1 :-
"Champion Jockey, Lester Piggott" – Eamon Roche
Best Pair £1 :-
"Ten Little Niger Boys" - Jack Murray and Aidan Hayes
Gate Prize:-
Desmond Murray

Mr. Stewart also donated a prize of 10/= each to every other child who took part in the fancy dress parade.

Dances

The C.Y.M.S. held dances in the Town Hall and in their own concert hall throughout the years as it was a good source of income for the club. It also helped maintain Wexford musicians in employment at home and it provided great entertainment for the Wexford people. It was a regular practice for prizes to be awarded based on the entrance tickets and on special occasions spot prizes, donated by businessmen members of the C.Y.M.S. would be dispensed.

C.Y.M.S. Dances at the Town Hall over the Years

The Society ran at least one dance in the Town Hall in 1941, another on the 17th November 1943 and one in 1945. In January 1946 the amusement committee applied to rent the Town Hall for St. Patrick's night for a dance and the Town Clerk informed them that the hall was already reserved by the Gaelic League for a dance that night. They ran a dance in October 1946 and the profit was £16-17-0. In September 1946 the amusement committee applied to the Town Clerk for the first available Sunday night after Christmas for a dance. Some problem arose at the time with regard to who had authority on the amusements committee and John F. O'Rourke, the Hon. Secretary of the amusements committee for some time, tendered his resignation and presented the Council with his statement of accounts. A general discussion ensued which resulted in John F. O'Rourke agreeing to withdraw his resignation on condition that a new amusements committee consisting of four members be formed. Furthermore, the caretaker was to be instructed that he was

not to take any orders from any other members except these four. The four members were - John F. O'Rourke, Hon. Secretary, William R. Turner, Thomas Barnwell and Tony Kelly.

In November of the same year the club decided to become a member of the 'Organisation of the Allocation of Dances for the Town Hall.' The fact that such an organisation existed goes to show how much the Town Hall was in demand in those days. There must have been numerous clubs and societies in existence in Wexford town when they needed to have such an organisation controlling the allocation of nights for dances in the hall.

In March 1947 the committee requested the use of the hall from the Town Clerk for the first available Sunday night after Lent. They held a dance there on Sunday the 28th September 1947 and also one on Sunday night December 21st.

Profit from a Ceili held on the 16th April 1948 was £13-12-0 and a dance held on the 25th April the same year made £19-3-0. In June 1948 John F. O'Rourke stated that the Society had joined the *'Wexford Dance Promoters' Protective Association'* and as a result the club was allocated Friday night 27th August and Sunday night 3rd October for their dances in the Town Hall. They also held a dance there on the 29th June and made a profit of £10-6-0 and £6-4-0 was made from a Ceili there on the 27th August. The Committee applied for the hall from the 1st to the 8th August 1948 for a week's carnival of dances.

On the 10th October 1948 there was a club dance at the Town Hall and at this stage sub-committees were formed to manage the running of these dances. It became known as the dance committee and members of the club's Council also helped at these dances. Wexford Corporation granted permission to the C.Y.M.S to rent the Town Hall from the 31st July to 7th August 1949 for the purpose of running a week's dances. The series of dances held at the Town Hall had made a profit of £115 and the Council commenting on this matter stated that *great work has been done by the dance committee. It was decided to present boxes of chocolates to each of the lady members of the entertainment committee who had worked so hard.* - 6th September 1949.

On the 2nd May 1950 the Hon. Secretary reported that he had hired Lowney's Band, Tommy and his Collegians and Doyle's Ceili Band for the week's dances to be held for the August Bank Holiday week and the dances all through this week made a profit of £100-0-2. During August Bank Holiday week 1951 *(5th to 12th August)* the cycling club section of the C.Y.M.S. held their annual gala dances in the Town Hall and the bands and dates they played were as follows:

Sunday 5th August	Lowney's Band
Monday 6th August	Tommy and His Collegians
Tuesday 7th August	Doyle's Ceili Band
Wednesday 8th August	Lowney's Band
Thursday 9th August	Lowney's Band
Friday 10th August	Doyle's Ceili Band
Sunday 12th August	Tommy and His Collegians

The list of bands and their fees throughout the August Bank Holiday week 1952 *(3rd to 10th August)* were:

Tommy and His Collegians	Payment not recorded
Rita and Her Band	Paid £6 per night.
Doyle's Ceili Band	Paid £4-10-0 per night.
New Eire Band	(L. O'Neill) Paid £6 per night.

Doyle's Ceilidhe Band

The C.Y.M.S. annual gala dance weeks were a great success. On Sunday night the prizes were presented to the winners after the finals of the various competitions. In the old time waltz competition silver cups were presented to Jackie Brennan and Miss B. Daly for first prize. In second place were Tom Redmond and Miss M. Hall and third prize of 10/- went to Jim Kelly and Miss P. Lewis. Fourth prize, a half-barrel of coal, went to T. Fortune and Miss P. McGuire. In the slow foxtrot Jim Kelly and Miss Keelan won 1st prize of £1 each and Mr. and Mrs T. Fortune were second, each receiving 10/-. Spot prizes were won by Messrs J. Saunders, John Street and T. Cadogan, The Quay, P. Brennan, New Ross, T. McNulty, R. Hynes, T. Breen, Wales, George Roche, The Faythe, D. Kelly, Hill Street, W. Whitty, Michael Street, S. Murphy, Hill Street and M. McCormack, North Main Street. Lady winners were the Misses Keelan, Back Street, K. Callaghan, Trinity Street, T. Carley, The Faythe, M. O'Neill, Distillery Road, M. Malone, A. Cleary, High Street, Miss Boyle, Miss Canavan and Miss Swords, John Street. The judges for the final were Mr. And Mrs. P. V. Carson and during the week the other judges included. M. Luccan, Guard Lawlor, Mr. and Mrs. Giddy and a Miss Hayes.

The club also held gala dances this year whether this is referring to the August Bank Holiday week or not one can only guess. They netted a profit of £125-5-11 for the club. During the gala dance week there were old time waltzing competitions held and the cups for these competitions cost the club's dance committee £10.

On the 2nd September a Mr. C. Moran made an application for permission to manage the mineral stall at the C.Y.M.S. dances and the matter was handed over to the dance committee for a decision. He did in fact acquire the permission he sought. The old timers reading this will share a nostalgic smile with me when they read *'mineral stall'*. Younger readers please note that in those bygone days alcoholic beverages were forbidden to be either sold or served on the premises during dances in the Town Hall or the Redmond Hall

Joe Lowney's Orchestra

Tommy and his Collegians

You simply drank mineral water which was orange juice or lemonade. Fellows fond of a drink or two whilst attending the Town Hall venue would run down to Mollie Mythen's public house just down the hill (*now the Thomas Moore Tavern*). In the late fifties when I was old enough to attend dances I too joined the *line of boyos' running down to Mollie's for 'a quick wan' in between dances.* However, if anyone had too much drink consumed they would not be allowed back into the dance

hall. In 1953 there appears to be no record of the club holding dances in the Town Hall. This does not necessarily mean that they did not have dances there. For instance I have noted that the club attempted to book the Town Hall for the August week. This application was dated 5th January 1953 but there is no record as to whether they got it or not. We do know that the C.Y.M.S. table tennis club ran a Ceili in the Town Hall on the 30th January of this year.

In 1954 the C.Y.M.S. held a week's dancing again during the August Bank Holiday week and the bands that played this week were:

Tommy and His Collegians	Played on the 2nd, 3rd, 4th, 5th, and 6th.
Mollie Turner and Her Band	Played on the 1st and the 8th
Tommy O'Neill's Band	Played on the 9th, 16th and 23rd November
	(*Fee was £6-10-0 per night*)

There was an old-There waltz competition held during the week and silver-cups were awarded to the winners and runners-up and a slow-foxtrot competition was held on the Thursday night, the winners and runners-up receiving a cash prize. The club invited Mr. and Mrs Jackie Brennan to judge the competitions and anyone who knew the Brendan's in those days would have known two brilliant

ballroom dancers. They were to be seen at every dance that was held around Wexford town. In the beginning of the year Council member Thomas Hayes proposed that the club should look into the possibility of booking the Town Hall for Tuesday nights on a regular basis. Nothing further is known of this suggestion.

New Eire Orchestra

In 1955 some of the dance committee members were - Thomas Hayes, George Bridges, Victor Bridges and John F. O'Rourke. 1955 was a very special year for the Wexford C.Y.M.S. club it being its centenary year and the club also hosted the National Convention for the C.Y.M.S. of Ireland. On the 4th January 1955 the Council applied to reserve the Town Hall for Whit Sunday to hold a special dance for the delegates from the national convention. If my records are correct I believe that this request was refused and they decided to hold the dance in the Concert Hall instead.

They also held the usual August Bank Holiday dances. An attempt was made to hire the famous Mayglass Ceilidhe Band for a Sunday night but it was unsuccessful more than likely due to heavy booking.

Tommy O'Neill's Band

Played on the 12th August
(*Fees were £6-10-0 per night*)

In 1956 the C.Y.M.S. were quoted fees from bands as follows:

Lowney's Band	£7-10-0 per night.
Tommy O'Neill's Band	£5-0-0 per night
Johnnie Reck's Band	£6-0-0 per night
Richard (Dick) Whitney's Band	£4-15-0 per night

The C.Y.M.S. cycling club held a dance in the Town Hall in the 1960s and you can read about this fiasco in the cycling chapter. For further information on C.Y.M.S. dancing please refer to the chapter on the Concert Hall activities

Johnny Reck's Band

Bands with C.Y.M.S. Connections

The 'Ceoltoiri Loc Garman' Ceili Band 1960

The Ceoltoiri Loc Garman Ceili Band'

In 1960 the young members of this band were: (*Left to Right*) Paddy Rossiter (*Drums*), Ollie Hall (*accordion, a C.Y.M.S. member*), Tony & Sean Rattigan (*both Violinists and C.Y.M.S. members*), Tommy Carroll (*Piano Accordion, C.Y.M.S. member*), Brendan Dowdall (*Piano Accordion, C.Y.M.S. member*), Marie O'Rourke (*Vocalist, sister of the author*), Sally Rattigan (*Piano*).

In actual fact this was the Rattigan family band, but with the amount of C.M.Y.S. members it contained it was practically a C.Y.M.S. band also. This young band went on to win the senior An Tostal All-Ireland Ceili Band Championships at Dunshambo, Co. Leitrim in the early 1960s beating more senior and experienced bands from all over Ireland.

Sean Rattigan, the leader of the band was not the type of man who would play second fiddle to anybody; he played both classical and traditional music. He won the All-Ireland solo violin championship in his early days and when the 'Dun Mhuire' Parish Hall in Wexford town was opened on the 4th December 1960, Sean was honoured by being chosen as one of the Wexford musicians to perform

a solo on the violin. He aptly chose 'Ave Maria' for the occasion. Sean or John as some of us call him is also an active member of the club to this day and is partial to a game of cards now and again.

Dick Whitney, a member of the club and a champion table tennis player of the Forties, wrote the lyrics for the ballad of 'Nicky Rackard'. Dick had his own dance band in the 1940s and he was a member of the 'New Eire Orchestra' at one time   There were numerous dance bands around in those days as dancing was all the go. Roy Doyle (snr.), the father of Roy the famous C.Y.M.S. cycling hero was also a fine musician who was on many of the bands from Wexford in the early 1960s, two that come to mind are Johnny Reck's and Lowney's bands.

Dick Whitney

The St. Iberius Catholic Club (C.Y.M.S.) Social Gatherings

Soirées, Communion Breakfasts & Reunions

1860s

We do not have the exact date for the first 'annual soirée' but in the minute book dated December 1859 we read that the 'annual soirée' was postponed until after Easter. This then tells us that the 'Annual Soirées' existed prior to 1859 and that was only four years after the Society was established. This being so, it would be safe to assume that the 'annual soirées' were a regular occurrence from the very outset. A soirée (swa'ra) is a social party or gathering for conversation to advance a Society's objects and was usually accompanied by music and some entertainment. The soirées that the Society held certainly lived up to this description.

On the 8th November 1860 the Society gave a public banquet for the County Wexford Soldiers of the 'Irish Papal Brigade'. The Central Council, Dublin sent a set of rules or suggestions that should be observed at the 'annual soirées' and this was intended to be implemented starting with the 16th November 1862 annual soirée held at the Town Hall. The list of suggestions were as follows:

1. **All politics to be avoided but an Irish and National tone preserved.**
2. **A judicious Chairman to be selected.**
3. **Friends of members to be admitted but to guard against improper parties (Persons)**
4. **Some distinguished person to be asked as a quest.**
5. **Some good music provided**
6. **Strangers (*non-members*) to be admitted on recommendation of member at the usual charge.**

These were the guidelines used for the Society's annual soirée and no doubt this standard was applied throughout the years. See next page for photocopy of the tea party (Soirée) of 1863 subscribers and a part list of names who had subscribed to the event.

The annual soirée that was held on the 17th February 1864 was into pyrotechnics which we know from an entry which records that *Capt. J. J. Doyle and Michael Hughes were appointed to superintend the fire works* for the coming St. Patrick's Night Soirée. So Mr. Hughes and Capt. Doyle were the first appointed 'Pyrotechnical Committee' in the Society. The fire works were intended to be let-off from the 'Ballast Bank' but this was decided against later on. The Council which organised the 1865 Soirée held on St, Patrick's Night managed to get Capt. Ennis to bring the tug opposite the Society on St. Patrick's Night for the purpose of letting-off the rockets from it. The club premises at this time were on Paul Quay. The club was also given twelve tar barrels to burn by Mr. Hall. Reporters from the People and the Independent newspapers were invited as guests and the drink consisted of six bottles of wine, a half-gallon of whiskey, two dozen bottles of lemonade and three dozen bottles of orange juice. Incidentally, Capt. Ennis was a member of the Society.

On New Years Night 1866 the Society staged an entertainment. Admission to non-members was 2/6 and members 1/6. Mr. Coulier (*a member*) supplied the drink for the soirée which consisted of half a dozen mineral water, one dozen ginger beer, one gallon of whiskey, four dozen bottles of orange juice and two bottles of sherry. They made a profit of £5-16-0 on the night.

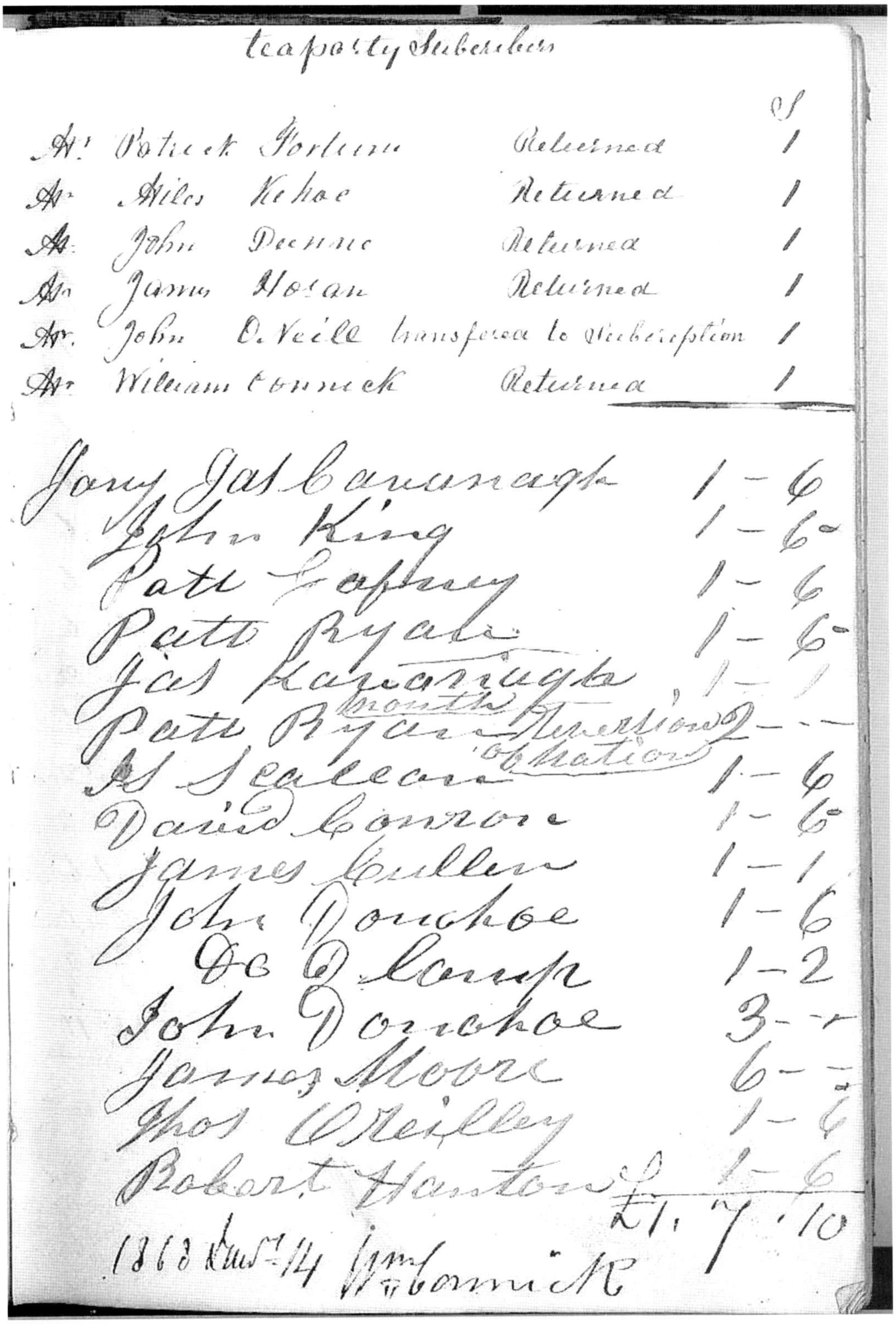

tea party Subscribers

Mr.	Patrick Fortune	Returned	1
Mr.	Miles Kehoe	Returned	1
Mr.	John Dunne	Returned	1
Mr.	James Hogan	Returned	1
Mr.	John O.Neill	transferred to Subscription	1
Mr.	William Connick	Returned	1

Jerry Jas Cavanagh — 1 – 6
John King — 1 – 6
Patt Gaffney — 1 – 6
Patt Ryah — 1 – 6
Jas Kavanaugh — 1 – 1
Patt Ryan — month Reversion ? – . –
Js Scallon oblation — 1 – 6
David Connor — 1 – 6
James Cullen — 1 – 1
John Donohoe — 1 – 6
Do Do Camp — 1 – 2
John Donohoe — 3 – r
James Moore — 6 – –
Thos O'Reilly — 1 – 6
Robert Hanton J — 1 – 6

£1. 7. 10

1863 Jany 14 Wm Connick 1

Tea Party Subscribers Example Page.

1880s

The annual soirée held on the 2nd January 1883 was one of the most successful the Society ever held. There were one hundred and fifty members in attendance and it was held in the original hall (*the Society's previous premises*) which through the beneficence of Richard Devereux, K.S.G. had been placed at the disposal of the Society for that night. The soirée organising committee this year consisted of the following members:

Edward Dixon, Robert Hanton, William J. Devereux and the Hon. Secretary Laurence Rossiter.

The soirée stewards working committee consisted of the following members:
Laurence Rossiter, William J. Devereux, James Stafford, J. Stafford, Patrick Byrne, Patrick Stafford, Patrick Cullen, James Sinnott, James Stamp and William Scallan.

Authors depiction of the Reunion Banquet as described in the text.

The Hall was decorated with flowers, evergreens, flags and bannerettes and at the end of the hall a commodious stage was erected, handsomely ornamented and overarched by a gracefully blended display of flags, bannerettes including the Papal flag and an Irish shield with harp, emblazoned in gold, on a green background. On the wall at the centre table was a life size portrait of the munificent Patron and friend of the Society, Richard Devereux, Knight of the Order of St. Gregory – one of D. G.

Fortune's masterpieces (*Fortune was the artist*). Various mottos, religious and national, were encircled with wreaths of holly among them were 'Ireland a Nation', 'A.M.D.G.' *(Ad Majorem Dei Gloriam)* meaning 'For the greater glory of God') and 'Faith and Fatherland'. The evening commenced at 7.30.p.m. when the Rev. Luke Doyle, President of the Society, took the chair. He drew attention to a letter issued by His Holiness during the year strongly recommending Young Men's Societies. His Holiness the Pope *(Leo XIII)* was toasted and the choir then sung 'God Bless our Pope'.

John Tennant next proposed a toast to the Bishop and the clergy of the Diocese. The Chairman then toasted the health of Richard Devereux, the founder of the Society (*Wexford Branch*). Others who were toasted were: Rev. P.M. O'Leary, The Stewards for all the various work undertaken. Hon. Secretary, Laurence Rossiter, The Rev. President, The performers, the Choir; William Connick, John Kehoe, Michael Maddock, John Furlong, William Codd, P. Cousins, Patrick Ryan, John Connick and J. Gahan.

The band (*musicians*) including Professor Patrick Breen, John Tennant and H. Leary were then toasted.

Bear in mind that this was a non-drinking Society and most of the members would not be accustomed to drinking the 'falling down water' *(whiskey)*. Surely these fellows would end up on the floor before they reached the last toast?

Patrick Breen

James Stafford

Professor Breen played 'The Pope's March' and William Codd read Lover's 'Loan of a Gridiron' in good style. John Tennant played several solos on the violin and Professor Breen presided at the pianoforte. Messrs Connick and Gahan sang 'Salvation Army duet' and Messrs. Connick, Kehoe, Connick (jnr.), Williams, Furlong, O'Connor and Company sang a number of songs, At 11.00.p.m. the entertainment was brought to an end with clasped hands singing 'Auld Lang Syne'. At the annual soirée of 1884 which was held in the original rooms in

Paul Quay, the programme, apart from the usual, contained a dramatic performance and a display of terpsichorean art. Unfortunately, they didn't give the name of the artistically inspired person who gave this exhibition in the science of dance. The soirée for the following year was held in the Old Hall again but on this occasion it was owned by a Mr. Davis of Enniscorthy who kindly loaned it to the Society for the night. Some of the expenses were recorded and I quote them hereunder as they detail the names of the gentlemen who supplied various fare for the evening.

William Scallan A member and Town Councillor	Supplied drink £5-5-6.
Mrs Robinson Wife of a member	Supplied the food £2-18-9
Pat Stafford A member	Supplied milk 3/-
Mr. Murphy A member	Supplied hire of labour 7/6
Professor Pat Breen A member	Supplied the music 5/-
Men	For carting etc £1-4-0

On Sunday evening the 15th January 1888 the reunion was held in the C.Y.M.S. rooms on Paul Quay. The room was decorated throughout with ivy and artificial roses which were interspersed with fern and evergreen. Amongst the decorations were portraits of faces once familiar. At the head of the room was the Papal arms and at either side hung the portraits of the late Richard Devereux, K.S.G., the great Patron and founding father of the C.Y.M.S. and the late Very Rev. James Canon Roche, P.P., Wexford. Though they had passed away their memory was still fresh in the minds of their fellow C.Y.M.S. members. The portrait of His Grace Most Rev. Dr. Walsh, Archbishop of Dublin occupied a prominent position.

Religion and nationalism blended together at these festive gatherings and were the driving force which would gain Ireland its freedom in years to follow. At the sidewall hung a splendid Irish flag which was painted by a young Wexford artist and upon this flag beside the harp, wolf-dog, round tower and church was a miniature green flag floating from a rock on which was inscribed the words 'Remember Davitt' and close beside this was a flag with the inscription 'Old Ireland for Ever'. The words 'Faith and Erin' with 'A Thousand Welcomes from the Catholic Young Men's Society' were also inscribed.

Undoubtedly there was a lot of hard toil put into the preparation of the hall for the reunion. Members of the sub-committee who organised and oversaw all the work were: Laurence Rossiter, Hon. Secretary, James Sinnott, James Stamp, Michael O'Connor, William McGuire, James Stafford, William Hutchinson, Patrick Cullen and John King. These men also acted as stewards and worked throughout the evening ensuring the comfort of the guests. The entertainment commenced at 7.00.p.m. sharp when over one hundred sat down to tea. This was the largest number of members ever to attend a reunion since their initiation. Rev. N. T. Sheridan presided and amongst the guests were - Rev. Luke Doyle, Adm. *(former President)*, Rev. P. M. O'Brien, *(son of John F. X. O'Brien, M.P.)*, Edward Walsh *(editor and proprietor of the People)*; John FitzSimon, John Tennant, John Hinton, T.C., William Connick, William Robinson, Robert Hanton and Moses Harpur.

The evening's entertainment commenced with the brass band of the C.Y.M.S. playing 'Home, Sweet Home'. This band had only been formed a few months previously and

was comprised of mostly young boys who surprisingly were very proficient even though only newly formed. The musical accompaniment was provided by P. J. Breen the parochial organist and under his excellent guidance this portion of the programme was admirably carried through. G. F. Dixon sang 'Jack's Farewell' and 'Our Jack's Come Home from Sea To-Day' and he was loudly applauded. J. J. Whelan, sang 'I've Such an Awful Cold' and the humorous song 'Money'. John Tennant played a violin solo and E.A. Whelan, also a violinist and a very talented one, played a very intricate solo 'The anchor in weighed' for which he received loud plaudits.

In response to repeated encores he sang 'Let me like a soldier fall'. P. Howlin, in character, sang 'The Irish Jaunting Car' and received a loud burst of enthusiasm from the members. Simon Hore danced a hornpipe and a step dance, as did Mr. Mullet who took the boards with a step dance and double. Master Hugh McGuire sang 'The Wonderful Musician'. Thus the first half of the entertainment ended with the band playing the Valse *(Swinging)*. (*Waltz two beats instead of three beats*]. The Rev. Sheridan rose and thanked everyone who took part and proposed toasts to various people present which were reciprocated. Rev. Luke Doyle the Society's former President rose and having thanked everyone for their kind words proposed a toast to William Connick *'the foundation stone and pillar of the Young Men's Society.'* Mr. Connick thanked everyone and sang 'Let Each Man Learn to Know Himself' with all the guests joining in the chorus. William Robinson sang 'The Visitors'. Rev. P. M. O'Leary spoke in praise of the C.Y.M.S. and John Hinton, T.C. concluded with some kind words.

The second part of the programme opened with a play performed by the members of the dramatic club entitled 'A Race for a Widow'. The characters were:-

M. Curry	As Cornelius Popjoy, a lawyer's clerk
G. F. Dixon	As Adolphus De Cremorne
J. Curran	As Mrs. Winnington, a widow with £300 a year
J. J. Whelan	As Mrs. Pepperpod
M. O'Connor	As Mr. Capsoum Pepperpod
T. J. Cullen }	
W. H. McGuire }	*Played other characters*
L. Crosbie }	

William H. McGuire

Some speeches followed to conclude this part of the programme thanking everyone for all they had done. Mr. Breen was given a special thanks as each year he kindly gave his valuable services in presiding at the piano.

The third part of the programme consisted of songs and a recitation by P. Howlin. The entertainment was then brought to a close with the band playing the National Anthem when the entire assembly rose to their feet and joined in the prayer 'God Save Ireland'.

1890s

The annual soirée was held on Sunday the 12rh January 1896 in the concert hall of the C.Y.M.S. premises and Mr & Mrs Scallan and Robert Hanton supplied the tables on loan for the occasion. A soirée was held on Sunday evening in the concert hall at Paul Quay on 17th January 1897.

The catering for the soirée banquet held on the 5th February 1899 in the concert hall was supplied by Hugh McCarthy of White's Hotel. They supplied the dinner

Mayor James Sinnott

with three drinks for a charge of 3/6 per person and all the drink needed to be supplied at trade price. Patrick Ryan, the Mayor of Wexford, placed the chairs of the Town Hall at the disposal of the club for the banquet. Both the Mayor and Hugh McCarthy were members of the Society.

1900s

There was a general reunion of the members held on Sunday the 3rd of February 1907. A supper for members was held in the concert hall on Sunday the 17th January 1908 after the Christmas holidays. John White was appointed to be in charge of the organising committee for this event. He requested that some gaslights be fitted-up in the concert hall in order to have sufficient light for the event. The Council granted this and also donated £3 towards the supper from the Society's funds *In order that some fowl might be provide.*

1910s

The following members were in attendance at the annual supper of the 'St Iberius Club' held in Wexford on the 5th Feb. 1910. The attendance included Rev. T. Cloney, Adm. Presided, Ald. J. Sinnott, Mayor, Ald. John Tyghe, and Messer's Robert Hanton, William Hutchinson, and Richard Goold, Hon. Secretaries, James O'Rourke, J. Dunne, J. Fennell, D. Murphy, N. Bolger, F. Horan and Michael O'Rourke (snr.). There were a total of 120 members attending the supper. On the 14th of February 1914 the St. Iberius Catholic club held their reunion consisting of supper, dramatic entertainment and singing. Miss Horan provided accompaniment on piano. The appointed organising committee consisted of Michael Kehoe and John Browne with power to add to increase their numbers as they wished. The charge was fixed at 3/- per member and the event was held in the concert hall.

1930s

There is very little documenting the 1920s and 30s. Kevin Cousins very kindly provided me with the following programme/menu for the reunion held at the C.Y.M.S. concert hall on the 16th April 1939. We can deduce from the information on the card that this reunion was held in the concert hall at Common Quay Street. The Most Rev. James Stauton, Lord Bishop of Ferns was the guest of honour and the catering was undertaken by the well-known restaurant of that time 'Love's Café' on North Main Street, just down from the Bullring approx. 100 yards from the C.Y.M.S. concert hall. You can just imagine the girls and lads from Love's Café rushing to and fro passing 'The Man in the Bullring' *(the memorial of 1798)* on their journey from the café to the concert hall, working like mad to insure that the various courses of the meal were delivered on time. It must have been a comical sight for the onlookers on the Main Street. Let us hope it was not raining.

John Dunne

James O'Rourke snr.

Nicholas Bolger

C.Y.M.S. Reunion Menu - 16th April 1939

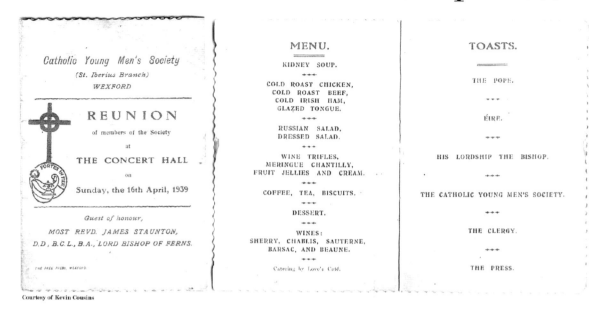

Catholic Young Men's Society
(St. Iberius Branch)
WEXFORD

REUNION
of members of the Society
at
THE CONCERT HALL
on
Sunday, the 16th April, 1939

Guest of honour,

MOST REVD. JAMES STAUNTON,
D.D., B.C.L., B.A., LORD BISHOP OF FERNS.

THE FREE PRESS, WEXFORD

MENU.

KIDNEY SOUP.

COLD ROAST CHICKEN,
COLD ROAST BEEF,
COLD IRISH HAM,
GLAZED TONGUE.

RUSSIAN SALAD,
DRESSED SALAD.

WINE TRIFLES,
MERINGUE CHANTILLY,
FRUIT JELLIES AND CREAM.

COFFEE, TEA, BISCUITS.

DESSERT.

WINES:
SHERRY, CHABLIS, SAUTERNE,
BARSAC, AND BEAUNE.

Catering by Love's Café.

TOASTS.

THE POPE.

ÉIRE.

HIS LORDSHIP THE BISHOP.

THE CATHOLIC YOUNG MEN'S SOCIETY.

THE CLERGY.

THE PRESS.

Courtesy of Kevin Cousins

1940s

A general discussion took place regarding the holding of a Fete in the Redmond Hall and it was decided that if a suitable date could be obtained early in October that a committee should be formed for that purpose. - 2nd July 1946. Also during this meeting a discussion took place regarding the question of the *'holding of the Communion Breakfast'* and the question was deferred for a further meeting. What became of any of these suggestions is unknown. Perhaps they never got off the ground because at the A.G.M held on the 9th February 1947 Thomas Banville said that he thought that a reunion of the members should be held as it was *Very popular with other clubs in the town* and there was a *strong feeling amongst the members, especially the junior members* that the *'C.Y.M.S. should have an Annual Reunion.'* The C.Y.M.S. of Ireland was founded on the 19th May 1849 and in 1949 the Wexford branch of the Society held a 'General Communion & Communion Breakfast' in celebration of the centenary. Approximately sixty members attended en masse at the Mass at 8.30.a.m in the Church of the Immaculate Conception, Rowe Street where they received Holy Communion. This was followed by the Communion Breakfast at the County Hotel, Anne Street.

C.Y.M.S. Communion Breakfast

"Mine's fried eggs, rashers, bangers and black pudding please."

The dining room was suitably decorated for the occasion with a place of honour given to the new flag of the Wexford C.Y.M.S. branch. This flag had been beautifully crafted by the nuns from the Convent of Perpetual Adoration. The President, Rev. Patrick Doyle, Adm., presided at the breakfast and in his speech said *the C.Y.M.S. was the foremost Catholic Action body of laymen in the County.* He thanked Shay Sinnott *[proprietor of the hotel and member of the Society]* and his excellent staff for the very fine breakfast they had served. In his speech John J. Donohoe, Hon. Secretary said *This morning is unique in the History of Wexford, insomuch as it was the first time a 'Communion Breakfast' had been held'* and he went on *"He hoped it was the forerunner of others to follow in years to come."*

168

1950s

The C.Y.M.S. re-union dinner dance was held on the 11th February 1951 and a sub-committee was formed to look into the organising of a re-union and an outing this year. The centenary of the founding of the C.Y.M.S. Wexford branch was celebrated in August 1955 and the reunion dinner dance was held in the Talbot Hotel on the 8th December 1955 on the Feast of the Immaculate Conception. The sub-committee appointed to organise this event were - Thomas Hayes, John F. O'Rourke, Thomas Kelly, John J. Donohoe and George Bridges. The admission charge was set at 15/= (*fifteen Shillings*) and Tommy O'Neill's Band provided the music.

The following is a list of some of the persons present plus their wives:

J. J. Donohoe, Chairman, John F. O'Rourke Hon. Secretary, Ald. John Cullimore, R. E. Corish, Mrs Thomas J. Hayes. Thomas Kelly, Edward F. O'Rourke, Mrs. Patrick J. O'Connor, Thomas O'Rourke, Michael Fortune, Jas O'Brien, Thomas McGuinness, William (Bill) Murphy, Michael (Mike) Kennedy, James Ffrench, Pat Whelan, Ray Whelan, Wally Cleary, Mrs Murth Joyce, Sean Kelly, C. J. Stone, Thomas Mahon, Mrs Michael Fortune, Mrs Thomas O'Rourke, Mrs. John Cullimore, Thomas White, Sam O'Rourke, Mrs Samuel O'Rourke, George Bridges, Paddy Kinsella, Dermot Hall, Con Sinnott, James McEneaney, Thomas Duffin (jnr.), William Couopy, Seamus Furlong, E. Doyle, William Kelly, Matty Luccan, Joan Cleary, Sean Radford, Miss P. O'Rourke. Willie Carley, Michael Lynch, Jackie Breen, W. Murphy, Pat O'Connell, Tom Cadogan, Seamus O'Rourke, M. Diffley, Pat Connolly, T. Byrne, Des Allen, Mr. & Mrs. Tommy Banville, Mr. Collopy, Frank O'Rourke, Dermot McGuire, Michael Mahon (jnr.), Richard Fortune and Michael A. O'Rourke.

Souvenir.

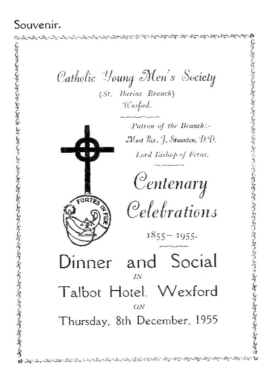

Catholic Young Men's Society

(St. Iberius Branch)
Wexford.

Patron of the Branch:-
Most Rev. J. Staunton, D.D.
Lord Bishop of Ferns.

Centenary
Celebrations
1855 ~ 1955.

Dinner and Social
IN
Talbot Hotel, Wexford
ON
Thursday, 8th December, 1955

Menu

"Cardinal-de-Salis"
Amontillado Sherry

Burgogne Aligote

"Corbieres Superieures"

Irish Whiskey
Power's Gold Label
"Red Breast"
John Jameson 12 years old

Grapefruit Cocktail

Cream of Tomato

Fillet Plaice
Belle Meuniere

Roast Stuffed Chicken,
Braised Wexford Ham,
Cauliflower a la Creme,
Peas au Beurre,
Pommes Fondant,
Pommes Puree,

Sherry Trifle

Fruit Salad
Coffee

Toasts:

The Pope

Ireland

C. Y. M. S. (ST. IBERIUS BRANCH)

Clergy

Our Guests

The foregoing list is an amalgamation of information from various sources. A newspaper report at the time omitted most of the ladies and many more that I remembered. I am sure that many more were present. I was only present for the dinner as I was not allowed to stay for the dance being only 15 years old. Young people of to-day will find that amusing but the fact was young people under age were not allowed where alcohol was on sale in those days.

C.Y.M.S. Reunion Dinner Dance at the Talbot Hotel 1955

Lt. to Rt.   Frances O'Rourke, Margaret Mahon, Tom Mahon, Madge Cleary,
Michael Fortune (the Chemist), Emily Fortune and Thomas O'Rourke

Reunion Dinner at the Talbot Hotel 1955

Mr. Michael Fortune the chemist and his wife Emily

Reunion night at the Talbot Hotel 1955

Frances O'Rourke   Margaret Mahon   Tom Mahon

C.Y.M.S. Reunion 1956 at Mernagh's Restaurant

Photograph Collection of Pat O'Connell

Back Row Lt. to Rt; Pat O'Connell, Paddy Brady, Front; Tom Cadogan, Jackie Breen.

The Children's Christmas Party 1952

172

Who's Who at the Party

1. Tom Mahon
2. Brendan Cullimore
3. Michael O'Rourke
4. Margaret O'Rourke
5. Unidentified
6. Unidentified
7. Unidentified
8. Unidentified
9. Charlotte Gaul
10. Unidentified
11. Unidentified
12. Is it Arthur Kelly ?
13. Ollie Hall
14. Dympna Wilson
15. Tony Rattigan
16. Joan Murphy
17. Sean Rattigan
18. Cyril Hogan
19. Desmond Fortune
20. Unidentified
21. Maureen Hendrick
22. Maureen Hendrick
23. Tom Doyle
24. Unidentified
25. Murphy ?
26. Mary Doyle
27. Ruby Doyle
28. Miss Murphy
29. Unidentified
30. Kathleen Duffin
31. Unidentified

32. Deirdre Donohoe
33. Unidentified
34. Unidentified
35. Unidentified
36. Unidentified
37. Unidentified
38. Doyle?
39. Clodagh Donohoe
40. Unidentified
41. Cleary?
42. Unidentified
43. Brendan O'Rourke
44. Unidentified
45. Philis O'Rourke
46. Nick Corish
47. Unidentified
48. Kevin O'Mahoney
49. Michael O'Rourke
50. Miss Wilson
51. Marie O'Rourke
52. Unidentified
53. Unidentified
54. Catherine Doyle
55. Margaret O'Rourke
56. Anne O'Rourke
57. Ethal Doyle
58. Jackoleen Donohoe
59. Unidentified
60. Breda White
61. Tommy Cullimore
62. Jack Doyle

173

The C.Y.M.S. reunion dinner dance 1956 for members, wives and lady friends was held on the 5th December in the Talbot Hotel. The cost per head to each member was 12/= and the music to be provided by Tommy O'Neill's Band. With regard to the finishing time for the event we read that Fr. O'Neill did not think it advisable for the Society to have *The social or dance part of the reunion continue till 2 a.m. As the commercial dance people in town might use this as an excuse to continue their dances after midnight.* After discussing the matter the meeting agreed that the dance should end at midnight and the reunion should then end with a few concert items and a singsong - 29th November 1956. You will note that the Council had indeed considered having the dance go on until 2.am.

Reunion Dinner 1950s

Jackie Donohoe, Hon. Secretary, Frances (Mrs. T. O'Rourke).

The C.Y.M.S. reunion dinner dance 1957 was held in the Talbot Hotel on Wednesday 4th December. Members were charged 12/= per person and they were *Allowed to take their wives and lady friends.* Also invited were Rev. M. J. O'Neill, Rev. J. Roche, Rev. Fr. Guardian and the local clergy and also the Mayor of Wexford, John Cullimore and Mrs Cullimore. There was a very poor attendance at this reunion.

The C.Y.M.S. reunion dinner dance 1958 was held on Wednesday the 3rd of December. It consisted of a dinner held in Mernagh's restaurant commencing at 7.30.p.m. followed by a social and dance in the C.Y.M.S. concert hall until 12.30.p.m. Invitations were sent out to the following: - the clergy, the Franciscans, Fr. T. Roche Ph.D., His Worship the Mayor, the Garda and the local press. Admission charge for the members was set a 10/- each. The Chairman John J. Donohoe presided and also in attendance were - Rev M. J. O'Neill, Adm., President; Rev. M. Doyle, C.C., Rev. T. Roche, Ph.D., Alderman John Cullimore, P.C. (*representing the Mayor*) Thomas Mahon, Hon. Secretary, William Murphy, Thomas O'Rourke, Walter (Wally) Cleary, Thomas Kelly, Harry P. Doyle, James O'Brien, George Bridges and Eugene McGrail, Vice-President. Tommy Roche, an Irish dancing champion, gave a demonstration in Irish dance and Paddy Scallan, Vincent Sherwood, Liam Bolger and Jackie Donohoe sang a few songs after which the dance commenced. I was fortunate enough to have attended this reunion.

St. Iberius branch C.Y.M.S. Reunion 1957

Left to Right: Tommy Sinnott, Mrs T. O'Rourke, Tom O'Rourke, unidentified, Mrs. T. Banville,
Tommy Banvelle, Mrs J. Cullimore, John Cullimore (Mayor), unidentified, unidentified, Jack Cullen
lady on the end of table Bridie Swords

The 1959 reunion dinner dance was held on the evening of 30th December and the meal was served in the table tennis room with the dance that followed being held in the concert hall on the premises at Common Quay Street. The organising committee as follows met in early October to discuss and arrange the event:

C.Y.M.S. Reunion Dinner Dance 1959 Organising Committee
John J. Donohoe, Hon. Secretary
Thomas O'Rourke
George Bridges
Desmond Allen
Thomas Mahon
P. Kelly

The ladies committee formed to organise the affair, set-up the tables and prepare the supper etc. are not mentioned by name. I cannot understand the Council omitting to record the names of all the ladies organising committees. These ladies did enormous work for the club throughout the years and always ensured that everyone enjoyed themselves at whatever activity they were involved in. Because I was there personally, I am able to name three of the ladies committee present whom I knew - Mrs John Cullimore, Mrs Maggie Mahon and Mrs Thomas O'Rourke. Unfortunately, I do not recall the names of the others.

Some of the Pongo working committee were involved in the relocating of the Pongo tables and seating up to the table tennis room. They then had to be erected and placed as per the ladies' instructions. The Pongo committee also helped set the tables under their watchful eyes. We did exactly as we were told, would we dare do anything else? If you put a knife or fork one millimetre out of place, you were in trouble. The Pongo men there on that particular day were Thomas O'Rourke, *(Commander-in-chief)*, Wally Cleary, Tom Mahon and I. A few other lads who were in the club were press-ganged into helping also. I cannot remember all of them but I believe there were Larry Roche, Francis Bolger and Michael *(Curley)* O'Rourke. We were all rewarded with a couple of bottles of Guinness for our trouble. To-day, helpers would put out their hand and ask for fifty Euros or more for the same work.

The fee for the dinner dance was set at 10/= each and there was to be no alcoholic drink to be consumed on the premises. Now before you utter in disbelief *'That must have been a really merry rave-up of a night'* let me inform you that some of the lads nipped across the road to Jimmy O'Brien's public house called 'The Slaney Bar' and availed of their preferred beverage there. It was alright with the Council so long as one behaved oneself. Incidentally Jimmy O'Brien was a C.Y.M.S. member and he was elected on to the Council in 1960. Eighty members supported this reunion plus their wives or girlfriends. It was a good night and I remember that we younger ones rock 'n' rolled as much as we liked and the older members were content to let us enjoy ourselves. It was a most enjoyable evening for everyone present.

Children's Christmas Parties in the 1950s

Children's Christmas parties were organised in the 1950s. (*See photograph of the 1952 party on the preceding pages*). The Children's Christmas party (December 1955) for the sons and daughters of the members was held on the 6th January 1956. The organising and the working committee which were appointed to organise and run the 1956 event were:

Organising Committee

Mrs. J. Cullimore, Mrs. T. J. Hayes, Mrs. Myles O'Rourke, Thomas J. Hayes, John J. Donohoe, George Bridges and Thomas O'Rourke.

Working Committee

Wally Cleary, Kevin O'Mahony, Thomas Mahon, Michael Mahon, Michael O'Neill, Michael O'Rourke (Author), Sean Doyle, Sam O'Rourke and Myles O'Rourke.

Music by the Slaney Band

Band members - Nicholas Doran, Liam Gaul (*accordions*), Oliver Hall (*accordion and* mouthorgan), Dan Duggan (*accordion*), Sean Rattigan, Tony Rattigan and Cyril Hogan (*Violins*), Eamon Hendrick (*piano and accompanist for singers*). Four of these young musicians later joined the Society - Ollie Hall, Sean and Tony Rattigan and Eamon Hendrick.

Marie O'Rourke sang 'Holy Night'
Myles O'Rourke (jnr.), sang 'Rudolf the Red-Nosed Reindeer'

Reunion Night at the C.Y.M.S. Concert Hall in the late 1950s

176

C.Y.M.S. Reunion 29th December 1959

(Lt. to Rt.) unidentified, Mrs. Margaret Mahon, Mrs. John Cullimore, unidentified, unidentified
possibly Paddy Brady, Tommy Cullimore, Kevin Cousins, Michael O'Rourke (the author)

C.Y.M.S. Reunion 29th December 1960

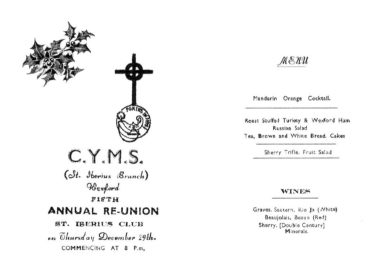

This invitation card was printed on the C.Y.M.S. 'Adana' printing press

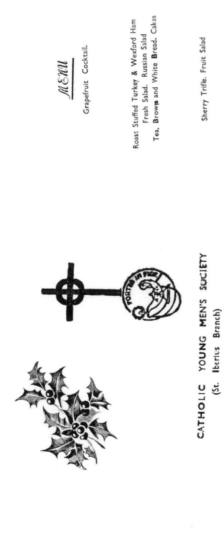

CATHOLIC YOUNG MEN'S SOCIETY

(St. Iberius Branch)

Wexford.

Fourth Annual

RE-UNION

IN

ST. IBERIUS CLUB

ON

Wednesday December 30th. 1959

MENU

Grapefruit Cocktail.

Roast Stuffed Turkey & Wexford Ham
Fresh Salad.   Russian Salad
Tea, Brown and White Bread. Cakes

Sherry Trifle. Fruit Salad

———

WINES

Graves, Sautern, Rio Ja (White)
Beaujolais, Beaun (Red)
Sherry. [Double Century]
Minerals,

The six who put their signatures on the card are : Peter Monaghan, Ray Flynn, Michael O'Rourke (myself), Frank O'Rourke, Desmond Allen, Desmond Fortune.

St. Iberius Branch C.Y.M.S. Reunion 1960

John Cullimore   Tom Mahon   Thomas O'Rourke

1960s

The annual reunion dinner dance of 1960 was conducted in a similar manner as the previous year. The ladies undertook most of the hard work in preparation once again. Jackie Donohoe reported *This year was the 5th Annual Reunion that the club have had since they were started.* However, only 57 members plus their wives and girlfriends attended. This prompted the Council to cancel the reunions for the following years because it was not getting the support that the Council thought it should. So there was no reunion for 1961 or 1962. Jackie was incorrect stating it was the 5th reunion since the club started them. The very first reunion was on the 3rd February 1907, there were reunions in 1914 and 1924 and following these three there were six held consecutively since 1955 making a total of nine annual reunions in all.

1970s

There was very little happening in the way of reunions during the two decades of the 70s and 80s. The only item I could get was this old photograph which was taken at a C.Y.M.S. function in the 70s.

C.Y.M.S. Function in the 1970s
Lt. to Rt. Back Row. Jackie Donohoe, Hon. Secretary, Tom O'Rourke, President.
Front Lt. to Rt. Mrs Jackie Donohoe, Frances (Mrs. T. O'Rourke).

Social Evening in the late 1980s

Myles O'Rourke - Harry Doyle - Nicky Lacey

Social and Presentation Evening 1980s

Mrs. O'Connor, Mrs. Crosbie, Sean 'Bosco' Mahoney and Myles O'Rourke

Celebrations after the Presentations 1980s

Harry Doyle, Myles O'Rourke, Terrence Crosbie, Sean 'Bosco' Mahoney, Ricky O'Rourke

1990s

In the 1990s the club began to hold an annual Christmas party for the members. The first one was held on the 4th December 1994 and on Wednesday 21st December 1994 the Christmas free draw for the members was held at 8.00.p.m. in the club. On the 20th December 1995 a very successful Christmas party was held and the Council hoped to make the event an annual social one. However, on the 3rd December 1996 it was decided at a Council meeting that there would be no Christmas party held this year due to lack of funding.

C.Y.M.S. Christmas Party 1990s

Myles O'Rourke   Dick Murphy

Presentation Night at the Regal Lodge May 1993

Lt. to Rt. Dick Murphy, Ronnie Pettit, Myles O'Rourke, Maurice Delaney

Presentation Evening Celebrations 1990s

Michael O'Rourke,   Milo Crosbie,   Maurice Delaney

(See appendixes number 7 and number 8 for full lists of 'Annual Soirée, Reunion and Banquet Records' from 1859 to 1997, also 'Entertainment Committees' from 1864 to 1959 on Pages 283 and 284)

C.Y.M.S. Excursions and Outings

1860s

On the 19th July 1860 the C.Y.M.S. annual excursion took place. The princely cost per person was set at one shilling (1/-) for those who took alcoholic drink and eight pence (8p) for those who were teetotal. An interesting fact is that all the initial trips undertaken by the Society throughout the 1860's were by boat or steamer. On this occasion the boat left the quayside at 6.00.a.m. sharp. The total expense to the Society for the excursion was £14-6-11. This is the first record that I discovered of the Society having an annual excursion.

The council discussed the preparations for the following year's annual excursion in June and the secretary was instructed to write to Richard Devereux requesting the use of the steam tug 'Erin' for an excursion trip to take place

on the first Sunday in July. This excursion went ahead as planned and the destination was Courtown Harbour at a charge of two shillings and six pence (2/6) each *Members were instructed to bring along their own knife and fork. The Catholic press (not mentioned by name) and Richard Devereux were invited to the pleasure trip.* For those unaware I should mention here that Richard Devereux was probably the biggest ship owner in Wexford town.

On Sunday the 27th September 1862 the C.Y.M.S. set out on their annual excursion by steamboat to the Saltee Islands on the 'Erin' which had been kindly loaned for their accommodation during the day by the said Richard Devereux. Initially, Mr. Robinson, a member of the Society, was to supply the dinner including two glasses of punch or porter. This would have been packed in hampers as was the custom of that time. However, on this occasion the plan was changed and it was agreed that the crew of the tug would supply dinner at a charge of fifteen shillings (15/=) each. The steamer left the quayside at Wexford Harbour at 12.00. noon sharp and as the 'Erin' bore her joyous cargo from the quay the Society's band struck up a variety of national and other popular airs as she dashed out to sea past the Tuskar Rock lighthouse and onward to Carne. Rev. J. Barry and Rev. J. Furlong of St. Peter's College accompanied the members. The council recorded *that any instance of intoxication be pro facto expulsion from the Society.* One cannot help but wonder had the council's ban on drink anything to do with the two illustrious guests on board? The party returned at approx. 6.00.p.m. delighted and invigorated after their day's excursion and were greeted by crowds of friends on the quay.

The Steam-Tug 'ERIN'

On the 8th June 1863 the council discussed the *'annual excursion trip'* and Mr. White suggested that they should send a deputation *to see Richard Devereux to ask him for the use of the steamer 'Erin' as there was a report abroad that her sale is intended.* Whether this trip took place this year or not is uncertain but there is an interesting piece recorded on the 13th June 1864 which informs us that the council were discussing the excursion for that year. It reads as follows *Brother Doyle was asked to speak with Mr. Loughlin, collector of customs about the 'Passenger Act', to find out if it would be legal for either of the steam tugs to take the members [C.Y.M.S.] on an excursion.* The estimated cost this year was set at 2/6 each member. Having perused the 1860s decade there can be no doubt that the Society did in fact use boat trips in the beginning for its excursions.

1880s

The excursion left the hall on Sunday 10th July 1881 at 10.00.a.m. with Castleboro as their destination. The cost was six shillings (6/=) each and only thirty three (33) members participated.

Expenses List

William Robinson supplied the dinners £3-17-0
William Scallan supplied the drink £1-14-6
Robert Hanton supplied the hired cars £4-12-6
(*These gentlemen were all members of the Society*)

The excursion of Sunday the 25th June 1882 was to Clonmines. The charge per head was five shillings (5/=) and sixty (60) members left the club at 9.30.a.m. on several large vehicles heading up William Street and the Faythe, past Johnstown Castle, past Murrintown, Sleedagh, Baldwinstown, Kilcowan, Rathangan, Duncormack, Wellington Bridge arriving at their destination Clonmines which was a journey of 19 miles.

Expenses List

David Robinson supplied the food £6-15-0
Stephen Doyle supplied the drink £3- 4-6
Robert Hanton supplied the hired cars £7-11-0

Owing to the kindness of Richard Codd whose house and offices were situated where one of the castles formerly stood, every facility was afforded to ensure the enjoyment of those participating. Everyone formed into small groups and visited the various ruined edifices dispersed over the area. William Robinson was in charge of the food hampers and having sated their appetites the sports commenced. This excursion was one of the most successful and memorable. The Rev. L. Doyle, C.C., President of the Society, accompanied together with Rev. T. O'Connor, C.C., Rev. P. M. O'Leary, C.C., Laurence Rossiter, Hon. Secretary, Robert Hanton, James Stafford, Patrick Byrne and Patrick Stafford who were active in organising the event.

The following members (*in alphabetical order*) were also in the party:

John Barnwell, Pat J. Breen, Pat Brennan, Pat Breslin, John Buckley, Nicholas Codd, William Connick, Edward Connors, William Corcoran, Nicholas Cosgrave, Pat Cousins, William J. Devereux, Edward Dixon, Myles Doyle, Pat Doyle, Stephen Doyle, John FitzSimons, Rich Furlong, W. Furlong, Nicholas Gahan, Pat Heffernan, James Hopley, Pat Hynes, James Joyce, John F. Kelly, John Kinsella, William Lambert, Joseph Lindsey, James Marlow, Patrick Marlow, Hugh McCarthy, James Moore, Stephen Mullet, John Murphy, Nicholas Murphy, Pat Murphy, Luke O'Connor, Michael O'Connor, Edward F. O'Rourke, Rich Phillips, Francis Quirke, Richard Ryan, Pat Ryan, Nicholas Scallan, William Scallan, Rich Stafford, John Tyghe, Pat Walsh, Edward Whelan and James Whelan.

The "A" Team for the Cricket Match:
J. Stafford, Captain (*he worked in Pettit's*), C. Redmond, B.9, James Stafford, C.3, P. Byrne F.O.W. 7, J. Cosgrave. P. Walsh, W. Corcoran, J. Stafford and W. Furlong.

The "B" Team for the Cricket Match:
H. Connor, J. Stafford, T. Stafford, J. Joyce, J. Barnwell, R. Stafford, J. Lindsey, M. Lambert, N. Gahan, R. Furlong and H. McCarthy.

Running Race (*150 yds. confined to C.Y.M.S. members*)
Twelve competitors. 1st Prize R. Furlong (an album), 2nd Prize W. Corcoran (a mythological curiosity)

Private Race (*150 yards*)
Mr. Cousins won the private race between Messrs Kelly and Cousins

Races confined to Residents of the Area (*450 yds. C.Y.M.S. members excluded*)
1st place Edward Morgan of Kilcavan, 2nd place J. Colothan from Clonmines. Six participated.

Juvenile Race (*C.Y.M.S. members excluded*)
1st place John Power from Garrycullen, 2nd place Matthew Whelan from Ballinruan.

Second Juvenile Race (same distance *C.Y.M.S. members excluded*)
1st place Thomas Murphy from Ballylannon, 2nd Place N. Whelan from Ballinruan.

Old Man's Race (200 Yds. *C.Y.M.S. members excluded*)
1st place Matthew McDonnell, 2nd Place William Wright from Tallaght. This race caused great mirth.

Tug of War

SNAP!

"'Humanity all in a heap"

Tug Of War (*six a side - The C.Y.M.S. versus the locals*)

Both sides were evenly matched and it would have taken much time to determine the winner had not Messrs Marlow and Breslin surreptitiously received assistance from some of the crowd that pressed in on the combatants. Fr. O'Leary at once gave the C.Y.M.S. side a helping hand and the additional strain now put on the rope proved too much, for it snapped, and those who first received unfair help were precipitated pell-mell on the grass in the most ludicrous fashion. This was what an American writer would call *'Humanity all in a heap'*.

High Jump

Several were engaged in this until the rope *(bar)* was raised to four feet. John Codd, Clonmines, Thomas Stafford, Ballymore and James Colothan, Clonmines gave the final leaps. Mr. Codd cleared four feet and nine inches which was sufficient to declare him the winner of the event.

Dancing

A capital display of *'poetry in motion'* was made in the commodious barn at Clonmines. The most notable was Mr. Breslin who danced an Irish double in fine style and Mr. Ryan who showed his ability in dancing a fine hornpipe.

At approx. 6.15.p.m. the bugles were sounded to summon everyone to the vehicles and the party departed from Clonmines at 6.30.p.m. amidst cheers from a large crowd which had gathered to wish the C.Y.M.S. men a safe journey home. The route taken was along the New Line, Ballymitty, Waddingtown, on the mountain road past Skeeterpark, past Forth Mountain, the Three Rocks and home.

On the 15th June 1886 the Council discussed the annual *'Drive'* (*excursion*) and they set the date for 11th July with the destination being the Blackstairs Mountains. The cost was seven shillings (7/=) each. By the 1st July the members objected to the Blacktairs Mountains but the Council decided to adhere to their decision. However, by the 5th July the Council finally had to *announce that the excursion was abandoned due to insufficient numbers of members who would go.* You can lead a horse to water but you can't make him drink it. A lesson that this Council learned the hard way.

On the 2nd May 1887 the following year the Council discussed the annual excursion and here is what they had to say: *It was suggested that the council have a chat with the members of the Society about the annual excursion in order to find out the place that they would want to go.* They had definitely learned their lesson from the previous year.

It was agreed to go to Tintern Abbey on the 10th July at a cost of six shillings (6/=) each. The meeting of 21st June 1887 discussed the forthcoming annual excursion that was referred to as *'The Drive'*. The arrangements were as follows - William Scallan was to supply the drink, Mrs Robinson and Miss O'Connor were asked to supply estimates for the dinner.

The following members were appointed as the organising committee -Michael O'Connor, James Stafford (snr), Nicholas White, Patrick Cullen, James Whelan, Michael Curry and William Hutchinson. William Scallan was the judge for the sports and Robert Hanton was the starter. The route to be taken would be through the Faythe and on to Johnstown. They would leave the club at 9.30.a.m. Seventy-one (71) members went on this trip.

Expenses List

Mrs Robinson	dinners	£11-2-0
John Eyre	car hire	£5-15-0
Robert Hanton	car hire	£2-6-0
John Tyghe	tumblers	£0-4-10
William Scallan,	drink	£7-15-0
John Whelan	car hire	£0-11-0
Pat Stafford	eggs	£0-1-0

In the discussion that took place on the 22nd May 1888 the Council considered the possibility of hiring *'The new tug, the 'Wexford'* for the annual excursion to the Saltee Islands. They appointed a deputation to go and see the Harbour Commissioners to ascertain the cost of same. There are no details of this meeting but we are left in no doubt that it was unsatisfactory as we read that the *Trip on the 'Wexford' was cancelled due to restrictions put on the hiring of it.*

Expenses for the Trip

John Eyre	Car Hire	£4-0-0
Robert Hanton	Car Hire	£2-8-0
Michael J. O'Connor	Dinners at Newtownbarry *(inclusive of drink)*	£5-12-3
S. Godkin & Co.	Seed Cake	4/-
Post Office	Telegram and Postage	1/2.

1890s

In May of 1894 the Council intended to take the trip to Woodenbridge and were making the usual enquiries concerning trains, dinners etc. etc. but due to lack of interest from the members the destination was changed to Kilmore Quay for Sunday the 1st July. Fr. O'Leary's band was invited to join in the excursion but on this occasion had to pay six shillings (6/-) for their fare. Prior to this their involvement in the excursions was free gratis. This excursion had to be cancelled as there was insufficient interest. Perhaps people were fed-up with Kilmore Quay and needed a change.

Glendalough

The 1895 excursion was bound for Kilmore on the 7th July and the cost was set at 6/- per head. The Council ruled that *No drink be given on the road going or coming back.* Needless to remark, this new rule did go down too well with the members because by the 18th June the Council rescinded it as *the majority of the members who were attending the excursion wished it so.* Had democracy arrived at the C.Y.M.S.? I would imagine the rule was simply for safety reasons and nothing more and as such it did make good sense.

The excursion visited Glendalough on the 12th July 1896 and the dinners and teas were supplied by a Mr. Richardson at two shillings and eight pence (2/8) each. The members were given four drinks in total - one on arrival and one on departure from Rathdrum and a further two in Glendalough. The Society incurred a loss of £4-6-4 on this trip.

In May the Council discussed the 1898 annual excursion. Destinations suggested were - Glendalough, The Devils Glen or a trip to the Saltee Islands. By June it was decided and arranged to hire the cars for a trip to Glendalough and they would return home via Roundwood, the Devil's Glen

and Rathnew. The hotels at Glendalough, Ashford and Newrath Bridge submitted their quotations for the dinners and teas and the following were given the contract - Mr. Richardson, Glendalough dinner at two shillings (2/-) each and Mr. Byrne, Ashford tea at eight pence (8p) each. Due to the poor interest in the previous year's excursions it was decided on this occasion to allow friends of members on the trip. The train left Wexford at 8.00.p.m. on the 12th July with forty nine members on it. The council also decided that cycling members of the club could have their bicycles transported to Rathdrum and brought from Rathdrum and the cyclists could participate in the other advantages of the excursion for a charge of seven shillings and six pence (7/6).

1900s

On the 15th June 1900 the Council discussed the annual excursion and it was suggested and decided that William Hutchinson, Hon. Secretary should write to Major Hamilton to ascertain if the club could get permission to visit 'Woodstock' as several of the members expressed a desire to go there. Alas, the Major replied on the 28th June in the negative stating *his instructions were not to allow the public to visit 'Woodstock' for the present.*

The annual excursion in the summer of 1901 had to be cancelled because there simply was insufficient interest in it. The reason given blamed the cyclists *Because most of the members had joined cycling clubs and avail themselves of their bicycles for their recreation.* Cycling was becoming so popular amongst the members that the council had to take note of it.

On the 3rd June 1902 the council decided to ask the cycling members of the club to organise an excursion for the last Sunday of June or first Sunday of July so that any member of the club could join in. Kilmore Quay was selected as the destination for the event to take place on

Sunday the 3rd July. The charge was set at 5/- per member and obviously the cyclists participating would pay a lesser fare. The Council were to *'Take the usual prizes for the sports.'* Prior to the event the Council ordered that *No drink to be given on the road either going to Kilmore or coming back.*

On the 25th of June 1903 it is recorded that the Council were organising an outing and had started to collect the names of those who would be interested. They decided that if sixty members or more showed an interest in the excursion then they would go ahead, if not the venture would be cancelled. Surprisingly enough they got more that sixty members interested and the organising of the event took place. *The question of bringing ladies on the excursion was mentioned but as the excursion was for members of the club only, it was considered this could not be entertained.* So there you have it ladies - like it says on the 'Yorkie' chocolate bar *'It's not for Girls'*. The Council's reason for not allowing ladies to come on the excursion is pretty weak wouldn't you say. By the 16th July the following arrangements were being made - R. Coady, Innistige (sic) quoted for the catering at Dinner 2/6 and Tea @ 9p per head and after some haggling he said he would supply dinner and tea for 3/- per head providing that there were more than fifty people and if not, then the charge was 2/6 each for dinner and 9p for tea. This was

agreed and P. Kelly, Commercial Quay was selected to supply the drink taken for the journey. Communication was also received from the manager and the stationmaster at New Ross regarding the railway fare and car hire. This was all considered acceptable and the excursion took place on the 19th July 1903.

On the 30th June the arrangements for the 17th July 1904 annual excursion were finalised to visit Cullenstown. Mrs McCoy of the 'Refreshment Rooms' at Cullenstown quoted 3/- per head for dinner and tea. The Council accepted this with the proviso that each person be supplied with a drink of ale, stout (*Guinness*) or mineral water with the dinner and she agreed to this. The excursion was to be by car and the cost 7/- per head but members who were travelling by bicycle would only pay 5/- each. By the 11th July the response from the membership was only fifteen members and the excursion had to be abandoned.

The excursion to Kilmore on Sunday the 5th July 1908 had forty-eight members. The minutes record *'No cyclists this time.'* So everyone would be travelling by car.

The fare was fixed at 5/- per head and scheduled to start from the club at 10.30.a.m.   They stopped for refreshments at Silversprings. It was expected to arrive at Kilmore at approx. 1.00.p.m. Dinner was at 1.30.p.m. tea at 6.00.p.m. and they would leave Kilmore at 8.00.p.m. They expected to be home in Wexford by 11.30.p.m
.

The following is the price list for the occasion:

Cost of each person for the excursion 5/-
Dinner and tea at Nicholas White's in Kilmore 3/-
J. Jameson XXX Whiskey 5/3 per quart.
Bishop Water Whiskey 5/- per quart.
Guinness Ex Stout 1/10 per dozen.
Bass Ale 2/6 per dozen.
Minerals (*water*) 1/6 per dozen.

1910s

On Sunday the 28th July 1912 the club held its excursion to Kilmore Quay. Nicholas White quoted 3/- per head for dinner and tea and this was accepted. Some of the members who took part were: Capt. Busher, Tim Carty, Mr Lawlor, Jem Roche (*the boxer*), Lar Furlong, Jimmy Browne (*the builder*), Tom Doyle (*the Free Press*), Tom Parle (*Rate Collector*), Richard Goold, Fr. Tom Moran, William Deasy, Johnnie Browne, Robert Hanton, Paul Roche (*the People Newspaper*), John Tom Sutton (*Kilmore Quay*), Mr. O'Leary (*from Park*), William Headship, Michael O'Rourke (*butcher*), Fr. James Codd, Tommy Godfrey, Bob Banville, John Rossiter, Pat Breen (*draper*), Fr. John Sinnott, Nick Bolger and Pat Leary.

Kilmore Excursion 1912

On the 13th January 1913 the council endeavoured to arrange an excursion to Glendalough. The organisers had spoken to the station master at Wexford as to the possibility of the trip taking place on a Sunday. Initially the station master intimated there were difficulties as Sundays were booked-up. Then the council decided to go to Kilmore at a cost of 5/- per head.   However, by the 14th July the stationmaster informed the club that the railway had agreed to put on a special extra train to cater for the club's excursion to Glendalough.   They would transport the party to Rathnew on the outgoing journey and pick them up at Rathdrum for the return journey

Expenses for the Trip

Car hire	5/6 per head
Dinner	2/- per head
Tea	<u>9p per head</u>

Rail fare, car hire, dinner and tea   8/6 per head in total

This total only adds up to 8/3 I cannot account for the other 3p.   I suspect it paid for a drink at the meals.   The members could pay for any other refreshments themselves outside dinner and tea.

On the 12th July 1914 the minutes record that *'The local branch of the A.O.H. Society were putting on an excursion to Cork and Lucenstown?'* for the first Sunday in August and they invited C.Y.M.S. members to join them and some members did.

Timothy McCarthy was the chief organiser for the 1916 excursion. The intention was to visit Kilmore Quay on the 16th July at a cost of 5/6 per member.   On the 5th of July the Council contacted White's Hotel, Kilmore Quay for a quote for the catering.   Mr. White quoted 4/- per head for dinner and tea but the Council replied that this was too expensive and offered him 3/6 instead.   The Council then discovered that the National Foresters Club had arranged their excursion for Sunday the 16th July to Kilmore and Cullenstown.   So the club decided to change their date to the 23rd July.   Meanwhile, Mr. White had replied accepting 3/9 per head for the catering.   This was agreed upon and fifty-two members went on the excursion this year.

On the 5th June 1917 the excursion to Kilmore Quay was arranged for Sunday the 1st July at a cost of 5/- per head. By the 19th of June it was discovered that many other parties had booked the same date which would mean that it would be difficult to *'Procure cars for the excursion'* so it was changed to Sunday 22nd July, it being the next available date.   Sixty-five members participated.

In 1918 the excursion was arranged for Sunday the 14th July to Kilmore Quay.   The arrangements committee secretaries John Browne and Timothy McCarthy enquired of Murthy McCarthy and Robert Hanton if vehicles would be available for that date.   The cost was fixed at 6/- per member and sixty-five members went on the excursion, some of whom were:
Michael Kehoe, Robert Hanton (snr.), Michael O'Rourke (*butcher*), Mr. O'Riordan, Rev. James Codd, Robert Barnwell, John Rossiter, Patrick Breen (*draper*), Rev. John Sinnott, Nicholas Bolger, Patrick O'Leary, Paul Roche, William Hutchinson, John Lambert, Capt. Laurence Busher, Martin O'Connor, Tim McCarthy, James Kehoe, Jem Roche (*the boxer*), Laurence Harpur, James Browne, Thomas Parle, Thomas E. Doyle, Richard Goold, Fr, Moran, Daniel Murphy, William Deasy and John Browne.

Timothy McCarthy

Rev. James Codd, C.C.

Ald. Robert Hanton

1920s

The annual excursion on Sunday the 15th July 1923 was a very special outing. It was the first occasion that motor cars were mentioned in relation to the clubs' excursions over the years. On the 19th June the organising committee reported that the motor cars would cost 15/- per member if this trip was to go to Duncannon via Ballyhack and Ramsgrange and from Duncannon via Tower of Hook, Fethard, Tintern, Wellingtonbridge and home. The fare was fixed at 20/- per head inclusive of dinner and tea. Fifty-eight members took part.

In June 1924 the organising committee were discussing a visit to Glendalough but by the 4th of July they were awaiting replies from the station master concerning particulars of transport to Bray, Co. Wicklow and from hotels and restaurants in Bray regarding refreshments. It transpired that no hotel in Bray would supply dinner and tea on Sunday, as they were always fully booked on Sundays. Eventually they discovered a hotels or restaurant which would accommodate their requirements on Sunday 3rd August at a cost of 2/6 per head for dinner and ¼ for tea.

Photo By Michael O'Rourke   Hook Lighthouse

It was also announced by the committee that efforts were being made to endeavour to organise a group from each club in town to total about two hundred and fifty people for an excursion from Wexford to Fishguard at 10/- per head.

1930s

The discussions regarding the arrangements for the 1930 excursion were under way with Robert Hanton estimating

that to supply 'Brakes' for an excursion to Kilmore would cost 50/- each including the driver's charges. I am surmising that 'Brakes' must have been an expression for these carts. Mr. Sutton, Kilmore Quay estimated dinner and plain tea would cost 4/- each member. The excursion took place on the 27th July at a cost of 9/- per member all inclusive, care hire and meals. On the 3rd March 1936 an excursion to the Isle of Man or other seaside resort per steamer was under discussion and it was decided to leave the matter in the hands of a small committee to see if they could make enquiries and bring it to fruition.

Sean Doyle

1940s

On 1st May 1949 Sean Doyle was elected to undertake the formation of a sub-committee concerning the proposed annual outing.

On 5th April 1949, on the advice of the Revd Chairman it had been decided *to confine the outing solely to the male members* of the Society. This is going to be a real bundle of laughs. We then read that the outing to Glendalough which had been arranged for July was *cancelled due to a lack of interest* from the membership. That's not surprising. I wonder if it ever occurred to the Rev. Chairman that the married men in the Society may well have wanted to give their wives a day's outing.

1950s

A bus outing of members, their wives and lady friends was suggested for late July subject to the approval of Fr. O'Neill. Meanwhile, a notice was to be erected in the case requesting members to sign their names if interested. Venues suggested were Glendalough, Tramore, Dunmore and Courtown Harbour. On the 3rd July 1956 Fr. O'Neill said he had no objection to the C.Y.M.S. outing provided it was well conducted and there was no misconduct by the members.

(See Appendixes No 9 and 10 for 'Excursion Arrangement Committees' and 'Annual Excursion Records' on Pages 286 and 288)

The Harmonium and Piano

On the 30th October 1865 Fr. Walter Lambert and Frank Lyons, a music teacher, consulted with Matthew J. Furlong on the possibility of purchasing a harmonium for the Society. By the 26th February 1866 the Club had purchased one and the Council were seeking for someone to teach it. A deputation from the Council visited Mr. Lyons who advised them that in the: *First place to discontinue playing the harmonium as much as possible,* as the instrument was being materially damaged and with regard to teaching members to play it he recommended *That first, the pupils learn the piano for three months, after that time they may play on the harmonium.* Frank Lyons agreed to teach the piano to four of the members for a charge of four guineas per quarter and the Council resolved *that the harmonium be played on Sunday evenings only by competent person.*

Matthew Furlong

In February 1869 the secretary Thomas White proposed and Mr. Martin seconded that *On condition that £10 be allowed for our present harmonium, a new one be provided at a cost of about £25, and that Frank Lyons be requested to solicit one for us at Dublin.* Nothing obviously came of this at that time because it is next recorded in 1870 when in November the Society received a letter from the Mechanics Institute referring to the harmonium which read:

Letter received from the Mechanics Institute dated 8th November 1869

'Mechanics Institute Wexford', November 1869.

Dear Sirs,
At a meeting of the 'Board of Directors of the Wexford Mechanics Institute and literary association' on this evening it was unanimously resolved. *"That the best thanks of the board directors be tendered to the council of the 'Catholic Young Men's Society' for their great kindness in granting the use of their splendid harmonium on the occasion of Mr. Meadow's reading in the 'Town Hall' last Friday evening.'*

Yours Faithfully,

Thomas M. O'Leary
Mr. Hanton, Hon. Secretary.

On the 29th August 1870 the harmonium must have been so much in use that the Council decided to procure a new one. They decided to sell the existing one and the Rev. President said that he would contact Rev. Roche P.P., Lady's Island and ascertain if he would be inclined to purchase it. The asking price was set at £20 and Fr. Roche did purchase it and paid the club £21 for it.

WHO DARE DISPUTE THIS STARTLING
INTELLIGENCE !
This is the Cheapest Piano in the World.

Walnut Case, Iron Frame, Check Action, Seven
Octaves. Price, £20 0s. 0d.

Specially Manufactured to my order, and only just received direct from the Makers.

PIANOS, £20 0 0
PIANOS, £75 0 0
PIANOS, £30 0 0
PIANOS, £35 0 0
PIANOS, £40 0 0
PIANOS, £50 0 0
PIANOS, £60 0 0
PIANOS, £70 0 0
PIANOS, £90 0 0
PIANOS, 100 GUINEAS

Harmoniums and American Pianos at all Prices

PIANOS which have given satisfaction to some of the most Respectable,
Intelligent and competent Judges in Ireland

For Tone, Touch, General Excellence and
Price,
THESE INSTRUMENTS
Will compare favourably with any Instruments in the World

SPLENDID NEW STOCK OF
Melodeons, Concertinas, Violins, Guitars,
Banjoes, &c.

NO   SECOND   PRICE.

Remember

FURLONG IS THE MAN

Who dares anyone to prove what he says is not correct

Note the Address :

M. J. FURLONG,

The Society had to hire a piano for an entertainment they conducted in the theatre in High Street in October 1888. This was hired from Matty Furlong a member and proprietor of The Stationary and Musical Instruments Depot on South Main Street at a cost of £1-5-0 for the two nights. The dramatic club held an entertainment on the 11th May 1896 for the sole purpose of raising funds to purchase a piano for the club.

On the 30th July 1896 the Council were debating whether to purchase a piano or not. They *decided to buy one so long as the price did not exceed £20.* The secretary Laurence Rossiter and John Donohoe were appointed to purchase the piano at Nicholas Neills of Francis Street. The asking price was £12-10-0, and following a discussion it was decided to go ahead and purchase. This John Donohoe should not to be confused with the John J. Donohoe, Hon. Secretary, known as Jackie of much later years. By the 12th October 1896 the piano was in

continuous use and giving great pleasure to the members. A singing class was started with over twenty five members active in it at that time and there was a weekly subscription of four pennies to become a member. It was also agreed that Mr, Donohoe would teach the class at 7/6 per week. This singing class was finished by the 14th February 1899 as per the A.G.M. notes but it re-commenced again almost immediately.

The club received a letter from Matthew J. Furlong *claiming £2-10-0 for damage done to his piano during the time the Society had a loan of it.* The Council discussed the matter and they decided to seek the opinion of solicitor Michael J. O'Connor and to be guided by him. The outcome of this dispute was that a settlement of 7/6 was agreed between Mr. O'Connor (*a fellow C.Y.M.S. member*) and Messrs. J. Sinnott & Son, Mr Furlong's solicitors. Mr. O'Connor carried out this work for the Society free gratis. Matty Furlong had been hiring pianos out to the Society since 1888 and possibly even prior to this date and it was a pity that matters had to end that way.

On the 3rd September 1902 Patrick Donohoe applied for the use of the concert hall and the piano for the purpose of choir practice for the forthcoming County Feis and this was granted. On 22nd December 1908 a bill for 10/- for the cost of the tuning of the piano was presented to the Council and it was decided to request both Charles E. Vize and Frank Breen who had been using the piano to contribute to the cost of tuning before the account was paid. Charles E. Vize was the famous photographer and a member of the club.

On the 18th November 1917 the Council was informed that a piano and pictures were to be sold by auction on Tuesday the 20th November from the estate of the late Mrs. Devereux of George's Street. Two representatives from the Council were sent with authority to purchase if anything was suitable, particularly the piano.

On the 14th January 1918 the McNally Concert Co. inquired if they could hire the club's piano for three nights at the Theatre (*Theatre Royal*) as *there was no other suitable piano available.* This request was granted at a charge of £3 for the three nights. This is interesting as elsewhere it is stated that many others were *absolutely forbidden to use the piano,* in fact they were not even to put a hand near it. Obviously, good pianos were very scarce in the town so it is understandable that the Council were so protective of it.

Charles E. Vize

The policy regarding the hiring of the piano was treated differently for charitable cases as on the 22nd January

1919 a J. Scallan from the Third Order rooms requested the loan of the piano for the purpose of practicing for a charity concert in aid of the rooms and the reply stated *The conditions of its use were explained to him.* There is no doubt that this request was granted because most often all charity requests were granted without question. The piano was also used by the Old Commercial Dance Class who hired the hall on Wednesday evenings weekly in October 1923 for dancing lessons. Its use was included in the charge of £1 per week for the concert hall. This appears to be the regular custom at this period as on the 11th November 1924 the Slaney Dance Class hired the hall on Friday evenings for dance practice at a charge of 15/= per night inclusive of the piano.

Dramatic Corps Record

1860s

The first type of entertainment or dramatic performance was of the variety type comprising of mostly singers and musicians. I cannot state categorically the exact date that a dramatic entertainment was first conducted by the Society but it is known that they staged an entertainment in the spring of 1868. A Miss Holbrook agreed to sing if she could be accompanied by Mr. Swaby (*a music teacher*).

However Mr. Swaby could not attend and as a consequence of this Miss Holbrook withdrew from the show. Frank Lyons, a music teacher, offered to take Mr. Swaby's place but, alas, Miss Holbrook still declined. Mr. Lyons trained a choral class for the event and cooperation was received from the Wexford Amateur Musical Club who also took part in the entertainment. Reserved seats cost 2/6 and seats for the general public were 1/6 with members paying 1/= for admittance.

1870s

On St. Patrick's Day 1871 the people of Wexford were awoken from their slumber early that morning by the two newly formed bands in the town. The new bands were named the Confraternity Band and the other not yet named was expected to be called the St. Patrick's Home Rule Band. The fife and drum band of the Wexford Militia joined them in marching up and down the town to the delight of the people who were quite proud to see the first two Wexford bands perform in such marvellous splendour considering that they had barely two weeks to practice. Amongst the crowds were two large groups of supporters belonging to Father Mathews' Temperance Movement and the O'Connor Repeal Group. The new bands at one stage played the National Anthem to the cheers of the crowds. There were Masses celebrated in the town and everyone wore the national emblem, the shamrock. One reporter wrote: *The festivities were brought to a close in the Young Men's Society's Hall, at Paul Quay, in a manner which deserves our heartiest praise to the members of this admirable institution.* The C.Y.M.S. provided the people with entertainment that surpassed all their former entertainments. Starting at 8.00.p.m. sharp James Horan, the stage manager commenced the evening's proceedings with the following prologue which created much amusement and laughter in the audience:

A welcome friends, to one and all
Who've come to-night to cheer our Hall,
And quaff with us the noble bowl
Of mind and mirth, and "flow of Soul".
'Tis thus St. Patrick loves, I ween
His sons should drown the shamrock green-
Not in those cups that have set the brand
Of bowl *we've* brewed is light and bright,
Spiced with wisdom, wit, and flight
Of soaring fancy-just the thing
To warm the soul's most genial spring;

And form the bright intellectual draught
No *boozing* tippler e'er hath quaffed.

"Venture and win" is manly teaching;
You'll find the lesson worth the preaching.
"John Duck", we trust, will yield ye fun,
And the saucy Pattle, whom he won
With such ado-is worth the money.
But what are both to Paddy Rooney?
The ultra-Irish Irishman.
That makes a blunder where he can.
But as for poor unhappy Dobbs
He simply gets what's due to snobs.

As amateurs, we'll do our best,
In scene, and song, and dance, and jest.
To give our Patrick's cup a zest-
So drink1 but mind do not get screwed
By o'er excess at the bowl we've brewed-
If you laugh too much at Duck or Rooney
You'll be fined in stitches –not in money-
Don't let a gold-laced sergeant, twig
Excessive mirth at the Irish jig
(We'll let the fines, tho-for this dance
Go towards the building at the Manse),
For this is a ticklish town to drink in,
One get's " a week as quick as winkin, -
And as far *fines*- I'm really told
The Mayor's Office's paved with gold;
And they say-from walking o, er the dollars
The things broke out on the sergeants collard-
But the golden ill might be abated
Were both the *youths re-vaccinated*.
Honour, however, to our worthy Mayor
Who makes all drunkards feel *"He's there."*

Then temper well your mirth and fun,
We'll find at length when all is done
We've spent a genial Patrick's night.
And, when dawns the morning light
'Tis not from "Quod" we'll greet the skies,
Racked in brain-with blood-shot eyes.
No-but fresh, and filled with happy dreams
And memories of the pleasant scenes.
We've witnessed here-whilst our loved Saint
And Patron, Patrick, sees no taint.
Or stain of ill, in the cheering way
We've honoured his blest Festive Day.

Two plays were performed by the Society's dramatic corps and the orchestra was supervised and conducted by Patrick Breen.
The plays and actors that night were:

The Outlawed Jacobite
P. Furlong as Sir Richard Wroughton
John Redmond as Major Murray
James Horan as John Duck
James Fewer as Lady Somerford
H. Stone as the widow Pottle landlady of 'The Crocked Billet'
William Kelly as Polly Pottle daughter of landlady

The farce The Omnibus
William Cummins as Mr. Ledger
Matthew Reck as Mr. Dobbs
William Kelly as Master Tom Dobbs
James Horan as Pat Rooney
James Kelly as the Farrier's Boy
Patrick Neill as Julis Ledger
James Fewer as Mrs. Dobbs
H. Stone as Miss Damper

The audiences were delighted with the evening's performances and then vacated the hall to view the illuminations on the Ballast Bank opposite Paul Quay just outside the C.Y.M.S. Hall.

1880s

The next reference to a dramatic club was on the 22nd September 1885 which meant there was a gap of seventeen years with no reference of any dramatic activities. It is difficult to accept that there was no entertainment staged during this period. Whilst there is no record in the minute books, I strongly suspect that some entertainment must have taken place. On the aforementioned date the Council was anxious to *get a 'Dramatic Class' started up again and they asked Mr. O'Connor to undertake the organising of this.'* They hoped that a play could be performed for the next soirée and we know from an entry on the 20th October that Mr. O'Connor did get matters started again as he requested the use of the concert hall for practice on two nights per week. Three years elapsed before any further mention.

On Monday evening the 13th February 1888 the C.Y.M.S. staged a variety entertainment at their new hall on Paul Quay before a large and select audience. The hall was tastefully decorated with flags and evergreens and Rev. N. J. Sheridan, the indefatigable and zealous President of the Society introduced the evening's entertainment. Some *'Magnificent Views, illustrating Ireland's Beauty, and Ireland's blight'* opened the event.

Very Rev. N. T. Sheridan, B. C. L,

The usual explanatory lecture had to be abandoned due to lack of time. The first picture presented was of William O'Brien, M.P. the indomitable champion of Ireland's rights followed by the Vale of Avoca, Glendalough, Lakes of Killarney and the Irish House of Commons together with many other picturesque and beautiful places in which Ireland abounds. Next were scenes of the evictions at Glenboigh and Woodford, of John O'Connor's burning rooftree and the widow Quirk's dismantled cabin. There were myrmidons of the crown, military and police engaged in the work of destruction and other villainy which was being carried out driving people from their homes. The horror and detestation that the audience felt was expressed in loud groaning. The audience rose to their feet in rapturous applause and the band played the 'Conquering Hero' when Mr. Parnell, the Irish leader, came into view. Following were pictures of D. Sullivan and Michael Davitt. The effect of the scenes on the audience was electrifying and the reporter present wrote *No more instructive lesson could be taught than what can be gathered from scenes like those at the Catholic Young Men's Society's entertainment that night.*

William Corcoran

196

Part two of the programme opened with the club band playing and singing 'Home Sweet Home.' George Dixon sang a beautiful solo 'Madeline' and his fine voice was in good form. At the close, Mr. Dixon received well-merited applause. James Whelan, in Irish character, rendered the comic 'Killaloe' in good style but he seemed to be more at home in the humorous piece 'Money'. Edward Whelan, in the 'Anchor's Weigh'd' and again in 'Queen of my Heart' was a great success. Next was the comic 'The Irish Jaunting Car' given by Patrick Howlin in a racy style and he also recited 'The Workhouse System'. He acquitted himself so ably with this as to gain the reputation of being an elocutionist of no mean order. Master Hugh McGuire delighted all in the comic 'I'm a Jolly Little All Round'.

The concluding part three consisted of a farce entitled 'A Race for a Widow or Two Gents Bamboozled'. A reporter present wrote *It is no exaggeration to say that never before had any Wexford audience presented to them the picture story of Ireland in a better arranged or more excellent manner.*

On the 1st and 8th October 1888 the dramatic club performed a play entitled 'The Shaughraun'. This play was performed in the Theatre in High Street *(obviously not yet named the Theatre Royal)*. The profit for the first night was £5 and £5-4-0 on the second. Hereunder is a list of people and their fees for various work executed in relation to this play:

Expense List

NAME	DESCRIPTION	AMOUNT
Mr. Sinnott	For theatre	£4-10-0
Mr. Sinnott	Men *(Labourers)*	17/=
Mr. L. Larkin	Pasting 150 bills around town	10/=
William Corcoran	Printing of bills	£2-10-0
Edward Walsh	Printing of bills	£1-10-0
John Green	Printing of bills	6/=
P. Murphy	Unknown	£1-0-0
William Crowther	Unknown	10/=
Myles Shanahan	Orchestra	£2-10-0
Matty Furlong	Hire of Piano Scripts, wigs and sundries	£1-5-0 £3-0-0

Mr. Sinnott is obviously the proprietor of the theatre. William Corcoran was the editor of the Irish Press later to become The Free Press on South Main Street. Edward Walsh was the owner/editor of the People Newspapers, North Main Street. John Green was the owner/editor of the Independent (*Wexford*) North Main Street. Matty Furlong was the proprietor of the Stationary & Musical Instrument Depot on South Main Street and he was the agent for both Boston and E. Bishop & Son pianos. All four of the aforementioned were members of the Society. Of the other four names mentioned i.e. L. Larkin, William Crowther and Myles Shanahan are definitely not on the membership list and with regard to P. Murphy there are twenty five P. Murphys on the register and only seven of those could possibly be the gentleman in question so the most we can deduce is that he may have been a member of the Society.

1890s

The Society held its annual reunion on the 4th January 1891 and the dramatic club provided a great evening's entertainments for the members. Over ten members took part in the vocals and Professor Patrick Breen and M. Hanrahan accompanied them. Eight actors performed a very laughable farce entitled 'L.L.' and Thomas Robinson's rendering of 'Auld Lang Syne' joined by all concluded the evening.

On Easter Monday night 1891 the Society's dramatic club conducted a most enjoyable entertainment to a large appreciative audience in the C.Y.M.S. Concert Hall, Paul Quay. The repertoire was diversified and lively and consisted of a comic drama, a farce and a musical melange of high-class character. Bernard's sprightly comic drama 'His Last Legs' formed the principle feature of the evening.

A reporter of the time wrote that *The C.Y.M.S. amateur thespians maintained their reputation as the best ever seen in Wexford.* The cast was:

Felix O'Callaghan as a spendthrift Irish Landlord
Thomas Harpur as Charles Rivers a Student
John J. Sutton as Dr. Banks
Daniel J. Healy as Mr. Rivers father of Charles
William H. McGuire as John his servant
John Williams as Mrs. Montague a Widow with a Fortune
William Murphy as Julia Banks
John Doyle as Mrs. Banks
John J. O'Neill as unknown

The musical interlude was the most enjoyable portion of the entertainment. It opened with a duet by P. B. Troy and James Furlong singing 'Larboard Watch, Ahoy!' in which the singers exhibited culture, voice and harmony of the highest order. Edward Whelan sang two solos 'Kathleen Mavourneen' and 'The Minstrel Boy'. The former he sang with much expression and good taste and the latter with appreciative verbs and effect and he was loudly encored. John Williams caught the ear of the audience at once with his rendition of 'What Will We Do With Our Girls' and yielded to an imperative demand for a repetition of the vital question. J. Furlong sang "A Sailor's Life for me" in fine voice and he received a vociferous encore to which he responded with a sympathetic and highly finished rendering of 'Go Where Glory Waits Thee'. Mr. Troy sang 'Then You'll Remember Me' and in response to loud and oft-repeated calls for 'The Boy's Of Wexford' sang the ancient legend with all the effect that is possible.

The performance concluded with a production of the farce 'Area Bella' which kept the fun flowing fast and furious for thirty minutes. The characters were:

J. Williams as Pitcher in the Police
J. J. O'Neill as Tosser in the Grenadiers
John Doran as Walker Charles a Milkman
J. Doyle as Mrs. Croaker "The Missus"
W. Murphy as Penelope the Area Bell

James Hanrahan provided the accompaniments with his accustomed good taste and ability and also gave a well liked exposition of pianoforte solo music during the evening, not the least pleasing of which were the 'All the Year Round' and Quadrilles by P. J. Breen.

An early gramophone

The gramophone evolved from the phonograph 'Talking Machine'

On the 29th October 1891 the records state *It was suggested to ask Mr. Lynd to give an entertainment with his "Phonographic', the next time Mr. Lynd visits Wexford Town on the 17th November 1891.* A brief note on this subject to acquaint the reader with what we are dealing with here. Edison made the first recording of a human voice in 1877. Bell and Tainter followed with their wax-coated cylinders and Bell invented his phonograph in 1877. Berliner invented his phonograph, which became known as a gramophone in 1885. So the *'phonographic'* referred to was an instrument that reproduces sounds from a grooved disc. It must have been a marvel for people to hear this wondrous invention that Mr. Lynd demonstrated and there could be no doubt that the concert hall would have been sold out for the occasion.

The dramatic club staged a play entitled 'The Drunkard's Warning' in the Theatre Royal on Wednesday evening the 29th January 1896 which was a great success and received good reviews in all the newspapers. The following were the cast involved:

Thomas Bent as Mr. Grandville a wealthy merchant

James Furlong as Edward Mordaunt his son-in-law
William H. Murphy as George Seymore clerk to Grandville
John Doyle as Tipton a confirmed inebriate *(drunkard)*
Thomas Murphy as Smasher his companion
Nicholas Gahan as a temperance landlord
Robert Harvey as warden
Thomas Salmon as Lousia Mordaunt
Martin Sutton as Emma Grandville
Patrick Dunbar as Laura daughter of Howard
Patrick Donohoe played some music during the interval. Edward Whelan sang 'Adieu Marie', Nicholas Gahan sang 'Norah Kearney', Robert Harvey sang 'Old Ireland's Head and Hands' and Thomas Bent sang 'That's The Cause of it'. The programme concluded with the farce 'Caught By the Cuff' the cast being Nicholas Gahan, Thomas Bent, James Furlong and Thomas Murphy.

Thomas Bent

Thomas J. Cullen was stage manager and Mrs Nicholas Gahan and Mrs. James Furlong were dressers preparing the ladies costumes. Frank Carty looked after the coiffures *(hair styles)*.

One of the play books used by the Dramatic Class possibly in the 1920s

The dramatic club staged an entertainment on the 11th May 1896, the profits of which were to go towards purchasing a piano. On the 22nd May 1896 Patrick Breen celebrated his silver jubilee, the twenty-fifth anniversary of his appointment to the position of organist for the Catholic parochial churches in Wexford.

The dramatic club entertained greatly at the annual soirée on Sunday the 19th January 1897. On the 20th December 1897, some eight to ten months after the club took possession of its new premises at St. Iberius House, they decided to stage a variety concert in the new hall for the official opening. You will remember that the strict rules governing the C.Y.M.S. forbade ladies to be on the premises. Well Rev. Fr. Aylward, the Society's President, sought and got permission from the Bishop to allow lady singers take part and he also suggested that *It might be in the interest of the Society if the council invited some Protestant singers to take a part*. The members of the organising committee appointed to take charge of the event were - Robert Hanton, Frank Carty, William Hutchinson and Richard Goold, the latter two being Hon. Secretaries on the Council.

Patrick Breen

List of Some of the Performers

Miss Jeffries, Miss Shanahan, Miss Maddock, Miss Cosgrave, J.W. Gilling, C. Walker, Mr. Fleming, D.J.R.J.C., J. Owen, M. A. Ennis, E. McGuinness and E. A. Whelan all from Wexford and the following from Dublin - Miss Murphy, E. P. Monck, E. V. Berry and Mr. Kearney. Due to the large numbers anticipated to attend it was decided by the Council to change the venue from the concert hall, which was deemed too small to accommodate everyone, to the theatre in High Street. The concert was held on the 20th January 1897 and admission was set at 2/6 each for the boxes and 1/= each for the pit and gallery. Having paid all their expenses the Society made a profit of 314 to add to their funds. I found the illustrated poster of the old Talbot Press Play in the club.

On Easter Monday evening 1898 the Camptown Serenaders conducted a performance in the concert hall. Recorded on the 22nd April is *a unanimous note of thanks was passed to His Worship the Mayor for his kindness in lending the seats of the Town Hall to the club for their concert hall for the entertainment held on Easter Monday Night.* Patrick Ryan was not only the Mayor of Wexford but also a member of the Society since 1883. The Camptown Serenaders staged another entertainment in the concert hall on the 26th May for the benefit of the

committee of the 1897 cycling carnival. The dramatic club sought permission to have ladies take part in a play they were rehearsing and informed the Council that their President Fr. O'Byrne would be present at their rehearsals and this should be sufficient guarantee that they would be carried-out in a satisfactory manner. The assurance of the presence of Fr. O'Byrne at the rehearsals was sufficient to persuade the Council to grant this request. On the 13th August 1899 the dramatic class staged an entertainment at Kilmore in aid of the parish Church

1900s

This decade began with the dramatic class conducting a performance on the 26th February at the Theatre Royal in aid of the Wexford Clothing Society. This was a charitable organisation which distributed clothes to the poor and needy of the town. It was later taken over by the St. Vincent de Paul Society. In March 1901 the Society held a smoking concert on St. Patrick's night and made a profit of £2-0-2 for the club funds. It is recorded on the 20th February 1902 that *Fr. O'Byrne handed in £3 from the Dramatic Class.* Obviously, they had staged some entertainment to make a profit. I should mention that the Fr. O'Byrne referred to is the same priest who later founded the Boys Confraternity band.

Patrick Ryan

On the 27th January 1904 an application was made from some of the members for the use of the concert hall for the purpose of forming a dramatic class and this was granted with the proviso that it did not interfere with all the other classes utilising the hall. This was yet again another revival of the dramatic section of the club. In March 1904 John Barker, secretary of the dramatic class, requested permission from the Council to use the concert hall for a performance on Friday 8th April. The Council despatched Michael Luccan, John White and Frank O'Connor to check the performance to ensure it was suitable and to make the necessary arrangements for it. The Council was informed that non-members of the club were taking part in the dramatic classes but the Council took no action at this stage. The dramatic class also conducted a performance on Monday night the 25th of April.

On the 13th September 1904 J. Barker applied to use the hall on behalf of the dramatic class again and the Council acceded with the proviso *that only members be in the class and if entertainment is been put on, the council must first view and agreed to it.* The dramatic class under the stewardship of P. Busher and Thomas Kennedy, the two Hon. Secretaries, was busy staging variety concerts some nine years later.

Edward F. O'Rourke

1910s

On the 25th March 1913 the entertainment performed on St. Patrick's night grossed £8-12-0 and with expenses of £4-9-8 there was a net profit of £4-2-4. £3 was donated to the Society's funds and £1-2-4 retained by the dramatic class. They also announced that they wished to expand the class and hoped to stage more entertainments in the near future. The Secretary's address at the A.G.M. of the 31st December 1914 has the following to report concerning the dramatic class *In the first place they [young members] have established a dramatic class which reflects the highest credit on themselves and on the club. In this respect the services of Edward F. O'Rourke cannot be overlooked.* It is clear from this statement that Edward O'Rourke had been involved with them for some time.

In January 1915 we read that *Edward F. O'Rourke applied for refund of £1 expended by him in connection with the dramatic class and the application was granted.'* In September the minutes state *Thomas Hayes, Hon. Secretary of the Dramatic Class wrote requesting*

permission of the council to bring young ladies into the dramatic class to take part in the plays and concerts that it was proposed to bring off at an early date. The meeting regretted that it could not accede to this request. In January 1916 Thomas Hayes, Secretary of the dramatic class, requested the use of the concert hall to hold an entertainment in aid of funds for the provision of comforts for Irish soldiers and sailors engaged in the war. This request, needless to remark, was unanimously granted.

At the A.G.M. of 13th February 1916 we are informed that *The dramatic class is vigorously progressing under the stewardship of Edward F. O'Rourke this year [1915] again.*

In April the Council decided to notify Edward F. O'Rourke who was in charge of the dramatic class that *None but members of the club would be allowed to take part in the practises of the class on the club premises in future.* The notification does not mention which gender but there can be no doubt that ladies are the non-members referred to. The dramatic class held a concert to raise funds for a *'new organ'* for Rowe Street church.

Thomas Hayes

The secretary of the class Thomas Hayes wrote to the Council requesting that they grant permission to allow some ladies on the premises for practice in the concert hall for the purpose of an entertainment they were holding in Castlebridge on Sunday 21st May in aid of the schoolhouse. He explained that the class had arranged for

this entertainment before he had received the notice that ladies would not be allowed on the premises in future and *Under these circumstances the council granted permission this one time.* In December Thomas Hayes requested the use of the concert hall for dramatic class practices. This was granted with the proviso that no non-members (*meaning ladies*) were present. There is no reference to any dramatic class activity for 1918 and 1919 but we do know that Nicholas Barnwell was the Hon. Secretary for those two years.

1930s

In April 1930 Nicholas Corish requested permission to start up a dramatic class in the club and this was granted. It is obvious that the dramatic class section had ceased to exist sometime between 1919 and this date. On the 11th June Nicholas Corish inquired if the Council would allow ladies to take part in any plays that they would perform and the Council passed this question over to Fr. Sinnott, the President, to give a ruling on. Permission was granted by Fr. Sinnott and the first play that the group performed was 'Look at the Heffernans' with a profit of £5-10-0.

1940s

At the A.G.M. of 1943 the following is recorded *Edward O'Brien said that he thought that a 'Smoking Concert' should be held, and it was decoded to leave the matter in the hands of the Amusements Committee.* Nothing further of this was referred to in the minutes but I wish some reader would enlighten me as to what constitutes a 'smoking concert'?

◄□►

1950s

A group of members revived the dramatic class in January 1953 but, unfortunately, we do not have any information concerning this group. There is only one reference to them in the minutes where they *asked for a grant of £10 as they wished to repair the stage and purchase curtains etc., for same.* - 13th January 1953. They were given the £10 grant from the Council and the stage they spoke about was obviously in the concert hall. Their first attempt at a play and accompanying concert met with little support from the members of the Society. We have no data on who all the players were but we do know the dramatic class committee comprised the following members; John J. Donohoe, Chairman, P. J. Roice, Hon. Secretary, Kevin O'Mahoney, George Bridges, and Oliver Kehoe. The next reference to this is on the 1st May 1956 when the Council congratulated members concerned with the concerts produced in the concert hall and went on to *offer future suggestions for concert.* Sounds like meddling! What budding thespian would want to be told what to do by a Council member?

P. J. Roice

The next attempt to re-start a dramatic section producing variety concerts was made out of necessity by the Pongo committee. It related to the licence issued under the Gambling & Lotteries Act 1956 for the Pongo and the concert hall as a whole. This was conditional on *other forms of entertainment are provided at the premises.*
Thomas O'Rourke on account of being the chairman of the Pongo committee now found himself also in the position of production manager of the C.Y.M.S. variety concerts which were active in this decade, with great success I might add. Thomas would be the first to admit that he hadn't a musical bone in his body but when it came to organisation and getting things done there was no one better equipped than Tom.

The popular tunes of the day were *'Twenty Tiny Fingers'* by the Stargazers, *'Love and Marriage'* by Frank Sinatra and *'The Yellow Rose of Texas'* by Mitch Miller. Some of the lads in the club used to mime to these and fool around and go through the actions as if they were singing the tunes. So the idea came to them - why not make an act of it and that is exactly what they did. I sat and watched a few of these shows and I have got to say that the miming act was brilliant. Thomas O'Rourke would put on these records behind the scenes and the lads would mime and pretend to be playing the various musical instruments with the harmonies etc. They were very good and one could be very easily fooled that they were actually singing and

....

On Sunday evening 17th June 1956 the C.Y.M.S. players held a most successful variety concert in Broadway before a very large and appreciative audience. This was their debut performance outside of the town and they deserved great praise for their outstanding success.

The producers were Thomas O'Rourke and William Murphy and Luke Wadding accompanied the following singers on the piano accordion:

Gerard Roche who sang 'The Rose of Tralee' (*Connected to the Slaneyside Ceilidhe Band*)

Marie O'Rourke who sang 'Kevin Barry' (*Connected to the Slaneyside Ceilidhe Band*)

Tom Mahon who sang 'Cool Water'

The Slaneyside Ceilidhe Band provided the music. I have Nick and Breda Doran to thank for the information relating to the band which was, incidentally, the Doran family band from Grogan's Road (*my next-door neighbours*). It was through the good offices of Thomas O'Rourke that the band was brought into the group and they stayed with the troop and completed all the engagements. The band members were very young with an average age of 16 years. Amongst them were two who went on to achieve musical acclaim in their new found roles. The female vocalist 14-year-old Marie O'Rourke joined the Rattigan family band known as the 'Ceoltoiri Loc Garman' ceili

playing the instruments. Later on other favourite songs were *'Memories are made of this'* by Dean Martin, 'The Ballad of Davy Crocket' by Bill Hayes, and *'It's Almost Tomorrow'* by Dream Weavers to mention but a few.

The troop consisted of the Pongo committee - Thomas O'Rourke, Bill Murphy, Thomas and Michael Mahon, Wally Cleary and other lads from the club such as Michael Kavanagh, Luke Wadding, Jack Radford, Eamon Doyle Willie Kehoe and Willie Carley who had some thespian experience. I can't remember them all. My sister Marie O'Rourke was singing with Doran's Ceili Band at the time and the band was taken along on all the entertainments. There was various sketches written by the lads themselves and Tom Mahon, Michael Mahon, Jack Radford, Eamon Doyle and Luke Wadding acted in many of them. Wally Cleary had back stage experience at the Theatre Royal so he was the stagehand cum electrician as I recall.

Early in 1956 the C.Y.M.S. troop staged their first variety concert in the concert hall and this was said to be an activity that had not been seen in the club for some time. The show went down very well indeed and after this initial success the group went *"on the road"*. The shows were put on in Broadway, Blackwater, Fethard, Oylegate, Ferns, Duncannon, Courtown Harbour, and Rosslare Strand. There was a joke going around the club that *the boys are playing on Broadway*

band who as the youngest ceili band in Ireland shot to fame by winning the senior An Tostal All-Ireland ceili band championship at Dunshambo, Co. Leitrim in competition with more mature and experienced bands from all over Ireland. Liam Gaul, playing button key accordion, entered the Feis held in the St. Iberius (C.Y.M.S.) Concert Hall in 1956 and won the competition. He went on to become all-Ireland champion. As a matter of interest the youngest cheeky young Jim Gaul emigrated to the U.S.A. in the late 1950s and joined the U.S. Air force. See the Band photograph on next page.

The 'Slaneyside Ceilidhe Band' June 1956.
Lt. to Rt. Maria Hayes (Piano), Marie O'Rourke (Vocals), Peter Murphy (Piccolo),
Liam Gaul (Button Key Accordion), Nicholas Doran (Piano Accordion, Band Leader),
Breda Doran (Drums), Ger Roche (Vocals), Jim Gaul (Piano Accordion).

Three very amusing sketches were performed which the lads had written themselves:

'A Day in the Life of a Doctor'.
Willie Kehoe played the Doctor, Michael Kavanagh played the nurse which evoked many a cat-whistle and loud laughter for the audience and Michael Mahon, Luke Wadding, and Tom Cadogan were the patients.

'The Club Around the Corner'
This was a mimic of the then popular show 'The School Around the Corner' compere by Paddy Crosbie. Willie Kehoe played Paddy Crosbie and Michael Mahon, Tom Mahon, Luke Wadding and Michael Kavanagh were the contestants.

'Army Life'
Michael Kavanagh played the Captain, Luke Wadding played the Sergeant Major and Sean Radford played the private in this farcical sketch.

Thomas O'Rourke was the master of ceremonies and Wally Cleary was electrical equipment technician and props man.

Vocalist Tom Mahon lubricates his tonsils while Luke Wadding belts it out on his piano accordion.

The locations in which the troop performed in those days were very rural and most people worked very long hours. These were pre T.V. days and they did not have much to entertain them. The radio if lucky enough to own one was the only contact with the outside world. The people were not street-wise like city folk. They were honest to God hard working Christian souls who lived a simple lifestyle so when these shows visited it was a great night out for them, the village hall would be packed to capacity and the shows were appreciated.

Michael Mahon

I recall being in the audience one night in Broadway when Tom Mahon was going through his act of miming to one of the popular records of the day. Unbeknown to him Thomas O'Rourke back stage, with impish delight, fiddled with the record player by placing his finger on the record which slowed it down ever so gradually and then he would let it speed up. This went on for a while to the annoyance of poor Tom Mahon who after all had to face the audience. Then it went down to slow motion and finally stopping suddenly. Of course this let the cat out of the bag as everyone in the audience now realised it was only a recording and Tom was only pretending to sing. The audience were in stitches and one *'not to bright'* old chap finally copped-on and shouted out to the audience *he's not singing at all, it's a recording!* The crowd burst into fits of laughter at this. The old boy was about one minute behind everyone else in realising the truth of the situation. And this was what most of the audience were now laughing at.

The group of players mentioned above are not the only men who were involved with the dramatic section. Eamonn Doyle acted in many of the sketches and sang a duet along with Willie Kehoe with guitar accompaniment. Eamonn tells me that a variation on the Doctor's sketch was a hospital sketch with Luke Wadding in bed.

There was also a 'Cowboy' sketch which was a mimic of Abbott and Costello (*popular in the movies at the time*) a type of slapstick humour. I remember Michael Mahon had one line which he kept repeating through the sketches. It appears it was a kind of catch-phase of a comedian on the radio then. The line was *'what about the working man'* and no matter what sketch Michael was in he would jump to his feet and shout this line, and the audience used to go into fits of laughter at it. It's funny how life turns out as Michael spent most of his working life as a union official so he was still asking *'What about the workingman.'* There was a sketch called 'The New Garda in the

Barracks' and I believe that Willie Kehoe played the Sergeant.

There was also the Dixieland Jazz Band sketch which was brilliant. I had the opportunity to see it on a few occasions sitting in the audience as my father had asked me to do this to see how people reacted to it. It started with Tom O'Rourke announcing the band (*some fictitious name or other*) and the boys armed with real musical instruments would be in place on the stage as the curtain was drawn. Meanwhile, backstage the ragtime record would be put on by Tom or Wally Cleary and the boys would mime and mimic the actions of the musicians. They would really give it their all jumping around, gyrating and emulating all the actions of a jazz-band. Everyone believed that the boys were actually playing the instruments as they really were great at this act. Initially some people actually thought they were being hoodwinked and they booed, but then they would realise that it was all an act and the crowd would start to laugh and clap, as it dawned on them how damn good the lads were.

Eamonn Doyle informed me about a magic act staged by Jackie Donohoe when they were in Kilmore Quay. It appears that Jackie took his act very seriously and thought of himself as an up and coming magician. He probably got the tricks out of a lucky bag (*remember them?*). Anyway Jackie was going through his act and due to the small stage he was nearer the front than usual. Alas, there was a group of young children in the front leaning in on the stage looking up under Jackie's hands trying to see what he was doing. It appears the kids could see the cards going up Jackie's sleeves and used to scream out telling everyone where the cards had gone. Jackie's second trick involved turning the backs of his hands towards the audience holding two balls between the fingers of each hand. They were in actual fact four half balls. Next Jackie would put his hands behind his back and closing the four half together to make two balls, he would then bring his hands to the front and open the palms up showing two balls. Hey presto! Two balls had vanished. But not tonight Josephine as the kids had spotted the half balls in his hand and told everyone in the hall. Jackie died on the stage that night.

John J. Donohoe

The acting careers of the troops did not last that long but for the length it did last it was great entertainment and there is great credit due to all those young men who revived the dramatic section of the club for the last time.

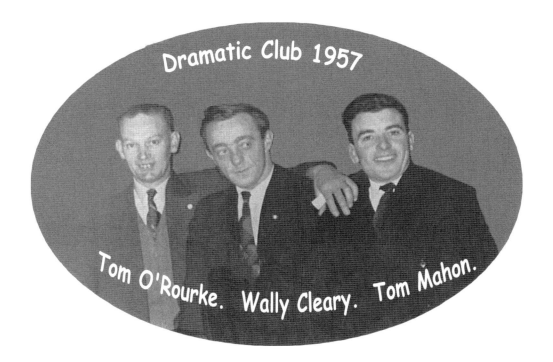

Dramatic Club 1957

Tom O'Rourke. Wally Cleary. Tom Mahon.

There never was any further dramatic class in the club after this 1950s troop and when the curtain went down on their last performance it was also curtains for the dramatic section in the club.

Incidentally Michael Kavanagh informed me that the troop had nicknamed themselves the 'Hooja Hot-Shots' and he claims that it was Tom O'Rourke who christened them that. He could not enlighten me as to what this nickname meant, or why they were called that. Tom Mahon corroborated Michael's story but like Michael, Tom could not tell me what the name stood for nor what the origin of it was. I wonder what the boys were on in those days?

Michael also related another anecdote to me concerning one night when they went to perform in a small hall that there was no piano stool for my sister Marie while she played the piano. Besides her singing Marie sometimes played the piano for the troop. Michael said that he had to go down on all fours and let Marie sat on his back while she was playing. There were other stories that I was told but I cannot repeat them without fear of being in trouble with the censor's office. One of them had something to do with the boys going outside in the dark to relieve themselves and a couple of cows. My lips are sealed.

(See Appendixes No 11, 12 and 13, for lists of 'Dramatic Management Committees', 'C.Y.M.S. Theatrical Amusements Record' and 'Productions and Actors' on pages 290, 292 and 294)

Singers and the Numbers they Sang

(Incomplete)

William Codd 'Lover's loan of a Gridiron.' 1883.
Miss Holbrook (?) accompanied by **Mr. Swaby** or **Frank Lyons** both music teachers
William Connick and **Nicholas Gahan** 'Salvation Army Duet' 1883
Messrs. Connick, Kehoe, Connick (jnr.), William Furlong, O'Connor and company various songs 1883. At the 1883 soiree 'Auld Lang Syne'
G. F. Dixon 'Jack's Farewell' and 'Our Jack's Come Home from the Sea Today"' 1888
J. J. Whelan 'I've Such an Awful Cold' and 'Money' 1888
E. A. Whelan 'Let Me Like a Soldier Fall' 1888
P. Howlin 'The Irish Jaunting Car' and many other songs 1888
Hugh McGuire 'The Wonderful Musician' the first part closed with the band playing the Valse (*Swinging Waltz two beats instead of three beats*) 1888
William Connick 'Let Each Man Learn to Know Himself' 1888
William Robinson 'The Visitors' 1888
Patrick Breen and **M. Hanrahan** 'Auld Lang Syne' at the Annual Reunion of January 1981

Rev. Fr. Aylward in January 1891 'Ould Ireland You're My Darling', 'Marsellaise!' and 'What is the use of Repining' (January 1892)
Thomas Bent 'I love 'er all the more' and 'Where have I seen that face before' January. 1897 and 'That's the Cause of it' 29th January 1896
Master Frank Breen a comic song (?) Jan. 1897
Rev. J. Browne 'Home Sweet Home' Jan. 1897
Frank Carty 'Johanna Magee'
The Choral Class 'God Bless our Pope' Jan. 1897
William Connick Jan. 1891 and Jan. 1897 'Let Each Man Learn To Know Himself'
George Dixon 'Madeline' February 1888
Patrick Donohoe and **Patrick Horan** a comic song 'Money Matters' Jan. 1897
Patrick Donohoe 'Song that broke my Heart' Jan. 1897
Michael A. Ennis, Patrick B. Troy and James Furlong . January 1891 'The Rolling Drum'.
Michael A. Ennis and **Patrick B.Troy**. January 1891 'I'na Sera D'amore', 'The Heart Bowed Down', 'Larboard Watch' and 'The Boy's of Wexford'
Michael A. Ennis. January 1891 'The Heart Bowed Down' and 'The Stowaway' January 1892
James Furlong. January 1891 'Go Where Glory Waits Thee', 'The Limerick Races', 'A Sailor's Life for Me', 'Go Where Glory waits Thee' and 'The Exile's Lament' Jan. 1897. 'The Star Spangled Banner' and 'The Harp' Jan. 1892
John Furling and **Mr. Maddock** 'The Minute Gun at Sea' January 1892
Nicholas Gahan 'Fr. O'Flynn' Jan. 1897 and 'Norah Kearney' 29th Jan. 1896

Robert Harvey 'Old Ireland's Head' and 'Hands' 29th January 1896 and 'I Know an Eye' and ' The Last Rose of Summer' January 1892
Patrick Horan 'Farewell for ever' Jan. 1897
Pat Howlin 'The Irish Jaunting Car' and 'The Workhouse System' February 1888
Master Hugh M'Guire 'I'm a Jolly Little All Round' February 1888
Frank O'Connor 'The Last Shot' Jan. 1897
Thomas Robinson January 1891 'Auld Lang Syne' and 'M'Guiness' Jan. 1897
The entire assembly 'God Save Ireland' Jan. 1897
Patrick B. Troy 'When Other Lips', 'Then You'll remember me', and 'The Boy's of Wexford' January 1891 and 'When Other Lips' and 'The Boy's of Wexford' 13th January 1892
William Walsh and **Frank Lyons** 'The Band Played Annie Rooney' Jan. 1897 and 'I Didn't know till afterwards' Jan. 1897
Edward Whelan (jnr.), January 19(?) 'Let Me Like a Soldier Fall', 'Kathleen Mavourneen' and 'The Minstrel Boy' on (29th January 1896) and he sung 'Adieu Marie' He sung 'Anchor's Weigh'd' and 'Queen of My Heart' in (February 1888)

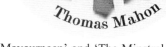

Edward Whelan (snr.), (January 1891) 'The Anchor's Weighed'
James Whelan 'Killaloe' and 'Money' February 1888
John Williams January 1891 (?) and 'Oh, Gentle Breathe the Tender' and 'What will we do with our, Girls'

Brendan Corish

Marie O'Rourke 'Kevin Barry' and 'Holy Night' 1950s and was the vocalist on the 'Ceoltoiri Loc Garman' Ceili Band 1960s
Myles O'Rourke (jnr.), sang 'Rudolf the Red-Nosed Reindeer' 1956.
Tom Mahon 'Cool Water' 1950s
Throughout the years there were many singers and musicians on church choirs, the Wexford Male Voice choir, Dance Bands, Ceili Bands, Variety Concerts and the Light Opera Society, etc., etc. The following are a few such members who deserve mention
Vincent Sherwood, Liam Bolger, Jackie Donohoe and Paddy Scallan sang various songs in 1958.
Jimmy Browne who was a popular Bishopswater publican. He won the All-Ireland Count John McCormack 'New Voices' Competition on Radio Eireann and was chosen to take a leading role in 'The Rose Castile' the first opera produced at the Wexford festival.

Jimmy Browne

Brendan Corish, the former Tánaiste and leader of the Labour Party was another great C.Y.M.S. singer in his day. He sang in the Gilbert and Sullivan productions on the stage in the Theatre Royal.

John Kirwan from Mary Street was a cattle dealer who had a great baritone voice. John was another member who sang mostly at religious functions and on the church choirs. There were a few anecdotes concerning John and one relates to him being at a fair one day and some bloke who did not think too much of men singing began to pass aspersions about John's manhood. This ignoramus seemed to have it in his head that only sissies sang and it was not 'a man thing'. Anyway, John turned around and landed him a right upper-cut sending him reeling back some yards before he fell on his rear end into the cow muck. That shut him up because the guy just got up and walked away and that was the end of that. Obviously John had managed to convince him that singing was indeed 'a man thing.'

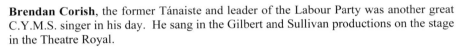

John Kirwan

Then there is our old pal **Nicky Lacey** who is a member of the Wexford Male Voice Choir. Nicky is known all over Co. Wexford for his rendition of the ballad of 'Nicky Rackard' sang to the air of Davy Crocket the lyrics of which follows on the next page:

Nicky Lacey

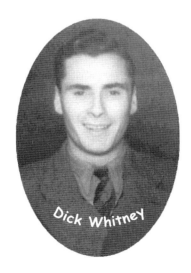

Dick Whitney

207

The Ballad of Nicky Rackard

Out in Killane upon a summer morn,
The greatest Gael in the land was born.
He learned to hurl, and so gifted was he.
He tipped 'em o'er the bar when he was only three.
Nicky, Nicky Rackard, saw his duty clear.

Away in St. Kieran's where he went to school,
He showed that he was nobody's fool;
There he picked up the tricks of the game,
That started the legend of his Famous name.
Nicky. Nicky Rackard, the man who don't know fear.

With brothers Bob and Billy on the county team,
He led the Wexford hurlers to Fulfil a dream.
The standard of the team mounted up and up.
Until they won the All-Ireland Cup.
Nicky, Nicky Rackard, king of the close in free.

On Sunday, May 6th, at old Croke Park,
The half-time score made things look dark;
But Nicky and the boys were up there to win,
And no power in Munster could make them give in.
Nicky, Nicky Rackard fighting for the National League.

The boys fought like tigers in the second half,
But Tipperary followers continued to laugh,
Soon they knew what was on the cards,
When points went in from over ninety yards.
Nicky, Nicky Rackard leading his mighty band.

Two points in the difference two minutes to go!
Dixon had a goal that staggered the foe,
We were in front and the seal was set,
When Nicky lashed another to the back of the net.
Nicky, Nicky Rackard gave us the National League

Nicky is the biggest, and Nicky is the best.
He beat the pick of Munster and the men of the West.
His deeds will be listed in the Hall of Fame,
And Irishmen for ever will remember his name.
Nicky, Nicky Rackard, his Fame will never die.

Nicky Lacey has been singing this song since May 1956 when Wexford won the National League beating Tipperary. It was on the way back from this match that **Dick Whitney** (*a band leader*) penned the words of this famous balled. Incidentally, Dick Whitney was another C.Y.M.S. member and a top class table tennis star of the early 1950s. (*See photographs in the table tennis chapter vol. 2*)

Nicky has been on the Wexford Male Voice Choir for many years. If you ask anyone in Wexford who sings the balled of Nicky Rackard they will respond immediately saying Nicky Lacey. Nicky has performed this balled in Oxford, Luton, London - all over England, Scotland and Wales. Also, in every county in Ireland, in New York, Boston and Canada. He sang it up in the sky (*flying across the Atlantic Ocean*) and probably attracted the attention of every angel in the heavens who probably were mesmerized at the melodious voice emanating from the plane.

Maurice O'Shea and Nicholas **Bolger** were members of 'The Camptown Serenader's' 1869. **John Donohoe** was the singing teacher on the choir 1896. **Jack Radford** is on the Wexford Male Voice Choir and he was also a violin maker.

History of the C.Y.M.S. Concert Hall

The entrance doors into the Wexford branch of the Halifax Building Society, Common Quay Street which exist to-day are the same entrance doors to the C.Y.M.S. concert hall which existed back in 1897 right up to the 1980s. The Society's billiards and card room were located upstairs directly above the hall. Some of the most eminent men of the town graced these chambers and tread these boards over the years. The most notable personages from overseas to perform there were world billiard champions Walter Lindrum and Tom Newman who gave an exhibition there on Sunday 6th April 1930.

The Old C.Y.M.S. Concert Hall

Situated in Common Quay Street
This premises was once the famous C.Y.M.S. concert hall,
a very popular venue for dances and various entertainments with the
the people of Wexford for over 90 years.

Initially there were many clubs and sections within the Society such as the dance and dramatic classes, the debating club, gymnastic, boxing and table tennis clubs to utilise the concert hall free gratis as the minutes of April 1954 state *The Hon. Secretary asked for permission to charge everyone (meaning members also) who wanted to use the concert hall. It was decided to charge £1 per day (all day up to 6 p.m.) and 10/= per night.* This was the beginning of the collection of money for the use of the concert hall from the Society's own members as well as from outside parties. The only exception to this rule was prior to 1915 when there was a gas meter installed in the concert hall for lighting purposes. One had to insert coins into the meter to provide light and this meter was removed by the Gas Company on the 7th March 1915 at the request of the Council. From then on there was a charge of 2/= per night for the gas light only. The use of the concert hall was separate. However, by the 19th March 1919 it is recorded that *The question of putting a charge on the concert hall to outsiders requiring the use of it was before the meeting and it was decided that when an application for the use of the hall was received in future. The question of making a charge for its use would be considered at the same time.* This meant that from then onwards only those who required the hall for charitable or religious reasons would be guaranteed to acquire it free gratis.

Charles E. Vise Photo   Mary O'Connor Collection

Martin O'Connor 1862 - 1938

By the 16th December of 1924 the Council had decided to charge 2/6 for the use of the concert hall to anyone, group or trades associations etc. and at a Council meeting of 9th October 1928 the question of charges arose again with the result that the following set charges were applied *Charges for the concert hall were fixed at 10 am to 6 pm at £1 and from 6 pm. to 10 pm. 10/= and the council reserved to itself the right to consider any particular application and*

alter the charge if necessary. The cash that accrued from the letting of the concert hall from outside parties was minimal indeed. For instance, for the year 1903 the complete proceeds from the concert hall were a mere £4 profit. Not something to get excited about.

In 1917 the 'Instrumental Music and Irish Costume' sections of 'Feis Carman' were held in the *'St. Iberius Hall'*.

At a meeting dated 8th October 1935 the Council saw fit to appoint an entertainment committee to organise some amusement for the members on Friday nights. The committee consisted of the following appointed members: Michael Collopy, John O'Keeffe, Thomas O'Rourke and John Donlan. This then was the first entertainment committee for the concert hall as prior to this there had been various amusement committees appointed to organise and manage individual entertainments which occurred from time to time. The first one I encountered in the minutes is recorded as follows *The 'Amusements Committee' with power to control the letting-out of the concert hall was formed on the 22nd March 1927, and it consisted of the following eight members: Messrs. Thomas Hayes, Edward F. O'Rourke, William Hynes, James Kelly, Michael Kennedy, John Cullimore, John Doyle and Martin O'Connor.*

In the 1920s up to the late 50s the 'in-craze' in the town was dancing and everyone seems to have suffered from dance fever. The concert hall was much sought after by almost every club and organisation in the town. Some of these dances went on quite late which was not exactly in keeping with the Society's squeaky-clean image. This was a cause of concern to some of the governing elders on the Council which caused them to make the following promulgation *To uphold the good name of the club it was decided that in future all dances in the concert hall should cease at 11.45 pm. And that the hall is closed by 12 o'clock midnight.* There is no doubt as to what dance the Council were referring to here as a charity dance that was held on the 7th May 1929 finished at 3.00.a.m. If my memory serves me right I can recall the dances in the early 1960s in the Redmond Hall or Town Hall finishing by midnight. Rather hypocritical to think that the older generation of that period used to complain about us young ones out at dances and making us feel badly about it whilst now I discover that some of those same people were dancing till 3.00.a.m. when they were young.

The C.Y.M.S. club was obliged by law to have current dance licences for the concert hall to enable them to run dances there or allow others to do so. They also had to purchase a performing rights certificate to play music there. In the early sixties they must have allowed their performing rights licence to lapse as on the 1st December of 1964 they received a letter from the Performing Right Society Ltd requesting them to pay the licence to continue playing records and music which was *'The intellectual property of the artists.'* Begrudgingly, the Council paid the licence on 12th January of 1965.

In the following chapter I have outlined the various people or groups that utilised the C.Y.M.S. concert hall throughout the years. I am recording this information purely as a social history exercise which I believe will be of interest to Wexford people in general. The hall had many uses throughout its time - drama, concerts, dances and shows etc. For the reader's convenience I have categorised the various groups and interests.

Drama Groups

On the 25th July 1900 Louis Hayes requested the use of the hall for rehearsals for a children's concert which Madam Hayes proposed to hold soon in the Town Hall. The Council decided to refuse this request stating that *the hall probably would be required for the use of the forthcoming '98 bazaar.* The Wexford Borough '98 Association Committee did in fact request the use of the hall as was anticipated.

In March of 1901 the Society ran a smoking concert on St. Patrick's Night and they made a profit of £2-0-2 for the club funds. Patrick Donohoe applied on the 3rd September 1902 for the use of both the concert hall and piano for the purpose of choir practice for the forthcoming county Feis and this was granted. Fr. O'Byrne occupied the hall on the 14th January 1903 for the Boys Confraternity Dramatic and Music Class. This was granted free gratis provided that they paid for the gas consumption during their practice. On the 6th January 1904 Fr. O'Byrne requested the use of both the concert hall and the billiard room to stage a performance of the boys' confraternity dramatic and music class. This was agreed to and granted of course. The Council looked upon the boy's confraternity as a breeding ground for the next up-and-coming junior members of the Society just as similarly the Catholic Boy Scouts was viewed in later years. Fr. O'Byrne's boys were such a success that he immediately applied for use of the concert hall for the 26th, 27th and 28th of April re-stage the show. This was again granted free gratis. However, something unforeseen occurred as Fr. O'Byrne cancelled and the show was staged in the Town Hall on the 13th April instead. On St. Patrick's night in 1904 P. J. Gregory, Hon. Secretary of the Gaelic League organised and staged a concert there and Fred Burke put on a variety concert in the hall in July 1905

In December 1906 a Mr. Quirke acquired the use of the hall for the purpose of *Giving entertainment, composed of*

Rev. James Cummins, C.C

Irish Subjects. He was charged 10/= per night. The Martinian Players, Dublin applied for the hall to stage a performance in Wexford in 1907. On 28th February 1907 St. Brigid's Band applied for use of it on Tuesday nights for the purpose of practicing for a concert which they proposed holding after Easter. Dr. Ormonde, variety entertainer, wrote on 5th January 1909 requesting it for the purpose of holding a public entertainment. This application was rejected.

On the 24th May 1909 Fr. Cummins had the hall for the boy's singing class practice in preparation for the forthcoming Feis in Enniscorthy. C. A. Whelan requested the use of it for the local ladies and gentlemen's choral class for the winter months in 1911. This request was refused however and no reason is given. By the 19th December of the same year the choral class were requesting permission to have a loan of the drum that had been loaned to the Irish National Foresters Wexford branch. They required it for a few weeks in the New Year and this request was granted. In 1913 Patrick Horan, Hon, Secretary of the Wexford Amateur Operatic Society staged a concert there for three nights and the charge was £1 per night.

Thomas Hayes

On the 22nd April 1913 a Mr. Barry of Rocklands Cottage wrote requesting the use of the concert hall for the dramatic class who were organising an entertainment in connection with the 'Aid Fund' for County Infirmary Bazaar.

In January 1916 Thomas Hayes, secretary of the dramatic class, applied for the use of the hall for the purpose of staging an entertainment for the provision of funds for the Irish soldiers and sailors engaged in the war. Needless to state this request was unanimously granted. In 1916 a concert was held to raise funds for a new organ for Rowe Street Church. On the 29th January 1918 J. T. Drought of Bank of Ireland, requested the use of the concert hall for dramatic class rehearsals. This also was granted. On the 14th January 1918 the McNally Concert Company inquired if they could hire the club's piano for three nights at the Theatre (*Theatre Royal*) as *'there was no other suitable piano available'* in the town. This request was granted at a charge of £3 for the three nights. This is interesting as elsewhere it is stated that many were *absolutely forbidden to use the piano.* In fact no one was allowed to put a hand upon it. It is obvious that good pianos were very scarce in the town. No wonder the Council were so protective of it. Their policy regarding the piano must have changed because on the 22nd January 1919 a. J. Scallan from the Third Order rooms requested the loan of the piano for the purpose of practicing for a charity concert in aid of the rooms. The reply states *The conditions of its use were explained to him.* There was no indication recorded as to whether they loaned the piano or not.

The Ladies Auxiliary Amusements Committee of the A. O. H. held an entertainment there on the 15th and 16th June 1919 in aid of charity. In October 1919 the Irish National Foresters, Wexford Branch held a practice there for a concert they were going to stage. On the 15th April 1924 the Third Order dramatic class requested the hall for a rehearsal of the play *'The New Curate'* which they were performing at Enniscorthy the following night and this was granted.

In 1926 there was a variety concert held there on behalf of the Mayor, Richard Corish (*a member of the Society*) in aid of the poor of the town. The Rev. A. V. Smyth of the Tate School had it on Friday night 17th December 1926 for the school concert. The Operatic Society held rehearsals there for a play they were staging at the Theatre (*I assume the Theatre Royal*). John White, secretary of the Wexford Amateur Operetta and Dramatic Society wrote on the 8th January 1929 requesting the use of the concert hall for rehearsals for a Gilbert and Sullivan Opera. They were offered two or three nights weekly over a period of twelve weeks at a cost of £3-10-0 inclusive of gas.

Richard Corish

The most interesting request of all was dated the 26th March 1929 when *Thomas Beaver, 41 William Street, on behalf of 'The Laughing Nigger Troup' requested the use of the concert hall for April the 4th and 5th for the purpose of putting on a concert and variety entertainment on those two nights.* This application was turned down with no reason given. This begs the question - was the council light-years ahead of us all with their *'Political Correctness'*? Or was this just coincidental and the real

reason for their refusal was unavailability of the nights in question. We will never know.

An application was received on the 14th October, 1930 from a P. Dempsey, Distillery Road requesting the concert hall for the purpose of staging a 'Dixie Minstrels' entertainment for the following Thursday night. This was also refused with no reason stated. Organist Miss Mary Codd held a practice for school children there in preparation for a concert arranged for December 1933. On the 6th April 1942 Dermot Cadogan, Director, C.M.C. Pantomime Productions wrote making application for the loan of timber and it was proposed to hire the timber to him for his forthcoming production at a cost of £2-10-0. The timber was not to be cut or *"dismantled in any way"*. I can only assume that the timber in question must be some of the large wooden painted scenery that was stored at the back stage in the Concert Hall.

The Trinity Players, Dublin performed a play there at one stage but after the first show the council stopped it and threatened to cancel their contract. One can just imagine the council stating something like *We are a Catholic club and will have no immorality goings on in our premises.* What happened you might ask? Well, it appears that these Dublin thespians had a lady who came on to the stage wearing a skin coloured and skin-tight cat suit. This was obviously all too risqué for the council so the show ended abruptly there and then. I know my father was one of the committee vanguards who approached the Trinity Players and was all for helping them pack their bags and throwing them out into the street in quick time. However all was not lost - an agreement was reached that the offending item in the show would be discontinued.

During the early days of the Wexford Festival fringe events were held here. Eamon Doyle informed me that he remembers John Molloy the comedian (*early R.T.E.*) and Ronnie Drew performing there. Drew played the guitar and sung at the time and he was later to become a lead singer with the Dubliners group.

The Dublin University Abbey Players rented the hall on a regular basis from 1955 to 1966 during the Wexford Festival week. They were paying £22 for the week in 1955 and by 1966 they were being charged over £5 to £6 per night. The following were there in 1962 - Wexford Golf Club, Luke Wadding for concert practice, the Post Office Drama Group for practice and Clover Meats Dramatic Group for practice. Mrs Dorrie Pettit was there in 1968

The Trinity Players hired the hall for the Wexford Festival Week 1965. A memo in the minute book states that it was decided to hire the hall to them on the same terms as last year. John Molloy Productions applied for the hall for festival week in 1966 but the club rented it to the regular people the Dublin University Abbey Players. The Wexford Festival Committee requested space to store costumes there in September of 1956. This was refused as no space was available.

Music and Dancing

On the musical side there was an Irish dancing club, Irish dancing classes and various groups who ran Irish dances. The club had Ballroom dancing teachers, a ballroom dancing committee and a dancing class section. Various clubs and bands besides the C.Y.M.S. held dances at the hall and the following activities were carried out over the years in the C.Y.M.S. concert hall.

Bands

In February 1907 St. Brigid's Band used the hall for band practice for forthcoming events. In January 1909 Fred Burke rented the hall for band practice and there was a Fife and Drum Band Contest there in 1959. Johnny Reck's Dance Band practiced there in 1959 and Michael Kelly's Band practiced there in 1967. The Supreme Dance Band used it for rehearsals and stored their equipment there in the 1970s.

Ballroom Dancing
1900s

On the 28th of January 1901 R. Redmond, secretary of the dancing class requested the use of the concert hall for a Cinderella dance. On this occasion poor Mr. Redmond was turned down point blank. On the 19th November 1909 C. J. McGovern and John Ryan (*both club members*) applied on behalf of the Commercial Dance Class for the use of the hall for one or two nights per week.

1910s

In October 1917 Miss Tierney, George's Street sought to rent the hall for dancing classes but alas the hall was in such high demand from the members that the Council had to refuse her. On the 5th of May 1918 the club's own amusement committee held a dance and a whist drive in the hall and they were instructed by the Council to ensure

(Lt. to Rt. from top) Dermot Kelly - Don Sadler
Con O'Rourke - John Lappin - Declan Kelly
Jimmy Flynn - Michael Hollman

that it finished by 12.00 midnight. Mrs. John English (*wife of a member*) and some of her lady friends applied on the 11th November 1919 for the use of the hall for one night weekly for dancing classes but for some unknown reason this was refused. There was a C.Y.M.S. dancing club with a dancing committee active in the club that used the concert hall on 2nd October 1918. They were ordered to finish the classes at 10.00.pm sharp each night. On the 16th December 1919 Nicholas Barnwell was the Hon. Secretary of the dance class and he applied to the Council for an extended dance to be held in January 1920 which was granted.

1920s

John Kehoe negotiated a new deal with the Council to cover the following year for the dance Class. John Kehoe requested *the use of the concert hall for every Wednesday night for dancing lessons 1924-1925* and this was agreed to at a charge of 15/= per week. By November 1920 Nicholas was no longer the secretary of the class and T. Keegan and W. Colfer were the secretaries and they used the hall *for the usual dancing lessons* in November 1920. J. J. Whitty, on behalf of the Old Commercial Dance Class wrote on the 10th October 1923 requesting the use of the hall on Wednesday evening weekly for dancing lessons. This was granted at a charge of £1 per week with the use of the piano. Mr. Whitty thought that this was too expensive so he wrote back offering £10 for the hall for the winter months (*this is one night per week*) for his dancing lessons. The Council replied offering him the hall at 15/= per night for this winter's lessons. Mr. Whitty obviously accepted this last offer because later he applied for other one-off nights to hold dances there. On the 15th January 1924 permission was given to the Commercial Dancing Class to use the hall on Sunday night 20th January until 1.00.a.m. for a dance they were holding for charitable purposes. Mr. Whitty and his Commercial Dance Class also received permission to run a dance to 12.00 midnight on St. Patrick's night of March 1924. By the 23rd September 1924 there was a new Hon. Secretary in charge of the Old Commercial the 7th October 1924 he requested the use of the hall on Sunday nights from 8.15.p.m. to 10.30.p.m. This too was passed and granted but only after Fr. Sinnott, the Society's President, was consulted on the matter and gave it the go-ahead. A couple of things can be said about the above. It is indeed surprising that Fr. Sinnott allowed the dance class on Sunday nights. He must have been a liberal minded priest. I can recall that even in the 1950s Sunday night was a no go area for certain activities and I would have thought that would have included dancing in 1924 especially in a staunchly Catholic establishment such as the C.Y.M.S. On the 11th November 1924 John Kavanagh on behalf of the Slaney Dance Class applied for the hall for Friday evenings for dance practice and this was granted at a charge of 15/= per night including the piano.

In October 1924 Laurence Grannell, William Street requested the use of the hall for holding dance practice on Sunday and Wednesday evenings from 7.30.p.m. to 10.30.p.m.. This was obviously refused as it coincided with John Kehoe's regular bookings. By the 24th February 1925 John Kehoe must have been replaced because on that date an M. Meyler wrote to the club on behalf of the Old Commercial Dance Class requesting *the use of the hall on St. Patrick's night for an extended dance.* By September 1925 John Carty, secretary of the Wexford Rugby Football Club held a dance and whist drive in the hall at the end of the month. They were charged 15/= for the night and instructed to vacate the hall and leave it cleaned by 12.00 midnight sharp.

On the 15th September 1925 when they were being charged less than most others for the hall John J. Kavanagh, President of the Wexford Harbour Boat Club requested the concert hall to hold dances on Friday nights from 8.00.p.m. to 11.00.p.m. This was granted at a charge of 12/6 per night. On the 6th October 1925 Murtha Meyler, secretary of the Old Commercial Dance Class requested the use of the hall on Wednesday and Sunday nights for dance practice. This was granted at 12/6 per night. Mr. Meyler also *asked for the hall for an extended dance on Wednesday evening 11th November plus the Gymnasium Room for catering purpose* for the same night and this was also granted. In December of the same year they held another extended dance on Tuesday night the 8th December from 8.00.p.m. to 12.00.p.m. Murtha Meyler, Secretary of the Commercial Dance Class held a charity dance there on the 2nd December 1925 and P. J. Gregory held charity dances there on Tuesday 19th January and Wednesday 6th April 1926. The Wexford

Harbour Boat Club under the stewardship of John Kavanagh held a dance there on the 5th February 1926. The Old Commercial Dance Class held a dance on St. Patrick's Night this year. Ellie Murphy rented the hall in March 1926 on Tuesday evening from 7.00.p.m. to 9.00.p.m. and Thursday evening from 4.00.p.m. to 6.00.p.m. weekly for the purpose of a juvenile dance class. She was charged 15/= per week. Kathleen Whelan held a Childrens' Fancy Dress Ball there on the 8th April 1926. John Kavanagh and his Slaney Dance Club held an extended dance there on Easter Monday night and he also used the supper room. I assume the supper room means the Gymnasium room. On the nights where food was being served that room was often used for that purpose. In my time the table tennis room was used for the preparation and serving of food especially on reunion nights.

On the 9th April 1926 Thomas Hayes held a dance to raise funds for St. Ibar's Football Club from 8.00.p.m. to 11.00.p.m. On 27th April Thomas held a dance to raise funds for the football team and I believe that this team was the C.Y.M.S.'s own team. Thomas was certainly a long-standing member of the Society. On the 27th April 1926 Michael Hall, secretary of the Wexford District Committee of Sinn Fein requested the hall for the following Sunday night in aid of the organisation. As the hall was already booked for that night it was not granted but had the following Sunday suited them they would have been welcome to it at the usual charge. I assume that they did not avail of this offer as nothing further is recorded in the minutes. Murtha Meyler on behalf of the Wexford Rugby Football Club hired the hall and the supper room for a dance on Wednesday night April 28th 1926. On the 14th September 1926 it is recorded that John J. Kavanagh, Hon. Secretary of the Wexford Harbour Boat Club was running dance classes there on Friday nights from 8.00.p.m. to 10.30.p.m. He also requested the hall for each week night commencing 27th September to holding a Fancy Fair. He settled for Wednesday and Sunday nights at 15/= per night. However on the 5th of October old Edward F. O'Rourke made an appeal on behalf of J. Kavanagh for a reduction in the charge of 15/= per night for the Fancy Fair which was being held to raise funds for the Boat Club. The Council agreed to reduce the charge to 25/= for the three nights.

Thomas J. Roche, an assistant teacher at the Christian Brothers School in George's Street held a charity dance there on Sunday night 26th September 1926 in aid of the provision of books for poor boys. This was granted free gratis as most charitable occasions were. Mrs Dowse, George's Street rented the hall every Tuesday from 2.00.p.m. to 7.00.p.m. commencing in October 1926 at a charge of 7/6 per day. On the 28th N. Lambert, secretary of the Rugby Football Club conducted the first dance of the year in the hall on the 1st January 1927 from 8.00.p.m. to 11.30.p.m. William Hayes, secretary of the Ramblers A.F.C wrote on the 25th January 1927 requesting the use of the concert hall for St Patrick's night for a dance. This was refused and the hall was given to the more regular customer P. Lambert, secretary of the Wexford Rugby Club, for a dance from 8.30.p.m. to 11.45.p.m. Two people applied for the hall to hold dances on the 24th March 1927 a Mr.

Meyler of Monck Street and a Nicholas Walsh. Nicholas Walsh got it at a charge of 12/6 for the night. On the 4th October 1927 it is noted that Messrs Millar and Hickey on behalf of the Killinick Harriers applied to rent the concert hall for their dance. This was granted but no date is recorded in the minutes as to when it was held.

A J. Saunders of Rathmines in Dublin wrote on the 15th November 1927 requesting the use of the hall for the purpose of holding dance classes there. He was a long way from home. The Council decided to refuse him. Major Walker applied on the 29th November of the same year requesting the use of the hall for a charity dance in aid of the dependants of ex-soldiers. The Wexford Rugby Football Club under the stewardship of their secretary P. Lambert conducted two dances there on the 12th and 19th

January 1928. On the 31st January of the same year Miss O'Connor, Westlands requested the use of the concert hall and the *'spare loft'* to hold a dance on the 8th February in aid of the fund for the Killinick Harriers and this was also granted. The Hockey Club's secretary P. J. Byrne ran the St. Patrick's night dance in the concert hall from 7.30.p.m. to 12.00 midnight. On Thursday 30th August 1928 the Wexford Agricultural Show under the stewardship of their secretary Henry Dempsey held a dance in the hall and from the 21st October 1928 to March 1929 the Wexford Rugby Football Club's two secretaries Mr. Meyler and Mr. Moore held several dances there.

On Sunday evening 10th of February 1929 Kathleen Whelan, George's Street held a childrens' dance from 4.00.p.m to 8.00.p.m. at a charge of 10/= with gas included. Fr. Allen held a childrens' Irish dance class on the 26th February 1929 from 3.00.p.m. to 6.00.p.m. at a charge of 5/= per week. This class seems to have been a regular one. Mrs Roche, North Main Street held a dance and bridge drive in the hall from 8.30.p.m. to 3.00.a.m. on Thursday night the 23rd May the same year in aid of the Loreto Convent building fund. After this late dance the Council moved to curtail late dances.

1930s

The Society of the Prevention of Cruelty to Children held a charity dance in the hall on the 2nd January 1931 and the C.Y.M.S. conducted dances there on a regular basis even prior to 1935. The club began what was described as an invitation dance class which was to be run on a regular basis throughout the winter evenings.

Jackie Donohoe

The committee who organised and ran these evenings were - J. J. Donohoe, M. J. Collopy, G.F. Kingsbury, J. Donlon,

J. J. Cosgrave. J.P. O'Keefe, Tom O'Rourke and M. Luccan. During these dance sessions there was a practice and teaching period. The band engaged for these evenings was Michael and his Accordion Band and they commenced on the 15th November 1935. It was reported at the A.G.M. dated 2nd February 1936 that the amusement committee earned a profit of £79-17-1 from the weekly dances. This was a fantastic amount of money in those days and the Secretary of the Amusements Committee said *This was the Big-Earner for the club at this time and without it, the club would be in trouble.* The last dance in the series prior to Lent was held on the 28th February 1936 and a very large crown attended. It was advertised with prizes and spot prizes and turned out to be a very enjoyable evening for all. The band played a pleasant programme of music and there were four prizes presented by the committee and two by jeweller George Z. Holmes. The following were the winners:

The lucky number - Martin Kehoe, Johnstown Castle and Alice Furlong, Davitt Road South
Spot prizes - Mr. Boggan, Newbay, Agnes Kelly, Michael Street; John O'Gorman, Wygram and Mary Mooney, Carrigeen Street.
M. J. Collopy acted as M.C. for the evening.

Eugene   McGrail

In August 1937 the Secretary applied for a dance licence for the Concert Hall. This was an annual exercise. In 1938 Kevin Morris, secretary of the Loch Garman Athletic Club, wrote inquiring if he could have the hall for Friday nights for dancing from 8.00.p.m. to 10.30.p.m. or 12.00.p.m. and on what terms. It was decided to allow him have the hall on Friday nights at 10/= per night from 8.00.p.m. to 10.30.p.m. or at 12/6 per night from 8.00.p.m. to 12.00.p.m.

1940s

In 1942 the club decided that they would not run a dance on St. Patrick's night but the reason for this decision is not recorded. Perhaps they did not wish to attract heavy drinkers into the club it being a night for heavier than usual drinking. On the 2nd September 1942 John Lowney was successful in acquiring the hall on Friday nights to hold dances with the proviso *That the dances were properly conducted and no person under the age of eighteen years was admitted.* In the 1940s there was a dancing section in the Society using the hall which covered ballroom dancing and Irish dancing.

The C.Y.M.S. Bridge Club got permission from the Council on the 2nd December 1947 to run a New Years Eve dance providing Fr. Doyle had no objections.

Both the table tennis club and the bridge club joined together to hold a series of weekly dances there in 1947. They made a profit of £22-10-6 from the dance on 21st December 1948 and an extra £15 was given to the Society's funds from the bridge club. Eugene McGrail, Patrick J. Hynes and Thomas Banville presented the spot prizes for the December dance.

1950s

In 1953 a Mrs. Kavanagh had the concert hall on Saturday afternoons during the summer term for dance classes. Her weekly rent was set at 2/6. In July 1954 a G. O'Brien, c/o Sheridan's, Newtown Hall sought permission to run dance classes there one night per week. Mrs Turner was given the concert hall on Tuesday nights at a cost of £1 per night to run a dance. She had to apply each week to ensure its availability. Both Mrs Turner and Mrs Kavanagh, regular renters, were informed that they *could not have the hall until after the convention.* In September 1955 Mr. Fortune, M. Turner and Mr. Hennessy made another application for the hall for dancing which was also refused because the club needed the hall themselves. A Mrs. Kavanagh was informed that she could not rent the concert hall after the 1st October 1955 and to make other arrangements. She applied again in September of 1957 but was refused once again as there were no nights available. The club at this stage was getting the Pongo up and running so the hall was needed. Johnny Reck's dance band held dances there and also practiced there in 1959.

1960s

The C.Y.M.S. held dances and their re-unions there in the 1960's. In 1965 a Mrs Mulcahy had it for ballroom dance classes and the soccer club held dances there in 1968.

Irish Dancing

The local branch of the Gaelic League held their reunion ceili dance in the concert hall on the 6th February 1936. Some of the officials of that club and who took part at that reunion are as follows:

Arrangement Committee - S. Dunne, W. Whitty, J. Browne and S. Murphy.
Singers and dancers - E. Murphy, K. O'Neill, M. Moran, S. Carley, P. Murphy, E. Murphy and S. Sharkey. M. & E. Tierney, J. Carbury.
Music – S. Murphy

The Gaelic dancing class was using the concert hall on the 4th January 1904 and the classes were confined to members of the Society only. The Feis was held there in May 1934 which the Gaelic League organised. In 1952 the Society had an Irish dance club who were attempting to promote Irish dancing amongst the club's members. On the 2nd June 1952 this club submitted their rules to the Council for approval. They were approved and adopted by the Council and the dance club was allowed to run weekly dances in the concert hall. The aims of the club were *to promote Irish dancing and to provide Christian recreation.* All the funds were to go to the C.Y.M.S. Council. The rules were as follows:

1) Admission by membership card only
2) Any member missing four consecutive nights ceases to be a member
3) No person admitted under the influence of drink
4) Members must uphold the standard of the classes whilst attending outside ???
5) The committee have the power to change or amend any rule with the approval of the Council
6) Misconduct or misbehaviour will not be tolerated
7) The Irish dancing committee have the power to appoint any person to act as M.C. on their behalf should the occasion arise
8) That all C.Y.M.S. members are entitled to attend the weekly dances
9) Visitors from other branches can attend the dances

The committee responsible for these rules was - George Bridges, Kevin O'Mahoney, Paddy Kelly plus two other club members. Tommy Roche, the Irish dancing champion and Irish dance teacher, held Irish dance classes there every Thursday afternoon in January of 1957. By February he had it on Monday nights from 6.15.p.m. to 8.30.p.m. His rent was 5/= per session. Incidentally, Tommy was a member of the Society and he resumed teaching Irish dance at the concert hall in 1969. In March of the same year a Mrs. K. Hillis sought the hall for Irish dance classes but was refused as there were no free nights available. The Gaelic League had it for Irish dances in 1963.

Tommy Roche winner of the Open Senior, Reel, Double and Hornpipe at Broadway 1954

Disco

The *'Groovy Sounds'* discotheque attracted big attendances to the hall each Wednesday evening. The Sarcfields Social Committee, attached to the club, organised the once weekly disco sessions in an effort to raise funds.

An Realt's Long Standing Tenancy in the Hall

An Realt the hall since April 1948 on set nights on a regular basis and paid their bill quarterly. They signed up to a *'new agreement'* on the 16th December of 1952 which stipulated:

1.   Every Wednesday night
2.   The 1st and 4th Sunday nights in the month
3.   Every Sunday morning.

This new agreement took effect from 1st January 1953 and they were informed by the Council in April 1955 that they were *not to play racquetball in the hall.* Racquetball was not the only ball game that they were playing. The hall had just been redecorated for the forthcoming national convention of the C.Y.M.S.I. The An Realt group received their marching orders in November 1961. The branch Council wrote to Miss B. Murphy their Hon. Secretary stating *That An Realt were going outside the terms of their agreement regarding the use of the concert hall and that the council wish them to obtain alternative accommodation.* - 7th November 1961,

I am very reliably informed that they were kicking a football around in the hall like a bunch of madmen and that a well-known Franciscan was involved. It was said that he kicked with the best of them and he being barefooted and wearing only sandals, as was the dress for the Friars in those days. This kind of horseplay, whacking a football at full force into the walls etc. obviously warranted the notice to vacate. There is nothing recorded to explain what happened to the notice to quit but they were still in occupation of the hall at the beginning of 1963. On the 7th January of that year they themselves served notice that they were terminating their tenancy. Perhaps they had located another venue which welcomed them kicking the football around.

Irish Language

On the 23rd November 1913 Rev. Mark O'Byrne C.C. wrote requesting the use of the concert hall for the Gaelic League for the purpose of holding Irish language classes. This was granted on the following conditions:

1)   That the evenings selected for the class do not clash with any evening that members of the club require the hall for any purpose.
2)   That no objectionable persons be brought into the hall in connection with the classes.

On the 2nd May 1915 the Gaelic League's permission to use the hall was *Cancelled owing to members of the club [the C.Y.M.S.] objecting to some of the persons who were using it.* Finally after a lengthy discussion it was proposed to allow *'these persons'* the use of the hall for their practice for the forthcoming Feis. The meeting decided to refuse the use of the hall to *The persons who had the use of the hall during the last week.* At the same time the meeting was prepared to consider an application from the Gaelic League (*Connradh na Gaeilge*) for the hall provided that no objectionable persons attend their practices.

On the 9th of May Fr. Mark O'Byrne wrote to the club regarding the use of the hall for Irish language classes and choral singing in preparation for the coming Feis. After consideration of the matter it was decided to send him a copy of the resolution of 23rd November 1913 granting him the use of the concert hall on the following conditions:

1. That the evenings selected for the classes do not clash with any evenings that the members of the club required the hall for any purpose.
2. That no objectionable persons be brought into the hall in connection with the classes.

That said it all - these *'objectionable persons'* will not be allowed or tolerated on the club premises no matter what anyone else thinks or says. The Council declared these people were persona non grata and that was an end of it. The Gaelic League retreated in shame after that and never showed their faces again until 14 years later in 1929 when they approached some Council members with the request to return to the club hall. They were advised to put their request into writing and this they did on the 3rd September

1929. On that day James Cadogan, secretary of the Gaelic League, wrote with their request to rent the concert hall for Irish classes including rent, cleaning, lighting and the use of the lavatories on the nights they required it. The Council's reply was as follows *It was decided to let (rent) the concert hall to the 'Wexford Branch of the Gaelic League' at a rent-including cleaning, lighting and the use of the toilets for £30 per annum subject to the following conditions.*

a)   The Council of this institute will reserve the hall for its own use for one night per week Wednesday or Thursday (*to be decided later*) and another occasional day with due notice to be given to your committee.
b)   Rent to be paid yearly in advance.
c)   On the acceptance of these terms a written agreement will be entered into in which a provision will be made that either side may terminate the tenancy at any time by giving 3 *(three)* months notice to the other side.

The Gaelic League accepted these terms for the tenancy and the contract was drawn-up by the Society's solicitors Messrs M. J. O'Connor & Co. The one night weekly which the C.Y.M.S. decided to retain for its own was Friday night. The contract commenced on the 29th September 1929 and this was the beginning of the Gaelic League's take-over of the concert hall. They abided by this contract right up to the 31st March 1945 when they terminated their tenancy with the club. However, they were to return to the concert hall again on Wednesday nights in 1960. They were paying 6/10 rent per week for the hall in 1936. In November of 1943, with permission

from the club, they sub-let the concert hall to Jack Kavanagh for roller skating. The Glun Na Taedhilge took up the tenancy in 1945 when the Gaelic League left but at an increased rent of £30 per annumn. A Thomas Fortune sought the hall from the Glun Na Taedhilge by November 1945 and by November of 1947 they were terminating their tenancy. Donncad O Laogaire, the Hon. Secretary of the Gaelic League, applied to take-over the tenancy once again and this was agreed but on the same terms as Glun Na Taedhilge had. However, after a lapse of only four months later the Gaelic League handed in their notice to terminate their tenancy of the hall on 1st April 1948.

Exhibition & Shows

Fr. Mark Byrne applied for the use of the concert hall for the County Wexford Feis in 1907. The Feis was also held in the hall on Whit Sunday and Monday in 1910 and on the 25th March 1913. P. J. Gregory was the Hon. Secretary of the Feis committee at this date and he also sought the hall on Whit Sunday and Monday 1916 to stage the Feis industrial exhibition. In 1920 Messrs Gregory and Cadogan, secretaries of the Feis committee held the Feis on Whit Sunday and Monday also. James Cadogan, secretary of the Feis committee in 1925 held the Feis in the hall again on Whit Sunday and Monday. Fr. Allen was the organiser of the Feis which was held there in 1928. In 1917 the instrumental music and Irish costume sections of Feis Carman was held there.

Wexford Cage Bird Society's annual show was held there every December from 1954 to 1971. In 1954 their rent was £3 per night. In 1956 they sought the hall for the 13th to the 16th December. However, the club could not accommodate them as the Pongo was in full swing then so the club rented them the table tennis room instead for £1 per night. They were refused the hall in 1972 as it was on a regular rental agreement by then.

The Christian Brothers held a boys' drill display there in either 1950 or 1951. I recall participating in it and also Jimmy Murphy, Solicitor, was another participant. A flower show was held there over the festival week of 1973. They had been refused the hall in 1972 due to it being on a regular rental agreement.

Film Shows

On the 19th December 1911 the club reprimanded the Gaelic League by reminding them that under the terms of their tenancy and the terms of our fire insurance policy that *No Cinematograph Display Art (motion pictures) was allowed to be shown in the Concert Hall.* Obviously the Gaelic League group had shown a motion picture without realising that it was prohibited. On the 2nd January 1913 a Mr. Cosgrave, secretary of Ireland's Own Animated

Pictures Co. requested the use of the hall and permission *to give an exhibition of the passion play* on the 1st and 2nd of January. This was granted and the charge was 15/= per night.

The following groups staged film shows in the hall – Fr. Jermayne O.F.M. in 1957 and the Wexford Rugby Club, the Co. Wexford cycling team and the Wexford Swimming club in 1962

The Club's Own Use

The branch's own activities in the hall were legion needless to say. I shall not refer to the Pongo here as it is dealt with elsewhere in the book. Activities which the hall was used for included plays, variety concerts, discos, children's Christmas party, table tennis competitions and presentations, dances, whist drives, reunion and supper dances to mention but a few. The hall was also used for bicycle race preparations prior to cycle races whereby cyclists left their clothing etc. there. The C.Y.M.S. cyclists also used it for winter training on the rollers (*which was a contraption you rode your bike on*). Nick Barnwell the main organiser of the C.Y.M.S.'s own commercial dance class also held their committee meetings there. The club's reunion and supper dance was held there from as early as 31st January 1910 when one hundred and twenty members attended.

Other Club and Association Meetings

The boys' confraternity had the hall on the evening of 14th September 1904 for their meeting. On the 31st May 1910 Thomas Doyle, president of the County Wexford Handball Association applied and was given the use of the hall to hold their committee meeting. In November of the same year the teachers of the Wexford Association were given permission to hold their quarterly meeting there   Miss Barry of Roxboro held a League of Pity meeting there on Thursday evening 20th February 1919 and a Mr. Mangan, secretary of the local branch of the Railway Clerks' Association sought it to hold their meeting there on the 1st February 1920 and he also requested a room for the first Sunday of each month for their meetings. This was granted at a charge of 5/= per evening. The Irish Clerical & Allied Workers Union also rented it for their meetings. On the 23rd November 1920 their secretary, a Mr. A. Murphy, also sought to have a room one night weekly for their meetings. This was granted at a cost of 2/6 per week for one of the small rooms. J. J. Kavanagh, secretary of the Wexford Harbour Boat Club held their A.G.M. there on the 6th April 1925 and they were only charged 5/=. This was very reasonable as the standard price was 15/= per night.

The Irish National Foresters held their International Convention in the hall in August 1926 and the Rugby Football Club rented it on Thursday nights for their meetings. They also rented it on the 8th December 1926 and the 6th January 1927. On the 11th June 1930 a Robert V. Kelly, secretary of the County Wexford Agricultural Society requested the use of the hall for their meetings once a weekly and this was granted at £5 per week. The Childrens' League of Pity had it for their A.G.M.'s in 1917, 1920, 1921, 1922, 1923, 1924, 1932 and 33. The Town Tenants meetings were held there in 1934 and the Order of Malta Ambulance Corps had it on the 4th September 1956. St. Aidan's Guild Muintir Na Tire held their A.G. M. there in 1963. The J. C. A. Town Association had it in 1966 and the Wexford Housing Action Committee in 1968.

Bazaar and Jumble Sales

On the 16th April 1900 a deputation from the '98 Memorial Committee consisting of N. J. Cosgrave, J. Godfrey and John White approached the Council requesting not only the hall but the entire club premises for the coming '98 bazaar. The Council unanimously agreed to let them have the club for this event. On the 16th August 1900 the '98 Memorial Committee' held the '98 Bazaar in the C.Y.M.S. club premises.

We should not be surprised to learn that this was granted because of the nineteen gentlemen on this committee no less than twelve were C.Y.M.S. members - James Stafford, Patrick Ryan, Hugh McGuire, Edward O' Connor, Robert Hanton, Simon McGuire, Thomas Godfrey, John Clancey, Patrick Hanrahan and David R. Keating. Incidentally, the gentleman with pen and notebook at the ready was Simon McGuire, the man who wrote the humorous verse concerning the C.Y.M.S. 1899 Bazaar.

The Wexford Borough '98 Association Committee

Lt. to Rt.   Front row: N. J. Cosgrave, H.C., Patrick Byrne, James Lee.
Second row: Ald. Jas. Stafford, Hon. Treas., Ben Hughes, T.C., Vice-Pres., Patrick Ryan, Mayor, Pres.,
Ald. Hugh McGuire, Vice-Pres. Edward O'Connor.
Third row: N. O'Neill, Robert Hanton, T.C., Simon McGuire, Hon. Sec., Thomas Godfrey, Hon. Sec.
Matthew Doyle, J. Clancy.
Back row: Luke Doyle, Joseph Hore, P. Hanrahan, James Kenny, David R. Keating.

In July 1906 there was a massive bazaar held at the club in aid of the St. John of God Convent. The entire club - the concert hall, billiard room and the yard were placed at the disposal of the bazaar committee. It was held over a period of two days on the 1st and 2nd of July 1906. The Boat Club ran a bazaar in the concert hall on the 20th August 1907 and also applied for the billiards room and other rooms as well as the concert hall to hold another bazaar there on the 12th November of the same year. Both the secretaries of the Boat Club wrote to the Society on the 17th December thanking the club for their kindness. In 1911 the Christian Brothers Bazaar committee had the billiards room, concert hall and yard for their bazaar. Mrs McGuire of Rowe Street held a Jumble Sale in the hall on the 28th March 1925. A Mr. Richardson applied for the use of the hall on the 18th January 1927 to run a Bazaar which was refused as there must have been no booking available

On the 8th January 1929 a D. Horan, secretary of the Junior Rugby Club, held a jumble sale there on the afternoon of 24th January 1929. Miss D. Sullivan held a jumble sale on Saturday the 31st May 1930 in aid of the Confraternity Band fund this was granted free gratis. In June 1954 the Castlebridge Branch of the J. C. A. applied to hold a jumble sale there and this was granted at a fee of £1 with the instruction that *no nails were to be driven into*

the walls. Would you believe it? On the 11th November the Castlebridge people sent a letter of apology to the club for cancelling their booking for the 30th October 1954 and *promised to forward payment in the near future.* Mrs Gaddren of Alvina Brook requested to use the hall for a jumble sale in August 1958 and this was refused. She sought the hall again in 1969 for the same purpose.

Whist Drives

The Amusement Committee (C.Y.M.S.) requested permission to hold a whist drive and dance in the hall on Sunday 5th May 1918 for the members and their lady friends and *After some discussion the application was granted but it was ordered that the hall should be closed not later than 12 O'clock on the same night'* and it was also ordered that *'any surplus funds of the whist drive and dance are to be handed over to the club.*

On the 26th December 1925 the Hockey Club held a whist drive in the hall and they paid 15/= for the night. Thomas Hayes ran whist drives there on the 12th and the 23rd of February 1925 on behalf of and in aid of the Christian Brothers and the Sisters of the Poor, St. John of God

Convent. John Carty, secretary of the Wexford Rugby Football Club, wrote on the 15th September 1925 requesting the use of the hall for the purpose of running a whist drive and dance at the end of the month. This was granted at a charge of 15/= per night with the proviso that the whist drive and dance must be over and the hall cleared by 12.00 midnight. Nicholas Walsh ran 45 drives on the 25th February and the 4th March 1927 at a charge of 7/6 each night. The Wexford Athletic Club held a whist drive there in 1933 and the Civic Guards ran a whist drive there on Friday nights in Lent in 1933 in aid of the County Board N. A. C. A. J. The Golf Club ran a card drive there in 1963.

Sport

A boxing contest was staged there on the 27th May 1927 with boxers from Dublin counted amongst the pugilists who fought that night.

On the 15th September 1903 Frank O'Meara and three other members requested the use of the concert hall for a gymnasium class which they hoped to start up in the club.

Dominic Kiernan

Their request was accepted but they were obliged to accept John White, a Council member, as the manager of the project. On the 8th March 1913 W. O'Brien from Arklow requested the use of the hall for a skating rink. This was roller-skating which was all the craze at the time and on into the 1920s. In March 1927 the Loc Garman Cycling and Athletic

Club staged a boxing tournament in the hall.

Mrs. Dunne, secretary of the County Board of Camogie, rented the hall on the 26th January and the 2nd February 1934 at a charge of 15/= per night. In November 1943 the Gaelic League (*the regular tenants*) were given permission to sub-let the hall to Jack Kavanagh for roller skating with the proviso that the C.Y.M.S. receive 50% of the weekly rent over and above the Gaelic League's own rent. The club also reserved the Friday nights for themselves. People from the dancing class were against the use of the hall for skating from the very start and advised against it and it soon became evident that the dance floor was being damaged exactly as they had predicted so the Council discontinued it.

The Christian Brothers school boxing tournament was afforded the hall free gratis in 1960 and 1961. The Wexford United Soccer Club rented it weekly on the same night in 1967 and St. John's Camogie Club was there in 1968. Dominic Kiernan, an ex Lord Mayor of Wexford, rented it for physical training in September 1968 and in 1975 both the Celtic Soccer Club and the North End United Football Club rented it.

Business

On the 13th September 1904 a Mr. Frizelle occupied the concert hall from October to March daily from 10.00.a.m. to 3.30.p.m for agricultural instruction classes. Several businesses rented it for various uses. On 23rd October 1934 the Cavendish Furniture Co. Ltd., Dublin made an application for the hall for the 19th January to the 2nd February 1935 to hold an exhibition of Irish made furniture. This application had to be refused because the Gaelic League occupied the hall for Irish classes on those days. T. D. Sinnott, the County Manager, requested permission to use it on Tuesday 10th June 1952. There is no record of whether he got it or not. Kevin Morris, auctioneer and an ex Mayor of Wexford, had it for one day monthly for the sale of furniture. Board Na Mona where there in 1960, Alexander Sloan & Co (Dublin) Ltd. were there from the 10th to 17th May 1965. The Drage Furniture Co., 60 Grafton Street, Dublin held a furniture exhibition there in April of 1966 and a Mr. Healey held a carpet sale in November of the same year.

Private

Guard John Kennedy held a childrens' party there and Thomas Howlin of Abbey Street held a private party there on 29th June 1963, as did Peter Murphy c/o Talbot Hotel, who held a birthday party in it in May of 1966.

Political

From the early 1900s up to 1916 the 'Wexford Gaelic League' organized a demonstration of national pride on St. Patrick's Day each year with a massive parade. On these occasions it was the custom of the C.Y.M.S. members to assemble at the concert hall and march in a body up to the Town Hall and join up with the main parade.

Mrs Scanlon, sister of Thomas Hayes (C.Y.M.S. member) had the hall for the purpose of supplying refreshments to the delegates attending the Redmond anniversary procession in 1924 and 25. In February 1938 the volunteers of the Irish Free State were looking for a drill hall for the local battalion of the volunteer force. As the Gaelic League held the tenancy the club would had to give priority accommodate to them before it could consider the volunteer force. There is no record of the outcome. On the 24th July 1955 a T. O' Connor, a civil defence officer, sought the hall for one night weekly during the winter months but the club had to refuse as the commencement of the Pongo was imminent. The hall was rented to a Mr. Corish for one week at a cost of £25 on the 4th June 1957.

Mrs A. Kehoe requested the use of the hall for a jumble sale in aid of the Republican prisoners dependents fund and the Society wrote to her stating *Owing to Article 4 of the Constitution of the C.Y.M.S of Ireland we could not allow the use of same.* - 4th March 1958. The constitution rules dated 1994 which I have in my possession have no bearing on what they wrote, nor has the St. Iberius club, General Rules of Management (*Rule 4*) any bearing on the foregoing. I have yet to see how this ruling could possibly have been justified. However I must accept that one of the golden rules of the Society from its very outset stated that no politics should be conducted in the society.
'Fine Gael' rented it for their election rooms and conducted their campaign from there in June 1969.

Miscellaneous

The Wexford Junior Mary's Needlework Guild wrote to the Council on the 31st August 1915 with the following resolution which was proposed by Mrs Horsbourgh and seconded by Lady Maurice FitzGerald *that the best thanks of this meeting be given to the secretaries and members of the 'St. Iberius Catholic Club' for their kindness in granting the use of the concert hall for the working parties of the guild.*
On the 29th December 1908 J. Godfrey, one of the secretaries of the Coursing Club, made an application for the use of the hall for the following evening for the purpose of holding the draw for the coursing meeting on the slob on New Years day.
On the 18th March 1925 Thomas Hayes (*member*) rented the hall at a charge of 15/= for Easter Sunday evening for a fancy dress carnival and tea party for children and adults and on the 5th October 1926 Edward O'Rourke (*member*) made an application on behalf of John Kavanagh *for a reduction of the charge of 15/= per night for three nights 'Fancy Fair' held for the purpose of raising funds for the 'Wexford Harbour Boat Club'.* The Council decided to reduce the charge to 25/= for the three nights. The Mass Radiography Association Limited requested the use of the hall from the 6th to 12th of April 1954. They were informed by the Council that both An Realt and the table tennis club had it reserved for two nights each, and suggested if they could to get another suitable venue but if not *then the C.Y.M.S. would make every effort to facilitate them.* – Dated 9th March 1954.

Miscellany

Miscellaneous Letters and Correspondence

Demonstrations of National pride

On the 3rd of February 1889 the following was instructed to be recorded in the minute book – *That we the members of the 'Wexford Catholic Young Men's Society' wish to express our sympathy with William O'Brien in his suffering and that we strongly condemn the Barbarous treatment, which he is enduring in Clonmel jail under the hands of Mr. Balfour his political opponent. (See Hugh McGuire's biography Vol. 2. for a very interesting and satisfactory conclusion to Mr. O'Brien's predicament)*

On the 4th March 1903 the 'Wexford Gaelic League' contacted the club requesting them to send two representatives to the Town Hall on Friday evening for the purpose of organising a demonstration on the national festival St. Patrick's Day. Frank O'Connor and Michael Kehoe were appointed to represent the club and the Council decided that all members who possibly could should march in the demonstration. These Gaelic League demonstrations were held annually as we can deduce from the following. On the 8th March 1905 William Goold and Frank O'Connor attended a meeting in the Town Hall and it was agreed that they would meet in the Concert Hall at 1.00.p.m. on St. Patrick's Day and march in a body of C.Y.M.S. men in procession behind a 'wagonette' which they had hired.

On the 31st January 1909 a letter was received from the 'Gaelic League' requesting the club to appoint two delegates to attend a meeting in the 'League Hall' Paul Quay on Monday evening 1st February at 8.00.p.m.

The purpose of this meeting was to establish and organise a committee to make the necessary arrangements for the proposed public meeting decided by the Wexford County Committee of the 'Gaelic League' to be held in the Town Hall on Sunday the 7th of February at 2.30.p.m. in connection with the Irish language and the new National University. Frank O'Connor and Capt. Busher were appointed as delegates to attend.

On the 7th March 1915 the National Foresters requested the club to appoint two delegates to attend their meeting to discuss the arrangements for a demonstration for home rule on St. Patrick's Day and Edward F. O'Rourke and John Browne were duly appointed. Reporting back on the meeting Mr. O'Rourke stated that *The demonstration was organised solely for the purpose of honouring Ireland's Patron Saint, and would take the form of a procession around the town*

ending with a religious service in the Church. The members were requested to take part. The reader must remember that at this time nationalistic feelings were running high and it was only one year away from the '1916 uprising'. This was a demonstration by the men of Wexford of their solidarity in their national pride. To describe it as a religious procession as opposed to a political demonstration would have been very wise at the time. In March 1916 the same meetings took place with Edward F. O'Rourke and John Browne representing the C.Y.M.S. Edward and John requested the members to take part in a demonstration on St. Patrick's Day by meeting at the club at 2.00.p.m. so the members could march in a body and on this occasion they did not refer to it as a religious procession they were quite open as to their purpose. Within weeks of this parade Padraic

Pearse, Commander-in-Chief of the Irish Republic Army read the proclamation from the steps of the G.P.O. Dublin. The war of Irish independence had begun.

On the 17th June 1917 the following resolution on the motion of Capt. Busher and seconded by John Browne was passed and copies ordered to be sent to John E. Redmond.

M.P., to Mrs. W. H. K. Redmond, to the 'Freeman's Journal', 'The Irish Times' and to the local newspapers *That on our own behalf and on behalf of the members of this Society we beg to tender to John E. Redmond Esq. MP, to Mrs. W. H. K. Redmond and to the members of the family our most sincere sympathy on the death of our illustrious and gallant fellow-townsman Major W. H. K.*

John Redmond M.P.

Redmond MP. He sacrificed his life in what he considered to be the noble causes of religions liberty and the freedom of small nationalities – in the latter case having, as his primary object the freedom of his own Native Country Ireland.

There was a massive anti-conscription protest held on the 21st April 1918 at the Old Pound [St. Peter's Square] the five eminent speakers who addressed the crowd of 5,000+ were Rev. Mark O'Byrne, Fr. Ryan, Richard (Dick) Corish, James Sinnott and James J. Stafford. What is most interesting about these speakers is that they are all C.Y.M.S. members with the exception of Fr. Ryan

Redmond Anniversary Commemorations

There was a letter dated 24th February 1925 from Mrs. Scanlon, Mary Street, applying for the use of the concert hall and kitchen for the purpose of supplying refreshments to the Belfast contingent attending the Redmond Anniversary Commemorations on the 8th March. This was granted at £2.

Easter Rising Commemorations

On the 5th April 1927 M. Flusk and P. Connick sent a circular requesting the Council *to send a representative to a procession to Crosstown [St. Ibar's Cemetery] on Easter Sunday in honour of the heroes who fell since 1916.* The Council decided to *Adhere to the principle of leaving the members to act on their own free will on the matter.* In 1932 James Rossiter, secretary of the County Wexford Easter Commemoration Committee invited the club to sent a representative on Easter Sunday. The Council responded with the same reply this year.

Anniversary of the 1798 Rebellion celebration

On the 26th October 1937 Mr. Byrne, Town Clerk wrote to the Society requesting that they send delegates to a meeting in the Town Hall for the purpose of *organizing a demonstration in celebration of the 140th Anniversary of the 1798 Rebellion.* It was decided to send some members representing the Society to the meeting.

1798

'98 Commemoration Celebrations

A letter from E. P. O'Brien, the Hon. Secretary of the '98 Commemoration Celebrations was received on the 11th April 1948. In it he refers to a forthcoming meeting to be held on Wednesday 14th April. Shay Sinnott was elected to represent the Society at this meeting and any other subsequent meetings regarding the celebrations.

Emergency Years

On 3rd November 1942 the Hon. Secretary received a letter from the County Manager requesting the Society to send representatives to a conference of the various unions and societies in the town. This conference was arranged for the purpose of considering the possible measures for completing the organisation of the A.R.P. services for the town. Both Patrick M. Whelan and Thomas Banville attended the conference as representatives of the Society.

A letter from P. McGuinness, A.R.P. Officer was read to the meeting. He requested that the Society hold a General Meeting with a view to having the representatives of the Emergency Services attend and appeal for recruits. This was agreed and a General Meeting of the members of the Society was held on 18th November at which Mr. McGuinness and the other representatives of the Emergency Services attended. Alas, to the disgrace of the Society, only around a dozen members attended the meeting and it had to be cancelled. There is no further mention of this particular incident recorded in the minutes, so one cannot be sure exactly what transpired. If this was the only item of written information regarding this particular occasion, one could not be blamed for thinking badly of the C.Y.M.S. membership. However, this couldn't be further from the truth especially when one reads the following extract of what Fr. Murphy had to say in his address to the Annual General Meeting of Sunday the 7th February 1943, barely two months later *While regretting the falling away in membership* he considered that this was in no way due to the fault of the members themselves, but owing to *so many young men and boys being members of the L.D.F., L.S.F., Red-Cross, A.R.P. and other services* which took up a lot of their time. Having read the above, can anyone doubt the commitment members gave to their town at a time when nothing seemed certain in the world?

C.Y.M.S. Pressure Group

On the 4th January 1944 a letter from the Hon. Secretary, C.Y.M.S. Study Circle, Tuam, Co. Galway was received. It stated that at a recent meeting the following resolution was unanimously adopted *That the members of this study circle are of the opinion. That the present situation in regard to children and the cinema is far from satisfactory. And that it is a matter of urgent necessity that steps should be taken to provide special suitable cinema programmes for children. Or at least that films should be classified so that children are excluded from unsuitable ones.* The foregoing resolution was also unanimously adopted by the Wexford branch at a Council meeting. The Hon. Secretary was directed to write to the Town Clerk accordingly and to also inform him that the Council considered that *in the granting of licences by the corporation for the exhibiting of pictures in the town. There should be an age limit on children attending pictures passed for exhibition to adults.* One has to wonder if it was pressure from these Catholic Action Groups which brought censorship to Ireland or was such censorship in place prior to this. The club received a reply letter from the Town Clerk on the 4th April which had enclosed a copy of a letter that he had received from the Department of Justice in connection with the censorship of films for children. Unfortunately for us, this letter is lost and there is no record of its contents. I have been reliably informed that there was no censorship legislation for films at that time and the local authorities were advised to send the fire and safety department to any cinema which refused to apply censorship and close them down on health and safety grounds by refusing to give them a licence.

A letter dated 26th January 1948 received from the National Council of the C.Y.M.S. of Ireland *regarding the nominations of members to the cultural and educational panel of the Seanad (Seanad Eireann - the upper chamber of the legislature of Eire)* was read, the contents of which were not recorded I must comment that I never realised just how much influence the C.Y.M.S. of Ireland must have had until I became involved in the research for this book. It was one mighty pressure group with access to many a politician's ear.

Defending the Morals of Wexford Girls

A vote of congratulations was unanimously passed with the Wexford Corporation on their resolution of protest passed at their meeting on the references made by Frank O'Connor in his article which appeared in the American magazine 'Holiday'. - 17th January 1950 Minute book. I wrote to Pat Collins, Town Clerk, requesting a copy of the notes of their council meeting of the 2nd January 1950 which refers to the article written by Frank O'Connor and Mr. Collins very kindly promptly sent me a copy. It appears that Frank O'Connor was a pseudo name and the article was written by a scriptwriter for Radio Eireann, who was also a Director of a state subsidized theatre. This person had painted a 'scurrilous picture of Ireland and in particular of the morals of the girls of Wexford.' The Corporation moved a motion to ask the Government to dispense with the services of this gentleman and the C.Y.M.S. were placing it on record that they agreed fully with the Wexford Corporation's actions on the matter.

Public Utilities and Technology Introduced into the Club
(See also Chapters on Billiards and Reading rooms)

1850s

On the 22nd September 1859 the secretary, according to the minutes, was ordered to *Pay Mr. Hughes's bill for putting in the pipe water, 6/-.* Nothing further is mentioned or known so it would seem that the water was piped into this property. The Society was situated at Allen Street at this date.

1860s

On the 29th February 1862 the following is recorded *The pipe water was ordered to be discontinued.* That's it! Not another word as to what is being discussed. What is obvious is that they are discontinuing the pipe water, but just what other water was available I hazard to guess. Neither am I aware if they were at the same premises that were mentioned in 1859, but it would appear they were.

1880s

In September of 1881 the Council discussed *Getting the water into the Society (premises)* and they decided to get it in and to *leave the cistern as it is.'* They must have had an underground water tank. They obviously went ahead and got this supply as by December they received the initial bill *(probably for instillation expenses)* which was £6-5-5.

They were unable to pay the bill so Mr. Hanton was instructed to approach Richard Devereux and request him to pay it. At this early period in the Society's history, they had very little funds and Mr. Devereux was most generous and altruistic in subscribing to and helping them whenever he was asked. Amazingly, on the 1st October 1883 the following is recorded *'The water rate for the last three years was ordered to be paid.'* Can you believe these guys? They had not paid a single penny for their water supply for three long years and now they were ordering their secretary to pay the water bill. It should also be noted that Richard Devereux had died in March 1883 so that source of financial assistance was gone.

13th April 1882
The Society purchased a Typographic Copying Machine from Mr. Timpson, for the sum of £2-10-0.

15th February 1883
The Society purchased a 'Weatherglass' [Thermometer] at a cost of £3.

1st July 1897

Tenders of the plumbing were sought from the following Club members
Michael McKenny............................ ...Did not tender
James Stamp.................................... ...Did not tender
James Sinnott....................................Estimated £19-5-2
Matthew Harpur................................ .Estimated £ 22-6-0
Mr. Sinnott got the contract.

1900s

In 1901 the cost of the consumption of gas for the year was under discussion. It was said that this was excessively high but the Council in reply stated that they considered it reasonable when taking into account the large and spacious apartments to be lit up. The Council considered there had been no extravagance. However, special meters were fitted in the card rooms and there were plans under way to ensure that people who used the concert hall would pay for the gas consumption.

September 1901
The Council decided *to have incandescent lights fitted on the gas in the card rooms and had 'Special Gas Meters' installed in the card room and the concert hall.*

On the **27th September 1905** the club had incandescent lights fitted on the gas in the card rooms. These were an improvement on the ordinary ones in existence at this time in that they glowed much brighter and produced a far more brilliant light. Of course, as the card rooms were on their own gas meters then, the Council were not overly bothered that the new lights would use more gas than the ordinary ones had previously. These lights were so good that on the 3rd April 1906 the Council wrote to Mr. Lyne, Manager of the Gas Company, enquiring as to the cost of having incandescent lights fitted on the billiard tables. The estimate that Mr. Lyne submitted to the club is not recorded but there is no doubt that the cost quoted was considered excessive and the matter was left in abeyance. The matter was next mentioned in 1919, some thirteen years later.

On the **8th of March 1906** this same subject was raised again. The high consumption of gas necessitated strict rules of usage from the Council who appointed a sub-committee to look into the matter and report their

Suggestions. The committee recommended the following alterations and regulations, which were considered necessary to guard against wastage and leakage and to limit the usage.
(1) The main supply cocks be turned off every night
(2) The main cocks not to be turned 'Full On' except when necessary
(3) The supply to the kitchen, back rooms and stove in the Council room to be cut off. An economy drive was well and truly in motion.

On the **21st of March 1906** the branch Council feared that the club might get into debt so they decided to *Levy a charge from the card players to provide funds for the club. A charge of 1p [penny] per night, per head was enforced from 1st January next year) 1906). And the slot gas meters now in the card room be removed when this charge comes into being.* This was the first time that members had to pay to play cards on the premises but the lighting had to be paid for and that was the end of it.

December 1907 the Council procured a 'Fixed Gas Pendant' for the reading room in place of the old one which was unsuitable for the incandescent burners.

1910s

The Society had a gas meter installed in the concert hall but by the **7th March 1915** they requested that the 'Gas Company' remove the gas meter from the hall. It was decided that a fee would be charged for the lighting instead. This proves to us that a gas meter was in operation in the concert hall prior to this date.

On the 5th of **September 1915** Thomas Underwood, Crescent Quay *(a member)* wrote requesting a share of the orders of the club for its gas fittings and plumbing work which the Council duly granted.

In **November 1919** the Council enquired of the Gas Company as to the cost of having gaslight over the billiard tables. Mr. Underwood on behalf of the Gas Company replied with an estimate of £56. This also was considered excessive and the matter left in abeyance. Just imagine it, £56 smackers in 1919 was big money.

1920s

On the **30th March 1920** a John Browne submitted plans and an estimate of £370 to install electric light in the club's premises. After consideration the Council decided to take no action in the matter unless the company made a proposal to install the light in the premises as an advertisement when it would have further consideration. Weren't the Council member's clever old fox's? The name of Mr. Browne's company was not recorded but as nothing came of this one must assume that Mr. Browne told the Council to take a running jump for them selves and could you blame him?

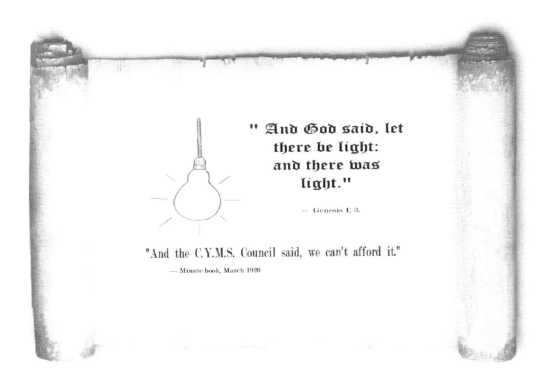

In **September 1923** a discussion took place as to the advisability of installing a plant *(probably a generator)* to light the club premises. This plant would cost approximately £80 and once erected the annual cost of maintaining it in working order would be very small. It would mean a saving of around £20 annually to the club. This was left to be discussed at a further meeting. On the **7th October** Mr. Murphy, electrician attended a meeting and gave particulars and prices of general electrical dynamos suitable for supplying the club premises with electric light. This meeting was also adjourned

In **September 1924** Wexford Corporation's electrical engineer wrote regarding a proposed undertaking for the supply of electricity to the principal houses in the town and it was decided that. Edward F. O'Rourke would meet the engineer to discuss the matter.

In **June 1927** the members signed a petition, with the Council's consent I hasten to add, requesting that the *council procure a loud speaker wireless set.'* It would be seven years before this request came to fruition.

On the **25th September 1928**, once again the subject of electricity was on the agenda Mr. Goold and Mr. Hayes were appointed to wait on [meet] the 'Electric Supply Co' for the purpose of getting particulars for the fitting-up of electric lights in the premises and the probable charge for same. In October of the same year a Mr. A. G. Brady, electrical engineer, 7-8 Eden Quay, Dublin, submitted an estimate of £88-17-9 for fitting up wires and bulbs for lighting of the club. The Council decided to postpone taking any action regarding the matter until a future date.

1930s

February 1934

The Society installed their very first 'Wireless Set' [radio set] in the Billiard and Snooker room. This set cost £36-15-0. The set was purchased from Nicholas Hore. The amusing thing about this was the Society was not yet connected to the electricity supply. But the Wexford Athletic Club who rented the gym from the Society did have a supply line in their room. So the C.Y.M.S. supply of electricity had to be purchased from them at the rate of 1/= per week for electricity consumed by the wireless apparatus from their tenants electric supply. Payment for this was set to begin on the 29th April 1934.

1938

In 1938 there was a disaster on billiard table No 2 when one of the gas mantles fell on to the table damaging the cloth. The Council considered the situation and as the installation of new gas mantles would be very costly they decided to look into the possibility of installing electricity. A representative from the Electricity Supply Board was invited to the club to estimate the cost of having electric light on the billiard tables. Talk about procrastinators - the Council was still pondering this question in December of 1941

1940s - The War Years

Fearing a failure of the Gas Supply it was decided on the 9th December 1941 to seek an estimate of the cost of installing electricity on the premises. They must have installed this supply as in 1943 there were complaints concerning the rationing of same.

7th July 1942.

It was decided to order-in a supply of turf and firewood until a supply of coal could be procured. Also in 1942 it was recorded that until further notice *the reading room fire will not be lit until after noon.* Coal costs money and with a war on there was a scarcity of it.

22nd September 1942 It was decided to purchase three ton of blocks *(firewood)* one ton each from the Wexford Timber Company, Harry Wilson and Paddy Kinsella. The clever old foxes at it again - ordering one ton from each Company knowing full well that one ton was probably the limit that you could order at any one time. This was good husbandry from the Council members.

4th May 1943

The E.S.B. supply of electricity to the club was obviously insufficient as it is recorded that the Hon. Secretary was instructed to write to them complaining that the supply to the club was inadequate. By the 2nd June an E.S.B. inspector visited the club and had a discussion with the Secretary. *He would not increase the quota allowed to the Society.* The Secretary pointed-out that it was absolutely impossible to carry-on with such a small quota and if that persisted then the club premises would have to be closed down. The inspector promised that he would report back on the situation. Due to the seriousness of the matter the Council decided to impose the strictest economy, advised the membership of same and requested their co-operation with the caretaker in this regard. It is very confusing to understand exactly what is going on here when one reads that the Council decided to have electricity installed in the Reading Room and the Council Chamber. On the one hand the Council are arguing with the E.S.B. authorities and informing them that the club will have to close because of the inadequate supply and on the other hand the Council are going to extend the supply further around other rooms.

4th January 1944

A quotation for the wiring of the reading room only was received from Mr. Levingston and the secretary then wrote to him requesting a quote for the J.O.C.'s room *(the gym)*, the reading room and the council chamber. The end result was that Mr. Quigley from North Main Street got the job. This was agreed on the 18th January 1944. By January 1945 the caretaker was allowed to light the fire in the reading room in the evenings. This implies that this practice had been stopped due, no doubt, to the coal shortage.

On the **7th October 1947** the Council wrote to the Department of Industry & Commerce *(Fuel section)* requesting permission to purchase coal. They returned a form to be completed which was duly attended to and mailed on the 4th November. By the 23rd of the same month the Society received a permit that allocated the Society ten CWT's (hundredweight) of coal per month.

December 1948
The club purchased their second wireless-set, 'New Wireless Set' *(radio)* from Mr. Hore at a cost of £25. You will remember they purchased their first one at a cost of £36-15-0 in April 1934. Fourteen years that one lasted so I suppose one can't complain at that. Take note the cost of a wireless set have come down in price.

1950s

In **1950** the Society got an electric clock for the billiard room. If nothing else this made the caretaker's job a little easier, at least he didn't have to hand-wind the spring-loaded old clock or wait for a sunny –day to look out into the garden at the sundial to know the time. The Table Tennis club received 'new' florescent lighting installed over the No. 1 table and also an electric fire for the room.

3rd January 1956
The Council purchased three gas heaters to be installed on the walls in the billiards room at a cost of £60.

1957
The Society had new showers installed not just for the sports men but for the members in general to use these showers. In those days few houses had a bath so the showers were a welcome amenity

1960s

7th of May 1963
The Society got their first Television set. It was acquired from R.T.V. Rentals Ltd.

Caretakers

The first person recorded as a caretaker in the Society was John Stafford on the 20th December 1858. The position of door porter for the Society was given to a man with the wonderfully biblical sounding name of Moses Abraham who was made door porter in December 1858. His duty was to open and close the door for members and to see to it that non-members did not enter the club.

List of Caretakers

Moses Abraham	Dec.1858	1860?	Door porter
John Stafford	20 Dec.1858	1863	The very first caretaker, later the librarian
Mr. Ahearne	25 Aug. 1863	?	Temporary caretaker
Mr. Cosgrave	10 Sept.1863	11 Apr. 864	Resigned
Walter Broadhurst	May 1864	2 July1866	Walter was let go
John Carroll	July 1866	?	On three month trial
John Nolan	27 Jan. 1873	1875	Caretaker and marker, first with this title
William Busher	1875	13 Oct.1881	Caretaker and marker gone by 13th Oct. 1881
Nicholas Murphy	Oct. 1881	8 Dec. 1881	Caretaker and marker let go
Matthew Sinnott	8 Dec. 1881	14 July1883	Caretaker and marker. Resigned his position
Thomas Lambert	21 Aug. 1883	Nov. 1890	Deceased November 1890
Nicholas Murphy	1888	?	Temporary caretaker
John Hanrahan	24 Nov.1890	10 Dec.1891	He was let go

John Hennelly	25 Apr.1892	13 Mar.1893	Caretaker and marker. He was let go
Peter O'Rielly	13 Mar.1893	?	Chief caretaker
Thomas Harpur	30 Aug. 1904	?	Temporary caretaker
Thomas Lambert	22 Sept.1897	7 June 1900	Assistant caretaker. Pensioned-off
John Rositer	1900	Jan. 1918	Chief caretaker left his job in January 1918
Peter O'Rielly	?	?	Assistant caretaker
Peter O'Rielly	15 Jan. 1918	Feb. 1921	Made chief caretaker. Deceased Feb. 1921
Martin Murphy	15 Jan. 1918	14 Jan.1919	Assistant caretaker laid off
Mr. R. Murphy	Jan. 1919	31 May1919	Assistant caretaker laid off
James Kehoe	14 Oct. 1919	?	Assistant caretaker laid off
James McMahon	1919	24 June1922	Assistant caretaker laid off
James Delaney	2 Feb. 1921	25 Mar.1925	Chief caretaker. Resigned
John Murphy	18 Dec. 1923	18 Mar.1925	Assistant caretaker. Resigned.
Kevin Morris	18 Mar. 1925	?	Assistant caretaker (future Mayor of Wexford)
John Fennell	14 Apr. 1925	27 Aug.1929	Caretaker, ill in hospital. Laid off
John Cullimore	June 1929	3 Jan. 1930	Temporary caretaker (future Mayor) resigned
Randal McDonald	18 Nov. 1929	3 Jan. 1930	Caretaker. Let go as no fidelity bond supplied.
William Hynes	3 Jan. 1930	?	Caretaker
Robert Banville	12 Jan. 1930	21 Jan. 1930	Stood in as temporary caretaker
John Cullimore	20 Oct. 1930	April 1932	Assistant caretaker & marker. Laid off
William Hynes	Jan. 1930	Oct. 1938	Caretaker. Resigned and emigrated Liverpool
Robert Barnwell	Oct. 1938	17 Dec.1939	Resigned, ill in Dec. Deceased February 1939
John Crosby	17 Dec. 1938		Temporary caretaker as Robert was ill
John Crosby	28 Feb. 1939	23 May1941	Caretaker. Let go
Frank Furlong	24 May 1941	?	Caretaker.
Christy Moran	23 Nov. 1947	April 1948	Acting assistant caretaker. Let go
Christy Moran	1948	?	Temporary caretaker for winter months only
Frank Furlong	1949	2 Jan. 1953	Caretaker. Resigned through illness
John Joseph Busher	5 Dec. 1950	?	One months trial
J. Stafford	3 Jan. 1953	?	Caretaker.
Joe Clancy	April 1953	8 Jan. 1954	Caretaker. Laid-off
Tom Doyle	12 Jan. 1954		Caretaker.
Peter Dunne	1956	7 June 1960	Caretaker. Resigned through illness
John Cleary	21 June 1960	7 May 1963	Caretaker. Laid-off
John Breen	Sept. 1961	?	Temporary caretaker covering holidays
Malachy Duggan	21 May 1963	1966?	Caretaker. resigned through ill health
Patrick Murphy	Nov. 1966	?	Temporary caretaker covering Mr. Duggan
W. J. Sadler	Nov. 1966	13 June1967	Caretaker. Resigned poor wages £4 per week.
William Gray	June 1966	Aug. 1967	Caretaker. Resigned ditto
Arthur Clarke	19 Sept.1967	1981	Caretaker
*** Gerard O'Rourke	11 Jan. 1982	18 Jan. 1983	Caretaker. Resigned
Jackie Breen	18 Jan. 1983	?	Temporary caretaker
Liam Underwood	22 Feb. 1983		Temporary caretaker
James(Jimmy)Robinson	1983	18 May1984	Caretaker. Let go
Myles O'Rourke	18 May1984	4 Sept.1984	Temporary stand-in caretaker
Martin Mahon	4 Sept. 1984	2 Nov.1984	Temporary stand-in caretaker
John Doyle	2 Nov. 1984	Jan. 1987	Caretaker. Deceased 1987
Myles O'Rourke	Jan. 1987	4 Mar. 1987	Temporary stand-in caretakers
Berty Mahon	Jan. 1987	4 Mar. 1987	Temporary stand-in caretakers
Thomas Hurley	4 Mar. 1987	Dec. 1987	Caretaker. He was hospitalised in Dec.
Myles O'Rourke	Dec. 1987	5 Jan. 1988	Temporary stand-in caretaker
Sean Parle	5 Jan. 1988	7 June 1991	Caretaker. Laid-off to save money
Myles O'Rourke	7 June 1991	4 Sept. 1999	Temporary stand-in caretaker. Deceased 1999
Liam Gordon	1999	2002	Chairman and temporary caretaker
Dick Murphy	2002	2008	Hon. Secretary and temporary caretaker

*** The practice of employing permanent full-time caretakers was discontinued around this time and was replaced by various members cleaning the premises. Liam Gordon and Dick Murphy carried out these duties from this period to the present time.

Caretakers Wages

13th of October 1881	Salary was 10/- per week	Plus 1/- in the pound on the earnings of the billiard table
22nd June 1906	Salary was 9/- per week	
7th of June 1906		The caretaker was asked to resign. Rev. Fr. P. Doyle had arranged for a small pension *'Paid from outside source'* and also the club would pay a small pension of 1/- per week from its funds.
11th July 1906	salary was 12/ per week	
15th January 1918	12/- per week	Plus accommodation on the premises
18th February 1919	12/- per week	Increased to 25/= a week if he take lodging outside the club premises.
8th February 1921	Wages 35/- per week.	
13th of May 1924		*'An order was given for a suit of clothes for James X (caretaker), on its usual conditions.'* By the 27th May the Council received the invoice from Healy & Collins *'for £5 for James's clothes.'*
6th October 1925	12/= per week	12th June 1926, received a wage increase which brought his wages up to 15/- per week.
27th March 1928	wages were 30/- per week	
29th November 1929	wages were fixed at 35/= per week	Caretaker had to *'enter into a fidelity bond as security.'* By the 3rd January 1930 Mr. X's fidelity bond had not been acquired so his employment was terminated
12th October 1938	wage of £2 per week	On condition he enters into a fidelity guarantee bond of £50 with an approved insurance company.

C.Y.M.S. MEMBERS
From the ranks of the
Catholic Boy Scouts of Ireland (C.B.S.I.)

The Catholic Boy Scouts of Ireland (C.B.S.I.) was founded in 1927 with the assistance of the religious order of the Knights of St. Columbanus. The Boy Scout movement is based on a number of fundamental principles which underline all its activities. These principles include adherence to spiritual values; loyalty to one's country, respect for the dignity of all people and the natural world. The organisation strove to develop each boy's character, resourcefulness and public spirit and the ethos of the movement made the organisation an ideal recruiting ground for future C.Y.M.S. membership. The Society lost no time in utilising this source of potentially new members from the very outset.

Badge of the Catholic Boy Scouts of Ireland

The 2nd Wexford (St. Columbanus) Troop was founded in October 1929 by the Wexford chemist R. J. Sinnott who was the first Scoutmaster. Others founder committee members were Edmond Hassett and Fr. Butler. Throughout the years many C.Y.M.S. members came from the ranks of this troop including our most famous C.Y.M.S. son, the late Tanaiste, Brendan Corish T.D. The Rev. John M. Butler, C.C., was made the Diocesan Chaplain of the Wexford Scouts in 1932 and was appointed President of the C.Y.M.S. in 1951. The photographs below show Murth Joyce *(one time Scoutmaster)*, Fr. Butler *(Scout Chaplain)* and Stevie Martin. *(Scoutmaster, Knight Errant Chief – Diocesan Commissioner 1968-1975, Member of the C.B.S.I. National Executive Board for 15 years, regional Chairman 1976-78, Regional Commissioner 2000-2003.)* Stevie joined the Scouts in 1936 and celebrated his 70th year as a Boy Scout in May 2006. That gives Stevie the privilege of being the longest serving Scout in Wexford and probably Ireland if not the world. Another long serving Scout is George Bridges who is an Honorary Life Member of the C.Y.M.S.

Murth Joyce

Fr. John M. Butler, C.C.
Diocesan Chaplin
1942

Stevie Martin

John O'Rourke

George Bridges

Nicky Lacey

The Scout Motto

'Bi Ullamh' which translates from the Irish to 'Be Prepared'

The Boy Scout Promise

On my honour, with the Grace of God I (Boys Name) promise to do my best: to love honour and serve Christ my King, his Holy Church and his Blessed Mother, to help my neighbour at all times and obey the Scout Law.

The Scouts Law (adopted 1969)

(1) A scout is Loyal; he is faithful to his scout promise, loyal to his fellow scouts and all others to whom loyalty is due.
(2) A Scout is Trustworthy; he respects his honour, keeps his word and does his duty.
(3) A Scout is Helpful, he does at least one charitable act a day.
(4) A Scout is friendly; he is a friend to all and a brother to every other scout.
(5) A Scout is Courteous; he is respectful and polite to all.
(6) A Scout is Kind and gentle to everybody. He is kind to animals that are also God's creatures.
(7) A Scout is Obedient; he promptly carries out the instructions of those placed over him.
(8) A Scout is Cheerful even under difficulties.
(9) A Scout is Thrifty, he saves so that he may pay his own way and be generous to those in need.
(10) A Scout is Brave; he always supports that which is right and good.
(11) A Scout is Pure in thought, word and deed.
(12) A Scout does all for the Glory of God.

Mickey Fortune

Frankie Moran

Tom Curran

List of Boy Scouts who became members of the C.Y.M.S. Society

Sean Barker, South Main Street (1930s-40s). Later became managing director of the family business. He attended the Aberystwyth camp in 1951.

George Bridges, Selskar Street (1930s). Chairman of the troop to this day. Later became Wexford businessman. Attended the Scouts' 75th Celebrations in June 2004. Retired and living in Clonard, Wexford.

Victor Bridges, Selskar Street (1936-43). Rode in the C.Y.M.S. colours in the cycling races of the early 1950s. Later ordained to priesthood and is presently a priest in the Parish of Liverpool.

Philip Broaders, (1940s). Later became a seaman / lightship man and businessman. Living South Main Street, Wexford. He attended the Scouts' 75th Celebrations in June 2004.

Very Rev. John M. Butler, Adm. He was one of the founders and Chaplain of the Catholic Boy Scouts (1929 - 1943). He attended the Aberystwyth camp in 1951. He was awarded the 'Order of the Silver Wolf' the highest award a Scout can achieve. He was also Chaplain of the Order of Malta Ambulance Corps (1940s) and became President of the C.Y.M.S. St. Iberius Branch, Wexford

Patrick (Paddy) Connelly, (1950s). He became ships' engineer and businessman. He attended the Aberystwyth camp in 195.

Brendan Corish, (1940s). He became a politician, leader of the Labour Party and Tanaiste. Deceased.

Patrick (Paddy) Connelly

Thomas (Tom) Curran, (1947). He became a seaman /engineer was on the Ferry to France. Deceased.
Andy Doyle, John's Road. (1943) He was employed at Coffey's shop on South Main Street. Deceased.
Johnny Doyle, Maudlintown. (1940s) He emigrated to Canada.
Sean Doyle, (1930s/40s) 13 High Street. Manager of P. J. O'Connor's, North Main Street.
Michael Firman, The Quay, (1950s) emigrated (returned) to England
Peter Firman, The Quay, in the Cubs (1952). Plumbing & Heating Engineer
Ger Foley. Selskar. (1940s). Wexford businessman Ardcavan.
Desmond Fortune, 82 North Main Street, in the Cubs (1952) He became a chemist.
Michael (Mickey) Fortune, 82 North Main Street. (1947). He attended the Aberystwyth camp in 1951.He became a seaman. Retired and residing in London.
Richard (Dick) Fortune, 82 North Main Street. (1947). He attended the Aberystwyth camp in 1951. He became a Master Mariner. Retired and residing in Cork.
Frank Furlong, He was the C.Y.M.S. club caretaker in the 1940s and an ex-British army man he was also the Annual Camp Cook for the Boy Scouts in the 1930s/40s.
Pat Hayes, Mulgannon (1943) Employed at Johnstown Castle. He was one of the founders of the Girl Guides.
Richard (Dick) Hanton, 25 John Street, (1942-43). He became Wexford businessman. Deceased.
Alan Hore, (1942-43). Proprietor of the 'Radio House/Bar South Main Street.
Murth Joyce, (1942). One-time Scoutmaster and he was also a member of the Order of Malta Ambulance Corps. He became a Wexford businessman. Deceased.
Oliver Kehoe, (1940s). Emigrated to Liverpool. Married George Bridges sister.
Kevin Kehoe, (1940s) He was Assistant Scout Master and was one of the first members of the Order of Malta Ambulance Corps .
Larry Kelly, Upper John's Street. (1943) He became seaman. Deceased.
Paddy Kelly, (1943) He was Scout Master in the 1940s. He was an office Clerk, he went to Limerick..

Michael Firman

Micheal Murray

Frank O'Rourke

Sean Nolan

Nicholas (Nicky) Lacey. The Faythe, (1948). He attended the Aberystwyth camp in 1951. Wexford. Attended the Scouts' 75th Celebrations in June 2004. Worked in Motor Industry in Oxford. Retired and residing in the Faythe, A life member of the C.Y.M.S.
Dick McCabe, Selskar. (1943). was a member of the Young Ireland team that won the minor football championship in the mid 1940s.
Stevie Martin, 35 Hill Street. (1940s –2008). One-time Scoutmaster. He attended the Aberystwyth camp in 1951 as assistant Diocesan Commissioner. Awarded the Order of the 'Silver Wolf' the highest honour a Scout can achieve. Attended the Scouts' 75th Celebrations in June 2004. Celebrated his 70th year as a Boy Scout in May 2006. He is probably the longest serving Scout in the world.. Retired and residing in Wexford
Tom McGuinness, Monck Street, (1940s) and was also a member of the Order of Malta Ambulance Corps. He boxed with the 2nd Wexford Scouts against the 45th Dublin troop in 1938. He was a shop assistant at Walker's, North Main Street. Deceased.
Bernard McGuinness, Monck Street, (1940s). Employed as an electrician at Quigley's, North Main Street. Deceased.
Frank (Frankie) Moran (1947). Ice cream parlour ,South Main Street/George Street. He attended the Aberystwyth camp in 1951. Became a radio Officer in the Merchant Navy. Retired and living in Perth, Australia.
Aidan Murphy, Selskar Street, (1942/43). Proprietor Painting Business
James (Jim) Murphy, (1943) was also a member of the Order of Malta Ambulance Corps . Proprietor Painting Business

Peter Firman   Des Fortune

Nick Murphy (1940s). Hurled with the Faythe Harriers. Emigrated to England.

Ray Murphy, Magdalen's Terrace (1943). Emigrated to Canada or the USA.

Micheál Murray, Selskar Street, (1940s). Later became a Royal Marine, UK. Was boxing champion in the marines (1950s/60s) he returned to Wexford. Deceased.

Sean Nolan, North Main Street, (1947). He attended the Aberystwyth camp in 1951. Became a jockey later worked in Cheese Factory Wexford. Deceased

Denis O'Connor, (1943). Photographer Main Street. Deceased.

Frank (Franko) O'Rourke, North Main Street, and (1947) Became Wexford businessman and resided at Carcur, Wexford. He attended the Aberystwyth camp in 1951. He also attended the Scouts' 75th Celebrations in June 2004. Deceased.

John O'Rourke, (1943). He attended the Aberystwyth camp in 1951.Emigrated to Gravesend, Kent. England. Deceased

Michael A. O'Rourke, *(the author)* North Main Street, (1947). He attended the Aberystwyth camp in 1951. Attended the Scouts'75th Celebrations in June 2004. Served on Oil Tankers deep sea and then worked in Motor Industry in Oxford. Retired to Wexford.

Larry Roche, (1940s). Became a Professor (?) taught at University College Dublin.

Kevin Rutledge, Maudlintown. (1943). Was Scout Master from 1946-48. He was a printer at the old 'Free Press' on South Main Street.

Tom Sherwood, Maudlintown, (1942) He became a priest. Deceased.

Vincent (Vinnie) Sherwood. Maudlintown, (1942-43). He attended the Aberystwyth camp in 1951. Emigrated To the USA. Worked for Wells Fargo Bank, returned and became clerk at Devereux's, School Street. Deceased.

R. J. Sinnott, the Wexford chemist was the founder and first Scout Master of the 2nd Wexford (St. Columbanus) Troop.

Billy Turner, (1940s). Employed at the Weather Station at Rosslare Harbour

Reggie Turner, Selskar, (1943). Had his own printing business and Grey Hounds breeder. Deceased.

Sean Wallace, 15 High Street, (1942)?? Living in Wexford.

Tom Walsh, (1940s). Seaman with Irish Shipping Ltd. Deceased.

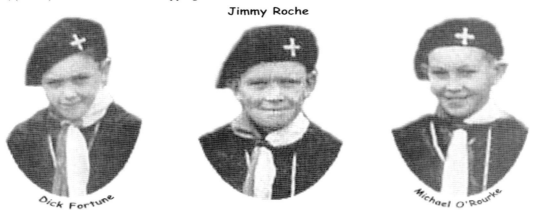

Jimmy Roche

Dick Fortune

Michael O'Rourke

In July 1951 the 2nd Wexford (St. Columbanus) Troop of the Catholic Boy Scouts of Ireland set sail for Wales. Their destination was Aberystwyth where they arrived on the 24th July. Leaders of the troop were; Harry Murry, Acting D.C., Steve Martin ,senior Scoutmaster and acting A.D.C., P. Foley ,Scoutmaster, John O'Rourke acting Scoutmaster. The troop was met by the Mayor of the town, Mr. Kenny, District Commissioner of the Aberystwyth Boy Scouts, Major Simpson, Co. Commissioner of the Cardiganshire Boy Scouts and G. S. M. Ferrell and high tea was provided. They were then transported to the campsite at Tycoch just 2-miles outside the town, which had been kindly, placed at their disposal by Lady Prysen. This was the first occasion the Wexford 2nd Troop had camped outside of Ireland and it was a very important occasion in Wexford town. Thousands turned out at the South Railway station to see the troop off. I was fortunate enough to have been in the troop.

Both Fr. John Butler and Scoutmaster Stevie Martin are the only two Wexford Scouts who have received the award of the 'Order of the Silver Wolf' in recognition of services to Scouting of the most exceptional nature. This is the highest award that can be achieved in the Catholic Boy Scouts of Ireland.

The above list is incomplete but there can be little doubt that there were many more C.Y.M.S. members who came from the ranks of the Catholic Boy Scouts.

A Good Scout Helps Himself

Besides their normal activities of doing a good deed-a-day; learning how to tie knots; using a compass and map reading; setting-up a camp, lighting a fire; pitching a tent etc. Scouts also learned basic first-aid methods which led them to the next natural progression to becoming members of the Order of Malta Ambulance Corps which many of them did. Back in the 1950s we always referred to this organisation as 'The Knights of Malta'. I've Gerry Breen to thank for correcting me on this matter who explained *'the knights of Malta is an order of chivalrous knighthood and there was only one Knight of Malta in Wexford. That was Dr. Tom Walsh, founder of Wexford Festival.'* Gerry then gave me the correct title for the order. Stevie Martin the expert on Wexford Scout and 'Order of Malta' history, while agreeing with Gerry, he pointed out that the official title of the organization is; 'The Sovereign Military Hospitaller Order of St. John of Jerusalem of Rhodes and of Malta'.

Intrigued with the above, I decided to do a bit of research myself and I came up with the following. 'The Knights of St. John' officially were the 'Order of the Hospital of St. John of Jerusalem'; also known as Hospitallers, Knights of Rhodes, or of Malta religious order founded by Papal charter (1113) to tend sick pilgrims in the Holy Land. It became a military order as well in 1140, and after the fall of Jerusalem was based successively on Cyprus (1291), Rhodes (1309), and Malta (1530) to provide a defence against Muslim sea power. Expelled from Malta by Napoleon in 1789, the Knights have been established at Rome since 1834. Conventionally, they are known as the 'Order of Malta'. There is a large number of similar-sounding named associations and organizations around the world today.

The Order of Malta Ambulance Corps attended all public functions in the town such as parades, processions, rallies, sporting events and were ready to administer first aid whenever required to do so. I have managed to secure a few photographs of some of these men, all former Scouts and C.Y.M.S. members. Incidentally, the Centenary of the Wexford C.Y.M.S. in 1955 coincided with the date of the Ambulance Corps of the Knights of St. John of Jerusalem and Malta.

Murth Joyce

Jim Murphy

Kevin Kehoe

Tom McGuinness

Society Members Who Received Awards

(Incomplete)

19th December 1858

John O'Brien, Hon. Secretary of the branch was presented with an address and gift on the occasion of his departure for the African Missions.

13th February 1869

Thomas Pitit Hogan was presented with an address for his services to the Society and his general exertions in aid of the charities of the town *(Wexford)*.

20th March 1871 - Knight of the Catholic Young Men's Society

Mr. N. J. Tucker was on this evening presented with a beautiful 'gold' medal brought by the Rev. President [Rev. Walter Lambert, C.C.] *from the Holy Roman Empire and created a Knight of the Catholic Young Men's Society. Mr. Tucker in an eloquent and suitable speech thanked the Rev. President for the high dignity and honour conferred on him* – Minutes Book 20th March 1871 *(For author's notes on this matter see 'Religion' page 73).*

Richard Joseph Devereux, K.G, (Knight of St, Gregory)
Circa 1870s / 80's

Richard Devereux did mammoth work for the religious orders and schools throughout Wexford. As his wealth grew so too did his altruistic spirit and his donations to charity. He was a founding father of the C.Y.M.S. of which much is recorded in this book. In recognition of his charitable works and service to the Church, Pope Pius IX created him a Knight of the Order of Pope St. Gregory the Great, an honour, which was truly well deserved. *(Author's note: I have not been able to discover the date of Richard Devereux's Knighthood)*

24th June 1899 Captain Laurence Busher

In early June 1899 during the movement of a boat in Wexford harbour by the pilot boat under the command of Capt. Laurence Neill and the tug boat 'Wexford' under the command of Capt. Laurence Busher, Capt Neill was knocked overboard and was in difficulties. Captain Busher, at great risk to his own life, jumped in after him to save his life. With difficulty Capt. Busher managed to get him aboard. On the 24th June 1899 **Capt. Laurence Busher** was awarded 'The Lloyd's Bronze Medal' for heroic conduct at sea.

The Lloyd's Medal for Heroic Conduct at Sea

Robert Hanton

On the 22nd January 1907 the following was ordered to be recorded in the minutes: *The heartiest congratulation of the council was tendered to the existing Vice-President & Treasurer of the Society Mr. Robert Hanton on his deciding to accept the Mayorship [sic] of the town for this year.*

Robert Hanton

Very Rev. John M. Butler, Adm. and Stevie Martin

Both were recipients of the 'Silver Wolf' award. The highest honour a Catholic Boy Scout can achieve.

John Kirwan, jnr. Irish Guards.

Awarded the 'British War Medal' and the 'Victory Medal' posthumously. He was killed on the 30th September, 1915 in the battle of Loos, Flanders.

The British War Medal and the Victory Medal 1914 - 1919

The Inscription on the reverse of the Victory Medal reads as follows;

" The Great War For Civilisation 1914 - 1919 "

28th January 1945 - Freeman of Wexford

Alderman Mayor Richard (Dick) Corish had the supreme accolade of the Wexford Borough conferred on him on the 28th of January 1945. Mr. Corish was Mayor of Wexford from 1920 until his death in 1945. He was the longest serving Mayor of Wexford having served for 25 years. He was one of three Wexford C.Y.M.S. members to have their names placed on the 'Roll of Honorary Freeman of Wexford'.

(Author's note: The Title is conferred on persons who have rendered distinguished service to the Church, State or municipality)

Richard Corish

238

1948 A.G.M. - Record Attendance

Joseph A. Fennell who died 1948 held the following record: *Mr Fennell held the record of never being absent from an Annual General Meeting since he joined the Society.* -- A.G.M. 1949.

7th July 1951 - Gold 'Forte in Fide'

Awarded to the oldest and longest serving C.Y.M.S. member in the World

In June 1951 the Gold Emblem of the Society was conferred on **Edward F. O'Rourke** *('the old Colonel O'Rourke')* by the Society's Headquarters in Dublin in recognition of his long and meritorious service to the branch. *The records of the Society in Dublin show that Mr. O'Rourke has the longest continuous service as a member in Ireland and probably in the World* – Wexford Free Press, 7th July 1951.

Photo] [Murray, Wexford.

President Rev. J. M. Butler, Adm. presenting Edward F. O'Rourke, Vice-President with the C.Y.M.S. gold emblem for 69 years service in June 1951.

On Friday evening 29th June 1951, the Feast of St. Peter and Paul, at the C.Y.M.S. St. Iberius branch, Wexford, Ireland's oldest member received his award from the newly elected President of the Wexford branch Very Rev. J. M. Butler, Adm. Besides the Gold Emblem he received a framed photocopy of the minutes of a meeting of the Council of the Society dated June 21st 1882 which recorded his acceptance into the Society. (*See photocopy next page*)

Old Edward was eighty-seven years of age at this award ceremony and he had clocked up sixty nine years service then. In 1955 at the C.Y.M.S. Convention of Ireland held in Wexford town, Edward F. O'Rourke was given a standing ovation. The National President, J. J. Campbell, M. A., from Belfast said: *Mr. O'Rourke was ninety one years of age and had served seventy-four years unbroken service with the Society.* Edward lived on to January 1959 when he died at the age of ninety-five years old with a service of seventy-seven years. He was, undoubtedly, the worlds' oldest serving C.Y.M.S. member.

21st June 1882

A meeting of the Council was held this evening at 9.0 Clock. the Revd President in the chair other present Wm Connick James Marlow Pat Walsh Robert Hanton Wm Scallan Edward Dixon and the Secretary. the minutes of the last meeting were read and confirmed. The following were elected Members of the Society Michael Kegan Wm Fitzpatrick James Whelan Edward Whelan Edward Rourke John Murphy and John Murphy, The Council decided the excursion should take the following route up William's street on to Johnstown Baldwins Town Duncormack and on to Blenmines,

Luke Doyle C.C.

Example page from the minutes book (3rd February 1869 to 22nd February 1891).
Mr. O'Rourke was presented with a framed copy of this page in 1951.

1952 Diploma in Social and Uneconomic Studies (Extra Mural)

Thomas Kelly, a long time Council member from Clifford Street, worked at Stafford's Timber Company on Crescent Quay. Thomas graduated and received his Diploma in Social and Uneconomic Studies *(Extra Mural)* at the Wexford Vocational School *(The technical School)* in early 1951. He was sponsored by the Wexford branch of the C.Y.M.S.

1953 – Awarded the Pro Bene Merenti Medal

Matthew (Matty) Luccan became the Sacristan of the Church of the Immaculate Conception, Rowe Street from 1917 up to his death in 1962. He received the Papal decoration Pro Bene Merenti in 1953 for his loyal service to the church. Matty's duties included ringing the bells for Mass daily and for the Angelus twice daily, mid-day and at six o'clock in the evening. He was a member of the Society for over fifty years.

3Rd February 1957, Gold 'Forte in Fide' Award

*George Bridges proposed and John J. Donohoe seconded that **Thomas O'Rourke** should receive a Gold Emblem award for his work for the Society over a large number of years. - A.G.M. 3rd February 1957.* Thomas went on to serve sixty six years with the Society.

3rd September 1957 - Mayor Elected

*A vote of congratulations was passed to **John Cullimore**, a member of the Society on him being elected as Mayor of Wexford, and in addition it was the wish of the council that a photo of him be obtained and hung in the club.* – 3rd September 1957.

John Cullimore was one of nineteen Society members who were Mayors of Wexford. He had the honour of greeting General Dwight D. Eisenhower, the retired President of the U.S.A. on 23rd August 1962 when the General visited Wexford.

John Cullimore

1960s - John Power Sports Stars of the Year awards.

C.Y.M.S. members received five of these awards:-

Roy Doyle won this award for cycling for two consecutive years 1965 and 1966. **Larry Codd** won the award in 1966 for Billiards the 'Mystery Award' winner. **Tommy Cullimore** won the award for cycling on two consecutive years 1967 and 1968.

Mr. F. J. O'Reilly, Chairman, John Power & Son Ltd., presenting the award for cycling to Roy Doyle of the C.Y.M.S. at the Talbot Hotel, November 23rd 1966.

Tommy Cullimore holding his 1967 John Power award being congratulated by his father Ald. John Cullimore.

Tommy Cullimore received his awards for two consecutive years for his extraordinary ability at cycle racing, in particular for his exploits in the Ras Tailteann 8-day cycle race representing Wexford. The photo depicts Tommy's proud father Ald. John Cullimore congratulating his son on his great achievement.

Freeman of the Borough of Wexford 1981

The Most Rev. Donal J. Herlihy, D.D., L.S.s., Ph.D. Lord Bishop of Ferns and Patron of the Catholic Young Men's Society was conferred with the freedom of the Borough of Wexford on the 10th June 1981.

Circa – 1978 – 1982 - Bene Merenti Medal

Ald. Nicholas P. Corish was a teacher at the C.B.S., one of the founders of the Labour Party in Wexford and Life President of the Trade Council. He was also Mayor of Wexford in 1955, one of the founders of the Invalid to Lourdes Association, a member of the C.Y.M.S. from 4th June 1918 until his death on the 17th April 1983. He was a devout Catholic involved in lay participation in Church affairs and was awarded by Pope John Paul II with the Bene Merenti Medal.

(Author's note; The Bene Merenti Medal is conferred on people who are deemed to have done 'Trojan Work' for the Church, Community and Parish.)

(See below an example of the award issues 1914 – 1922.)

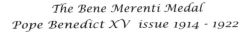

The Bene Merenti Medal
Pope Benedict XV issue 1914 - 1922

OBVERSE   *REVERSE*

10th June 1990 - Freeman of Wexford

The Most Rev. Brendan Comiskey, D.D., Lord Bishop of Ferns and Patron of the Wexford C.Y.M.S. had the supreme accolade of the Wexford Borough conferred on him on the 10th June 1990. He is one of three Wexford C.Y.M.S. men to have had their names placed on the 'Roll of Honorary Freeman of Wexford'.

May 12th 1984 - Freeman of Wexford

Brendan Corish, T.D., was conferred with the Freedom of the Borough on May 12th 1984. He was an Honorary Life Member of the Society. He was a former leader of the Labour Party *(1960-1982)* and served as Tanaiste *(Deputy Prime Minister)* from 1973-1977.

Mayor Peter Roche and Brendan Corish the day Brendan was conferred with the Freedom of the Borough May 12th 1984

Photograph Ray Flynn

Gold 'Forte in Fide' Award

On the 11th of April 1994 Seán Radford, the Chairman of the Council, presented the President and Treasurer, **Myles O'Rourke** with a gold "fortes in fide" Society emblem for his long-standing service to the Society.

18th February 1996, Gold 'Forte in Fide' Award

Henry F. Doyle was awarded a gold 'Forte in Fide' emblem for his sixty years service to the Society.

Gold 'Forte in Fide' Award

Nicky Lacey received a "fortes in Fide" Gold emblem award for his long service to the Society on the 21st March 2000.

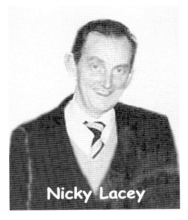

Many Gold Medals and Awards

Philip and **Martin Pierce** the proprietors of the famous Pierce's Foundry and Ironworks on Mill Road , the largest employer in the town, received many gold medals for excellence in the manufacture and export of farm machinery from all over the world. They were awarded several gold medals for excellence at the Dublin and Paris exhibitions in 1882.

Martin and Philip Pierce

8th December 1962
James J. Stafford, K.S.G. (Knight of St. Gregory)

His Holiness, Pope John XXIII, conferred the Knighthood of the Most Holy Order of St. Gregory the Great on James J. Stafford of Cromwell's Fort, Wexford on the 8th December 1962.

The honour was bestowed for his outstanding service to the Catholic Church. The citation was sent to the Most Rev. Dr. Staunton, Lord Bishop of Ferns *(the Society's Patron)* who presented it to Mr. Stafford on Friday 1st February 1963 at the Bishop's House, Wexford.

Pope John XXIII

"John XXIII, Supreme Pontiff.

We willingly accede to the requests made to us, believing that you have deserved well of the Catholic Church and cause, contributing to its welfare and progress. Therefore, to give public expression to our pleasure and our will, we choose you, James J. Stafford, of the Diocese of Ferns, and create you a knight of the Order of St. Gregory the Great, and we proclaim the same; and we give you the right to use all the privileges which go with this honour."

– The text from Rome, issued "apul S. Petrum", 8th December, 1962.

 # The Catholic Young Men's Society

versus

The Typographical Association

The C.Y.M.S. Council of the day decided to purchase a small printing machine which they had seen advertised for sale. *(One wonders who printed the advertisement.)*.

This machine was only capable of printing small handbills and tickets etc. It was not the club's intention to conduct a print business but rather to print their own work in an effort to save some expenses. It is important

The ADANA' printing press

that the reader is aware of this before perusing the following developments which led to the dispute. The first mention of this was at a meeting on 1st May 1956 where the possibility of purchasing a small printing machine was discussed. The outcome of that discussion was *that J. J. Donohoe was instructed to make enquiries with regards the price and suitability of one for sale by W. J. Kelly, Rosslare Strand. For the next meeting.* The next meeting held on the 4th June resulted in William Murphy proposing and H.

F. Doyle seconding *'that the 'Adana' printing machine be purchased from Mr. Kelly for a sum of £14-18-3.'* This proposition was *'carried unanimously'* by the Council of the day.

At a meeting of the 19th June 1956 the matter of the printing machine was discussed in greater detail. John Cullimore,

William Murphy

Thomas Hayes *(a leading union man of the print union)* and

Sean Doyle all spoke against the Society having a printing press, as it would according to them *Damage the printing trade in town and embarrass members of the Society who were in that trade.* Jackie Donohoe, William Murphy, Oliver Hickey and others expressed the opposite opinion and further stated that *it was foolish for the Typographical Association to be concerned about such a small press with its very limited output and capabilities.* Fr. O'Neill expressed the view that *members had a right to do as they choose and that the trade union had no right to interfere.* This meeting concluded having reached the decision that the *Organizer* [union leader] *of the Typographical Association be allowed to inspect the machine and to meet with Fr. O'Neill* [the branch President] *Thomas Kelly, Hon. Sec. and Thomas Hayes* (Council member who incidentally was the aforementioned union leader] *to discuss the matter further.*

There was a group of printers *(all members of the Typographical Association)* who were club members at the time. One of these was Michael Mahon. I knew Michael very well and he was a useful member of the Society. Michael and I had both been involved in the table tennis club and we

Michael Mahon

were both on the Pongo working committee for some years. Many of the members were in a slight dilemma over this issue. Whilst no one wished to see people like Michael being forced to leave the club by their union, nevertheless, one was loyal to the Council and fully behind them in refusing to allow an outside body dictate to the club what it could or could not do.

At a Council meeting held on the 3rd July 1956 Fr. O'Neil

reported on the meeting which had transpired between the representatives of the Typographical Association and the Hon. Secretary Thomas Kelly and himself. At the meeting Fr. O'Neill informed the union representatives that *The C.Y.M.S. would not dispose of the 'Adana' printing machine, but would give them an assurance that it would be used only for club purposes and that it would not be used by any outside body.* The representatives did not appear to be prepared to accept that assurance and one wonders if the reason for their non-acceptance was because they knew full well the reputation of the C.Y.M.S for its charitable work. Perhaps the union thought that if the club had a printing press that eventually some deserving charity would come along with cap-in-hand seeking help with printing their tickets or whatever? One could understand the union thinking along these lines.

Oliver Hickey proposed and Jackie Donohoe seconded that

a letter be sent to the Typographical Association *giving them a written assurance that the machine which will be kept under lock and key, will be used only for the society's work and not for any outside body.* Fr. O'Neill proposed that *they* [the union] *be asked as a gesture of goodwill. To allow their members who are members of the C.Y.M.S. To help in working the printing machine.* The latter suggestion of Fr. O'Neill must have raised the hackles of even the doves in the union negotiating team, not to mention the hawks, who must have gone ballistic at the suggestion?

A prompt reply letter was received from the Typographical Association which read *It would not be possible to allow our members who were also members of the C.Y.M.S. to help in working the club's printing press.* By December of the same year matters had deteriorated. Up till then it had involved a bit of posturing and sabre waving but now the Typographical Association fired the first shot in a battle that

would see the C.Y.M.S. come out victorious with the majority of its members firmly supporting it. A hand full of unfortunate members, who were also members of the Typographical Association, were forced to leave the society indefinitely.

In early December 1956 the Council received a letter from the Typographical Association which stated *they were calling on their members who were also members of the C.Y.M.S to resign from the society, since the C.Y.M.S. had insisted on working that printing press.* The secretary, Thomas Kelly, was instructed to reply expressing *'their amazement'* at the letter, since their representatives had stated that *objections was to the use of the machine by outside bodies and since a written assurance was given to the effect that the machine would be used solely for the society activities.* The secretary was further instructed to inform the T.A. that the *council considered it a grave injustice on their members being forced to resign from the society.*

By the 8th December another letter was received by the club from Thomas Hayes of Thomas Street *resigning from the society and the council due to the purchase of the printing press and the closing of the reading room.* [Thomas was a very valued C.Y.M.S. member who organised endless charitable events both in the club and externally. He was, also, the union representative for the T.A.]. The Secretary was instructed to write to Thomas *asking him to reconsider his decision* -- 8th December.

Another letter was received on the same date from Eugene McGrail which urged the Council to *arrange a meeting between the printer's union and themselves.* There was no action taken on this suggestion? On the 8th January 1957 a letter was received from the Typographical Association stating that *they did not give permission to use the printing machine and again asking the society to dispose of the machine.* The letter was marked *'Read.'* On the 15th January a letter was received from Thomas Hayes stating the *he was unable at present to reconsider his decision to resign.* Clearly Thomas was standing on a point of principle, but at the same time he was leaving the way open for himself to

return should the dispute be settled in a mutually agreeable manner.

Thomas was not the only member who was concerned with the matter. The Council received a letter from John F. O'Rourke [former Hon. Secretary] on the 27th January which put the dispute firmly on the agenda of the forthcoming A.G.M. to be held in February. John's letter read *That the printing machine purchased by the council during the year be offered for sale to a committee of the printers union and that no effort be made to use same in the future.* – Proposed and signed by John J. O'Rourke, seconded and signed by W. R. Turner.

On Sunday night 3rd February 1957 at 8.30.p.m. the Society's Annual General Meeting was held. I personally was one of those who packed the card area of the billiards room on that night. Each side in the dispute had called all their supporters in for the debate. Many people spoke at the meeting but not all are recorded in the minutes. Michael Mahon pleaded his case admirably as I recall but it is not recorded. John F. O'Rourke, in proposing the motion stated *I would like to point out that as a result of purchasing the machine. Five members would have no alternative but to leave the society.* He continued by asking *Was the branch going to lose these members, with some others for the sake of saving £2 per year on printing?* Surely, this was a bit of hyperbole by John. I would have thought that the press would have saved the Society far in excess of a mere £2 per year. *(Incidentally, John resigned his membership of the Society on a matter of principle and he joined the Thomas Moore Branch of the Irish National Foresters' as did most of those who left the C.Y.M.S over this issue.)* In seconding the resolution W. R. Turner thanked those members who opposed purchasing the machine which *although very small was capable of cutting across the livelihood of members of the printing trade on which 450 people depended for their support.* He went on to point out that *members of the Typographical Union, under the rules of that society, are not allowed to associate with any such machine.* He continued: by informing the meeting that *He had been a member* [of the C.Y.M.S.] *for forty years, and appealed for justice and if the society kept the machine he must leave on principle.* Sean Doyle, spoke-up and supported the motion. Nick Corish also supported the motion and asked the members to *let bygones be bygones and dispose of the printing press.*

Jackie Donohoe, the branch Chairman, proposed an amendment that *the society retain the machine as no out-side*

body had a right to interfere with the society or the private lives of its members. Jimmy O'Brien, a Council member, seconded that amendment. Nick Barnwell stated that the printers' union accused the C.Y.M.S. of setting a headline *(precedent)* in purchasing the machine. He did not think so, as other firms and bodies in the town had these machines for the last twenty years, and he went on to state *Some years ago a private individual who had a printing machine was allowed to advertise in the local papers* [i.e., People and Free Press], *and members of the T.A. supported this man in his business; Why then did the printers object to the C.Y.M.S. and withdraw their members from the society?*

The President, Fr. O'Neill, stated that *The first principle was that a society or an individual had a right to manage their own affairs.* He went on to say that he agreed with trade unions and realised their importance but he must hold an even balance and *disagreed with their action in calling their members to resign. This he believed raised the matter to a different level. The issue now is if we are going to allow an outside body to interfere in the affairs of the society.* This pretty much brought the meeting to it conclusion

Rev. Michael J. O'Neill, Adm.

but before it ended Fr. O'Neill once again stressed *an outside body had no right to interfere in the internal affairs of the society* Fr. O'Neill made it quite clear that he was not in favour of giving-in to the dictates of the Typographical Association, nor any members who were sympathetic to their case. The meeting concluded with the printers standing-up with a few supporters and ceremoniously vacating the room.

It was a sad period for the club which lost many good fellow members. The majority of members considered this dispute to be hair picking by the Typographical Association and backed the Council fully in its stand. The club survived and continued to grow in strength and the C.Y.M.S. printing press continued to roll, if you'll excuse the pun.

The card printed on the club 'Adana' Printing Press in 1960 published on the following page is what the Typographical Association claimed was *Capable of cutting across the livelihood of members of the printing trade.* I leave the readers to judge for themselves. Consider this – there was only one reunion per annum with an average of sixty members supporting it – that means sixty cards! Come on lads are you for real?

At a meeting held on the 7th May 1957 Jackie Donohoe proposed that the following motion be sent to the National Council for the convention *That the Wexford branch of the Typographical Association are wrong in refraining their members from remaining in the society while the society is*

the owner of a small 'Adana' printing press. In June the Council decided that the aforementioned letter be taken by the Wexford delegates to the Dublin convention and put before the National Council. As it transpired they posted the letter prior to attending the convention. The whole business dragged-on for a full year and if you think it ended at the meeting of 7th May 1957 you would be wrong

because almost two years later we read that on the 8th April 1959 Ald. John Cullimore stated *he had been approached to know if the Society would sell the printing machine to the Typographical Association to enable the members of the printing trade to re-join. It was decided to defer the matter for the attendance of the Rev. President* - Minute Book Here we have the Typographical Association making overtones to the society concerning a matter that had ended two years previously and three years after it had originated. The *'Rev. President'* mentioned was none other than the Very Rev. Michael J. O'Neill, Adm. On Wednesday 15th April the Council met and the matter relating to the printing machine came up for discussion and the ruling on this was

short and to the point. It read as follows: *...it was decided that the machine was not for sale.* It is quite obvious from this, that the C.Y.M.S. Were standing on a matter of principle and stated quite clearly that *this club was not going to be dictated to by any trade union and certainly not by a trade union which operated a closed-shop policy. This was enforced by the Typographical Association* (printers union) *at the 'People' Newspaper printing works at that time.* This then was the final word on the matter.

Young people of to-day who have easy access to computers will wonder what all the ado over a small printing press, capable of only printing a few tickets and small handbills, was about. Most households to-day possess a personal computer and most young people use word processing and desktop publishing almost every day. A ten-year-old kid could produce as much print work in one hour as the 'Adana' printing press could do in one year and at a tenth of the price I venture. One wonders how the Typographical Association weathered the storm of the advent of the P.C. and what their stance was relating to that technological wonder. Obviously, they had to accept the changing times as we all do. One thing is certain - there was no restriction placed on their members who joined the C.Y.M.S. in the 1980s because Michael Mahon rejoined the club that year after an absences of twenty-five years and he was more than welcome back as far as I understand.

Below is a photograph of Thomas Hayes at work in the People newspaper works. When one compares the size of these presses against the diminutive 'Adana' press in the C.Y.M.S. one cannot help but recall the Biblical story of David the shepherd boy against Goliath the Philistine giant.

A sample card printed on the 'ADANA' press

Courtesy of Tomas Hayes

250

Mail Delivery Service

We read an interesting piece dated the Sunday 4th January 1857, which refers to the 'Society's Letter Carrier'. It reads: *The council decided to give the letter carrier 2/6 as a Christmas box.* This was the first mention that members could have their mail delivered to the society's premises and the 'Letter Carrier's' job was to deliver it to the gentlemen's place of business no doubt. Why these gentlemen would want mail delivered to their gentlemen's club instead of to their homes is beyond me, but there you are, that service was in place for the members.

This matter popped up again in 1908 where we read: *It was brought to the notice of the council that a telegram delivered to the club recently for one of the members in the morning was not delivered to that member until after 6 P.M. when it was ordered that all telegrams coming to the club for any of the members should be delivered at once by the caretaker.--* Dated 1st December 1908. So by this date the caretaker was now the 'Letter Carrier' and the services was a well established custom.

In my time at the club I can recall the caretaker was still delivering letters and notices from the Council to the member's home addresses, but this covered matters pertaining to the Society's own business and had nothing to do with the general postage and mail service. In actual fact, a call at your door from the caretaker would be bad news because usually he would be delivering final notices on unpaid subscription or notification that your presence was requested to appear before the Council for something or other.

Colophon Page

The C.Y.M.S. is a famous Wexford social club and Society and is the only one of its kind left in the town. The Society belongs to the people of Wexford and its time that the people of the town got involved again with the club and bring back the vibrancy into it and the comradeship as in days gone past. There is so much potential and variety of activities to become involved in, all it takes is a few dynamic men or women to get things moving. A club is what the members make it and passive membership will end in a downhill motion. This is not only happening to the Wexford branch, it is nationwide. Just imagine that back in 1856, one year after the Wexford branch came into being, there were 127 branches in Ireland. Sadly, today there are fifteen branches in the country and some of these are just hanging-on by the skin of their teeth.

Whether this book is considered as having 'done something for the club' I do not know. But I can truthfully state that this work was undertaken with no financial inducement, but purely as a personal service to the club and to honour all its members past and present. I am very proud to be a C.Y.M.S. member and able to support the club in this small way. I do not know whether this book will be read by anyone other than the club members, ex-members and perhaps their respective families., but if that is the sum total of my readership then I will, at least, have enlightened them on 153 years of some of Wexford's colourful social history and given the reader an insight into the numerous activities and antics of some of the finest young men that Wexford has ever produced. That achievement alone will serve as my reward.

I wish all the members of the Wexford C.Y.M.S. well and I can only hope that the members of the next 153 years live up to the achievements of the men of the past because 'they are a hard act to follow'.

Acknowledgements

Grateful thanks to all the following:

A very special word of thanks and appreciation to my ever patient wife Margaret O'Rourke for her support and encouragement whilst I was immersed in this work.

Persons interviewed

The late **Thomas O'Rourke,** 13 Grogan's Road (*General history 1920s-1990s*); the late **Frank O'Rourke,** 'Slaney View House', Carcur., Wexford (*Cycling history 1957-1964*); **Roy Doyle,** Mansfield Drive, Wexford *(Cycling history 1964-67);* **Tom O'Hara,** St. Aidan's Crescent, Wexford (*Cycling & Football history 1960s-1980s*); **Thomas Mahon,** St. Peter's Square, Wexford (*General history 1950s to-date*); **Ger Foley,** Crosstown, Wexford (*Table Tennis history 1940s – 1950s*); **George Bridges,** Clonard, Wexford (*General history 1940s to-date*); **Ray Flynn,** South Main Street (*General History 1950s-1960s);* **Eamon Doyle,** Athlone, Co. Westmeath *(Dramatic Section and general history 1950s).*; **Rodney Goggins,** Liam Mellows Park, Wexford (*Billiards & Snooker history 1980s to-date*); **Nicky Lacey,** The Faythe, Wexford (*Billiards & Snooker history 1970s – 1990s*); **Dick Murphy,** Davitt Road, Wexford *(Hon. Secretary C.Y.M.S. Wexford Branch* for his kind cooperation and access to the minute books and photo archives); **Billy Roche,** Pineridge, Wexford (*For information relating to his grandfather the late Jem Roche the boxer*); **Kevin Cousins,** St. John's Road, Wexford (*General history 1950s -1960s*); **Francis Creane,** Saltmills *(Co. Wexford Billiards & Snooker League 1980s-1990s);* **James & Sylvia O'Connor** Spawell Road, Wexford (*For information relating to the O'Connor family's involvement*); **Michael Kavanagh,** Fort Mountain *(Dramatic Section and General history 1950s);* **Tommy Cullimore,** Coolree, Wexford *(Cycling history 1960-68);* **Gerry Breen,** Rocksborough, Wexford *(Information concerning People newspaper editors*); The late **Liam Lahiff,** Hill Street. *(G.A.A. information);* **Hilary Murphy,** Parklands, Wexford. (Information concerning *Richard J. Devereux*). **Victor James Stafford** *(information and photographs concerning the Stafford Family).***Stevie Martin & Nicky Lacey** *(information concerning the Boy Scouts).*

Persons who donated photographs and other memorabilia

Thomas Mahon, St. Peter's Square, Wexford *(General1950s to-date);* **Ray Flynn,** South Main Street, Wexford (General & *Municipal photographs*); **C.Y.M.S. Archives** *,(Wexford Branch)* ; **Paddy Donohoe,** Carriglawn, Wexford ; **Michael Cullen,** Coolcotts *(Photographer of the modern Billiards & Snooker archives);* **Tom O'Hara,** St. Aidan's Crescent, Wexford ; **Pat O'Connell,** Liam Mellows Park, Wexford ; **Roy Doyle,** Mansfield Drive, Wexford; **Kevin Cousins,** St. John's Road, Wexford; the late **Thomas O'Rourke,** 13 Grogan's Road, Wexford; the late **Frank O'Rourke,** 'Slaney View House', Carcur, Wexford; **Rodney Goggins,** Liam Mellows Park, Wexford; **Nicky Lacey,** The Faythe, Wexford **Billy Roche,** Pineridge, Wexford; **John, Theresa & Michael O'Rourke,** Corish Park, Wexford; **Mary O'Connor,** King Street, Wexford; **Mrs Margaret O'Toole,** Rathnure, Enniscorthy, Co. Wexford; **Mrs. Breda Moloney,** Ardnacuan Estate, Whiterock, Wexford; **Mrs. May McGuinness,** Bishopswater, Wexford; **Marie O'Rourke-Mitchell,** Oak Tree Rise, Newlands, Wexford; **Denise O'Connor-Murphy**. Pinewood Estate, Wexford; **John Reeks,** Port Elizabeth, South Africa; **Knock Museum,** Co. Mayo; **Knock Shrine,** Co. Mayo; **Kevin O'Rourke,** Cardiff, Wales; **John Walsh,** Enniscorthy; **Robert Brady,** Enniscorthy ; **Ger Foley.** Crosstown, Wexford ; **Tommy Cullimore,** Coolree, Wexford ; **Pat Collins,** Town Clerk. Municipal Buildings, Wexford; **John Power,** Kilmore, Co. Wexford; **Nicholas & Breda Doran,** Grogan's Road, Wexford; the late **Liam Lahiff,** Hill Street. Wexford; **Mrs. Eileen Kelly,** Rosslare, Co. Wexford; **George Bridges,** Clonard, Wexford; **Dominic Kiernan,** Crescent Quay, Wexford; **An Anonymous donor**; **Mrs. Anne Ffrench,** White House Park, Rosslare Strand, Co. Wexford; **Mrs Marie Sherwood,** Blackhorse, Drinagh., Wexford; **Jim Kelly,** Ardcavan. **Tomás Hayes,** Whiterock Hill. **Murth Joyce,** Killeens. **Dermot Kelly,** Viking Print. **John Hayes,** Distillery Road. , **Canon Seamus De Val,** Bunclody. Co. Wexford. **Gertrude Molloy,** William Street. **Tom Hassett,** Wygram, Wexford. **Kehoe & Associates,** (Auctioneers, Valuers) Commercial Quay, Wexford. **Eamon Doyle,** 'Waesfjord'. Retreat Heights, Athlone. **John Moran,** Carrig Lawn, Wexford. The late **Gerard Stafford,** Kerlogue House, Rocksborough. Wexford. **Victor James Stafford,** Dublin. **Nicholas Furlong,** Drinagh, Wexford. **Josie Redmond,** Beechville, Wexford. **Dick Kelly,** Hillview, Wexford. **Gerry Breen,** Rocksborough, Wexford

Photographers whose work was donated by the aforementioned people

William Andrews, 13 High Street; **Charles E. Vize,** Main Street, Wexford & Enniscorthy; **John Scallan,** John's Gate Street, Wexford; **Michael Murray,** Selskar, Wexford; **Dean Art Studio,** Main Street, Wexford; **Pat Hayes,** 7 William Street, Wexford; **Denis O'Connor,** 94 South Main Street, Wexford; **Michael Cullen,** Belvedere Grove, Wexford; **Michael Kavanagh,** Fort Mountain, Wexford; **Ray Flynn,** South Main Street, Wexford; **Beehan,** Rathmines, Dublin 6; **John Walsh,** Enniscorthy, Co. Wexford; **Eagle Photo Service,** Waterford; **George Craig,** Belfast, N. Ireland; **Ellie Studios,** Dublin; **J. G. Murphy,** Wexford; **J. Evens,** Wexford; **Kennelly Photo Works,** Tralee, Co. Kerry; **Prosper Morren,** Louvain, France; **Joseph Simpson,** Port Elizabeth, South Africa; **Crame & Co.** Enniscorthy, Co. Wexford; **Pat O'Connell,** Liam Mellows Park, Wexford; **John Hayes,** Distillery Road; **J. P. Murphy, A.P.Sc.** South Main Street; **Harris & McKnaught photographers,** Port Elizabeth, Cape Colony.; **R & P Photographic Services,** England; **Michael A. O'Rourke,** Bulgan, Glynn, Enniscorthy, Co. Wexford.

Others sources contacted

Leinster Billiards and Snooker Association, 117 Morristown, Newbridge, Co. Kildare
Republic of Ireland Billiards & Snooker Association, House of Sport, Longmile Road, D12
Francis D. Creane, former Hon. Secretary, Co. Wexford Billiards & Snooker League Association
Presbytery, 12 School Street, Wexford
Bishop's House, Fr. John Carroll, Secretary
Archivist of the Diocese of Ferns, Canon Seamus De Val, 1 Irish Street, Bunclody. Co. Wexford
Archivist & Librarian of the The Holy See. (Cardinal Jean-Louis Tauran), Vatican City, Rome, Italy
Wexford County Library HQ, Management Services, Ardcavan. Celestine Rafferty
Wexford County Library, Research Facilities, Wexford.
National President of the Catholic Men and Women's Society of Ireland, Eamon Hennessy
Bishop's House, Port Elizabeth, Republic of South Africa, Anneliese Beekers, Diocesan Secretary
Diocesan Archivist, Port Elizabeth, Republic of South Africa, John Reeks
National Secretary of the Catholic Men's Society, United Kingdom, Christopher Bolger.
Knock Museum, Co. Mayo. Caroline Naughton
National Archives of Hungary, Budapest, Dr. Eva Kisasszondy
Fr. Brendan O'Rourke, C.Ss.R. Rathgar, Dublin.

Bibliography

Books & Journals

Catholic Young Men's Society of Ireland Constitution. 1934
Catholic Young Men's Society of Ireland Constitution. 1947
Catholic Young Men's Society of Ireland Constitution. 1962
Catholic Young Men's Society of Ireland Constitution. 1984
'Life of Dean O'Brien' *(Founder of the C.Y.M.S)* by M. J. Egan, published in Dublin 1948
'The Catholic Church in Wexford Town – the Coast 1984' by Jarlath Glynn
'The Catholic Circle' Official organ of the C.Y.M.S., England
'History of the Wexford Men's Confraternity of the Holy Family' by Rev. J. W. O'Byrne, C.C. 1910
'The Secular Priests of the Diocese of Ferns' by Canon John V. Gahan
'Centenary Record of Wexford Twin-Churches, 1858-1958' by Fr. Berney
'History of the Diocese of Ferns' 1916 by Grattan Flood
'Vow To Vigil Keep' *(Perpetual Adoration Nuns of Wexford)* by Clericus Amicus, 1950, Gill & Son, Dublin.
'The Franciscans in Wexford' by Fergal Grannell, O.F.M.
'Bishop James Brown's Silver Jubilee Souvenir Issue 1909'
'Bishop James Staunton Souvenir Book 1981'
'Bishop Herlihy's Jubilee Souvenir Book 1981'
'The Irish Missionary Movement. A Historical Survey, 1830-1980' by Edmund Hogan
'The Life and Times of the Right Rev. Dr. Ricards' 1908, South Africa by A. Wilmot
'The South African Catholic Magazine' South Africa
'St. Aidan's College Grahamstown – A History' by Prof. Francis I. Coleman

'**History of the Catholic Church in Uitenhage – The Town of Tolerance - The Fourth Parish in South Africa**' by Rev. Father Pierce

'**The Past**' No 15 (1984) Articles by Jarlath Glynn

'**The Journal of the Wexford Historical Society**' No 16, 1996-97, 'Pierces of Wexford' by M O'Sullivan

'**Wexford County- Guide and Directory**'. Bassett, G.H. 1885.   Dublin 406 pp

'**Wexford Port – A History**' By Nicholas Rossiter. 1989

'**Walk Wexford Ways**' by William Roche, Nicky Rossiter, Kevin Hurley and Tomás Hayes, 1988

County Wexford in the Rare oul' Times', Nicholas Furlong & John Hayes

'**A Municipal History**' Mulgannon Publications 1987, 251p by Padge Reck

'**Families of Co. Wexford**' by Hilary Murphy, 1986

'**Philip Pierce & Co. 1939-100 Years of Progress, Centenary 1839**' by Pierces Company Wexford

'**Rambles in Eirinn 1907-1929**' by William Bulfin, Dublin, 456 pp

'**An Rothar**' (The Irish Cycling Journal) Vol. 1, No. 3, February 1968

'**National Cycling Association (N.C.A.)' Twenty-First Birthday Book 1938-1959**' by Kerry Sloane

'**Bikes & Bikemen**' (Ireland's only cycling magazine) early 1960s

'**An Ras Tailteann' Souvenir Programmes for 1950s – 1960s**

Newspapers

'**The Independent**' (Wexford)

'**The Irish Independent**'

'**The People Newspaper**' (Wexford)

'**The Free Press**' (Wexford , 1896 to the last issue on 12th February 1971 when the People Newspapers took over

'**The Wexford Evening Post**' (No 1 Vol. 1, 7th March 1826) Wexford County Library

'**Wexford Herald**'

'**The Woodford & Chigwell Times**' Wanstead, London

'**Uitenhage Times**' South Africa

'**La Femme**' South Africa

'**Port Elizabeth Telegraph**' South Africa

'**Diamond Fields Advertiser**' South Africa

'**Port Elizabeth Evening Post**' South Africa

'**The Catholic Chronicle**' East London South Africa

Unpublished Sources

Minute Books of the C.Y.M.S. Wexford 1858-2000

Minute Book of the C.Y.M.S Shareholders Billiard Table 1875-1888

Minute Book of the C.Y.M.S. Debating Club 1888-1894

General Memoranda by John Stafford, C.Y.M.S. Librarian 1858-1867

C.Y.M.S. Book of Guilds by William Scallan. 1863

C.Y.M.S. Register of Members Names Books 1920-2000

Interview notes and recordings of the late Thomas O'Rourke 1980s

The late Frank O'Rourke's Cycling Diaries and Photo Archives (1950s 1960s)

The Roy Doyle Cycling Diaries and photograph Archives (1964-1967)

Ger Foley, Table Tennis Diary photograph Archives (1942-1953)

Minutes of the Co. Wexford Billiards & Snooker League Association 1980s-1990 by Francis D. Creane

Minutes of the Celtic Football Club 1970s by Tom O'Hara

APPENDIX 1

Elected Council Members 1855 to 2008

The very first meeting held in August 1855 elected a Committee of 12 equals:
Very Rev. James Roche, P.P., V.F., Spiritual Director
Mr. Thomas Alphonsus Hoope, *(Director of the Christian Brothers)* acting Chairman
James A. Johnson, Esq., *(was elected the first President, but he respectfully declined and suggested that a provisional committee of 12 equals should be elected. This was agreed and Mr. Johnson was prevailed upon to act as the Hon. Secretary.)*
Nicholas Cousins
Matthew Simpson
William Connick
John O'Brien
Richard Furlong
Robert Doyle
Edward Bent
John Sinnott
William Murphy
Edward W. Fitzpatrick
John Shannon.

The C.Y.M.S. Provisional Committee (16th August) 1855:
Very Rev. James Roche, P.P., V.F., Spiritual Director
James A. Johnson, Esq. Elected Chairman & Hon. Secretary *(He left and joined the 'Redemtorist Congregation' and studied for the priesthood).*
John O'Brien was elected Assistant Provisional Secretary.
(The same committee as above with the following exception)
 John Cullen was *(Nominated Assistant Secretary December 1855)* and nominated Secretary on the 22nd February 1856 by Rev. James Roche

The C.Y.M.S. Committee 1st March 1856:
Very Rev. James Roche, P.P., V.F., Spiritual Director (he nominated all the committee as he wished to place the right people into the right positions to help put the Society on a sound footing)
Very Rev. William Doyle, President *(resigned 1st March)*
Mr. Rigley, Director of the Christian Brothers, Chairman *(resigned 16th February)*
Ald. Robert Creane, Esq. M.D. Vice-President. *(He resigned 1st March)*
William Connick *(nominated Vice-President on the 1st March)*
Edward Dixon *(nominated Vice-President 1st March)*
John O'Brien, Hon Secretary
William Power, Hon Secretary
Richard Keating *(nominated to Presidency 18th February).*
Matthew Simpson. *(Nominated Assistant Secretary)*
Denis Quinn
Nicholas Tennant
Michael Walsh
Mr. Connor
Mr. Bolger
Robert Doyle
Thomas White

'Young Men's Society Council' 1857:
Very Rev. James Roche, P.P., V.F., Spiritual Director
Rev. James Barry, President
William Connick, Vice-President
John O'Brien , Hon. Secretary
William Power, Assistant. Secretary
John Dunne
Matthew Simpson
Joseph Connors
Thomas White
John Cogley
Nicholas Crowe
John Tierney
Edward Dixon
Nicholas Cousins

'Young Men's Society Council' 1858 :
Very Rev. James Roche, P.P., V.F., Spiritual Director
Rev. James Barry, President (*resigned 3rd Nov.*)
William Connick ,Vice-President
John O'Brien, Hon Secretary (*resigned 19th December and went to South Africa*)
William Power, Hon. Secretary
William Scallan, Acting Hon. Secretary
John Pitt
John Dunne
Matthew Simpson
Joseph Connors
Thomas White
Nicholas Crowe
Stephen Doyle (*Gone by 20th October*)
James Condon
Nicholas Cousins
Peter Fardy
John Murphy
John Browne (*replaced Doyle 20th October*)
Very Rev. Walter Lambert, President (*3 November*)

'Young Men's Society Council' 1859 :
Very Rev. James Roche, P.P., V.F., Spiritual Director
Rev. Walter Lambert, President
William Connick, Vice-President
Thomas White, Hon. Secretary
John Pitt (*resigned 11th October*)
John Dunne
Joseph Connors
William Scallan
Nicholas Crowe
Peter Fardy
William Power (*died this year*)
Miles Kehoe (*resigned 11th October*)
William J. Tucker
Rich Furlong (*co-opted October*)
Nicholas Cousins (*co-opted October*)
The practice at this time was that the Chairmanship was rotated with everyone taking their turn.

'Young Men's Society Council' 1860 :
Very Rev. James Roche, P.P., V.F., Spiritual Director
Rev. Walter Lambert, President
William Connick, Vice-President
Thomas White, Hon. Secretary & Treasurer

William Scallan, Hon. Secretary
Peter Fardy
John Dunne
Matthew Simpson
Rich Furlong
William J. Tucker
Nicholas Cousins
Nicholas Crowe
John Tennant
Joseph Connors
Very Rev. James Barry (*sat in on some of these meetings*)
Rich Ryan, Warden
Mr. Brown, Warden
Brother Dempsey (*co-opted 5th February*)

'Young Men's Society Council' 1861 :
Very Rev. James Roche, P.P., V.F., Spiritual Director
Rev. Walter Lambert, President
William Connick, Vice-President (*elected Treasurer on the 9th January*)
Thomas White, Hon. Secretary & Treasurer was *ill for a period and resigned office and his place on the Council on 26th December*)
William Scallan, Hon. Secretary (*resigned position 27th August. It was not accepted*)
Peter Fardy (*elected Hon. Secretary 5th September*)
John Dunne
Rich Furlong
William J. Tucker
Nicholas Cousins (*acting Hon. Secretary during Mr. White's Illness. Resigned the position 23rd May*)
John Tennant
Joseph Connors
Brother Dempsey
Rich Ryan, Warden
Mr. Brown, Warden
Mr. McCann (*elected to Council 12th August*)

'Young Men's Society Council' 1862 :
Very Rev. James Roche, P.P., V.F., Spiritual Director
Rev. William Murphy, President
William Connick, Vice-President
Richard Devereux Esq., Treasurer
Joseph O'Connor, Hon. Secretary
Peter Fardy (*elected Hon. Secretary 29th April*)
John Dunne
William J. Tucker
John Tennant
Rich Ryan, Warden
M. J. Mc Cann
William Martin
Patrick Fortune
James Moore
James Grace

'Young Men's Society Council' 1863 :
Very Rev. James Roche, P.P., V.F., Spiritual Director
Rev. William Murphy, President (*resigned 24th February*)
Rev. Jeremiah Hogan, C.C. (*elected President 1st March*)
William Connick, Vice-President
Richard Devereux Esq., Treasurer
Thomas White, Hon. Secretary

J. E. Hore, Assistant Hon. Secretary *(resigned position 10th December)*
John Dunne
William Joseph Tucker *(resigned position on council, 6th January)*
William Martin
Patrick Fortune
William Dromgoole
Stephen Doyle
Patrick White
Miles Kehoe
William Scallan *(co-opted 5th February)*
Thomas O'Reilly *(co-opted 5th February)*

'Young Men's Society Council' 1864 :
Very Rev. James Roche, P.P., V.F., Spiritual Director
Rev. Jeremiah Hogan, C.C., President *(Left by 23rd October?)*
William Connick, Vice-President
Thomas White, Hon. Secretary
William Martin
John Dunn
William Dromgoole
Stephen Doyle
Capt. J. J. Doyle
William Scallan
Thomas O'Reilly
Thomas Roche
James Roche *(elected Assistant Hon. Secretary 13th January)*
Michael Hughes *(resigned his membership on 14th March)*

'Young Men's Society Council' 1865 :
Very Rev. James Roche, P.P., V.F., Spiritual Director
Rev. Walter Lambert, President
William Connick, Vice-President
Thomas White, Hon. Secretary
Richard J. Devereux, Treasurer
William Martin
John Dunn
William Dromgoole
Stephen Doyle
Capt. J. J. Doyle
William Scallan
Thomas O'Reilly
Thomas Roche
James Roche *(elected Assistant Hon. Secretary 13th January)*
Michael Hughes *(resigned his membership on14th March)*
R. Murphy *(co-opted March?)*

'Young Men's Society Council' 1866 :
Very Rev. James Roche, P.P., V.F., Spiritual Director
Rev. Walter Lambert, President
William Connick, Vice-President
Thomas White, Hon. Secretary
William Scallan, Hon. Secretary
Thomas O'Reilly
James McArdle
Richard Murphy
Isaac Scallan
William Martin

James Moore
Nicholas Crowe
Capt. P. J. Doyle
Rev. Cullen *(elected Spiritual Director of the Guilds 11th May)*

'Young Men's Society Council' 1867 :
The Right Rev. Dr. Furlong, Patron
Very Rev. James Roche, P.P., V.F., Spiritual Director
Rev. Walter Lambert, President
William Connick, Vice-President
Thomas White, Hon. Secretary *(resigned on 4th February for reasons beyond his control. The Council refused to accept his resignation and allowed him to hold the position and attend meetings when convenient for him)*
William Scallan, Hon. Secretary
Thomas O'Reilly
James Moore
Richard Murphy
Nicholas Crowe
Patrick White
William Martin
James M'Ardle
Capt. P. J. Doyle
Isaac Scallan

'Young Men's Society Council' 1868 :
The Most Rev. Dr. Furlong, Patron
Very Rev. James Roche, P.P., V.F., Spiritual Director
Rev. Walter Lambert, President
William Connick, Vice-President & Treasurer
James M'Ardle, Hon. Secretary
James Moore
William Martin
Thomas O'Reilly
Richard Murphy
Isaac Scallan
P. J. Gaffney
Nicholas Crowe
Robert Hanton
William Scallan

'Young Men's Society Council' 1869 :
Rev. Walter Lambert, C.C. President
William Connick, Vice-President
Thomas White, Hon. Secretary
William Martin Hon. Secretary *(resigned his position on the 18th March 1869)*
William Scallan,
Patrick White
Isaac Scallan
Thomas O'Reilly
Nicholas Crowe
James M'Ardle *(died Feb. 1869)*
Robert Hanton, Warden *(acting Hon. Secretary from 18th March 1869)*
Edward Dixon
Mr. P.J. Gaffney

'Young Men's Society Council' 1870 :
Rev. Walter Lambert, C.C. President

William Connick, Vice-President & Treasurer
Robert Hanton, Hon. Secretary
William Martin
William Scallan,
Isaac Scallan
Thomas O'Reilly
Thomas White
Richard Murphy
James Moore
James Horan
Mr. Crane
Mr. Tucker

'Young Men's Society Council' of 1871 & 1872 (probably consisted of the same Council as above)

Rev. Walter Lambert, C.C. President
William Connick, Vice-President & Treasurer
Robert Hanton, Hon. Secretary
William Martin
William Scallan,
Isaac Scallan
Thomas O'Reilly
Thomas White
Richard Murphy
James Moore
James Horan
W. Crane
Mr. Tucker

'Young Men's Society Council' 1873 :

Rev. Walter Lambert, C.C. President
William Connick, Vice-President & Treasurer
Robert Hanton, Hon. Secretary
William Scallan,
Isaac Scallan
Richard Murphy
James Moore
Philip Pierce
H. Conway
Edward Dixon
W. Crane
Mr. ? Murphy

'Young Men's Society Council' 1874 (probably consisted of the following)

Rev. Walter Lambert, C.C. President
William Connick, Vice-President & Treasurer
Robert Hanton, Hon. Secretary
William Scallan,
Isaac Scallan
Richard Murphy
James Moore
Philip Pierce
H. Conway
Edward Dixon
W. Crane
James Murphy

'Young Men's Society Council' 1875 :

Rev. Walter Lambert C.C. President

William Connick, Vice-President & Treasurer
Robert Hanton, Hon. Secretary
Pat Brien
Isaac Scallan
Richard Murphy
Edward Dixon
John Tyghe
James Moore
Laurence Rossiter
Philip Pierce
James Crosby

'Young Men's Society Council' 1876 :

Rev. J. F. Doyle. President (*resigned 1st December*)
William Connick, Vice-President & Treasurer
Robert Hanton, Hon. Secretary
Richard Murphy
Edward Dixon
John Tyghe
James Moore
Laurence Rossiter
Philip Pierce
James Murphy
John Holbrook
W. Devereux
J. Carty
Rev. J. Browne, C.C. (*elected President on 1st Dec. 1876*)

'Young Men's Society Council' 1877 (This Council was the one elected during the dispute)

Rev. J. Browne, C.C. President
William Connick, Vice-President & Treasurer
William Murphy, Vice-President
Robert Hanton, Hon. Secretary
James J. Kelly, Hon. Secretary (*resigned 7th May in dispute*)
Richard Murphy (*resigned over dispute and refused to serve on this Council*)
Edward Dixon
Laurence Rossiter (*appointed Assistant Hon. Secretary 5th June*)
Philip Pierce
John Holbrook
William J. Devereux
Nicholas Scallan
Michael Browne
Patrick Walsh

'Young Men's Society Council' 1878 :

Rev. J. Browne, C.C. President
William Connick, Vice-President & Treasurer
Laurence Rossiter, Hon. Secretary
Edward Dixon
Philip Pierce
William J. Devereux
Nicholas Scallan
Patrick Walsh
John King
Stephen Doyle
Edward Walsh T.C.
William Scallan

Wexford Branch C.Y.M.S. Council of 1879:
Rev. J. Browne, C.C. President
William Connick, Vice-President & Treasurer
Laurence Rossiter, Hon. Secretary
Edward Dixon
Philip Pierce
William J. Devereux
Patrick Walsh
Stephen Doyle
John King
Edward Walsh T.C.
William Scallan
Peter Hanton

Wexford Branch C.Y.M.S. Council of 1880:
Rev. J. Browne, C.C. President
William Connick, Vice-President & Treasurer
Laurence Rossiter, Hon. Secretary
Edward Dixon
William J. Devereux
Patrick Walsh
Stephen Doyle
William Scallan
Peter Hanton
James Moore
Nicholas Scallan
Patrick J. Breen

Wexford Branch C.Y.M.S. Council of 1881:
Rev. Luke Doyle, C.C. President
William Connick, Vice-President & Treasurer
Laurence Rossiter, Hon. Secretary
Edward Dixon
William J. Devereux
Patrick Walsh
Stephen Doyle
William Scallan
Peter Hanton
James Moore
Robert Hanton
James Stamp

Wexford Branch C.Y.M.S. Council of 1882 :
Rev. Luke Doyle, C.C. President
William Connick, Vice-President & Treasurer
Laurence Rossiter, Hon. Secretary
Edward Dixon
William J. Devereux
Patrick Walsh
Stephen Doyle
William Scallan
Peter Hanton
Robert Hanton
James Marlow
James J. Stafford

Wexford Branch C.Y.M.S. Council of 1883 :
Rev. Luke Doyle, C.C. President
William Connick, Vice-President & Treasurer
Laurence Rossiter, Hon. Secretary
Edward Dixon

William J. Devereux
Patrick Walsh
William Scallan
Peter Hanton
Robert Hanton
James Marlow (*expelled 3rd February*)
James Horan
Matthew Harpur
James J. Stafford, Snr. (*co-opted 21st June to replace Mr. Marlow*)

Wexford Branch C.Y.M.S. Council of 1884:
Rev. Luke Doyle, C.C. President
William Connick, Vice-President & Treasurer
Laurence Rossiter, Hon. Secretary
William J. Devereux
Patrick Walsh
John Tyghe
John King
James Sinnott
William Scallan
James Stafford, Snr.
Patrick Walsh
James Horan
James Stamp

Wexford Branch C.Y.M.S. Council of 1885:
Rev. Luke Doyle, C.C. President (*resigned 26th May*)
William Connick, Vice-President & Treasurer
Laurence Rossiter, Hon. Secretary
Robert Hanton
Michael O'Connor
William Scallan
William J. Devereux
James Horan
James Stafford, Snr.
Edward Dixon
John King
Peter Hanton
Rev. N. T. Sheridan. C.C. (*elected President 26th May*)
William Hutchinson (*elected Assistant Hon. Secretary 21st July*)

Wexford Branch C.Y.M.S. Council of 1886:
Rev. N. T. Sheridan. C.C. President
William Connick, Vice-President & Treasurer
Laurence Rossiter, Hon. Secretary
Robert Hanton
Edward Dixon
William Scallan
John King
Michael O'Connor
Peter Hanton
William Robinson
James Stafford ,Snr.
John FitzSimmons
William Hutchinson (*elected Assistant Hon. Secretary. 23rd February*)

Wexford Branch C.Y.M.S. Council of 1887 :
Rev. Nicholas T. Sheridan. C.C. President
William Connick, Vice-President & Treasurer

Laurence Rossiter, Hon. Secretary
John King
Robert Hanton
Edward Dixon
Nicholas White
Michael O'Connor
William Scallan
Peter Hanton
James Sinnott
James Stafford, Snr.
William Hutchinson *(elected Assistant Hon. Secretary. 9th March.)*

Wexford Branch C.Y.M.S. Council of 1888 :
Rev. Nicholas T. Sheridan. C.C. President *(resigned to take up position in St. Peters College 15th October)*
William Connick, Vice-President & Treasurer
Laurence Rossiter, Hon. Secretary
John King
Robert Hanton
James Sinnott
Michael O'Connor
James Stamp
James Stafford, Snr.
Edward Dixon
Peter Hanton
Rev. Patrick Doyle, C.C. *(elected President on 15th October)*

St. Iberius Catholic Club Council of 1889 :
Rev. Patrick Doyle, C.C. President
William Connick, Vice-President & Treasurer
Laurence Rossiter, Hon. Secretary
James Kavanagh
Robert Hanton
James Stafford ,Snr
Michael O'Connor
James Stamp
James Sinnott
Michael Nolan
William R. McGuire
James Horan

St. Iberius Catholic Club Council of 1890 :
Rev. Patrick Doyle, C.C. President *(Left by August?)*
William Connick, Vice-President & Treasurer
Laurence Rossiter, Hon. Secretary
James Kavanagh
Robert Hanton
Michael O'Connor
William R. McGuire
William Hutchinson
John Tyghe
Michael Nolan
Michael Kehoe
William J. Robinson
Frank Norton
Rev. Fr. E. Aylward Adm .*(acting President from August)*

St. Iberius Catholic Club Council of 1891 :
Rev. Fr. E. Aylward Adm. President
William Connick, Vice-President & Treasurer

Laurence Rossiter, Hon. Secretary
Robert Hanton, T.C.
James Kavanagh
Michael Kehoe
William J. Robinson
Michael O'Connor
Michael Nolan
John Cosgrave
William Scallan, T.C.
James Stafford, Snr. J.P.

St. Iberius Catholic Club Council of 1892 :
Rev. Fr. E. Aylward Adm. President
William Connick, Vice-President & Treasurer
Laurence Rossiter, Hon. Secretary
Robert Hanton, T.C.
William J. Robinson
William Scallan, T.C.
Patrick Walsh
Michael Kehoe
Michael Nolan
James Stafford, Snr.
Matthew Harpur
John Holbrook

St. Iberius Catholic Club Council of 1893 :
Rev. Fr. E. Aylward Adm. President
William Connick, Vice-President & Treasurer
Laurence Rossiter, Hon. Secretary
Robert Hanton, T.C.
William J. Robinson
William Scallan, T.C.
Patrick Walsh
Michael Kehoe
Michael Nolan
James Stafford ,Snr. J.C.
Matthew Harpur
John Holbrook
John Tyghe J.C.

St. Iberius Catholic Club Council of 1894 :
Rev. Fr. E. Aylward Adm. President
William Connick, Vice-President & Treasurer
Laurence Rossiter, Hon. Secretary
Robert Hanton, T.C.
William J. Robinson
Patrick Walsh
Michael Kehoe
James Stafford, Snr. J.C.
Matthew Harpur
John Holbrook
John Tyghe J.C.
Patrick Doyle

St. Iberius Catholic Club Council of 1895 :
Rev. Fr. E. Aylward Adm. President
William Connick, Vice-President & Treasurer
Laurence Rossiter, Hon. Secretary
Robert Hanton, T.C.
William J. Robinson
Patrick Walsh
Michael Kehoe

James Stafford, Snr. J.C.
John Holbrook
William Hutchinson
Richard Goold
Frank Carty

St. Iberius Catholic Club Council of 1896 :
Rev. Fr. E. Aylward Adm. President
William Connick, Vice-President & Treasurer
Laurence Rossiter, Hon. Secretary
Robert Hanton, T.C.
William J. Robinson
Patrick Walsh
Michael Kehoe
John Holbrook
William Hutchinson
Richard Goold
Frank Carty
John Tyghe, J.C.

St. Iberius Catholic Club Council of 1897 :
Rev. Fr. E. Aylward Adm. President *(resigned July went as PP to Blackwater)*
William Connick, Vice-President & Treasurer
Laurence Rossiter, Hon. Secretary *(died in Office 12th July)*
William Hutchinson, Hon. Secretary *(elected July)*
Richard Goold, Hon. Secretary *(elected July)*
John Tyghe, T.C. H.C.
Robert Hanton, T.C.
William Scallan, T.C.
Patrick Walsh
William J. Robinson
Thomas Robinson
Capt. James Smith
Francis Carty
Edward Hendrick

St. Iberius Catholic Club Council of 1898 :
Rev. P. Doyle Adm. President
William Connick, Vice-President & Treasurer
William Hutchinson, Hon. Sec.
Richard Goold, Hon. Sec.
John Tyghe, T.C. H.C.
Robert Hanton, T.C.
William Scallan, T.C.
Patrick Walsh
William Robinson
Thomas Robinson
Capt. James Smith
Francis Carty
Edward Hendrick

St. Iberius Catholic Club Council of 1899 :
Rev. P. Doyle Adm. President
William Connick, Vice-President & Treasurer
William Hutchinson, Hon. Sec.
Richard Goold, Hon. Sec.
John Tyghe, T.C. H.C.
Robert Hanton, T.C.
William Scallan, T.C.
Patrick Walsh

William Robinson
Thomas Robinson
Capt. James Smith
Francis Carty
Edward Hendrick

St. Iberius Catholic Club Council of 1900 :
Rev. P. Doyle Adm. President
William Connick, Vice-President & Treasurer
William Hutchinson, Hon. Sec.
Richard Goold, Hon. Sec.
Robert Hanton, T.C.
Patrick J. Walsh
William J. Robinson
Thomas W. Robinson
Capt. James Smith
Edward Hendrick
Michael Kehoe
Frank O'Connor
Michael Luccan

St. Iberius Catholic Club Council of 1901 :
Rev. Patrick Doyle, Adm., President.
W. J. Robinson, Vice President
Robert Hanton, Treasurer.
W. Hutchinson, Hon. Secretary.
Richard Goold, Hon. Secretary.
Michael Kehoe
Frank O'Connor
Capt. James Smith
John Tyghe
Edward Hendrick
John Harpur
Patrick J. O'Connor
Patrick J. Walsh
John White

St. Iberius Catholic Club Council of 1902 :
Rev. Patrick Doyle, Adm., President.
W. J. Robinson, Vice President
Robert Hanton, Treasurer.
W. Hutchinson, Hon. Secretary.
Richard Goold, Hon. Secretary.
Michael Kehoe
Frank O'Connor
Capt. James Smith
John Tyghe
Edward Hendrick
John Harpur
Patrick J. O'Connor
Patrick J. Walsh
John White

St. Iberius Catholic Club Council of 1903:
Rev. Patrick Doyle, Adm., President.
W. J. Robinson, Vice President
Robert Hanton, Treasurer.
W. Hutchinson, Hon. Secretary.
Richard Goold, Hon. Secretary.
Michael Kehoe
Frank O'Connor
Capt. James Smith

John Tyghe
Edward Hendrick
Patrick J. O'Connor
Patrick J. Walsh
John White

St. Iberius Catholic Club Council of 1904 :
Rev. Patrick Doyle, Adm., President.
Robert Hanton, T.C., H.C., Vice President & Treasurer.
W. Hutchinson, Hon. Secretary.
Richard Goold, Hon. Secretary.
Michael Kehoe
Frank O'Connor
Capt. James Smith
John Tyghe, T.C. H.C.,
Patrick J. O'Connor
John White
Patrick Walsh
Maurice O'Shea
Michael Luccan
Michael Kehoe

St. Iberius Catholic Club Council of 1905 :
Rev. Patrick Doyle, Adm., President.
Robert Hanton, T.C., H.C., Vice President & Treasurer.
W. Hutchinson, Hon. Secretary.
Richard Goold, Hon. Secretary.
Michael Kehoe
Frank O'Connor
Capt. James Smith
John Tyghe, T.C. H.C.,
Patrick J. O'Connor
John White
Patrick Walsh
Maurice O'Shea
Michael Luccan

St. Iberius Catholic Club Council of 1906 :
Rev. Patrick Doyle, Adm., President.
Robert Hanton, T.C., H.C., Vice President & Treasurer.
W. Hutchinson, Hon. Secretary.
Richard Goold, Hon. Secretary.
Michael Kehoe
Frank O'Connor
Capt. James Smith
John White
Michael Luccan
Joseph Murphy
Laurence Harpur
John Dunne

St. Iberius Catholic Club Council of 1907 :
Rev. Patrick Doyle, Adm., President.
Robert Hanton, Mayor of Wexford. Vice President & Treasurer.
William Hutchinson, Hon. Secretary.
Richard Goold, Hon. Secretary.
Peter Hutchinson
Frank O'Connor
John White
Capt. Laurence Busher
Laurence Harpur

Capt. James Smith
John Dunne
Michael Kehoe
John Tyghe

St. Iberius Catholic Club Council of 1908 :
Rev. P. O'Connor, Adm., President (*died in Office January 1908*)
Robert Hanton, Mayor of Wexford. Vice President & Treasurer.
William Hutchinson, Hon. Secretary.
Richard Goold, Hon. Secretary.
Peter Hutchinson
Frank O'Connor
John White
Capt. Laurence Busher
Laurence Harpur
Capt. James Smith
John Dunne
Michael Kehoe
John Tyghe
Rev. T. Clooney, Adm. (*became President February*)

St. Iberius Club & Catholic Young Men's Society Council of 1909 :
Rev. T. Clooney, Adm, President.
Robert Hanton, Mayor of Wexford. Vice President & Treasurer.
William Hutchinson, Hon. Secretary.
Richard Goold, Hon. Secretary.
Peter Hutchinson
Frank O'Connor
John White
Capt. Laurence Busher
Laurence Harpur
Capt. James Smith
John Dunne
Michael Kehoe
John Tyghe

St. Iberius Club & Catholic Young Men's Society Council of 1910 :
Rev. T. Cloney, Adm, President.
Robert Hanton, J. P., Vice President & Treasurer.
William Hutchinson, Hon. Secretary.
Richard Goold, Hon. Secretary.
Rev. J. W. O'Byrne, C.C
John White
John Wadding
P. J. Carroll, T.C.
Capt. Laurence Busher
Capt. James Smith
Michael Kehoe
Ald. John Tyghe (*died September*)
John Shirlock

St. Iberius Club & Catholic Young Men's Society Council of 1911 :
Rev. T. Cloney, Adm, President.
Robert Hanton, J. P., Vice President & Treasurer.
William Hutchinson, Hon. Secretary.

Richard Goold, Hon. Secretary.
Rev. J. W. O'Byrne, C.C. *(transferred to Boolavogue)*
John White
Capt. Laurence Busher
Capt. James Smith
P. J. Carroll, T.C.
Michael Kehoe
John Shirlock
Laurence Harpur
Timothy McCarthy

St. Iberius Club & Catholic Young Men's Society Council of 1912 :

Rev. Thomas Hore, Adm., President.
Robert Hanton, J. P., Vice President & Treasurer.
William Hutchinson, Hon. Secretary.
Richard Goold, Hon. Secretary.
P. J. Carroll, T.C.
Capt. James Smith
Capt. Laurence Busher
Michael Kehoe
Laurence Harpur
John White
John J. Shirlock Rev.
Timothy McCarthy
Rev. J. W. O'Byrne, C.C. (re-elected to Council but unable to attend)
Rev. James Goold *(co-opted to replace Fr. O'Byrne)*

St. Iberius Club & Catholic Young Men's Society Council of 1913 :

Rev. Thomas Hore, Adm., President.
Robert Hanton, J. P., Vice President & Treasurer.
William Hutchinson, Hon. Secretary.
Richard Goold, Hon. Secretary.
Michael Kehoe
Rev. James Codd, C.C.
Capt. Laurence Busher
Capt. James Smith
James Kehoe.
Laurence Harpur
John White
Timothy McCarthy
John Browne

St. Iberius Club & Catholic Young Men's Society Council of 1914 :

Rev. Thomas Hore, Adm., President.
Robert Hanton, J. P., Vice President & Treasurer
William Hutchinson, Hon. Secretary
Richard Goold, Hon. Secretary.
Michael Kehoe
Rev. James Codd, C.C.
Capt. Laurence Busher
Capt. James Smith
James Kehoe.
Laurence Harpur
John White
Timothy McCarthy
John Browne

St. Iberius Club & Catholic Young Men's Society Council of 1915 :

Rev. Thomas Hore, Adm., President.
Robert Hanton, J. P., Vice President & Treasurer. *(died towards end of term)*
William Hutchinson, Hon. Secretary.
Richard Goold, Hon. Secretary
Michael Kehoe
Rev. James Codd, C.C.
Capt. Laurence Busher
Capt. James Smith
James Kehoe.
Laurence Harpur
John White
Timothy McCarthy
John Browne

St. Iberius Club & Catholic Young Men's Society Council of 1916 :

Rev. Thomas Hore, Adm., President.
Michael Kehoe, Vice President
William Hutchinson, Hon. Secretary.
Richard Goold, Hon. Secretary
The National Bank, Treasurer *(the Bank was elected treasurer. Fact!)*
Rev. James Codd, C.C.
Capt. Laurence Busher
Capt. James Smith *(Died September)*
Laurence Harpur
John Browne
James J. Kehoe
Timothy McCarthy
Patrick Breen *(co-opted 20th Feb. to fill vacancies)*
John White (left town)
James Kelly *(co-opted 20th Feb. to fill vacancies)*

St. Iberius Club & Catholic Young Men's Society Council of 1917 :

Rev. Thomas Hore, Adm., President.
Michael Kehoe, Vice President
William Hutchinson, Hon. Secretary.
Richard Goold, Hon. Secretary
The National Bank, Treasurer
Capt. Laurence Busher
Laurence Harpur
John Browne
Patrick Breen
Rev. James Codd, C.C
James J. Kehoe *(resigned from Council 27th July)*
James Kelly
Timothy McCarthy

St. Iberius Club & Catholic Young Men's Society Council of 1918 :

Rev. Thomas Hore, Adm., President.
Michael Kehoe, Vice President
William Hutchinson, Hon. Secretary.
Richard Goold, Hon. Secretary
The National Bank, Treasurer
Rev. James Codd, C.C
Capt. Laurence Busher
John Browne

Patrick Breen
Frank Carty
James Kelly
Timothy McCarthy
Patrick O'Connor
William O'Leary

St. Iberius Club & Catholic Young Men's Society Council of 1919 :

Rev. Thomas Hore, Adm., President.
Michael Kehoe, Vice President
William Hutchinson, Hon. Secretary
Richard Goold, Hon. Secretary.
The National Bank, Treasurer
Rev. James Codd, C.C
Capt. Laurence Busher
James Kelly
Patrick O'Connor
John Browne
Timothy McCarthy
William O'Leary
Patrick Breen
Francis Carty

St. Iberius Club & Catholic Young Men's Society Council of 1920 :

Rev. Thomas Hore, Adm., President.
Michael Kehoe, Vice President
William Hutchinson, Hon. Secretary.
Richard Goold, Hon. Secretary.
The National Bank, Treasurer
Rev. James Codd, C.C
Capt. Laurence Busher
James Kelly
Patrick O'Connor
John Browne
Timothy McCarthy
William O'Leary
Patrick Breen
Francis Carty

St. Iberius Club & Catholic Young Men's Society Council of 1921 :

Rev. Thomas Hore, Adm., President.
Michael Kehoe, Vice President
William Hutchinson, Hon. Secretary
Richard Goold, Hon. Secretary.
The National Bank, Treasurer
Rev. James Codd, C.C
Capt. Laurence Busher
James Kelly
Patrick O'Connor
John Browne
Timothy McCarthy
William O'Leary
Patrick Breen
Francis Carty

St. Iberius Club & Catholic Young Men's Society Council of 1922 :

Rev. Thomas Hore, Adm., President. (*left town, promoted to Parish Priest 11 April*)
Michael Kehoe, Vice President
William Hutchinson, Hon. Secretary
Richard Goold, Hon. Secretary.
The National Bank, Treasurer
Rev. James Codd, Adm. President. *(became President in 13th June)*
Capt. Laurence Busher
James Kelly
Patrick O'Connor
John Browne
Timothy McCarthy
William O'Leary
Patrick Breen
Francis Carty
Rev. Fr. Wickham (*co-opted to Council to fill vacancy 9th May*)

St. Iberius Club & Catholic Young Men's Society Council of 1923 :

Rev. James Codd, Adm., President.
Michael Kehoe, Vice President
William Hutchinson, Hon. Secretary.
Richard Goold, Hon. Secretary.
The National Bank, Treasurer
Rev. Matthew Wickham, Rector
Edward O'Rourke
Martin O'Connor
Joseph A. Fennell
John Cullimore
William Hayes
James Kelly
John Browne
William O'Leary

St. Iberius Club & Catholic Young Men's Society Council of 1924 :

Rev. James Codd, Adm, President.
Michael Kehoe, Vice President
William Hutchinson, Hon. Secretary
Richard Goold, Hon. Secretary.
The National Bank, Treasurer
Rev. Matthew Wickham, Rector
Edward O'Rourke
Martin O'Connor
Joseph A. Fennell
John Cullimore
William Hayes
Rev. John Sinnott (*co-opted 29th Jan.*)
John Browne
William O'Leary
John Kavanagh (*co-opted 12th Feb. to replace James Kelly*)

St. Iberius Club & Catholic Young Men's Society Council of 1925 :

Rev. James Codd, Adm, President
Michael Kehoe, Vice President
William Hutchinson, Hon. Secretary
Richard Goold, Hon. Secretary
The National Bank, Treasurer

Rev. Matthew Wickham, Rector
Edward O'Rourke
Rev. John Sinnott
John Browne
Joseph A. Fennell
Martin O'Connor
Nicholas J. Hore
William O'Leary
John Cullimore
William Hayes

St. Iberius Club & Catholic Young Men's Society Council of 1926 :
Rev. John Sinnott, Adm., President
Michael Kehoe, Vice President & Treasurer
William Hutchinson, Hon. Secretary *(tendered his resignation as Secretary on 25th Jan. as he was leaving for Enniscorthy)*
Richard Goold, Hon. Secretary
John Breen
John Cullimore
John Doyle
Joseph A. Fennell
William Hayes
Thomas Hayes
William O'Leary *(died in October)*
Edward O'Rourke
Martin O'Connor

St. Iberius Club & Catholic Young Men's Society Council of 1927 :
Rev. John Sinnott, Adm., President
Michael Kehoe, Vice President & Treasurer
Richard Goold, Hon. Secretary.
John Browne
Joseph A. Fennell
Nicholas Furlong
Thomas Hayes
Martin O'Connor
William Hynes *(co-opted 8th February)*
John Doyle *(co-opted 8th February)*

St. Iberius Club & Catholic Young Men's Society Council of 1928 :
Rev. John Sinnott, Adm., President
Michael Kehoe, Vice President & Treasurer
Richard Goold, Hon. Secretary
William Hutchinson, Hon. Secretary *(was requested to return)*
John Doyle,
Nicholas Furlong
Joseph A. Fennell
Thomas Hayes
Joseph Cunningham   }
John Browne   }
John Kelly   } *(all five co-opted 28th February*
Patrick Breen   }
Edward O'Rourke   }

St. Iberius Club & Catholic Young Men's Society Council of 1929 :
Rev. John Sinnott, Adm., President
Michael Kehoe, Vice President & Treasurer
Richard Goold, Hon. Secretary
William Hutchinson, Hon. Secretary *(was requested to stay on)*
John Doyle
Nicholas Furlong
Joseph Kinsella
Edward O'Rourke
Patrick Breen
John Browne
Christopher Delaney
John Kelly
Thomas Hayes

St. Iberius Club & Catholic Young Men's Society Council of 1930 :
Rev. John Sinnott, Adm., President
Michael Kehoe, Vice President & Treasurer
Richard Goold, Hon. Secretary
Joseph A. Fennell, Hon. Secretary
John J. Donohoe, Hon. Secretary
Christopher Delaney
Joseph B. Kinsella
Nicholas P. Corish
Edward O'Rourke
William R. Turner
Nicholas Furlong
Patrick Breen
Patrick (Paddy) Brady
John Kelly

St. Iberius Club & Catholic Young Men's Society Council of 1931 :
Rev. John Sinnott, Adm., President
Michael Kehoe, Vice President & Treasurer
Richard Goold, Hon. Secretary
Joseph A. Fennell, Hon. Secretary
John J. Donohoe,
Christopher Delaney
Nicholas P. Corish
Edward O'Rourke
William R. Turner
Nicholas Furlong
Patrick Breen
Patrick (Paddy) Brady
Daniel Costello

St. Iberius Club & Catholic Young Men's Society Council of 1932 :
Rev. John Sinnott, Adm., President
Michael Kehoe, Vice President & Treasurer
Richard Goold, Hon. Secretary
William Hutchinson, Hon. Secretary
Thomas O'Rourke
John J. Donohoe
Nicholas P. Corish
William R. Turner
Nicholas Furlong

Patrick Breen
Daniel Costello
John Kelly *(co-opted 19th April)*

St. Iberius Club & Catholic Young Men's Society Council of 1933 :

Rev. John Sinnott, Adm.., President
Michael Kehoe, Vice President & Treasurer *(Resigned February)*
Richard Goold, Hon. Secretary
William Hutchinson, Hon. Secretary (e*lected acting Vice President & Treasurer February)*
Thomas O'Rourke
John J. Donohoe
Nicholas P. Corish *(elected Hon. Secretary February)*
Patrick Breen
Michael J. Collopy
Thomas Redmond
John O'Keeffe
John J. Cosgrave
John J. Kehoe
John Dolan *(co-Opted 13th February)*

St. Iberius Club & Catholic Young Men's Society Council of 1934 :

Very Rev. John Sinnott Adm. President
Richard Goold, Vice-President
William Hutchinson, Hon. Secretary
John J. Donohoe, Hon. Secretary
Patrick Breen
Nicholas P. Corish
Michael Collopy
John J. Cosgrave
John Donlon
William J. Kehoe
Thomas O'Rourke
Thomas Redmond
John O'Keeffe

St. Iberius Club & Catholic Young Men's Society Council of 1935 :

Very Rev. John Sinnott Adm. President
Richard Goold, Vice-President & Treasurer
William Hutchinson, Hon. Secretary
John J. Donohoe, Hon. Secretary
Patrick Breen
Nicholas P. Corish *(resigned due to his responsibilities)*
Michael Collopy
John J. Cosgrave
John Donlon
William J. Kehoe
Thomas O'Rourke
Thomas Redmond
John O'Keeffe
Note: Mr. Corish was requested to reconsider his resignation March 1935 but he was unable to do this. It would appear that the Council allowed him to remain a Council member in his absence from 1935 to 1939 because his name was still given as a Council member. Or did he finally rescind his resignation?

St. Iberius Club & Catholic Young Men's Society Council of 1936 :

Very Rev. John Sinnott Adm. President
Richard Goold, Vice-President & Treasurer
William Hutchinson, Hon. Secretary
John J. Donohoe, Hon. Secretary
Patrick Breen
Nicholas P. Corish *(resigned February due to other commitments)*
Michael Collopy
John J. Cosgrave
John Donlon
John Kehoe
Thomas O'Rourke
Thomas Redmond
John O'Keeffe
James Kelly *(co-opted to fill vacancy, in May)*

C.Y.M.S. (St. Iberius Branch) Council of 1937

Very Rev. John Sinnott Adm. President
Richard Goold, Vice-President & Treasurer
William Hutchinson, Hon. Secretary
John J. Donohoe, Hon. Secretary
Thomas O'Rourke
Nicholas Barnwell
Patrick Breen
Nicholas P. Corish
James P. Quirke
John J. O'Keeffe
Michael J. Collopy
W. R. Turner
Michael O'Rourke *(the Faythe)*
Philip Wilson

C.Y.M.S. (St. Iberius Branch) Council of 1938

Very Rev. John Sinnott Adm. President
Richard Goold, Vice-President & Treasurer
William Hutchinson, Hon. Secretary
John J. Donohoe, Hon. Secretary
Nicholas Barnwell
Patrick Breen
Nicholas P. Corish
James P. Quirke
John J. O'Keeffe
Michael J. Collopy
W. R. Turner
Michael O'Rourke *(the Faythe)*
Philip Wilson
Henry Compton

C.Y.M.S. (St. Iberius Branch) Council of 1939

Very Rev. John Sinnott Adm. President
Richard Goold, Vice-President & Treasurer
William Hutchinson, Hon. Secretary
John J. Donohoe, Hon. Secretary
Nicholas Barnwell
Patrick Breen
Nicholas P. Corish
James P. Quirke
W. R. Turner
Michael O'Rourke *(the Faythe)*
Philip Wilson

Henry Compton
John McMurrogh

C.Y.M.S. (St. Iberius Branch) Council of 1940
Very Rev. John Sinnott Adm. President
Richard Goold, Vice-President & Treasurer
William Hutchinson, Hon. Secretary
John J. Donohoe, Hon. Secretary
Nicholas Barnwell
Patrick Breen
James P. Quirke
W. R. Turner
Philip Wilson
John McMurrogh
Edward O'Brien

C.Y.M.S. (St. Iberius Branch) Council of 1941
Very Rev. John Sinnott Adm. President
Richard Goold, Vice-President & Treasurer *(died in office November)*
William Hutchinson, Hon. Secretary
John J. Donohoe, Hon. Secretary
Patrick Breen *(elected Vice-President November)*
W. R. Turner
Edward O'Brien
Eugene McGrail
John Cullimore *co-opted on 4th March)*

C.Y.M.S. (St. Iberius Branch) Council of 1942
Rev.. George J. Murphy, Adm. President
Patrick Breen, Vice-President
William Hutchinson, Hon. Secretary *(died during the year)*
John J. Donohoe, Hon. Secretary
W. R. Turner
Eugene McGrail
John Cullimore
Patrick Gaul
William G. Collopy
John F. O'Rourke

C.Y.M.S. (St. Iberius Branch) Council of 1943
Rev. George J. Murphy, Adm. President
Patrick Breen, Vice-President
John J. Donohoe, Hon. Secretary
John F. O'Rourke *(elected Asst. Hon. Sec. 2nd June)*
W. R. Turner
Eugene McGrail
John Cullimore
Patrick Gaul
William G. Collopy
Henry F. Doyle *(co-opted on 2nd March)*

C.Y.M.S. (St. Iberius Branch) Council of 1944
Rev. George J. Murphy, Adm. President
Patrick Breen, Vice-President
John J. Donohoe, Hon. Secretary
John F. O'Rourke, Asst. Hon. Sec.
W. R. Turner
Eugene McGrail
John Cullimore
William G. Collopy

Henry F. Doyle
Thomas Hayes
Patrick J. Curran *(co-opted on to the Council 7th March)*

C.Y.M.S. (St. Iberius Branch) Council of 1945
Rev. George J. Murphy, Adm. President
Patrick Breen, Vice-President *(died in November)*
John J. Donohoe, Hon. Secretary
John F. O'Rourke, Asst. Hon. Sec.
William R. Turner
Eugene McGrail
William G. Collopy
Henry F. Doyle
Thomas J. Hayes
Patrick J. Curran

C.Y.M.S. (St. Iberius Branch) Council of 1946
Rev. George J. Murphy, Adm. President
Edward O'Rourke, Vice-President & honorary life Member.
John J. Donohoe, Hon. Secretary
John F. O'Rourke, Asst. Hon. Sec.
William R. Turner
Patrick Lennon
Nicholas Barnwell
James Gordon
Thomas Banville
Thomas O'Rourke
Henry F. Doyle
Laurence (Lar) Roche
Eugene McGrail
Patrick J. Curran

C.Y.M.S. (St. Iberius Branch) Council of 1947
Rev. George J. Murphy, Adm. President *(left town in April)*
Rev. Patrick Doyle, Adm. President *(from 6th May)*
Edward O'Rourke, Vice-President & honorary life Member.
John J. Donohoe, Hon. Secretary
John F. O'Rourke, Asst. Hon. Sec.
William R. Turner
Thomas Banville
Eugene McGrail
Patrick J. Curran
Patrick J. Hynes

C.Y.M.S. (St. Iberius Branch) Council of 1948
Rev. Patrick Doyle, Adm. President
Edward O'Rourke, Vice-President & honorary life Member.
John J. Donohoe, Hon. Secretary
John F. O'Rourke, Asst. Hon. Sec.
Edward P. O'Brien, Hon Auditor
Thomas Banville
Eugene McGrail
Patrick J. Curran
Shane Sinnott
James Gordon
John Barmes
Henry F. Doyle
William Murphy

Thomas McGuinness

C.Y.M.S. (St. Iberius Branch) Council of 1949
Rev. Patrick Doyle, Adm., President
Edward O'Rourke, Vice-President & honorary life
Member.
John J. Donohoe, Hon. Sectary.
John F O'Rourke, Asst. Hon. Sectary.
Edward P. O'Brien, Hon Auditor
James Gordon
George Bridges
Eamon Cleary
Thomas Kelly
William Murphy
Eugene H. McGrail
Henry F. Doyle
Sean Doyle

C.Y.M.S. (St. Iberius Branch) Council of 1950
Rev. Patrick Doyle, Adm., President
Edward O'Rourke, Vice-President & honorary life
Member.
John J. Donohoe, Hon. Sectary.
John F O'Rourke, Asst. Hon. Secretary
Edward P. O'Brien, Hon Auditor
James Gordon
George Bridges
Eamon Cleary
Thomas Kelly
William Murphy
Eugene H. McGrail *(resigned his position on 3rd Oct.)*
Henry F. Doyle
Thomas Kelly
Sean Doyle

C.Y.M.S. (St. Iberius Branch) Council of 1951
Rev. Patrick Doyle, Adm., President
Edward O'Rourke, Vice-President & honorary life
Member.
John J. Donohoe, Hon. Sectary.
John F O'Rourke, Asst. Hon. Secretary
Edward P. O'Brien, Hon Auditor
Eugene H. McGrail
Thomas McGuinness
Gerald Foley
William Murphy
Thomas O'Rourke
George Bridges
Thomas Kelly
Eamon Cleary
Sean Doyle

C.Y.M.S. (St. Iberius Branch) Council of 1952
Rev. J. M. Butler, Adm., President
Edward O'Rourke, Vice-President & honorary life
Member.
John J. Donohoe, Hon. Sectary.
John F O'Rourke, Asst. Hon. Secretary *(he resigned his position on the Council on 1st May)*
Edward P. O'Brien, Hon Auditor

George Bridges
Eamon Cleary
Thomas Kelly
William Murphy
Thomas O'Rourke
Gerald Foley *(was removed 3rd Jul,y Rule 15 of the general Rules)*
James Gordon
Sean Kelly
Sean Doyle *(co-opted onto council 1st May to fill the vacancy)*
Patrick J. Roice *(co-opted 3rd July to fill the vacancy)*

C.Y.M.S. (St. Iberius Branch) Council of 1953
Rev. J. M. Butler, Adm., President
Edward O'Rourke, Vice-President & honorary life
Member.
John F O'Rourke, Hon. Secretary
Edward P. O'Brien, Hon. Treasurer & Auditor
George Bridges
Thomas Kelly
William Murphy
James Gordon
Henry F. Doyle
Patrick Kelly

C.Y.M.S. (St. Iberius Branch) Council of 1954
Rev.. J. M. Butler, Adm., President
Edward O'Rourke, Vice-President & honorary life
Member
John F O'Rourke, Hon. Secretary
Thomas Kelly, Assistant Hon. Sec.
John J. Donohoe, Hon Auditor & Chairman *(co-opted onto council 9th March)*
Victor Bridges
Kevin O'Mahoney
George Bridges
Thomas Hayes *(co-opted onto council 11th April)*
Rev. M. J. O'Neill Adm
Thomas O'Rourke }
W. R. Turner } *All three were co-opted to Council on 9th March and*
M. McCormack } *none had taken their seat by April*

C.Y.M.S. (St. Iberius Branch) Council of 1955
Rev. M. J. O'Neill Adm, President
Edward O'Rourke, Vice-President & honorary life
Member.
Thomas Kelly, Hon. Sec.
John F O'Rourke, Hon. Sec. *(co-opted on to the Council 22nd Feb.)*
John J. Donohoe, Hon Auditor & Chairman
Thomas Hayes
George Bridges
Victor Bridges
Kevin O'Mahoney *(co-opted on to the Council 22nd Feb.)*

C.Y.M.S. (St. Iberius Branch) Council of 1956
Rev. M. J. O'Neill Adm, President
Edward O'Rourke, Vice-President & honorary life
Member.

John F. O'Rourke, Hon. Secretary *(resigned over Printing Dispute)*
Thomas Kelly, Hon. Sec.
John J. Donohoe Hon Auditor & Chairman
Thomas Hayes *(resigned over Printing Dispute 15th Jan. 1957)*
George Bridges
Jack .J. Breen
Wally Cleary
John Cullimore
Henry (Harry) F. Doyle
Sean Doyle
Oliver Hickey
Tom Mahon
William Murphy
Jimmy O'Brien

C.Y.M.S. (St. Iberius Branch) Council of 1957
Rev. M. J. O'Neill Adm., Presiden
Edward O'Rourke, Vice-President & honorary life Member
Thomas Kelly, Hon. Sec.
John J. Donohoe, Hon Auditor & Chairman
George Bridges
Jack .J. Breen
Wally Cleary
John Cullimore
Henry (Harry) F. Doyle
Oliver Hickey
Tom Mahon
William Murphy
Jimmy O'Brien
Thomas O'Rourke

C.Y.M.S. (St. Iberius Branch) Council of 1958
Rev. Michael J. O'Neill Adm., President
Edward O'Rourke Vice-President & Honorary Life Member *(died during year)*
Thomas Kelly, Hon. Sec.
Thomas Mahon, Hon. Treasurer
John J. Donohoe, Hon. Auditor
Ald. John Cullimore P.C. *(Mayor of Wexford)*
Henry F. Doyle
Thomas O'Rourke
Wally Cleary
William Murphy
Eugene H. Mc Grail
Jimmy O'Brien
George Bridges

C.Y.M.S. (St. Iberius Branch) Council of 1959
Rev. Michael J. O'Neill Adm., President
Eugene H. Mc Grail Vice-President
Thomas Kelly, Hon. Treasurer
Thomas Mahon, Hon. Sec.
John J. Donohoe, Hon. Auditor
Ald. John Cullimore P.C.
Henry F. Doyle
Thomas O'Rourke
Wally Cleary
William Murphy
Desmond Allen
Patrick Kelly

Jimmy O'Brien
George Bridges

C.Y.M.S. (St. Iberius Branch) Council of 1960
Rev. Michael J. O'Neill Adm., President
Eugene H. Mc Grail Vice-President
John J. Donohoe Hon. Sec. & Treasurer
Ald. John Cullimore P.C.
Henry F Doyle
Thomas O'Rourke
Thomas Kelly
Wally Cleary
William Murphy
James O'Brien
Thomas Mahon
Patrick Kelly

C.Y.M.S. (St. Iberius Branch) Council of 1961
Rev. Michael J. O'Neill Adm., President. *(he resigned Sept.)*
Eugene H. Mc Grail Vice-President
John J. Donohoe, Hon. Sec. & Treasurer
Ald. John Cullimore P.C.
Henry F. Doyle
Thomas O'Rourke
Thomas Kelly
Thomas Mahon
James O'Brien
Wally Cleary *(co-opted on to the council)*
William Murphy, *(Co-opted onto the council)*
Luke Wadding *(co-opted on to the council)*
The Very Rev. Thomas Murphy Adm. *(was President by 5th Sept 1961)*

C.Y.M.S. (St. Iberius Branch) Council of 1962
Very Rev. Thomas Murphy Adm., President
Eugene H. Mc Grail, Vice-President
John J. Donohoe, Hon. Sec. & Treasurer
Ald. John Cullimore, P.C.
Henry F. Doyle
Thomas O'Rourke
James O'Brien
John O'Connell
William Murphy *(co-opted June 1962)*
Kevin Cousins *(co-opted June 1962)*

C.Y.M.S. (St. Iberius Branch) Council of 1963
Very Rev. Thomas Murphy Adm., President.
Eugene H. Mc Grail, Vice-President
John J. Donohoe, Hon. Sec. & Treasurer
Ald. John Cullimore, P.C.
Henry F. Doyle
Wally Cleary
James O'Brien
John F. O'Connell
Kevin Cousins
Arthur Kelly *(resigned 7th May 1963)*
Thomas O'Rourke *(co-opted at election.)*
Capt. Michael Doyle *(co-opted April 1963)*
Tom Mahon were *(co-opted April 1963)*
George Bridges *(co-opted on 7th May 1963)*

C.Y.M.S. (St. Iberius Branch) Council of 1964

Very Rev. Thomas Murphy Adm., President
Eugene H. Mc Grail, Vice-President
John J. Donohoe,   Hon. Sec. & Treasurer
Wally Cleary
Kevin Cousins
Ald. John Cullimore, P.C. *(co-opted at the meeting)*
Tom Mahon *(co-opted at the meeting.)*
Capt. Michael J. Doyle   }
Thomas O'Rourke   } *(all three refused to go*
forward this term)
 John F. O'Connell   }
George Bridges (c*o-opted on 3rd May 1964)*

C.Y.M.S. (St. Iberius Branch) Council of 1965

Very Rev. Thomas Murphy Adm., President
Eugene H. Mc Grail ,Vice-President
John J. Donohoe,   Hon. Sec. & Treasurer
Ald. John Cullimore, P.C.
Harry F. Doyle
James O'Brien
Wally Cleary
Kevin Cousins
Capt. Michael J. Doyle
George Bridges *(co-opted at Meeting)*
Thomas Tierney (c*o-opted later)*
Thomas A. Carton *(co-opted later)*
Thomas O'Rourke *(co-opted 15th June. He did not*
accept.)

C.Y.M.S. (St. Iberius Branch) Council of 1966

Very Rev. Thomas Murphy Adm., President
Eugene H. Mc Grail, Vice-President
John J. Donohoe,   Hon. Sec. & Treasurer
Ald. John Cullimore, P.C.,
Harry F. Doyle
James O'Brien
Wally Cleary
Kevin Cousins
Capt. Michael J. Doyle
Thomas Tierney
Thomas O'Rourke *(co-opted 7th Feb..but again declined)*

C.Y.M.S. (St. Iberius Branch) Council of 1967

Very Rev. Thomas Murphy Adm., President.
Eugene H. Mc Grail, Vice-President
John J. Donohoe, Hon. Sec. & Treasurer
Ald. John Cullimore, P.C.,
Harry F. Doyle
James O'Brien
Kevin Cousins
Capt. Michael J. Doyle
Thomas Tierney
Thomas O'Rourke
George Bridges
Robert Devlin
Tom O'Hara

C.Y.M.S. (St. Iberius Branch) Council of 1968

Very Rev. Thomas Murphy Adm., President
Eugene H. Mc Grail, Vice-President
John J. Donohoe, Hon. Sec. & Treasurer
Ald. John Cullimore, P.C.,

Harry F. Doyle
Capt. Michael J. Doyle
Thomas Tierney
Thomas O'Rourke
Timothy Kehoe
George Bridges *(co-opted on 5th March 1968)*
Tom O'Hara *(co-opted on 5th March 1968)*

C.Y.M.S. (St. Iberius Branch) Council of 1969

Very Rev. Thomas Murphy Adm., President.
Eugene H. Mc Grail, Vice-President
John J. Donohoe,   Hon. Sec. & Treasurer
Harry F. Doyle
Capt. Michael J. Doyle
Thomas O'Rourke
Robert Devlin
George Bridges
Sean Tyghe
Tom O'Hara
Donal Sadler
Thomas Butler
Liam O'Grady

C.Y.M.S. (St. Iberius Branch) Council of 1970

Very Rev. Matthew J. Berney, Adm., President
Eugene H. Mc Grail,Vice-President
John J. Donohoe,   Hon. Sec. & Treasurer
Capt. Michael J. Doyle
Robert Devlin
Sean (John) Tyghe
George Bridges
Liam O'Grady,
Thomas O'Rourke *(co-opted 3rd March 1970)*

C.Y.M.S. (St. Iberius Branch) Council of 1971

Very Rev. Matthew J. Berney, Adm., President
Eugene H. Mc Grail, Vice-President
John J. Donohoe,   Hon. Sec. & Treasurer
Robert Devlin
Sean (John) Tyghe
William Power
Thomas O'Rourke   }
Capt. Michael J. Doyle   } *(all three co-opted 6th*
April, 1971)
George Bridges   }

C.Y.M.S. (St. Iberius Branch) Council of 1972

Very Revd. Matthew J. Berney, Adm., President
Eugene H. Mc Grail, Vice-President
John J. Donohoe,   Hon. Sec. & Treasurer
Sean (John) Tyghe
William Power
Capt. Michael J. Doyle
John A. Roche
Liam O'Grady
Liam Keane
Thomas Butler
Thomas Ryan
Thomas O'Hara
Thomas J. Grant
Thomas O'Rourke *(co-opted 7th March 1972)*

C.Y.M.S. (St. Iberius Branch) Council of 1973

Very Rev. James B. Curtis, Adm., President
Eugene H. Mc Grail, Vice-President
John J. Donohoe, Hon. Sec. & Treasurer
Noel Morris
Liam Keane
Thomas Butler
Thomas Ryan
Thomas O'Hara
Thomas J. Grant
Thomas Connor
Capt. Michael J. Doyle }
Thomas O'Rourke } *(all three co-opted in February 1973)*
Robert Devlin }
Sean (John) Tyghe *(co-opted 6th March 1973)*

C.Y.M.S. (St. Iberius Branch) Council of 1974

Very Rev. James B. Curtis, Adm., President.
Eugene H. Mc Grail, Vice-President
John J. Donohoe, Hon. Sec. & Treasurer
Thomas O'Rourke
Capt. Michael J. Doyle
Sean (John) Tyghe
Samuel O'Rourke *(co-opted on 5th March)*
George Bridges *(co-opted on 5th March)*

C.Y.M.S. (St. Iberius Branch) Council of 1975

Very Rev. James B. Curtis, Adm., President
Eugene H. Mc Grail, Vice-President
John J. Donohoe, Hon. Sec. & Treasurer
Thomas O'Rourke,
Capt. Michael J. Doyle
Sean (John) Tyghe
Samuel O'Rourke
George Bridges

St. Iberius C.Y.M.S. Branch Council 1976 :

(No minutes are recorded for this year. The following is guesswork)
Thomas O'Rourke, Chairman
John J. Donohoe, Hon. Sec. & Treasurer
Capt. Michael J. Doyle
Sean (John) Tyghe
Samuel O'Rourke
George Bridges
Eugene H. Mc Grail, Vice-President *(His name does not appear after this year and as there are no minutes one must assume that he died)*

C.Y.M.S. (St. Iberius Branch) Council of 1977

(Only two meetings held this year on 19th Oct. and 13th December 1977 with the following present:)
Thomas O'Rourke, Chairman
John J. Donohoe Hon. Sec. & Treasurer
Capt. Michael J. Doyle
Samuel O'Rourke
George Bridges
Myles O'Rourke
Henry F. Doyle
Jackie Breen
Matthew Stafford *(co-opted on the 13th Dec. 1977)*

C.Y.M.S. (St. Iberius Branch) Council of 1978

(Only three meetings held this year. The following members were present:)
Thomas O'Rourke, Chairman
John J. Donohoe, Hon. Sec. & Treasurer
Capt. Michael J. Doyle
Samuel O'Rourke
Myles O'Rourke
Henry F. Doyle
Matthew Stafford

C.Y.M.S. (St. Iberius Branch) Council of 1979

(There were no meetings held this year. No minutes recorded but we are safe in assuming that the following did hold some meetings to conduct the Society's business etc.)
Thomas O'Rourke, Chairman
John J. Donohoe , Hon. Sec. & Treasurer
Capt. Michael J. Doyle
Samuel O'Rourke
Myles O'Rourke
Henry F. Doyle
Matthew Stafford

C.Y.M.S. (St. Iberius Branch) Council of 1980

Thomas O'Rourke, Chairman
John J. Donohoe, Hon. Sec. & Treasurer
Capt. Michael J. Doyle
Samuel O'Rourke
Myles O'Rourke
Henry F. Doyle
Matthew Stafford

C.Y.M.S. (St. Iberius Branch) Council of 1981

Thomas O'Rourke, Chairman
John J. Donohoe, Hon. Sec. & Treasurer
Capt. Michael J. Doyle
Samuel O'Rourke
Myles O'Rourke
Henry F. Doyle
Matthew Stafford
George Bridges

C.Y.M.S. (St. Iberius Branch) Council of 1982

Very Rev. John McCabe Adm., President
Thomas O'Rourke, Chairman
John J. Donohoe, Hon. Sec. & Treasurer
Samuel O'Rourke
Myles O'Rourke
Matthew Stafford
George Bridges
Tommy Tierney
Sean O'Donohoe
Michael Murphy *(co-opted on the 18th May 1983)*
Tom Mahon *(co-opted on the 18th May 1983)*

C.Y.M.S. (St. Iberius Branch) Council of 1983

Very Rev. John McCabe Adm., President
Thomas O'Rourke, Chairman
John J. Donohoe, Hon. Sec. & Treasurer
Samuel O'Rourke

Myles O'Rourke
Matthew Stafford
George Bridges
Tommy Tierney
Sean O'Donohoe   *(died 1983)*
H.F. Doyle
Jim Crowley *(co-opted to fill the vacancy on 4th Oct. 1983)*

C.Y.M.S. (St. Iberius Branch) Council of 1984
Very Rev. John McCabe, Adm., President
Thomas O'Rourke, Chairman
John J. Donohoe, Hon. Sec.
Samuel O'Rourke   *(resigned from Council 4th Sept. 1984)*
Myles O'Rourke
Thomas Tierney *(resigned his place on 25th Sept 1984)*
Thomas Mahon
Matthew Stafford
Jim Crowley   *(also asked to resign his place on Oct 1984)*
Henry F. Doyle
Fergus Kehoe
George Bridges   *(co-opted to fill the vacant place 4th Sept. 1984)*
Ger Healey *(co-opted on 23rd Oct. 1984)*
 James Breen   *(co-opted on 23rd Oct. 1984)*

C.Y.M.S. (St. Iberius Branch) Council of 1985
Very Rev. John McCabe, Adm., President
Thomas O'Rourke, Chairman
John J. Donohoe, Hon. Sec.
Myles O'Rourke
Thomas Tierney
Thomas Mahon
Henry F. Doyle
Fergus Kehoe
Ger Healey
Liam Underwood   *(died before Aril 1985)*
Matthew Stafford   *(co-Opted to Council to fill the vacancy)*

C.Y.M.S. (St. Iberius Branch) Council of 1986:
Very Rev. John McCabe, Adm., President
Thomas O'Rourke, Chairman
John J. Donohoe, Hon. Sec.
Myles O'Rourke
Thomas Mahon
Matthew Stafford
Henry F. Doyle
Ger Healey
Joe Delaney
Michael Mahon

C.Y.M.S. (St. Iberius Branch) Council of 1987:
Very Rev. John McCabe, Adm., President
Thomas O'Rourke, Chairman
John J. Donohoe, Hon. Sec.
Myles O'Rourke
Matthew Stafford

Henry F. Doyle
Ger Healey
Thomas Mahoney
Dick Murphy
Peter Crowley
Sean Radford

C.Y.M.S. (St. Iberius Branch) Council of 1988
Very Rev. John McCabe, Adm., President
Thomas O'Rourke, Chairman
John J. Donohoe, Hon. Sec.
Myles O'Rourke
Matthew Stafford
Henry F. Doyle
Sean Radford
Pete Crowley   *(co-opted on 5th Apr. 1988)*
Thomas Mahon   *(co-opted on 5th Apr. 1988)*

C.Y.M.S. (St. Iberius Branch) Council of 1989 :
Very Rev. John McCabe, Adm., President
Thomas O'Rourke, Chairman
John J. Donohoe, Hon. Sec.
Myles O'Rourke
Matthew Stafford
Thomas Mahon
Dick Murphy
Henry F. Doyle
Sean Radford
Nicky Lacey *(co-opted on 4th Apr. 1989)*
Richard Walsh   *(co-opted on 4th Apr. 1989)*

C.Y.M.S. (St. Iberius Branch) Council of 1990
Very Rev. Hugh O'Brien, Adm., President
Thomas O'Rourke, Chairman
John J. Donohoe, Hon. Sec.
Myles O'Rourke
Thomas Mahon
Dick Murphy
Henry F. Doyle
Sean Radford
Nicky Lacey
Richard Walsh

C.Y.M.S. (St. Iberius Branch) Council of 1991
Thomas O'Rourke, Chairman   *(died in January)*
John J. Donohoe, Hon. Sec.
Myles O'Rourke
Thomas Mahon   *(acting Hon Sec. Sept. He resigned before Nov. 1991)*
Dick Murphy   *(acting Hon. Sec. from 12th Nov. 1991)*
Henry F. Doyle   *(elected President & Chairman 5th Feb. 1991)*
Sean Radford
Nicky Lacey
Richard Walsh
Matt Stafford *(resigned)*
Very Rev. Fr. Hugh O'Byrne *(now occupying position of Chaplain)*

C.Y.M.S. (St. Iberius Branch) Council of 1992
Henry F. Doyle, President
John J. Donohoe, Hon. Sec.
Dick Murphy, Acting Hon. Sec.
Myles O'Rourke
Sean Radford
Nicky Lacey
Very Rev. Fr. Hugh O'Byrne (*now acting as Chaplain*)
Martin Donovan (*co-opted*)
Paddy Connick (*co-opted*)
Jim Kehoe   (*co-opted*)

C.Y.M.S. (St. Iberius Branch) Council of 1993
H. F. Doyle (Harry), Chairman
John J. Donodoe, Hon. Sec. (*died during term*)
Richard Murphy (*Hon. Sec. 2nd May 93*)
Sean Radford
Myles O'Rourke
P. Connick
T. Mahoney
Terrance Crosbie
Martin Donovan
Tony O'Connor
P. Crowley
Nicky Lacey

C.Y.M.S. (St. Iberius Branch) Council of 1994
Myles O'Rourke, President & Treasurer
Dick Murphy, Hon. Sec.
Sean Radford, Chairman
Nicky Lacey
Tom Mahoney
Paddy Connick
Michael O'Rourke
Dermot O'Rourke
Terrence Crosbie
Chaplain Rev. H. O'Byrne

C.Y.M.S. (St. Iberius Branch) Council of 1995
Myles O'Rourke, President & Treasurer
Richard (Dick) Murphy, Hon. Sec.
Sean Radford, Chairman
Nicky Lacey
Ricky O'Rourke
Sean Mahoney
Terrance Crosbie
H.F. Doyle
Michael Cullen
Chaplain Rev. P. Cushen
(*Paddy Connick and Michael O'Rourke resigned and will not run for this year 1995*)

C.Y.M.S. (St. Iberius Branch) Council of 1996 :
Myles O'Rourke, President /Treasurer
Dick Murphy, Hon. Sec.
Liam Gordon
Michael Cullen
Henry F. Doyle
Der. O'Rourke
Sean Radford
Sean Mahoney

Nicky Lacey
Chaplain Rev. P. Cushen
Terrence Crosbie   (*will not run for election this year.*)

C.Y.M.S. (St. Iberius Branch) Council of 1997
Sean Radford, President /Chairman
Myles O'Rourke, Treasurer
Richard Murphy, Hon. Sec.
Nicky Lacey, Vice President
Liam Gordon
Joe Walsh
Marty Donovan
Michael Cullen
Henry F. Doyle

C.Y.M.S. (St. Iberius Branch) Council of 1998
Myles O'Rourke, Treasurer
Richard Murphy, Hon. Sec.
Liam Gordon
M. Donovan
J. Walsh
Sean Radford
Nicky Lacey
Michael Cullen
H. F. Doyle.
Chaplain Rev. James Fegan A.D.M.

C.Y.M.S. (St. Iberius Branch) Council of 1999
Nicky Lacey, President
Liam Gordon, Vice-President
Myles O'Rourke, Treasurer
Richard Murphy, Hon. Sec.
Michael Cullen
Shane Mitchell
Marty Donovan
David Roche
Stuart Grannell
Myles O'Rourke   (*died during year*)
On the 22nd Sepember the following four new Council members were included:
Alan Dempsey, Jason Vaughan, Tommy Flynn and Paul Clancy

C.Y.M.S. (St. Iberius Branch) Council of 2000 and 2001 (two year term) :
Liam Gordon, Chairman
M. Donovan, Treasurer
Richard Murphy ,Hon. Sec.
Terence Crosbie, Vice-Chairman
Nicky Lacey
Alan Dempsey
Jason Vaughan
Tony Ryan
P. Clancy

C.Y.M.S. (St. Iberius Branch) Council of 2003 and 2004 (two year term) :
Liam Gordon ,Chairman & Caretaker
Dick Murphy, Hon. Secretary
Marty Donovan , Treasurer   *died in Office*)

Catholic Men and Women's Society *(St. Iberius Branch) Council 2005 and 2006* *(two year term) :*
Liam Gordon, Chairman & Caretaker
Dick Murphy, Hon. Secretary
Nicky Lacey
Rodney Goggins

Catholic Men and Women's Society *(St. Iberius Branch) Council 2007 and 2008* *(two year term) :*
Liam Gordon, Chairman   Dick Murphy, Hon. Secretary   Nicky Lacey   Rodney Goggins

Appendix 2

Speakers and Lecturers at the Club

Very Rev. Dean O'Brien of Limerick, founder of the Society, lectured on the 10th February 1856 at Dr. Sinnott's School, George Street.

Dr. Anderson of the Catholic University of Dublin, lectured at the same place and time.

Very Rev. Fr. Murry (*later became Archbishop of Dublin*) lectured at the same place and time.

Very Rev. James Roche, P.P. Wexford gave two lectures in 1858 on the subject of 'The Church of St. Lateran' and 'The churches of Wexford Ancient and Modern'.

Fr. Doyle lectured 12th August 1858 at George Street School.

Fr. Doran lectured 27th October 1858.

Fr. Murphy lectured on the 31st October and 7th November 1858.

Dr. Nichols (USA) delivered his second lecture to the C.Y.M.S. members in the Town Hall on Tuesday evening the 21st of December 1858 on 'The Social Life and Institutions of America'.

Fr. Rochford lectured on Monday 14th February 1859.

Dr. Ryan lectured 19th May 1859.

Rev. John Lambert Furlong lectured for the Society from the 1850s right up to the late 1870s and all his visits are not recorded. Some of these lectures were 'The friends and foes of civilization in the past' Part II and 'The inroads of Mohammedanism during the whole course of the middle ages'.

Dr. Murray lecture held on the 12th April 1860 in the Town Hall.

Rev. John Lambert Furlong lectured on the 27th June 1860.

Fr. Hore of the Franciscan Convent gave a lecture on May 1862.

Dr. Murry gave a lecture in the Town Hall early 1862.

Rev. John Lambert Furlong lectured on Monday evening the 1st December 1862 at the Town Hall on the subject of 'The friends and foes of civilization in the past' Part III and 'The Reformation'.

Thomas D'Arcy McGee gave a lecture in Wexford in 1865.

Mr. N. Philan, Esq. delivered a lecture at the club hall in January 1873. William Redmond, M.P. was in attendance at this lecture.

Rev. John Lambert Furlong lectured 6th May 1878 at the Theatre, High Street on the subject of 'Revolution and Pious IX' Part 1.

Very Rev. James Roche, P.P. of Wexford and the Spiritual Director of the C.Y.M.S. gave a lecture on the 3rd June 1878.

Myles O'Cleary, M.P. lectured in November 1878.

Rev. John Lambert Furlong lectured 16th January 1879 on the subject of 'Revolution and Pious IX' Part 2 and 'The Roman Republic'. Held in the Town Hall with the Band of the Catholic Wexford Total Abstinence Association in attendance.

Rev. John Lambert Furlong lectured 26th January 1879 on the subject 'Revolution and Pious IX' Part 3 and 'The Roman Republic'. Held in the Theatre in High Street.

His Lordship Dr. Richards lectured 21st January 1880.

Fr. Crean of St. Peter's College lectured at the reading room 2nd March 1880. Both George Dixon and Ben Williams sang.

Fr. Roche of London gave an interesting Magic Lantern Exhibition on Wednesday 26th July 1882.

Lecture on Ireland illustrated by Oxy-Hydrogen lime Light with music, singing and a short farcical play. Held at the C.M.Y.S. Hall, Paul Quay on the 14th February 1888.

Sir Thomas Esmonde gave a lecture in October 1888.

Rev. Patrick F. Kavanagh, O.S.F. lectured on St. Patrick's Night 1890 at the Concert Hall on the subject of 'Patriotism'.

Mr. Lynd provided an entertainment with his 'Phonographic' at the Concert Hall C.Y.M.S. on the 17th November 1891.

Mr. Cosgrave secretary of 'Ireland's Own Animated Picture Co.' gave a picture exhibition of the 'Passion Play' in the C.Y.M.S. on the 1st and 2nd June 1913.

Madame Alicia Adelaide Needham, A.R.A.M., A.R.C.M. the well-known composer lectured on her travels in Italy and Germany before and after the Great War.

Fr. Finn, S.J. gave a lecture on temperance in the concert Hall of St. Iberius House, C.Y.M.S. open to the public in 1929.

Rev. Patrick Doyle, C.C. (*of the C.Y.M.S. Study Circle*) gave various lectures from 1936 to 1939.

Rev. William Gaul, S.T.L. of St. Peter's College Wexford gave various lectures from 1936 to 1939.

Fr. O'Neill, Adm. the President gave many lectures on the history of the Wexford C.Y.M.S. in the late 1950s.

Bro. T. F. Rowlet, Hon. Propagandist in the National Executive Committee of the Catholic Young Men's Society of Ireland gave an interesting lecture at the Council's meeting held on the 23rd June 1959.

Appendix 3

List of Suppliers of Newspapers and Periodicals

Mr. Gainfort, 29 North Main Street, pre 13th December up to 31st December 1877

Mr. Peter Hanton, General Fancy Warehouse, 3 North Main Street. He shared the order with Myles Doyle from 7th January 1877 to 22nd June 1899 and given the order for six months starting 11th December 1934.

George Holbrook, 5 North Main Street from 22nd June 1899

Myles Doyle, Bookseller, Stationer & General Merchant, 9 & 11 North Main Street. He shared the order with Peter Hanton from 13th January 1877

Myles Doyle's business stamp used on magazines and papers supplied to the C.Y.M.S.

Thomas Buckland, 50 South Main Street, his contract ended on the 1st January 1923

Mr. J. H. Doyle, 58 North Main Street, had the order in the 1920s

John Stafford, North Main Street, supplied from 28th December 1922 to April 1923

Miss Maud Kirwan, Carrigeen (*Sister of Toddy*). She rented the club shop on the Quay and supplied the papers and magazines from 1st January 1930

Patrick Whelan, 96 North Main Street, had the order at various times in the 1920s to 1940s

Nicholas Murphy, 84 or 86 North Main Street, had the order at various times in the 1920s to 1940s.

Mr. Dermot Hall, 58 North Main Street was given the order for six months starting December 1948.

Librarian and Library Committees

16th August 1855. First Librarian appointed
John O'Brien was nominated by Fr. James Roche (the Spiritual Director).

Early November 1855. Provisional Librarian
Master John McGee, a junior member, was nominated. He resigned on the 13th November 1855

1859 - The Book Censor Committee
William Connick, VP.
William Scallan, Hon. Secretary.
Peter Fardy
Richard Ryan, Warden.
Nicholas Cousins,
This group were appointed as a Book Censor Committee to look at the reading material in the library. Their mandate was to *'See if there are any books therein objectionable and that all things are right in connection with that department.'*

November 1855 to 1860s - Librarian
John Stafford

1858 - Cataloger of the library Books
James Cullen

24th February 1863 - Library & Book Committee
Thomas J. Roche
Patrick White
Richard Ryan
James Kehoe
John Dunne

January 1864 - Library & Book Committee
William Scallan.
Patrick White
James Roche

January 1865 - Library & Book Committee
William Scallan
Richard Murphy
William Connick
Thomas White

April 1865 - Library & Book Committee
James McArdle
Mr. Murry
William Scallan

April 1866 - Library & Book Committee
Robert Hanton
James Hore
Thomas O'Reilly

January 1868 - Library & Book Committee
Myles Murphy
William Scallan
James Moore

February 1884 - Library & Book Committee
Robert Hanton
James Stafford
Patrick Byrne
William Hutchinson
John King
James Sinnott.
Laurence Rossiter

1885 - Library & Book Committee
John King
Robert Hanton
James Stafford
William Hutchinson
Mr. Byrne
James Sinnott
Capt. Thomas Lambert was the librarian

30th July 1896 - Library & Book Committee
Michael Kehoe
Mr. Morris
Frank Carthy
William Hutchinson
Richard Goold
Laurence Rossiter

15th February 1900 - Library & Book Committee
Richard Goold
William Hutchinson
Michael Kehoe
Michael Luccan

John White
Nicholas Bolger
P. J. Walsh

1904 - Acting Liberian
Rev. Fr. Doyle was acting librarian

April 1907 - Library & Book Committee
John Dunne
John White

February 1910 - Library & Book Committee
Rev. Fr. O'Byrne
John White
John Shirlock

John Wadding
Mr. Frizille

February 1913 - Library & Book Committee
Rev. James Codd, C.C., Chairman
Michael Bolger
Joseph Fennell
John Dunne
James J. Kehoe

1944 - Library & Book Committee
Edward O'Brien
Joseph Fennell
Thomas Hayes.

Appendix 4

Band Members and Committees

6th June 1859 - Fife and Drum Band Committee
Fr. Jeremiah Hogan, Chairman
John Brown J.P.C., Hon. Secretary.
Two members from the Guild of St. Joseph (Unknown)
Two members from the Guild of St. Mary (Unknown)
Two members from the Guild of St. Patrick (Unknown)
Two members from the Council (Unknown)

23rd March 1861 - Fife and Drum Band Committee
Fr. James Roche, P.P., Chairman
John Dunne
Rich Ryan
Mr. Jones, teacher of the flute
Mr. Bolger, teacher of the drums
William Martin (given an honorary membership for organising the band)

15th August 1861 - Brass Band Organiser
William Martin, L.M. Chairman
Mr. Jones, teacher of the flute
Mr. Bolger, teacher of the drums

6th March 1862, Brass Band Committee
Probably the same as above
Joseph Kinsella (given an honorary membership for joining the band)
Thomas Murphy was a member of the band

St. Patrick's Day 1871
This is the very first time the band called themselves the Confraternity Band

31st January 1887 - Brass Band Committee
Laurence Rossiter, Chairman
William Hutchinson
James Whelan
Mr. Murphy, band master and teacher

January 1888 - Brass Band Committee
Edward Whelan, Hon. Secretary of the band
William Hutchinson, Hon. Secretary of the band
Mr. Murphy, band master and teacher
James Neill was a member of the band

13th July 1889 - Brass Band Committee
R. Curran (given an honorary membership for joining the band)
Mr. Kelly (given an honorary membership for joining the band)
Mr. Lucking (given an honorary membership for joining the band)

January 1890 - Brass Band Committee
Mr. R. Curran
Mr. Kelly
Mr. Lucking

1890 - Brass Band Committee
Appointed to hand-over the band instruments to Fr. O'Leary's newly formed confraternity band.
Myles Connick
Robert Hanton
John Tyghe
R. Curran
Mr. Kelly
Mr. Lucking

25th June 1903 - Boy's Confraternity Band (Boy's Brigade)
Fr. O'Byrne, founder and director
This must have been the forerunner to the confraternity band proper

1926 - Confraternity Band
Rev. Martin O'Connor, C.C., re-establishing the band date?
The band was celebrating its Annual Reunions from this date onwards

Appendix 5

Entertainment/Amusements Committees

Organiser of Amusements in Concert Hall 1907
John White

Visiting Committee 7th April 1918
Capt. Busher
P. J. O'Connor, Snr.

Amusements Committee 13th February 1923
Rev. P. Doyle C.C.
Edward F. O'Rourke
Joseph Fennell

Amusements Committee 7th February 1928
John Doyle
Thomas Hayes
(*With power to appoint others to their numbers*)

Amusements Committee
25th September 1928
John Doyle
John Kelly
Aidan Kelly
John Cullimore
(*With power to appoint others to their numbers*)

Amusements Committee 1930
Nicholas Corish, Secretary
Others?

Amusements Committee 6th October 1932
Nicholas Corish, Secretary
W. R. Turner
Joseph Kinsella

Entertainments Committee October 1935
Michael Collopy
Thomas O'Rourke
John O'Keeffe

John Donlan
This committee was appointed by the Council

Entertainments Committee October 1936
Michael Collopy
Thomas O'Rourke
John O'Keeffe
John Donlan

Amusements Committee September 1946
William R.Turner, Chairman
John J. O'Rourke, Hon. Secretary & Treasurer
Thomas Barnwell
Tony Kelly

Amusements Committee 1947
John J. O'Rourke, Hon. Secretary & Treasurer
Unknown but most likely the same committee

Concert Hall Committee 1952
Thomas Kelly
Thomas O'Rourke
Thomas Mahon
P. J. Roice
John F. O'Rourke
George Bridges

Whist Drive Committee 1952
Thomas Kelly
Thomas O'Rourke
Thomas Mahon
P. J. Roice
John F. O'Rourke
George Bridges

Pongo Working Committees 1955 to 1964.
Took over the responsibility of fund raising from 1955 to 1964 .(*See Pongo section for full details of its working committees.*)

Appendix 6

Pongo Working Committees Throughout the Years

'Housie Housie' Working Committee 1949
Names unknown. Not recorded. Most likely some of the Council members.

Pongo Think-Tank & Organising Sub-Committee of October 1954
Thomas Kelly, Chairman
Thomas O'Rourke, in charge of game
George Bridges, negotiated to get the game
Thomas Hayes
G. Leahy
P. J. Roice
Victor Bridges

Pongo First Working Committee 1955
Thomas O'Rourke, Chairman
Thomas Kelly (*Society's Hon. Secretary*)
Lar Roche
Others Unknown, not recorded

Pongo Working Committee 1956
Thomas O'Rourke, Chairman
William Murphy
Wally Cleary
Tom Mahon
Michael A. O'Rourke, ball boy
Michael Mahon, ball boy (*Joined late in the year*)

Pongo Working Committee 1957
Thomas O'Rourke, Chairman
William Murphy
Wally Cleary
Tom Mahon
Michael A. O'Rourke, ball boy
Michael Mahon, ball boy (*Resigned 3rd. February due to printer's dispute.*)

Pongo Working Committee 1958
Thomas O'Rourke, Chairman
William Murphy
Wally Cleary
Tom Mahon
Michael A. O'Rourke, ball boy

Pongo Working Committee 1959
Thomas O'Rourke Chairman
William Murphy
Tom Mahon
Wally Cleary
Michael A. O'Rourke
Michael Murphy, ball boy

Pongo Working Committee 1960
Thomas O'Rourke Chairman
William Murphy
Tom Mahon
Wally Cleary
Myles O'Rourke
Michael Murphy, ball boy
Tommy Cullimore, ball boy

Pongo Working Committee 1961
Thomas O'Rourke, Chairman
William Murphy
Tom Mahon
Wally Cleary
Myles O'Rourke
Michael Murphy, ball boy
Tommy Cullimore, ball boy

Pongo Working Committee 1962
Thomas O'Rourke Chairman
William Murphy
Tom Mahon
Wally Cleary
Myles O'Rourke
Michael Murphy, ball boy
Tommy Cullimore, ball boy

Pongo Working Committee 1963
Thomas O'Rourke, Chairman (*Resigned*)
William Murphy, (*Filled position of Chairman*)
Tom Mahon
Wally Cleary
Myles O'Rourke
Michael Murphy, ball boy
Tommy Cullimore, ball boy

Pongo Working Committee 1964 (The final year)
William Murphy, Chairman (*William asked to step-down at beginning of year*)
Tom Mahon
Wally Cleary
Myles O'Rourke
Michael Murphy, ball boy
Tommy Cullimore, ball boy
Thomas O'Rourke (*called back by Council as Chairman at beginning of year*)

Finished November of 1965
This Pongo Committee was disbanded and the game discontinued on the advice of Thomas O'Rourke to the Council, due to unacceptable losses incurred.

Appendix 7

Annual Soirée, Reunion and Banquet Records
(*Incomplete*)

Annual Soirée for 1859 was postponed until Easter
16th November 1862 annual soiree' held at the Town Hall
8th February 1863 annual soirée held at the Town Hall
1864 soirée held on St. Patrick's Night
8th November 1864 public banquet for Irish Papal Brigade held at Town Hall
St. Patrick's Night 1864 soirée fire works display outside the club on Paul Quay
St. Patrick's Night 1865 soirée fire works and rockets from tug outside Paul Quay.
New Years Night 1866 annual soirée held in club Hall *(Paul Quay?)*
4th January 1891 annual reunion held in rented Hall.
8th November 1860 public banquet
1863, tea party April 1867 on Low Easter Sunday evening annual soirée
18th April 1868 complimentary supper for James McArdle
8th January 1882 annual soirée
12th December 1882 annual soirée
2nd January 1883 annual soirée
14th January 1883, annual Soirée
13th January 1884 annual Soirée
1885 annual soirée was cancelled
10th January 1886 annual soirée
9th January 1887 annual soirée
15th January 1888 annual soirée
1889 no annual soirée held
11th January 1890 annual soirée
1890 no annual soirée held
10th January 1892 annual soirée held in Concert Hall
14th January 1893 annual soirée held in Concert Hall
13th January 1894 annual soirée held in Concert Hall
12th January 1895 annual soirée held in Concert Hall
1896 no annual soirée held
17th January 1897 annual soirée held in Concert Hall
Sunday 12th January 1896 annual soirée held in the Concert Hall of the C.Y.M.S.
5th February 1899 annual soirée held in Concert Hall
3rd February 1907 general reunion
17th January 1908 annual supper
5th February 1910 annual supper in Concert Hall
5th February 1911 annual supper in Concert Hall
15th February 1914 annual supper & reunion in Concert Hall
10th February 1924 annual reunion
1939 reunion
1946 communion breakfast
February 1951 annual reunion
Children's Christmas Party 1952
17th December 1955 C.Y.M.S. Wexford Centenary reunion dinner dance held in Talbot Hotel
5th December annual reunion dinner dance 1956 held in the Talbot Hotel
December 1956 children's Christmas party held in the Concert Hall
4th December 1957 annual reunion dinner dance held in the Talbot Hotel
3rd December 1958 annual reunion dinner dance - meal in Mernagh's restaurant and Dance held in the Concert Hall
30th December 1959 annual dinner dance - meal and dance held in C.Y.M.S.
1960 annual reunion dinner dance held in club
4th December 1994 annual Christmas party
20th December 1995 annual Christmas party
December 1994 annual Christmas party
December 1995 annual Christmas party
December 1996 annual Christmas party
December 1997 annual Christmas party

Appendix 8

Entertainment Committees

Pyrotechnical Committee - St. Patrick's Night 1864
Capt. J. J. Doyle
Michael Hughes

Pyrotechnical Committee - St. Patrick's Night 1865
William Connick
William Martin
Mr. Kehoe
P. White

Stage Entertainment Committee - New Years Night 1866 Soirée
P. J. Gaffney
James Moore
James McArdle

Annual Soirée Organising Committee 1883
Laurence Rossiter, Hon. Secretary of the Society
William J. Devereux
Edward Dixon
Robert Hanton

Stewards Working Committee - Annual Soirée 1883.
Laurence Rossiter, Hon. Secretary of the Society
William J. Devereux
James Stafford
James Stafford
Patrick Byrne
Patrick Stafford
Patrick Cullen
James Sinnott
James Stamp
William Scallan

Annual Soirée Organising Committee 1886
James McArdle, Hon. Secretary of the Society
William Scallan
Michael O'Connor
John King
Robert Hanton
James Stafford
Plus one other unknown

Annual Soirée Organising Committee 1887
Laurence Rossiter, Hon. Secretary of the Society
William Hutchinson, Asst. Hon. Secretary
William Scallan
Michael O'Connor
John King

Robert Hanton
James Stafford

Annual Reunion Organising Committee 4ᵗʰ January 1891
Laurence Rossiter, Hon. Secretary of the Society
William Hutchinson
James Kavanagh
Michael Nolan
M. Kehoe
Michael J. O'Connor
D. J. Healy
James Stafford
Robert Hanton

Annual Soirée Organising Committee 1894
William Scallan
James Stafford Jnr.
Michael Kehoe
Thomas Harpur
William McGuire
Patrick Walsh

Annual Soirée Organising Committee 1895
William Scallan
James Stafford, Jnr.
Michael Kehoe
William Hutchinson
William H. McGuire
Richard Goold
Frank Carty

Annual Supper Organising Committee 1908
John White, Chairman
Others unknown

Annual Supper & Reunion Organising Committee 1914
Michael Kehoe
John Browne
Others unknown

Annual Reunion Committee 1924
Edward F. O'Rourke, in charge
Others unknown

Childrens' Christmas Party 1952 Organising Committee
Thomas Mahon
Thomas O'Rourke
Harry Doyle
George Bridges
Thomas Kelly

John J. Donohue

Wexford C.Y.M.S. Centenary Reunion Dinner Dance 1955 Organising Committee
Thomas Hayes
John F. O'Rourke
John J. Donohue
Thomas Kelly
George Bridges

Childrens' Christmas Party 1956 Organising Committee
Mrs John Cullimore
Mrs Thomas J. Hayes
Mrs Myles O'Rourke
Thomas J. Hayes
John J. Donohoe
Thomas O'Rourke
George Bridges

Childrens' Christmas Party 1956 Working Committee
Sean Doyle
Kevin O'Mahony
Michael O'Neill
Thomas Mahon
Michael Mahon

Wally Cleary
Michael A. O'Rourke
Myles O'Rourke
Sam O'Rourke

Annual Reunion Organising Committee 1959
John J. Donohoe, Hon. Secretary
Thomas O'Rourke
George Bridges
Desmond Allen
Thomas Mahon
P. Kelly

Annual Reunion Ladies Working Committee 1959
Mrs John Cullimore
Mrs Maggie Mahon
Mrs Thomas O'Rourke

Annual Reunion Working Committee 1959
Thomas O'Rourke, Chief Organiser
Thomas Mahon
Wally Cleary
Michael A. O'Rourke
Larry Roche
Francis Bolger
Michael (*Curley*) O'Rourke

Appendix 9

Excursion Arrangement Committees

Excursion Arrangement Committee 1860 and 1862
Council members - names unknown

Excursion Arrangement Committee 1863
Thomas White, Chief Organiser
Unknown

Excursion Arrangement Committee 1864
Thomas White, Chief Organiser
Stephen Doyle
Unknown

Excursion Arrangement Committee 1881
Rev. Luke Doyle, C.C.
Laurence Rossiter, Hon Secretary
Robert Hanton
James Stafford
Patrick Byrne
Patrick Stafford
William Robinson, in charge of food

Excursion Arrangement Committee 1882
Rev. Luke Doyle, C.C., President
Laurence Rossiter, Hon secretary
Robert Hanton
James Stafford
Patrick Byrne
Patrick Stafford
William Robinson, in charge of food

Excursion Arrangement Committee 1883
Laurence Rossiter, Hon. Secretary
Robert Hanton
Pat Walsh
Edward Dixon
William Robinson

Excursion Arrangement Committee 1887
Michael O'Connor
James Stafford, Snr.
Nicholas White
Patrick Cullen
William Hutchinson
James Whelan
Michael Curry

Athletic Officials (Excursion 1887)
William Scallan, Judge.
Robert Hanton, Race Starter

Excursion Arrangement Committee 1895
Laurence Rossiter
Robert Hanton
Michael Kehoe
William J. Robinson
James Stafford, Snr.

Excursion Arrangement Committee 1896
Frank Carty
William J. Robinson
James Stafford, Snr.
Pat Walsh, Snr.
Pat Walsh, Jnr.
Edward Hendrick

Excursion Arrangement Committee 1916
Timothy McCarthy, Chief Organiser
Other members unknown

Excursion Arrangement Committee 1918
Timothy McCarthy, Chief Organiser
John Browne
Other members unknown

Excursion Arrangement Committee 1920
Timothy McCarthy, Chief Organiser
John Brown
William O'Leary
Frank Carty
Joseph A. Fennell
Other members unknown

Excursion Arrangement Committee 1922
Timothy McCarthy, Chief Organiser
John Brown
William O'Leary
Other members unknown

Excursion Arrangement Committee 1923
Timothy McCarthy, Chief Organiser
Edward F. O'Rourke
William Hynes
John Brown
John Cullimore
William Leary
Martin O'Connor

Excursion Arrangement Committee 1924
Timothy McCarthy, Chief Organiser
Edward F. O'Rourke
William Hynes

Joseph A. Fennell
Other members unknown

Excursion Arrangement Committee 1942
Sean Doyle, Chief Organiser
Other members unknown

Excursion Arrangement Committee 1949
Sean Doyle, Chief Organiser
Others unknown

Excursion Arrangement Committee 1957
(Pongo Committee took over the arrangements)
Thomas O'Rourke, Chief Organiser
William Murphy
Thomas Mahon

Wally Cleary
Michael A. O'Rourke
Michael Mahon

Excursion Arrangement Committee 1958
(Pongo Committee took over the arrangements)
Thomas O'Rourke, Chief Organiser
William Murphy
Thomas Mahon
Wally Cleary
Myles O'Rourke
Michael A. O'Rourke
Tommy Cullimore
Michael Murphy

Appendix 10

Annual Excursion Record
(Incomplete)

19th July 1860
The annual excursion by boat. Destination?
First Sunday in July 1861
Annual excursion by the steam tug 'Erin' to Courtown Harbour
27th September 1862
Annual excursion by steamer to Tuskar Rock
Summer 1863
No information. Most probably a steamer trip
Summer 1864
No information. Most probably a steamer trip
10th July 1881
By hired cars to Castleboro
25th June 1882
By hired vehicles (*carts*) to Clonmines, 60 members
8th July 1883
By hired cars to Mount Leinster, Blackstair Mountains. 48 members went. Six shillings and sixpence (6/6) each.
13th July 1884
By hired car to the old church of Bannow Bay. 59 members went. Six shillings and six pence (6/6) each. Hotel bill for the dinner cost £9-0-0, Car hire cost £8-5-0 and Drink bill came to £1-16-4.
5th July 1885
By hired cars to Castleboro. 49 members went at six shillings and six pence (6/6) each. John King's bill for drink was £7-19-0. Mr. Hanton's bill for car hire was £6-7-6 and Mr. Robinson's bill for dinner came to £7-19-0.
11th July 1886
Abandoned due to insufficient numbers
10th July 1887
By hired car to Tintern Abbey
10th July 1888
By hired cart to Johnstown Castle. 71 members went
1889
By the new tug boat the 'Wexford' to the Saltee Islands. Cancelled due to restrictions put on the hiring of it. The new arrangements were for
23rd July 1889
By train to 'Rathdrum'. This was also cancelled and there was no excursion this year
13th July 1890
By car hire to Newtownbarry. 47 members went
5th July 1891
Hired car to Kilmore Quay. Charge 6/- each. Mr. White at Kilmore Quay supplied the dinners and teas at 2/9 each. The party held some athletic events after dinner
1892
By boat the S. S. Menapia to Waterford. This was cancelled. The new destination was Kilmore trip to *"James Wooden House"* by hired car on the
3rd July 1892.
Cyclists also took part in this trip
1893
By hired cars to Courtown Harbour. 7/- per head. Dinner and tea at Mr. Funge's restaurant at 2/9 each. This intended trip was cancelled
1st July 1894
Initially to travel to Woodenbridge but the trains not be arranged. They then decided on Kilmore, but the trip had to be cancelled through lack of interest
7th July 1895
Trip to Kilmore again. The newly formed Cricket Club was in action at the sports that day

12th July 1896
By train to Rathdrum and hired car to Glendalough. The Society lost £4-6-4 on the trip. The cyclists we invited to go with this excursion

12th July 1898
By hired cars to Glendalough. 49 members went

1900
Tried to arrange to go to Woodstock but it was cancelled as Major Hamilton would not allow it

18th of June 1911
By hired car went to either Kilmore or Cullenstown

Sunday 3rd July 1902
By hired car to Kilmore Quay, charge five shillings (5/-) each. Cyclists went on this excursion

19th July 1903
Train journey? 60 members attended

5th July 1908
By car to Kilmore Quay. 48 members went at a charge of five shillings (5/-) each

28th June 1912
By car to Kilmore Quay at three shillings (3/-) each

14th July 1913
By car to Kilmore Quay. Charge five shillings (5/-) each

25th July 1915
By car to Kilmore Quay. Charge six shillings (6/-) per head

23rd July 1916
By car to Kilmore Quay, 52 members attended at a charge of five shillings and six pence (5/6) each

22nd July 1917
By car to Kilmore Quay. Charge five shillings (5/-) each and 65 went on the trip

14th July 1918
By cars to Kilmore Quay. Six shillings (6/-) each

25th June 1922
By car to Kilmore Quay. 40 went on this excursion

15th July 1923
By motor car, this is the first time that motor cars were used by the club, up to now the cars mentioned were horse drawn. The charge was set at £1 and the drive was to go to Duncannon via Ballyhack, Ramsgrange, Duncannon, Tower of Hook, Fethard, Tintern, Wellington bridge and home

27th July 1930
By bus to Kilmore Quay. Charge nine shillings (9/-) each

3rd July 1956
By bus to Glendalough. Members their wives and girl friends allowed to go on the trip

1950s?
The Pongo group outing by bus to Glendalough, Co. Wicklow

1950s?
The Pongo group outing by bus to Tralee, Kerry

Appendix 11

Dramatic Management Committees

Stage Committee - 13th February 1865
P. Fortune
P. White
William Scallan

Music & Singing Class - 1866 to 1869
Frank Lyons, Choir & Music Teacher

The Camptown Serenader's Committee – 18th to 26th May 1869
Maurice O'Shea, Hon. Secretary
Nicholas Bolger, Hon. Secretary

The Old Dramatic Corps Committee - 1869 to 1896
Prof. Breen, in charge
James Furlong, Hon. Secretary

Dramatic Club Committee - September 1885
Mr. O'Connor, organiser

Dramatic Corps Committee - 25th May 1886
Prof. Breen, in charge
James Furlong, Hon. Secretary

Dramatic Corps Committee - March 1888
There were 12 members of the club, names unknown.

Dramatic Club Committee - April 1899
Fr. O'Byrne, Chairman (*up to the 1900's*)
James Whelan, Hon. Secretary
John Carty, Hon. Secretary

Dramatic Class Committee - 1902
Fr. O'Byrne, Chairman
P. Busher
Thomas Kennedy
Members unknown

Dramatic Club - 13th September 1904
P. Busher, Hon. Secretary
Thomas Kennedy, Hon. Secretary

Dramatic Class Committee - 1904
John Barker, Hon. Secretary
Members unknown

The String Band or the Violin Club - 1891
Founded by Prof. Patrick J. Breen, music teacher

Dramatic Corps Committee - 13th January 1892
John Donohoe
Frank Carthy, stage manager and make-up artist

Piano Purchase Committee - 30th July 1896
Laurence Rossiter, Hon. Secretary (*Council*)
Mr. John Donohoe

Singing Class Teacher - 12th October 1896
Mr. John Donohoe (*piano*), Hon. Secretary

Choral Class Committee - 19th January 1897
Mr. John Donohoe (*piano*) Hon. Secretary
Patrick (Pat) Donohoe, musician
Donohoe Brothers, musicians were connected with this group.

Organising Committee Concert Hall Opening - December 1897
William Hutchinson, Hon. Secretary
Richard Goold, Hon. Secretary
Robert Hanton, dramatic club Hon. Secretary
Frank Carty, dramatic club Hon. Secretary
Frank O'Connor

Dramatic Performances Vetting Committee - September 1904
Michael Luccan
John White

Dramatic Class Committee - September 1913
Edward F. O'Rourke, Chairman
P. Busher, Hon. Secretary
Thomas Kennedy, Hon. Secretary

Dramatic Class Committee - 1914
Edward F. O'Rourke, Chairman
Thomas Hayes, Hon. Secretary
Members unknown

Dramatic Class Committee - 1915
Edward F. O'Rourke, Chairman
Thomas Hayes, Hon. Secretary
Members unknown

Dramatic Class Committee - 1916
Edward F. O'Rourke, Chairman
Thomas Hayes, Hon. SecretaryMembers unknown

Dramatic Class Committee - 1919
Edward F. O'Rourke, Chairman
Nicholas Barnwell, Hon. Secretary
Members unknown

Amusements Committee - September 1924
William Hynes, Chairman
John J. Kavanagh, Hon. Secretary
Mike Kennedy
Murtha (Murth) Meyler
Patrick Meyler
William Devereux
Thomas J. Hayes
Thomas B. Keegan

Dramatic Class Committee - April 1930
Nicholas Corish, Chairman
Members unknown

Dramatic Class Committee - 1953
John J. Donohoe, Chairman
P. J. Roice, Hon. Secretary
Kevin Mahoney
George Bridges
Oliver Kehoe

Dramatic Class Committee - 1918
Edward F. O'Rourke, Chairman
Nicholas Barnwell, Hon. Secretary

Dramatic Class Committee - 1958
Thomas O'Rourke, Manager/Chairman
William Murphy, Assistant/Manager
Michael Mahon
Thomas Mahon
Jack (Sean) Radford
Michael Kavanagh
Luke Wadding
Wally Cleary
Eamon Doyle
Willie Kehoe
Tom Cadogan
Others unknown

Dramatic Class Committee - 1959
Thomas O'Rourke, Manager/Chairman
William Murphy, Assistant/Manager
Michael Mahon
Thomas Mahon
Jack (Sean) Radford
Michael Kavanagh
Luke Wadding
Wally Cleary
Eamon Doyle
Willie Kehoe
Tom Cadogan
Others unknown

Appendix 12

C.Y.M.S. Theatrical Amusements Record
Entertainments, Variety Concerts, Plays and Shows
(Incomplete)

St. Patrick's Night, 1865   Entertainment

Easter Monday night 1868   Entertainment, music and singing

St, Patrick's Night, 1869, Entertainment. Mr. Callion, read the prologue. £15-2-11 Profit.

19th April 1869, Entertainment, held in the C.Y.M.S. hall, admission 1/-.

Sunday the 15th January 1871, Entertainment by 'Dramatic Corps' and the Band. Profit £14.

At the Soirée of 1883, Singing and music.

19th January 1897, entertainment held at the C.Y.M.S. Annual Reunion, at the concert Hall, Paul Quay. Both the dramatic club and the Choral Class (C.Y.M.S.) partook in the entertainments that evening.

St. Patrick's Night 1871, Entertainment. Held at the C.Y.M.S. Hall, Paul Quay. James Horan, read the prologue, Mr. P. Breen conducted the orchestra; proceeds went to the building of a Manse

Low Easter Sunday 1881, a Concert held in the hall for members and their friends.

Monday the **8th June 1886** performed a Play titled 'Rory O'More' by the 'Dramatic Club' held in the Theatre in High Street. For the benefit of the Library. Prof. Breen in charge. Profit £8-11-6.

1886, performed a Play, titled 'Barney the Baron' by the 'Dramatic Players' held in the Theatre in High Street.

1886, Entertainment by the 'Dramatic Players' held in Murrintown.

1886, Entertainment by the 'Dramatic Players' held in the hall at Paul Quay.

Monday evening the **13th February 1888**, a 'Variety Entertainment' by the 'Dramatic Club' at 8 o'clock in the hall, Paul Quay. Reserved seats 2/-, front seats 1/-.

Monday 1st October 1888, a Play titled 'The Shaughraun' by the 'Dramatic Club'. At the Theatre in High Street. Profit £5-0-0.

8th October 1888, a Play titled 'The Shaughraun' by the 'Dramatic Club'. At the Theatre in High Street.

4th January 1891, Gave an entertainment at the C.Y.M.S. reunion this evening.

7th November 1891, a 'Phonographic Entertainment' by Mr. Lyons.

1891, 2   Entertainment by 'The Dramatic Club' in the hall.

13th January 1892,entertainment plays and vocals at the Annual soirée held in concert Hall, Paul Quay.

March 1892, a Play by 'The Dramatic Club' in the concert hall, Profit £4-3-11.

Wednesday evening 5th October 1892, a Play by 'The Dramatic Club' at the Theatre in High Street. Profit £15-8-7.

March 1893, Entertainment by 'The Dramatic Club' for the benefit of the Christian Brothers.

1894, a performance by 'The Dramatic Club' held in the concert hall.

Monday 4th June 1894, a performance by 'The Dramatic Club' held in the Theatre in High Street. Profit £12.

Monday evening 6th June 1894,a Play titled 'Kathleen Mavausneen' by 'The dramatic Club' at Wexford Theatre. It was a full house.

12th September 1894, Entertainment by 'The Dramatic Club' at the Theatre in High Street. For the benefit of Fr. O'Leary's Confraternity Band. Profit £18-2-6.

1895 there were two entertainments staged this year. One at the theatre Royal and the other out at Castlebridge.

11th May 1896, Entertainment by 'The Dramatic Club' held in the Theatre in High Street.

Sunday the 19th January 1897, the C.Y.M.S. drama club performed the entertaining screaming farce titled "That Rascal Pat"

20th January 1897, a Variety Concert by 'The Dramatic Club' and many guest singers and musicians. Held at the Theatre in High Street. Admission 2/6 each for Boxes and 1/- each for the pit and Gallery. Profit £14.

Easter Monday 1897. Entertainment given by the 'Camptown Serenader's' for the 1897 Cycling carnival.

20th January 1898, Entertainment by 'The Dramatic Class' and held at the 'Theatre Royal'

Easter Monday 1898, Entertainment by 'The Camptown Serenades' in the concert hall.

Monday evening 11th April 1898, the opening entertainment for the Concert Hall, performances by 'The Minstrel Troop'

March 1898, Entertainment by the 'Choral Class' in the Concert hall.

Easter Monday Night 1898, Entertainment by 'The Camptown Serenaders'. Held in the concert hall.

St. Patrick's Night 1899, Entertainment by 'The Camptown Serenader's' in the concert hall. Profit £24-4-6.

1899, a Performance by the 'Choral Class' in concert hall. Profit £16-8-8.

1899, Entertainment by 'The Dramatic Club' in the concert hall. Profit £11-6-10.

13th August 1899, entertainment by 'The Dramatic Club' at Kilmore in aid of the Parish Church.

26th February 1900, Entertainment by the 'Dramatic Class' in the 'Theatre Royal' in aid of the 'Wexford Clothing Society', a charity.

St. Patrick's Night, 1901, Held a smoking Concert in the concert hall.

Monday 6ᵗʰ May 1901, Performance by 'The Camptown Serenader's' at the Theatre in High Street. Profit £11-0-1.

2ⁿᵈ February 1901, a 'Smoking Concert' by the 'Dramatic Club' in the hall

February 1902. An entertainment, by 'Dramatic Class'. Profit £3

Friday 8th April. 1904, performance by the 'Dramatic Class' in the concert hall.

Monday night the 25th April. 1904, performance by the 'Dramatic Class' in the concert hall.

St. Patrick's night 25th March 1913, entertainments put on by the 'Dramatic Class'. Takings £8-12-0.

January 1916, entertainment by the 'Dramatic Class' in the concert hall. In aid of the funds for the providing of comforts for the Irish Soldiers and Sailors engaged in the war.

Sunday 21st May 1916, performance by the 'Dramatic Class' held in Castlebridge in aid of the schoolhouse.

June 1930, play by the new 'Dramatic Group' performed "Look at the Heffernans". Profits £5-10-0.

1943, a 'Smoking Concert' by the 'Dramatic Class', in the concert hall.

Pre 1st May 1956, Variety Concert, (first one) by the 'Dramatic Class' in concert hall.

Pre 1st May 1956, Variety Concert, (second one) by the 'Dramatic Class' in concert hall.

17ᵗʰ June 1956, Varity Concert by the C.Y.M.S. dramatic Section. At Broadway.

1950s, Varity Concert by the C.Y.M.S. dramatic Section. At Ballycogley

1950s, Varity Concert by the C.Y.M.S. dramatic Section. At Kilmore

1950s, Varity Concert by the C.Y.M.S. dramatic Section. At Bree

1950s, Varity Concert by the C.Y.M.S. dramatic Section. At Blackwater.

1950s, Varity Concert by the C.Y.M.S. dramatic Section. At Fethard.

1950s, Varity Concert by the C.Y.M.S. dramatic Section. At Ferns.

1950s, Varity Concert by the C.Y.M.S. dramatic Section. At Oylegate.

1950s, Varity Concert by the C.Y.M.S. dramatic Section. At Duncannon.

1950s, Varity Concert by the C.Y.M.S. dramatic Section. At Courtown Harbour.

1950s, Varity Concert by the C.Y.M.S. dramatic Section. At Rosslare Strand.

Various Names used by the Dramatic Section

The Dramatic Club	Established in 1883
Choral Class	1868, Frank Lyons was the music teacher
Choral Class	1897, John and Patrick Donohoe were in charge of this section
The Dramatic Corps	October 1869
The Brass Band	January 1871
The Dramatic Players	1886
The String Band or	
The Violin Club	1891
Choral Class	1898
The Minstrel Troop	1898
The Camptown Serenader's	May 1901
The Dramatic Class	1902
Dramatic Club	1904
C.Y.M.S. Dramatic Section	1950

Appendix 13

Productions and Actors
(Incomplete)

***The Outlawed Jacobite* performed St. Patrick's Day 1871**
P. Furlong
John Redmond
James Horan
H. Stone
William Kelly
William Cummins
Matthew Reck
James Kelly
Patrick Neill
James Fewer

***A Race for a Widow* performed 1888**
M. Curry as Comelius Popjoy, a lawyer's clerk.
G. F. Dixon as Adolphus De Cremorne.
J. Curran as Mrs. Winnington, a widow with £300 a year
J. J. Whelan as Mrs. Pepperpod
M. O'Connor as Capsoum Pepperpod
T. J. Cullen, W. H. McGuire and L. Crosbie played other characters

***A farce entitled L.L.* performed January 1891**
J. J. Sutton
J. O'Neill
William McGuire
T. Harpur
John Williams
Daniel J. Healey
J. Doyle
W. Murphy

***A farce entitled Area Bella* performed January 1891**
John Williams
John J. O'Neill
John Doran
James Doyle
William Murphy

***Comic drama entitled His Last Legs* performed 4th January 1891**
Flex O'Callaghan
Thomas Harpur
John J. Sutton
Daniel J. Healy
William H. M'Guire
John Williams
William Murphy
John Doyle

John J. O'Neill

***A three act farce entitled The Irish Doctor* performed 13th January 1892**
J. S. Carthy
Denis Murphy
John J. O'Neill
William J. Murphy
John Doyle
P. O'Connor
John Williams
Laurence Kirwan
Michael O'Keefe
William Carberry
Frank Carthy, stage manager and make-up artist.

***Play The Drunkard's Warning* performed 29th January 1896**
Thomas Bent
James Furlong
Robert Harvey
Patrick Dunbar
William H. Murphy
John Doyle
Thomas Salmon
Thomas Murphy
Nicholas Gahan
Martin Sutton

***Comic farce Caught by the Cuff* performed 29th January 1896**
Nicholas Gahan
Thomas Bent
James Furlong
Thomas Murphy
Thomas J. Cullen, stage manager
Mrs N. Gahan and Mrs. J. Furlong, dressers preparing the costumes
Frank Carty, hair stylist

***A screaming farce entitled The Rascal Pat* performed January 1897**
James Furlong
Thomas Bent
Thomas Salmon
Patrick Dunbar
James J. Cullen, stage manager

Variety Concert
staged 19th December 1897
Wexford Cast
Miss Shanahan
Miss Jeffries
Miss Maddock
Miss Cosgrave
J. W. Gilling
C. Walker
Mr. Fleming, D.J.R.J.C.
Mr. J. Owen
Michael A. Ennis
E. McGuiness
Edward A. Whelan

Dublin Cast
Miss Murphy
E. P. Monck
E. V. Berry
Mr. Kearney

Comic Sketches in the Variety Concerts staged 1950s
Tom Mahon
Michael Mahon
Michael Kavanagh
Sean Radford
Eamon Doyle
Luke Wadding
Willie Kehoe
Tom Cadogan
Jackie Donohoe, magician 1950's

Other Dramatic Class Members

P. White *(Stage Manager)*, **William Scallan** *(Stage Manager)*, **P. Fortune** *(Stage Manager)*, **James Furlong** and **John White** were members of the dramatic class in 1865
John Baker, Michael Luccan, Frank O'Connor, and **John White** were members of the dramatic class in 1904.
P. Busher and **Thomas Kennedy** were members of the dramatic class in 1904-13
Thomas Hayes and **Edward F. O'Rourke** were members of the dramatic class in 1904-16
Nicholas Barnwell was a member of the dramatic class in 1919
Nicholas Corish was a member of the dramatic class in 1930s
Thomas O'Rourke *(Manager/ Director)*, **Wally Cleary** *(Stage Manager)*, **Kevin O'Mahoney, Luke Wadding, Michael Kavanagh, Oliver Kehoe, Michael Mahon** and **Tom Mahon** were members of the C.Y.M.S. dramatic troop in the 1950s

Musicians
(Incomplete)

Mr. Smith was a member of the C.Y.M.S. brass band 1859
Mr. Bolger was a teacher of drums for the C.Y.M.S. brass band 1861
Mr. Jones was a teacher of the flute for the C.Y.M.S. brass band 1861
Mr. Lucking was a member of the brass band January 1861
John Dunne, Mr. Kelly, William Martin, James Roche, Rich Ryan and **Joseph Kinsella** were all members of the C.Y.M.S. brass band 1861
Thomas Murphy was a member of the brass band January 1863 and was the teacher of the band by January 1888
James Neill was a member of the brass band January 1888
Brass Band (C.Y.M.S.) played "Home Sweet Home", "God Save Ireland" and the "National Anthem" 13th February 1888
R. Curren was the conductor of the C.Y.M.S. brass band 1889
Matt Stafford was a member of the Loc Garman Band from the 1960s to recent times.
Professor Patrick Breen, John Tennant and **H. Leary** were the musicians at a soiree in 1883
John Tennant played a violin solo 1888
E. A. Whelan played a very intricate solo on the violin "The Anchor in Weighed" in 1888
Mr. Swaby was a music teacher for the club
Frank Lyons was a music teacher for the club and a member in the 1890s
Professor Patrick J. Breen played "The Pope's March" on the piano at soiree in 1883. He was the parochial organist and provided all the musical accompaniments at the soiree in 1888. He was a teacher of the string band and violin class in 1891 and he played piano 1892.

M. Hanrahan played piano January 1891
John & Patrick Donohoe provided the music Jan. 1897, John was the conductor of the band.
James Hanrahan played "All the year Round" on piano January 1891
Matthew Furlong, Main Street loaned the piano on many occasions.
Mr. O'Mahony was a musician 13th January 1892
Charles E. Vize and **Frank Breen** both played piano with the dramatic class 1902
Luke Wadding played piano accordion 1950s
James F. Roche was the drummer on a Dance Band in the late 1950s.
The Slaneyside Ceilidhe Band 1950s
Sean and **Tony Rattigan** played violin on the 'Ceoltoiri Loc Garman' Ceili Band 1960s
Tommy Carroll and **Brendan Dowdall** played piano accordions on the 'Ceoltoiri Loc Garman' Ceili Band 1960s
Brendan Lowney was a member of Lowney's Dance Band 1960s

Dancers
(*Incomplete*)

Mr. Ryan danced a hornpipe 1882
Mr. Breslin danced the Irish Double 1882
Stephen Mullet danced a step dance and double January 1888
Simon Hore danced the horn pipe and a step dance January 1888
James Redmond danced a step dance 13th January 1892
C.J. McGovern and **John Ryan** were keen ballroom dancers in 1909
Nicholas Barnwell was a keen ballroom dancer in 1919
John Kehoe, Thomas Hayes, Thomas Keegan and **William Colfer** were all keen ballroom dancers in the 1920s
Tommy Roche, was an Irish Dance champion in the 1950s.

Wexford Festival Opera
(*Incomplete*)

Many C.Y.M.S. members had connections with the Wexford Festival Opera. When Dr. Tom Walsh proposed the notion of starting up a Wexford Festival there was two C.Y.M.S. men who supported and assisted him in the venture.
Dr. James Desmond Ffrench was the co-founder, the first Artistic Director and Honourary Medical officer of the Festival. He was also Chairman of the Wexford Festival Council for many years. The other member was Eugene McCarthy, the proprietor of White's Hotel, Wexford. The following list is incomplete:

Dr. J. D. Ffrench, co-founder, first Artistic Director, Honorary Medical Officer and Chairman of the Council for many years.
Eugene McCarthy, one of the first supporters for the venture.
Brendan Corish, T.D., Wexford Festival Council member.
Ald. Kevin C. Morris, Mayor of Wexford. Wexford Festival Council member.
Raymond E. Corish, Wexford Festival Council member.
Fintan Michael O'Connor, LL.B., Wexford Festival Council member.
T.D. Sinnott, Wexford Festival Council member.
William Victor Stafford, Wexford Festival Council member.